Communications
in Computer and Information Science   1876

Rationale

The CCIS series is devoted to the publication of proceedings of computer science conferences. Its aim is to efficiently disseminate original research results in informatics in printed and electronic form. While the focus is on publication of peer-reviewed full papers presenting mature work, inclusion of reviewed short papers reporting on work in progress is welcome, too. Besides globally relevant meetings with internationally representative program committees guaranteeing a strict peer-reviewing and paper selection process, conferences run by societies or of high regional or national relevance are also considered for publication.

Topics

The topical scope of CCIS spans the entire spectrum of informatics ranging from foundational topics in the theory of computing to information and communications science and technology and a broad variety of interdisciplinary application fields.

Information for Volume Editors and Authors

Publication in CCIS is free of charge. No royalties are paid, however, we offer registered conference participants temporary free access to the online version of the conference proceedings on SpringerLink (http://link.springer.com) by means of an http referrer from the conference website and/or a number of complimentary printed copies, as specified in the official acceptance email of the event.

CCIS proceedings can be published in time for distribution at conferences or as post-proceedings, and delivered in the form of printed books and/or electronically as USBs and/or e-content licenses for accessing proceedings at SpringerLink. Furthermore, CCIS proceedings are included in the CCIS electronic book series hosted in the SpringerLink digital library at http://link.springer.com/bookseries/7899. Conferences publishing in CCIS are allowed to use Online Conference Service (OCS) for managing the whole proceedings lifecycle (from submission and reviewing to preparing for publication) free of charge.

Publication process

The language of publication is exclusively English. Authors publishing in CCIS have to sign the Springer CCIS copyright transfer form, however, they are free to use their material published in CCIS for substantially changed, more elaborate subsequent publications elsewhere. For the preparation of the camera-ready papers/files, authors have to strictly adhere to the Springer CCIS Authors' Instructions and are strongly encouraged to use the CCIS LaTeX style files or templates.

Abstracting/Indexing

CCIS is abstracted/indexed in DBLP, Google Scholar, EI-Compendex, Mathematical Reviews, SCImago, Scopus. CCIS volumes are also submitted for the inclusion in ISI Proceedings.

How to start

To start the evaluation of your proposal for inclusion in the CCIS series, please send an e-mail to ccis@springer.com.

Udo R. Krieger · Gerald Eichler ·
Christian Erfurth · Günter Fahrnberger
Editors

Innovations for Community Services

23rd International Conference, I4CS 2023
Bamberg, Germany, September 11–13, 2023
Proceedings

 Springer

Editors
Udo R. Krieger (iD)
University of Bamberg
Bamberg, Germany

Christian Erfurth (iD)
University of Applied Sciences Jena
Jena, Germany

Gerald Eichler (iD)
Deutsche Telekom Technology
and Innovation
Darmstadt, Germany

Günter Fahrnberger (iD)
University of Hagen
Hagen, Germany

ISSN 1865-0929 ISSN 1865-0937 (electronic)
Communications in Computer and Information Science
ISBN 978-3-031-40851-9 ISBN 978-3-031-40852-6 (eBook)
https://doi.org/10.1007/978-3-031-40852-6

This Springer imprint is published by the registered company Springer Nature Switzerland AG
The registered company address is: Gewerbestrasse 11, 6330 Cham, Switzerland

Foreword

The International Conference on Innovations for Community Services (I4CS) is back in Germany for its 23rd edition in 2023. After 2021, the Steering Committee assigned it again to Bamberg University. Due to pandemic reasons, we were not able to meet physically at this famous World Heritage site two years ago. The selection of conference locations by alternating foreign and German venues is supported by the members of the Program Committee (PC) who offer suitable locations to live our passion. The Steering Committee had the honor to hand over the organization responsibility again to Udo R. Krieger and, therefore, to determine the city of Bamberg in Franconia, Germany as venue. Located on the River Regnitz, the cathedral city perfectly meets the current year's motto "Creating Digital Spirit".

Although we prefer to meet our community in person, we will offer once again the opportunity to join us virtually. This hybrid approach was introduced with The Hague conference edition in 2022 to open the valuable scientific program to a broader community as well as our PC members.

In June 2001, Herwig Unger and Thomas Böhme founded the Workshop on Innovative Internet Community Systems (IICS) at the Technical University of Ilmenau, Germany. It continued its success story under its revised name I4CS since 2014. IICS/I2CS published its first proceedings in books of the Springer Lecture Notes in Computer Science series (LNCS) until 2005, followed by Gesellschaft für Informatik (GI), and Verein Deutscher Ingenieure (VDI). I4CS had commenced with the Institute of Electrical and Electronics Engineers (IEEE) before it switched back to Springer's Communications in Computer and Information Science (CCIS) series in 2016 and created a permanent partnership in 2018. The unique combination of printed proceedings and the SpringerLink online edition generates high interest of external readers with increasing numbers of downloads.

We are proud to reach the envisaged number of scientific presentations, combined with a keynote, two invited talks, and a great social conference program to strengthen the cultural community spirit. The proceedings of I4CS 2023 comprise six sessions that cover the selection of 15 full plus four short papers out of 38 submissions, received from authors of eleven countries. Furthermore, invited papers are added. Interdisciplinary thinking is a key success factor for any community. Hence, I4CS 2023 covers the established plurality of scientific, academic, and industrial topics, bundled into three revised key areas: "Technology", "Applications", and "Socialization".

Technology: Distributed Architectures and Frameworks

- Data architectures and enablers for community services
- Blockchain and decentralized technologies
- 5G/6G technologies and ad hoc mobile networks
- Data models, artificial intelligence, and big data analytics
- Distributed and hybrid quantum computing

Applications: Communities on the Move

- Social networks, news, and mobile work
- Open collaboration and eLearning didactics
- Recommender solutions and context awareness
- Augmented reality, robotics, and location-based gaming
- Intelligent transportation, logistics, and connected cars

Socialization: Ambient Work and Living

- Remote work challenges and eHealth-assisted living
- Smart energy and home control
- Smart cities and municipal infrastructure
- Internet of things and sensor networks
- Cybersecurity and privacy concerns

Based on the reviewers' ratings, the I4CS Steering Committee issues the "Best Paper Award", while the "Best Presentation Award" is selected by the conference participants' voting. All on-site Program Committee members agree on the winner of the "Young Scientist Award", which goes to the most convincing student's work.

Many thanks go to the 25 members of the Program Committee, representing 13 countries worldwide, for their 138 reviews, especially to its chair Udo R. Krieger, our Conference Chair Christian Erfurth with academic and scientific focus, and our Publication Chair Günter Fahrnberger, collaborating closely with the Springer CCIS publishing team.

Next year's I4CS location has not yet been determined by the Steering Committee. Please check regularly the permanent conference URL http://www.i4cs-conference.org/ for more details! Proposals on emerging topics as well as applications of prospective Program Committee members and potential conference hosts are kindly welcome to request@i4cs-conference.org.

Kind regards on behalf of the entire Steering Committee and the Editors' Board.

I4CS Innovations for Community Services

September 2023

Gerald Eichler
I4CS Steering Chair

Preface

As Program Chair, it is my pleasure to present this CCIS volume with unique contributions on distributed architectures and frameworks for community services, on advanced applications regarding digital communities on the move, and on new trends of socialization covering the ambient work and living of digital societies. The related papers were presented at the 23rd International Conference on Innovations for Community Services (I4CS 2023), held during September 11–13, 2023, at the University of Bamberg in the UNESCO World Heritage Site of Bamberg, Germany. The historical spirit of this ancient medieval residence in the Bavarian region Upper Franconia which is on the way to become a smart digital city invigorated the meeting among the open-minded people of our community.

The conference I4CS 2023 was inspired by the exciting cultural and intellectual heritage of our world, in particular the recognition of the invariant dignity and unchangeable human rights of all beings. We are living together in a rapidly evolving physical world and associated digital worlds, but the latter habitat is challenged by many different physical and digital threats these days. The conference has again continued its reflection on a multi-dimensional, interdisciplinary approach to improve the digital evolution of modern societies. After the challenging period of the pandemic during the last years, the conference theme "Creating Digital Spirit" expressed the hope of many people that the rapid evolution of Internet and cloud technologies as well as the outstanding technical capabilities of machine learning will enable us to effectively support our physical and intellectual well-being within a united global society. The mission statement of the global I4CS community and its research efforts are dedicated to this unique multi-dimensional, interdisciplinary evolution of digital societies towards a global identity of humans and their invariant trust of being able to create new generations of generous, helpful, good-hearted humans and associated digital twins with similar behavior.

Following a thorough single-blind review procedure by at least three reviewers for each submission, the Program Committee of the I4CS conference has compiled an interesting scientific program. It includes 15 full and four short papers out of 38 submissions.

- "Exploring the Landscape of Federated Learning Systems and Applications: Advantages, Challenges, and Security Concerns" by Alexandra Dmitrienko, Chair of Secure Software Systems at the University of Würzburg,

    as well as the two invited talks

- "Advancing AI in Healthcare: Empowering Radiology through Image-Based Approaches" by Christian Ledig, Chair of Explainable Machine Learning at the University of Bamberg
- "Detecting Hidden Innovative Networks in Hacker Communities" by Joachim Klerx, Foresight & Policy Develoment Department at AIT Austrian Institute of Technology GmbH, Vienna

As Program Chair and representative of the Steering Committee, I want to express our gratitude to all members of the Program Committee for their dedicated service, maintaining the quality objectives of the conference, and for the timely provision of their valuable reviews. We thank all the authors for their submissions, all the speakers for their inspiring presentations, and all the participants for their contributions and interesting discussions. We express our sincere appreciation to the University of Bamberg as conference host as well as to all the members of the local Organization Committee. Their devoted efforts contributed to the success of this conference during a challenging period for our society. Last but not least, we acknowledge the support of the EasyChair conference system and express our gratitude to its management team, which always serves the digital community in an altruistic way. Further, we thank Springer regarding their technical support and excellent management of our CCIS publishing project.

Finally, it is our hope that readers will find the I4CS 2023 proceedings informative and useful with respect to their research and development activities in the future. It may effectively assist them in creating a fresh digital spirit which reflects the needs of all humans to continue their lives in a peaceful, habitable physical world and its associated inspiring digital universe.

September 2023   Udo R. Krieger

Organization

Program Committee

Sebastian Apel	Technical University of Applied Sciences Ingolstadt, Germany
Gilbert Babin	University of Montréal, Canada
Gerald Eichler	Deutsche Telekom Darmstadt, Germany
Christian Erfurth	University of Applied Sciences Jena, Germany
Günter Fahrnberger	University of Hagen, Germany
Hacène Fouchal	University of Reims Champagne-Ardenne, France
Sapna Ponaraseri Gopinathan	i.k.val Softwares LLP, India
Michal Hodoň	University of Žilina, Slovakia
Mikael Johansson	CSC - IT Center for Science, Finland
Kathrin Kirchner	Technical University of Denmark, Denmark
Udo R. Krieger	University of Bamberg, Germany
Peter Kropf	University of Neuchâtel, Switzerland
Ulrike Lechner	Bundeswehr University Munich, Germany
Andreas Lommatzsch	Technical University of Berlin, Germany
Karl-Heinz Lüke	Ostfalia University of Applied Sciences Wolfsburg, Germany
Raja Natarajan	Tata Institute of Fundamental Research, India
Deveeshree Nayak	University of Washington Tacoma, USA
Dana Petcu	West University of Timisoara, Romania
Frank Phillipson	TNO, The Netherlands
Jörg Roth	Nuremberg Institute of Technology, Germany
Amardeo Sarma	NEC Laboratories Europe GmbH, Germany
Pranav Kumar Singh	Indian Institute of Technology Guwahati and Central Institute of Technology Kokrajhar, India
Julian Szymanski	Gdansk University of Technology, Poland
Rob van der Mei	CWI, The Netherlands
Leendert W. M. Wienhofen	City of Trondheim, Norway

Exploring the Landscape of Federated Learning Systems and Applications: Advantages, Challenges, and Security Concerns (Keynote Speech)

Alexandra Dmitrienko(iD)

University of Würzburg, Würzburg, Bavaria, Germany
alexandra.dmitrienko@uni-wuerzburg.de

Abstract. Machine Learning (ML) methods have reached a level of maturity where they are being widely deployed across various domains, aiding users in classification and decision-making tasks. In this presentation, we will showcase the numerous advantages ML offers for applications dedicated to detecting security threats on mobile platforms. However, it is important to address the security and privacy concerns that arise when utilizing ML methods. One particular focus of our talk will be on Federated Learning (FL), which is a distributed form of ML that enhances privacy preservation during the training of ML models. We will conduct a comprehensive evaluation of the security and privacy risks associated with FL, delving into the intricacies of targeted and untargeted poisoning attacks, as well as the countermeasures employed to mitigate these threats. Our discussion will highlight the ongoing challenges in this field, such as the ability to differentiate between poisoned models and benign but uncommon models, particularly those trained on datasets with different data distributions. We will also address the issue of adaptive attackers who, once aware of the detection method, can add an additional training loss to minimize any changes in the detection metric, effectively evading detection. To stimulate further dialogue and exploration, we will outline promising research directions and open avenues for future research work.

Keywords: Machine Learning (ML) · Federated learning systems

Advancing AI in Healthcare: Empowering Radiology Through Image-Based Approaches (Invited Talk)

Christian Ledig

University of Bamberg, Bamberg, Bavaria, Germany
`christian.ledig@uni-bamberg.de`

Abstract. In recent years, the integration of artificial intelligence (AI) in healthcare has shown tremendous promise, particularly in image-based applications such as radiology. This invited talk is concerned with the continuously increasing need to responsibly integrate AI technology into healthcare applications, while emphasizing its transformative potential. The healthcare industry is faced with the challenge of processing and analysing and evergrowing volume of imaging data. AI-driven image analysis can offer a possible solution by enabling clinical experts to more efficiently and more accurately interpret medical images. However, the adoption of AI in the healthcare sector comes with significant technical challenges, regulatory obligations as well as societal implications. The talk will highlight opportunities and difficulties that must be considered when implementing AI in clinical applications, a particular benefit being the potential to improve access to consistent, more accurate and more objective diagnoses.

Keywords: AI-driven image analysis

Contents

Quantum Computing

Internet of Things

Short Papers

Detecting Hidden Innovative Networks in Hacker Communities (Invited Talk)

Joachim Klerx[✉][iD] and Claudia Steindl[iD]

Austrian Institute of Technology (AIT), Vienna, Austria
{joachim.klerx,claudia.steindl}@ait.ac.at

Abstract. Innovation networks have always been in the core of human wealth, because of their contribution to increased economic efficiency. Hacker communities in particular have been proven to be the fastest and most successful innovation network. This paper presents a method to extend the concept of innovation networks, by elements of innovation from the digital ecosystem and more specifically the crypto ecosystem and to use artificial intelligence to discover the specific hidden part of the innovation networks. By using specific sources from the internet about community communication on platforms in surface web, deep web and dark nets, in addition to publication analytics and patent analytics, the hidden part of the innovation networks will be made visible and accessible to further analytics. This understanding the innovation methods from hacker communities is essential for the digital transformation in public services, universities, and other organizations.

Keywords: Foresight · Horizon scanning · Artificial intelligence · TRACE · Crypto ecosystem · Digital ecosystem · Hidden networks · Innovative networks · Hacker communities · Disruptive innovation analysis

1 Introduction

The digital revolution has unleashed a new era of innovation where hacker communities play a pivotal role. They are the linchpin in the rapid expansion and evolution of technologies such as blockchain, cybersecurity, and other aspects of the crypto ecosystem. However, understanding these communities and their innovation networks remains a complex task, given their diverse, distributed, and often opaque nature. This paper aims to demystify these networks and provide a framework for understanding their innovative mechanisms and impact.

This paper summarizes the technical and conceptual considerations for high performance source identification crawler in surface-, deep-, and darknets, which are developed and improved in the EU project TRACE[1]. First results from tests and insights into the capabilities from the infrastructure are presented to discuss the technical concept and the new potential for artificial test investigation, (to not interfere) and which are realistic enough to create a near real background. The objectives of this publication are to:

---

[1] TRACE, Developing AI solutions to disrupt illicit money flows, https://trace-illicit-money-flows.eu/.

© The Author(s), under exclusive license to Springer Nature Switzerland AG 2023
U. R. Krieger et al. (Eds.): I4CS 2023, CCIS 1876, pp. 1–26, 2023.
https://doi.org/10.1007/978-3-031-40852-6_1

- present results from scanning the internet for innovation networks of hacker communities,
- contribute to understand the typical structures of these communities,
- and derive political implications for the innovation policy of the EU.

Innovation networks, specifically those that arise from hacker communities, have already been recognized as somewhat critical and maybe problematic, because of some being illegal, but anyway they deliver important contributors to the innovation potential in the context of the digital transformation. There is no doubt, illegal activities are a dangerous for society and needs to be prosecuted. But hacker communities as a whole embody a unique combination of attributes that makes them invaluable in the pursuit of a thriving digital society. These communities are obviously a repository of significant talent and technical acuity. The individuals within these networks demonstrate an extensive understanding of digital technologies, often being at the cutting edge of the field. Their ability to exploit and improve these technologies provides an important resource that Europe can harness to drive forward its digital transformation agenda. These communities are characterized by their agility and speed of innovation. The rapidity with which they pioneer new methods and solutions ensures that they remain at the forefront of technological advancement. This places them in a pivotal position to assist European policymakers in keeping ahead of the pace of digital innovation.

This publication is going to look into legal and illegal activities of hacker communities to provide empirical evidence for a fact-based political strategy about how hackers innovation could support the digital transformation. The methodical development in this paper focuses on hidden network detection with knowledge graph generation to provide empirical support for future strategies in innovation policy.

2 High Performance Crawling Infrastructure for Knowledge Discovery

The first and most important step in automatic knowledge discovery is data collection. Collecting data from different sources from the internet, including deep web and darknet for the construction of a knowledge graph is a complex task that comes with various considerations. Our data is collected from various darknet sources, such as forums, marketplaces, or onion sites. These sources contain information about hacker which is either not readily available on the surface web or which is hidden because of search engine blacklisting.

The horizon scanning system, which was used for the knowledge discovery, is developed at AIT since 2015 and contains at this time more than 700 million data points on global geopolitical and innovation activities. It is constantly being expanded. The global coverage makes it possible to identify regional thematic priorities and classify them in relation to different countries. Figure 1 shows the basic structure of the so called CATALYST (Collaborative Trend Analytics System) system.

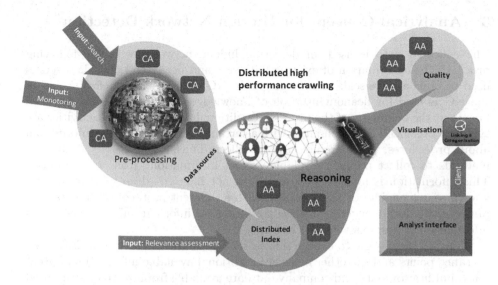

Fig. 1. Technical overview of the CATALYST infrastructure

The process of data collection is starting with collecting agents (CA), which are used to collect information from the surface web, deep web and the different dark nets. This data from the internet comes in a rather unstructured format, such as text from homepages, forum posts or chat logs. To be useful in a knowledge graph, this data needs to be cleaned, structured, and classified automatically by natural language processing (NLP), entity recognition, and emotion mining.

Therefore, once collected, based on a given search strategy, the assessment agents (AA) are doing some reasoning processes and updating processes within the distributed central index. After quality check the results are visualized in the analyst interface for further processing. The most important part in constructing the knowledge graph are unique and non-unique identifiers. Just as with data from other sources, darknet data can be represented with both unique and non-unique identifiers within a knowledge graph. A unique identifier e.g. is a specific URL, a unique email address, while non-unique identifiers could include common usernames, names, company names or hacker group names.

In order to identify potential "topics" for the knowledge graph generation, the texts need to be classified. The content elements usually include references to weak signals for future requirements, innovations, threats or trends and are supplemented with weak signals that indicate changes. As a result, the identified content elements are condensed into thematic maps that condense the knowledge generated about possible hidden networks and activities within the networks.

3   Analytical Concept for Hidden Network Detection

The collected data is used for detecting hidden networks with the following process. The combination of existing data sets and newly collected data sets is used to build a large scale knowledge graph (KG). The "network effects" within the KG is used for deanonymization of knowledge objects, which are not well known at the beginning of the process. Traditional and new hacker activities are typically organized in communities with a certain level of secrecy and information about procedures, which are not easy to collect. Thus, it is necessary to develop methods to collect publicly available "secret information" from a community. This information is hidden because of it is not indexed (deep web) from well-known search engines or it is provided with a different protocol (dark nets). By purpose, we do not attempt to access "protected information", e.g. encrypted information or systems with access control.

Figure 2 shows how to collect this secret information. The red fields are the entrance points and the other fields are additional available information. Patent data, publication data and company data are available from different structured databases. The internet data is collected with the CATALYST infrastructure. By systematically combining this data, it is possible to get more information about the hacker communities than expected by the typical community members, as the following picture shows. The most important elements of the community are the following four different ecosystems:

- The knowledge ecosystem is the most important one to extract future capabilities from the hacker community.
- The crypto knowledge system exposes possible financial relations between different actors.
- The business ecosystem is the system, which is easier to monitor than the other ecosystems to get realistic behavioral data about future business concepts of the hacker community.
- And finally, the innovations ecosystem shows how new business models are developed in the community.

The actual analytical process is supported by a wide variety of different methods, including high performance crawling, data mining, big data analytics, social network analytics, clustering and horizon scanning. The horizon scanning process is one of the most important processes as it is responsible for the "weak signal" detection[2]. As result, a knowledge graph is generated, which is used to identify the "hidden elements" from the hacker community, like company ownership, academic activities and other to recognize strategic roles of actors within the community.

For performance reason, the source knowledge graph generation is embedded in the process of crawling, following the typical architecture [2] from cybercrime entity detection. A future development perspective might be the Differential

---

[2] European Foresight Platform (EFP), http://foresight-platform.eu/community/forle arn/how-to-do-foresight/methods/analysis/horizon-scanning/.

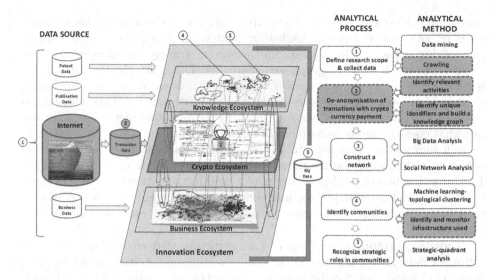

Fig. 2. Expanded framework of a multi-layered ecosystem mapping [3]

Evolution Algorithm based Intelligent Multi-Agent architecture (DEAIMA) [1], proposed by Weslin Devasirvatham and Joshva Devadas Thiyagarajanc. However, it is essential at some point in the optimization procedures to improve the reliability for operational use. The best possible crawler will not be used, if the crawler is not reliable.

By incorporating these processes into a focused crawling system, it was possible to create a crawler which can efficiently and effectively navigate the web, selecting and prioritizing URLs that are most relevant to the target topic(s), and gathering high-quality information while minimizing the resources spent on off-topic content.

4 First Results on Knowledge Graph Generation

Hacker communities have demonstrated unprecedented abilities to foster innovation at a speed unmatched by traditional organizations. Their ability to navigate and leverage the evolving landscape of the internet - the surface web, deep web, and the dark net - provides them with unique opportunities for innovation. Previous works have attempted to understand the workings of these communities, with a focus on individual platforms or isolated segments of the network. However, a holistic perspective of the entire network, including its hidden aspects, has been lacking.

To discover hidden networks by targeting specific keywords and websites associated with criminal activity, the crawler needs to identify the types of websites and forums where criminals might be communicating, such as online marketplaces for illegal goods or forums for discussing criminal activity. For the hacker community the search strategy was rather complex as the term hacker or hackers is by no means complete. "hackathon pentesting" would have been a simple jet working strategy. After setting up the search strategy, the crawler are used to generate the knowledge graph automatically. The next step is to search for specific keywords and target the corresponding websites, gathering information on individuals and organizations involved in criminal activity. This information includes usernames, email addresses, IP addresses, and other identifying information that could be useful to map out the network. Once the crawler has gathered enough information, it is used to create a graph as a basis to visualization the network, highlighting the connections between individuals and organizations. This was then be use to identify key players within the network and target them for in deep understanding their innovative activities. The next section will go more into the details of this process and describes the result on one selected network.

Knowledge graphs are a form of data structure that enables the representation of data in a graph-like structure, providing an intuitive, semantic, and contextual framework for data storage and retrieval. At the core of a knowledge graph is a collection of entities (nodes), their attributes, and relationships (edges). This format allows data to be interconnected in a way that mirrors how humans tend to understand the world by making associations between different elements. Examples of well-known knowledge graphs include Google's Knowledge Graph. This graph shows that the data structure is a good representation of the extracted knowledge from an unstructured data set. High value information are for the hacker dataset are **unique knowledge objects**, like email addresses, dank accounts, crypto addresses and **non-unique knowledge objects**, which often provides additional information, that helps to develop the overall understanding of the network dynamic. However non-unique knowledge objects without context cannot be considered as evidence. Figure 3 shows with red marker the selected and with yellow the considered unique identifiers.

A unique identifier (UI) in a knowledge graph is a label that uniquely distinguishes an entity within the graph (see Fig. 4). The UI ensures that each entity within the graph is distinct, even if different entities share common attributes. For instance, two individuals might share the same name, but they will have unique identifiers within the knowledge graph to prevent any confusion.

Non-unique identifiers, on the other hand, are attributes that do not necessarily uniquely identify an entity within the graph. These attributes may be common among multiple entities. Examples could include characteristics such as an individual's name, age, or occupation. In the knowledge graph about the hacker community, for instance, a non-unique identifier might be a malicious software used, as many groups might use the same software.

The first results of a simple KG did show that the information for deep web and dark nets is highly valuable, but difficult for analytics. By creating the first TOR knowledge graph (KG) it became clear that the TOR hidden service nodes are not interlinked. As visible in the following picture, TOR hidden services do usually only have self-references.

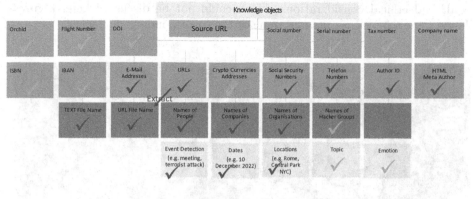

Fig. 3. Knowledge objects from knowledge graph

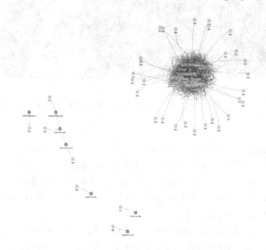

Fig. 4. Knowledge graph

In conclusion, the combination of unique and non-unique identifiers, as well as information from various sources, makes knowledge graphs a powerful tool for representing and navigating complex, interrelated data in a way that is intuitive and mimics human understanding.

Information from the darknets can provide an additional, though often challenging, source of data for a knowledge graph. The darknet refers to parts of the internet not indexed by search engines which requires specific software to access. Networks within the darknet, such as Tor, are commonly associated with privacy, security, and anonymity, but this is only the case if strict uncomfortable user rules are followed. Collecting data from the darknet for the construction of a knowledge graph was a complex task that did come with various technical, legal, and ethical considerations, which could not be discussed here. Figure 5 shows some selected results and some of the corresponding challenges.

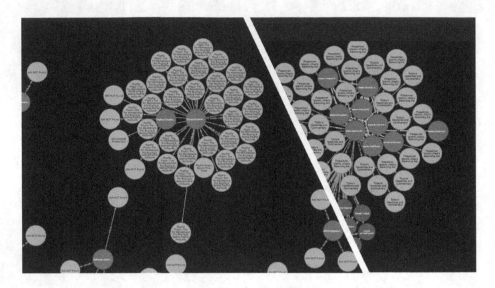

Fig. 5. TOR hidden service small part of the TOR KG

The main challenges are, that TOR hidden services are not well interlinked. A possible strategy to improve the results is to identify and download sources from surface web and deep web which point to the TOR hidden services. First estimates from Google search let expect additional 500.000 surface web nodes, which link to TOR hidden services.

Another issue is that name entities on TOR hidden services seems to be used as fake names. A small test did show that most of the names on TOR are not connectable to human profiles. In the opposite, a test KG from the surface web did show, that the name entity extraction did show better results. The reason for this needs further evaluation in the process of crawler development.

With the data basis available at the date of publication, it looks very promising to use surface data and deep web data to unveil the structure and the identities of hidden services in TOR. The pattern of the community does show a global structure with globalized services and networks. Therefore, essential information is simply missing at present. Hopefully, the crawler development can contribute to fill this gab. For the provision of new sources on the Internet and their relevance, new protocols and services like the decentralized finance (DeFi) protocols are becoming increasingly significant. This makes clear, that embedding Crypto Ecosystems and global Innovation Ecosystems are of utmost importance to support future community mapping activities.

5   Selected Results on One Specific Case

In the following description, an example is presented on how unique identifiers helps to create our knowledge graph (KG) through a unique/non-unique key identification and match the respective entities or relationships accordingly. In this way, information from different data sources can be brought together and linked with each other in building a coherent knowledge network in the KG. All knowledge objects are marked in gray. The weak signals are marked in red letter. The results from knowledge graph generation should not be considered somehow similar to an investigation. So, all information in the following is just an example of the process and should not be considered as investigation. **If names from person, companies or nations are mentioned together with illegal activities, this should be considered as result from a knowledge graph generation process. This can not in any way supplement prosecutors or court decision.**

For example, by starting with the hacker username "Slavic" could identify the innovation network of one of the most wanted hackers in the world. He is particularly well suited as a pattern because he has been active for many years (historical component)[3], very successful (innovative component, political component) and still engages investigators like no other (evidence-based component)[4], as he continues to be in freedom until now.

Slavic stole over 100 million US dollars, allegedly manipulated the 2016 US elections on behalf of the Russian government and developed one of the most dangerous malware viruses at the age of 22[5]. In 2015, the FBI put a USD 3 million bounty on his head[6]. Yet his identity remained unknown for years. He is one of the most wanted hackers in the world[7]. To this day, there are critical voices that doubt that Slavic has been unmasked[8].

5.1   1st Phase (2006 - Fall 2009): A New Malware Emerges

The hunt for Slavic began in the fall of 2009 when FBI Special Agent James Craig was dealing with strange cases of digital theft. In the first case, $450,000 was stolen from payment service providers First Data and Telecash and in the second case, $100,000 from the First National Bank of Omaha[9].

The strange thing was that these thefts were carried out from the victim's computer and IP[10]. In addition, the original logins and passwords were used.

---

[3] https://www.youtube.com/watch?v=YuBSzOm2p3w&t=11s.
[4] https://www.youtube.com/watch?v=WXf2JOEakPY.
[5] https://www.youtube.com/watch?v=Vn4VA5-n8AM.
[6] https://www.fbi.gov/wanted/cyber/evgeniy-mikhailovich-bogachev.
[7] https://www.ibtimes.co.uk/worlds-most-wanted-hacker-evgeniy-bogachev-fuelled-kremlins-espionage-efforts-report-1611188.
[8] https://www.youtube.com/watch?v=DGTN60hBRoM&t=5s.
[9] https://www.youtube.com/watch?v=DGTN60hBRoM.
[10] https://www.youtube.com/watch?v=VMSriXdAxuM.

After Craig had examined the companies' computers closely, his fears were confirmed. They were infected with a malware called Zeus. At this point, Craig was not yet aware of the innovative malware he had discovered here.

First discovered in 2006, this malware was considered an absolute masterpiece by both criminals and security experts. Unobtrusive, effective and destructive. Its author was known on the internet under the name Slavic[11].

Zeus is a so called "Man-in-the-browser (MitB)-attack-malware" that steals online banking credentials and conducts unauthorized fund transfers[12]. It has also been used to execute technical support scams. Attacks have been successful on Firefox and Internet Explorer web browsers and have targeted Amazon, Bank of America and the U.S. Department of Transportation.

The Zeus malware infected computers as follows: e.g., fake emails from the tax office or fake tracking links of your DHL or UPS delivery[13]. The goal of these emails was to trick you into downloading a file. Once this happened, the computer was infected, and the hackers had far-reaching possibilities of influence. Not only could all login credentials (usernames and passwords) as well as the respective account balance be recorded, but also websites and other forms could be modified without the user noticing. With the infected computer, the user was shown the old account balance. Only when the user logged into that website with another computer, the robbery of the money became obvious. But that was not the end of the story. Whoever was infected with Zeus was automatically a member of a botnet (see Fig. 6)[14]. Slavic did something that was atypical for hackers up to that point and ultimately made Zeus a criminally successful skill: he did maintenance work and improvements - he regularly updated Zeus, patched it, added new features to his malware and fixed bugs.

Summary of Identified Knowledge Objects (see Fig. 7):

- Economic interests: yes
- Victims: known cases, hacked websites (organization/company):
  - First Data, Telecash
  - First National Bank of Omaha
  - Firefox
  - Internet Explorer
  - Amazon
  - Bank of America
  - U.S. Department of Transportation
  - DHL
  - UPS
- Hacker names/nick names: Slavic
- Software/technique used:

---

[11] https://www.youtube.com/watch?v=DGTN60hBRoM.
[12] https://threatpost.com/man-browser-inside-zeus-trojan-021910/73568/.
[13] https://www.youtube.com/watch?v=DGTN60hBRoM.
[14] https://securityboulevard.com/2019/11/zeus-virus-aka-zbot-malware-of-the-month-november-2019/.

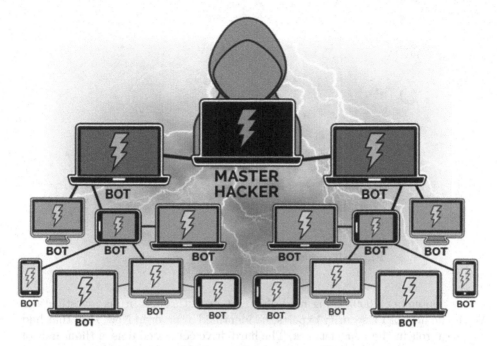

Fig. 6. Illustration of hierarchic Zeus botnet

- Man-in the browser (MitB)-attack-malware
- Botnet, Bot network
- DDoS attacks
- Training, education & skills:
  - Updating software
  - Fixing bugs
- Investigator/investigating authorities/company: James Craig (FBI agent)
- Malware: Zeus

5.2 2nd Phase (Fall 2009 - Fall 2010): First Round of Investigations

However, shortly before Craig began his investigation in 2009, Slavic appeared to change tactics[15]. He formed a group of criminal hackers around himself and launched them with a new vision of Zeus. "Jabber Zeus" - Jabber is a kind of instant messenger (like WhatsApp), only with the advantage that it can be operated completely independently of a company or institution. I.e., Jabber operated completely privately and unsupervised. This allowed the hackers to coordinate their attacks with one another. With that, Slavic carried over all the cybercrime cases that the FBI had previously seen.

---

[15] https://www.wired.com/2017/03/russian-hacker-spy-botnet/.

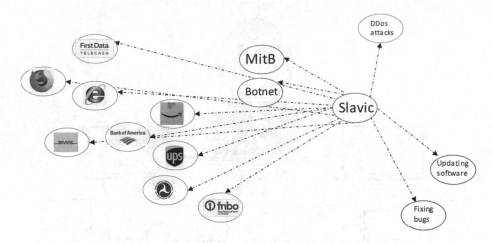

Fig. 7. Identified knowledge objects of 1st phase

In September 2009, Craig made his first breakthrough in his investigation. With the help of IT security experts, he identified a server in New York that had a central role in the Zeus network. The hard drive contained tens of thousands of lines of chat transcripts in Russian and Ukrainian. They had found the criminals' Jabber servers. This would give investigators a direct look behind the criminals' curtain.

In the chat logs, investigators found in 2010 not only hundreds of stolen credit cards, but also evidence that the criminal operations went far beyond the digital world. Somehow, Slavic and his hacker group had to get their hands on the stolen money without attracting attention. To do this, they used so-called "money mules"[16]. It worked as follows: A person, who at first had nothing to do with the hackers, opens a new account at a new bank. A few days later, they start withdrawing smaller amounts (so that the bank does not get suspicious). This way, Slavic was able to smuggle the money through legitimate bank accounts unnoticed. In addition, investigators determined that the U.S. was only one market of many. Salvik had built a multinational fraud network. Officials found money laundering activity in Romania, the Czech Republic, the United Kingdom, Ukraine, and Russia. In total, investigators were able to attribute thefts to the group in the amount of $70–80 million[17]. The suspicion was that the total amount was much higher. Craig was making good progress with his investigation of the Jabber Zeus gang[18]. The FBI, along with the Department of Justice, was able to identify several members (see Fig. 8[19]. "thehead" specialized in managing all the gang's money. "petr0vich" was responsible for the hacker's

---

[16] https://nautil.us/the-100-million-bot-heist-237260/.

[17] https://www.youtube.com/watch?v=DGTN60hBRoM.

[18] https://www.youtube.com/watch?v=ejKb-bsjO1I.

[19] https://therecord.media/alleged-zeus-cybercrime-leader-arrested-in-geneva-to-be-extradited-to-us.

IT administration and web hosting, while "tank" was Slavic's right-hand man and helped with organizational administration.

Ivan Viktorvich Klepikov
Aliases: "petr0vich",
"nowhere"

Alexey Dmitrievich Bron
Alias: "thehead"

Vyacheslav Igorevich
Penchukov
Aliases: "tank", "father"

Fig. 8. Members of the hacker group

By the fall of 2010, the FBI was poised to take down the network. With 39 arrests worldwide, the FBI thought they had destroyed the criminal group around Slavic. A mistake. Mastermind Slavic continued to operate in the dark. While there were countless photos of everyone else involved, Slavic remained a phantom[20].

Additional knowledge objects identified (see Fig. 9):

- Malware: Jabber Zeus (= new version of Zeus)
- Communication channels used: Jabber
- Suspicion points for money laundering: Money mules
- Geographic notes:
  - Russia
  - Ukraine
  - Romania
  - Czech Republic
  - United Kingdom
- Fraud: Stolen credit cards
- Investigator/investigating authorities/company:
  - Department of Justice

---

[20] https://www.youtube.com/watch?v=Vn4VA5-n8AM.

- FBI
- Hacker Group: Jabber Zeus (gang)
- Names of the hackers:
  - Ivan Viktorvich Klepikov
  - Alexey Dmitriech Bron
  - Vyacheslav Igorevich Penchukov
- Hacker names/nick names:
  - petr0vich, nowhere
  - thehead
  - tank, father
- Arrested: yes - 39 hackers (not Slavic)
- Photos/images/videos: yes (not Slavic)

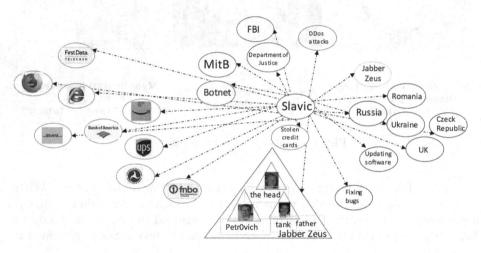

Fig. 9. Identified knowledge objects of 2nd phase

5.3 3rd Phase (Fall 2010 - Fall 2014): Second Round of Investigations

Just a year after the FBI captured key members of the Jabber Zeus hacking group, a new variant of Zeus emerged: "Game-Over Zeus"[21].

This new version was even more dangerous than its predecessor. With Jabber Zeus, all infected computers still communicated with a central server. If this server was disabled, the entire network was paralyzed. The new version used peer-to-peer technologies. Simply put, the infected computers were able to communicate with each other. If one were to shut down a central control server, the other infected computers could simply be redirected to another server. The entire

---

[21] https://www.proofpoint.com/us/threat-reference/gameover-zeus-goz.

network was designed from the start that it could not be destroyed by conventional means. This "invincible" system belonged to elite hacker group "Business Club" with its leader Slavic. He was back - after just one year - stronger than ever.

The business club focused mainly on banks - with devastating damage. Just like the Jabber-Zeus attacks before it, the malware stole bank account credentials and transferred large sums directly to the fraudsters' accounts. There were two main differences: first, the large botnet attacked the bank at the same time with a so-called DDoS attack to distract the bank (no one was supposed to discover the missing money in a timely manner) and second, much larger amounts were stolen (see Fig. 10[22]).

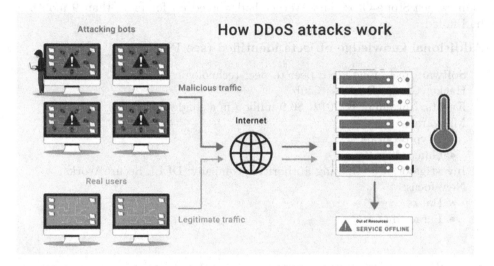

Fig. 10. The new malware DDOS attack strategy

On November 6, 2012, for example, the FBI observed how the game-over network had stolen \$6.9 million in a single transfer[23]. However, banks did not remain the only target of the business club. In fact, many of the infected computers were not used for online banking at all, so directly did not yield any money at all for the hacking group. To solve this problem, Slavic had an idea: he designed a malware called "Crypto-Locker" that encrypted the hard drives of the affected computers, making it impossible for users to access their data. If you wanted your data back, you had to pay between \$300 and \$750 in Bitcoins. According to the company DELL Secure Works, this malware alone has infected over 250 000 computers. Between 2011 and 2013, various cybersecurity companies and researchers made three attempts to break the Game Over Zeus network. However, Slavic apparently fended off these attacks without any problems.

---

[22] https://gcore.com/materials/how-to-protect-against-ddos-attacks/.
[23] https://www.youtube.com/watch?v=DGTN60hBRoM.

In January 2013, German security expert Tillman Werner[24] and Brett Stone-Gross[25] teamed up to attack the Game-Over network[26]. The plan was to redirect said peer-to-peer network, centralize it and then bring it under their control on a new server. This way, they hoped to break the communication link between Slavic and the bot network. At first, everything went well. Hour by hour, the experts could see more and more computers coming under their control. They were able to control up to 95% of all networked computers during this attack. But Slavic had an ace up its sleeve: A small portion of the infected computers were still able to communicate with Slavic's control server. In the second week of the attack, Slavic was thus able to apply an update to the entire network and regain complete control. The researchers had to watch live as piece by piece the entire Game-Over-Zeus peer-to-peer network reassembled before their eyes. The plan, which Stone-Gross and Werner had worked on for more than 9 months, had failed.

Additional knowledge objects identified (see Fig. 11):

- Software/technique used: peer-to-peer technologies
- Hacker Group: Business Club
- Events: November 6, 2012 ($6.9 million in a single transfer)
- Malware:
  - Crypto-Locker
  - Game-Over-Zeus
- Investigator/investigating authorities/company: DELL Secure Works
- New focus:
  - Banks
  - Large amounts

5.4   4th Phase (Fall 2014–2015): Success Without Arrest

After months of tracking leads employees from FOX IT (Michael Sandee)[27] found a promising, obscure email address[28].

The team was able to trace this email address back to a UK server that Slavic used to run the business club's websites[29]. Further investigations and court orders led authorities to a Russian social media website - where said email address was linked to a real name: Evgeniy Bogachev (also Evgeniy Mikhaylovich Bogachev, Yevgeniy Bogachev).

---

[24] https://www.sueddeutsche.de/digital/it-sicherheit-botnetze-killen-fuer-das-fbi-1.3692050.

[25] https://www.sans.org/profiles/brett-stone-gross.

[26] https://www.proofpoint.com/us/threat-reference/gameover-zeus-goz.

[27] https://de.scribd.com/document/343628416/FoxIT-Whitepaper-Blackhat-Web, https://www.youtube.com/watch?v=st8gQ-grxr0.

[28] https://nltimes.nl/tags/evgeniy-bogachev.

[29] https://www.youtube.com/watch?v=WAdK-ONnI4k.

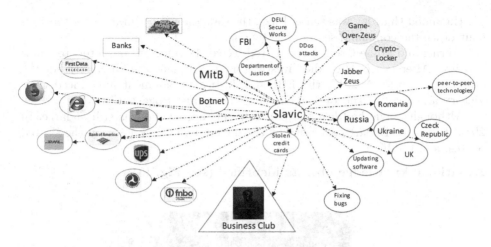

Fig. 11. Identified knowledge objects of 3rd phase

At first, this name was meaningless to the investigators, and it would be weeks before they realized that this was Slavic's real name. As it turned out, Slavic (alias lucky123459, Pollingsoon, Monstr, IOO and/or Nu11) was a then 30-year-old man who lived in Anapa - a Russian resort on the Black Sea. They had finally found him. But one thing puzzled investigators: how could the world's most wanted hacker (see Fig. 12[30] live such an open and pompous life in the public eye without being caught directly by Russian authorities? Upon further investigation, officials discovered that the Game-Over network was not only used to steal bank accounts, but it also specifically searched the infected computers for classified information that could be useful for military operations, for example.

Apparently, not the fellow members of the hacker network knew about this "additional function", but only Slavic himself. The FBI and FOX IT team could not prove any concrete connections between Bogachev and the Russian secret service. But it was obvious that a certain entity sent Bogachev certain terms/keywords to search for specifically. Thus, Bogachev was not only one of the biggest cybercriminals for the investigators, but also a Russian spy and thus "untouchable" for them[31].

In 2014, the FBI planned an unprecedented attack against the Game Over Zeus network. Together with more than 70 Internet providers in numerous countries (such as Canada, United Kingdom, Japan or Italy), they planned to strike on Friday, May 30 - this international inter-agency collaboration named Operation Tovar[32]. For over a year, the experts had decoded every line of malware,

[30] https://money.cnn.com/2014/06/02/technology/security/gameover-zeus-botnet.

[31] https://www.cbsnews.com/news/evgeniy-mikhailovich-bogachev-the-growing-partnership-between-russia-government-and-cybercriminals-60-minutes/.

[32] https://www.ibtimes.co.uk/gameover-slavik-cybercrime-kingpin-behind-zeus-malware-1451095.

yet the mood that day was tense. First, the Canadian and Ukrainian authorities shut down the command servers one by one.

Werner and Stone-Gross carefully redirected the infected computers to a new synchro. After nearly 60 h, the investigators' team knew they had succeeded[33]. On Sunday, June 2, 2014, the FBI and Justice Department announced their victory and released the 14-count indictment against Bogachev[34].

Although Slavic had lost the battle for his botnet, he was still at large. In 2015, the State Department put out the largest bounty ever set by the United States, at \$3 million.

Additional knowledge objects identified (see Fig. 13):

Aliases: Yevgeniy Bogachev, Evgeniy Mikhaylovich Bogachev, "lucky12345", "slavik", "Pollingsoon"

DESCRIPTION

Date(s) of Birth Used: October 28, 1983
Height: Approximately 5'9"   **Hair:** Brown (usually shaves his head)
Weight: Approximately 180 pounds   **Eyes:** Brown

Fig. 12. Wanted by the FBI: Bogachev

- Investigator/investigating authorities/company/collaboration:
  - FOX IT
  - Michael Sandee
  - Operation "Tovar"
- Geographic notes:
  - UK (server)
  - Anapa
- Names of the hackers:
  - Evgeniy Bogachev, Evgeniy Mikhaylovich Bogachev, Yevgeniy Bogachev
- Hacker names/nick names:
  - Slavic (alias lucky123459, Pollingsoon, Monstr, IOO and/or Nu11)
- Military & government interests: yes
  - Red flags: Malware infected computers for classified information
  - Russian secret service/Russian spy
- Malware: more spellings
  - GameOver ZeuS, Gameover Zeus

---

[33] https://www.youtube.com/watch?v=GBXc5QSGBls.
[34] https://www.fbi.gov/news/stories/gameover-zeus-botnet-disrupted.

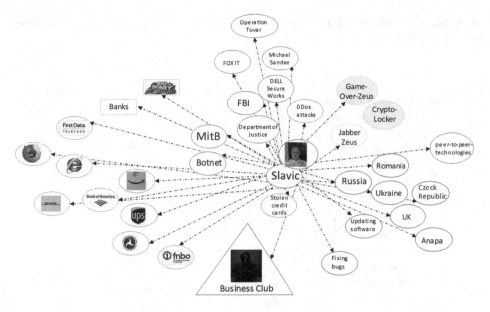

Fig. 13. Identified knowledge objects of 4th phase

5.5 5th Phase (2015 - Now): A Life of Luxury

To this day Bogachev lives at large[35]. His business interests go further than just Russia. At one point, he reportedly owned two villas in France. He also kept a fleet of cars parked around Europe, so he would never have to rent a vehicle while on vacation. He also owns many luxury cars, but reportedly prefers his Jeep Grand Cherokee[36]. The US suspects that the Russian government is protecting him and keeping him on their soil so that he can help boost their own espionage capabilities[37].

Additional Knowledge Objects Identified: None
To summarize the case from an innovation strategy perspective, the knowledge objects did show, that the case was an innovation race between hacker and prosecutor in five stages (Fig. 14), starting with a new man in the middle malware and the first improvement with a central control unit. This was defended, by shooting down the control server. The next attempt was to have a more secure communication infrastructure, by using the Jabber message service, followed by a peer-to-peer communication and crypt locker. This was addressed by using advanced network techniques to channel the communication, an unsuccessful attempt. Finally, it became clear, that the hacker was backed by a secret service,

---

[35] https://www.nytimes.com/2017/03/12/world/europe/russia-hacker-evgeniy-bogachev.html?smprod=nytcore-iphone&smid=nytcore-iphone-share&_r=2ls.

[36] https://officechai.com/stories/fabulous-life-evgeniy-bogachev-worlds-wanted-hacker/.

[37] https://www.youtube.com/watch?v=WAdK-ONnI4k.

in exchange for classified information. The whole process is ongoing and did last more than 17 years, up to now.

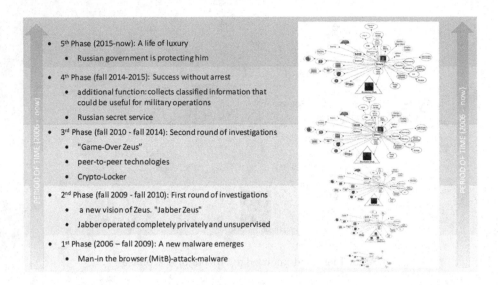

Fig. 14. Example - Slavic in summary

This shows, that without a proper innovation management public services can stay behind, for a long time. The hacker community around Bogachev is a new type of network managed organization, with a commercial approach to a resilient network organization. The weak point of these organization are the visible network activities. By addressing and undermining the money flow, these networks typically collapse.

Therefore, by looking more into the details of money laundering in the context of hacker communities, there are interesting patterns. If the money is earned with illegal activities or illegal behavior, like malware, crime as a service or crypto locker, this money needs to be cleaned for further usage. In this further process the money from an illegal activity is used in unregistered legal activities, avoid being punished for the illegal activity. Thus, it is important to make a distinction between the legal and illegal parts of the hacker communities and their corresponding **crypto systems** (see Fig. 15). The identification of cases for money laundering will most likely lead to additional identification of illegal behavior in the hacker community.

Fig. 15. Legal and illegal sides of a crypto ecosystem

With regard to community formation, legal and illegal forces have an impact on innovation in the crypto ecosystem. By fare not all hackers are willing to engage in illegal activities. But some of the illegal hacker got their education in the legal hacker community. This important distinction is done in the community (white hacker, gray hacker and black hacker) but rarely appear in public and common explanatory models. Given the fact, that this is highly relevant for the identification of organized crime networks, further research is needed. Classic data sources - such as those of patents, publications, or business data - are no longer sufficient to uncover innovative networks, when it comes to illegal hacking and cybercrime. The different sub parts of the community is using different channels to exchange their knowledge. Therefore, are the crawler developed to work with internet, deep web and dark nets, but as result from the crawling activity, this is not enough. The interlinkage between surface web and dark net is not as simple as expected, caused by experts, which knows very well how to hide.

6 Political Implications for the Digital Transformation in the EU

In addition to the "common assumptions" about the hacker communities and their contribution to the digital transformation, mentioned at the beginning of the publication the hacker communities contribute significantly, to innovations in cybersecurity, either for the good or for the bad. Given their aptitude for identifying and addressing security vulnerabilities, interaction with these communities could potentially enable policymakers to enhance the security of digital infrastructures and systems, a crucial element of any digital transformation strategy, only in the case that hacker are motivated to support national interests. As the example case did show, this could go wrong. In any way the open-source ethos permeates these communities, fostering a culture of knowledge sharing and collaborative problem solving. This approach stimulates innovation by creating a communal pool of knowledge and tools, allowing diverse individuals and organizations to build upon shared resources. This approach has already entered the EU innovation strategy[38], but needs to be differentiated, when it comes to state motivation. As was presented, a state could very well profit from hacker experience. But this experience could be misused and ends up in a very powerful next generation organized crime activity.

The diversity inherent in hacker communities also holds considerable value to nations regarding their innovations. A variety of perspectives on technology and its applications can ensure that digital transformation is as inclusive as possible, catering to a broad range of needs and potential impacts. Hacker networks contribute to the democratization of innovation by making it accessible to all, irrespective of traditional power structures. This encourages grassroots innovation, which is key to a broad-based digital transformation. Finally, these communities foster a culture of experimentation, endorsing risk-taking, learning, and constant iteration, which are fundamental to innovation. This environment stimulates novel ideas and breakthroughs that may otherwise be missed by traditional top-down approaches.

First analytics did show that there is a structural change, ongoing in the hacker community, caused by disruptive innovations in the digital ecosystem. All activities are highly globalized, and the community makes use of the different national regulations in a very effective way. To identify future hacker groups in the global hacker community, it is worthwhile to look more closely into the digital ecosystem and to discover innovations which might be used for money laundering in the future. We understand a digital ecosystem to be a socio-technical system that uses mechanisms of the platform economy to connect its own and external services with possible stakeholders in a central instance. Digital ecosystems thus differ significantly from traditional ecosystems. They change the economy and society in equal measure and stimulate emerging technologies.

The crypto ecosystem is a system where participants are connected and supported each other within a blockchain. Blockchains have surged in popularity ever since bitcoin introduced the world to cryptocurrency. There has never been a new technology that has grown this fast. The blockchain technology is the strong beating heart, the cryptocurrency the money that fuels this ecosystem. The fragmentation of the individual sub-ecosystems is large and the different definitions are not always clear-cut.

---

[38] Future governance of the European Research Area (ERA) - Council conclusions (adopted on 26/11/2021), 14308/21.

"Just as the technology of printing altered and reduced the power of medieval guilds and the social power structure, so too will cryptologic methods fundamentally alter the nature of corporations and of government interference in economic transactions[39]."

In the next step of development, we will therefore clarify the different levels and elements as well as their mutual interaction. Afterwards, those special aspects of crypto ecosystems that are relevant for the innovation-driving forces in the networks operating will be addressed. Figure 16 illustrates the interaction of the individual elements of a digital ecosystem. It consists of three, overlapping areas and a core - the crypto ecosystem - whose heart is blockchain technology.

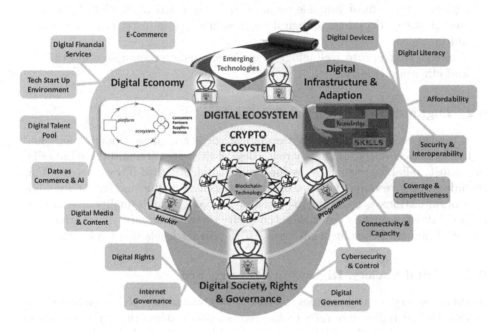

Fig. 16. Elements of a digital ecosystem

6.1 Digital Economy

Early in the digital era, the term knowledge economy was used to denote a combination of the Information and Communications Technology (ICT) sector, digital

---

[39] Timothy C. May, The Crypto Anarchist Manifesto, tcmay@netcom.com, https://groups.csail.mit.edu/mac/classes/6.805/articles/crypto/cypherpunks/may-crypto-manifesto.html.

media and e-commerce. The emergence and evolution of the digital economy is characterized by key trends[40]:

- The digital economy is often referred to as a platform economy. The platform business model is the emblem of digital transformation.
- In the digital economy, organizations differentiate themselves by creating digital experiences for customers.
- In the digital economy, traditional and linear value chains with limited partner engagement are now giving way to scaled-up, integrated ecosystems that use software platforms to deliver value, create resiliency, and foster innovation through connected products, assets, people, and processes.
- The digital economy is primarily a data-driven economy. Indeed, in the digital age, data is the most valuable resource and it is a critical enabler of personalized customer experiences, digital business models, industry ecosystems, and automation.
- The role that crypto technology plays in enhancing economic opportunities and efficiency is huge.

6.2 Digital Infrastructure and Adaption

The digital economy as well as the digital society requires organizations and individuals to connect seamlessly regardless of their location and therefore relies on robust, reliable, responsive, secure, and scalable digital infrastructure. This includes all the resources that make digital systems possible and how individuals and organizations access and use those resources. A high-quality, nationwide digital infrastructure is crucial for the entire digital economy. Adaptations are essential here and thus form the basis for the higher levels in all value chains.

6.3 Digital Society, Rights, and Governance

In this area, crypto technologies interact with government, civil society and the media. Digital rights here refer to the rights and freedoms that individuals can exercise online, including rights to privacy and data ownership. When it comes to governance, we differentiate: Internet governance touches on a range of public policy issues, including commerce, civil liberties, cybersecurity and sovereignty. Digital governance, on the other hand, refers to the use of digital technologies as an integral part of governance modernization strategies to create public value[41]. Significantly, an open-source ethos permeates these communities, fostering a culture of knowledge sharing and collaborative problem solving. This approach

---

[40] Safder Nazir, Accelerating the Digital Economy: Four Key Enablers 2021-07-28, Senior Vice President - Digital Industries, https://e.huawei.com/br/eblog/industries/insights/2021/accelerating-digital-economy.

[41] USAID, DIGITAL ECOSYSTEM FRAMEWORK, https://digitalprinciples.org/wp-content/uploads/Digital_Strategy_Digital_Ecosystem.pdf, 2021, https://www.usaid.gov/sites/default/files/documents/Digital_Strategy_Digital_Ecosystem_Final.pdf.

can stimulate innovation by creating a communal pool of knowledge and tools, allowing diverse individuals and organizations to build upon shared resources.

In conclusion, hacker communities and their innovation networks, offer an invaluable resource for European innovation policy as it navigates the complex terrain of digital transformation. These communities provide an alternative perspective, practical technical knowledge, and a dynamic approach to problem-solving that can significantly aid policy initiatives. But there is an inherent risk involved, when the motivation of hackers turn into illegal activities. This has already been addressed by the criminal law, but maybe future improvements are necessary.

7 Outlook

The proposed method to detect hidden innovation networks, by using the network effect within the formal and informal communication on the internet, the deep net and dark nets was very successful and did give deep insights into the inner structure of innovation networks, which are using digital ways of communication and knowledge management. The innovation networks identified have been proven to be fast and efficient in using their digital methods. It is up to further research, whether this is the reason, that the identified networks are so efficient, by creating this high pace of innovation.

As we move further into the digital age, the role of hacker innovation networks within the European innovation policy landscape is expected to grow, spurred by an increasing recognition of their value. Looking forward, we can anticipate several key trends. The collaboration between hacker communities and European policymakers is likely to intensify. Policymakers, seeking to leverage the unique skill sets, rapid innovation capabilities, and extensive knowledge of these communities, will likely forge closer ties, facilitating better dialogue and cooperation. This collaboration might take various forms, ranging from more formal partnerships and consultations to less formal, but equally critical, exchanges of ideas and information. However as mentioned, this comes with a risk.

In the realm of cybersecurity, the expertise within hacker communities will become an even more vital resource. As digital transformation continues to unfold, the security of digital infrastructure and systems will remain a top priority. We can anticipate an increasingly proactive role for these communities in helping to identify and address potential vulnerabilities and threats.

As a next step, further test cases need to be explored and the analytical details could by improved, by using more advanced artificial intelligence. It is very likely, that the missing part of the high pace of innovation could be identified. But to quantify the actual contribution of the hidden part in an innovation network, it is necessary to compare different innovation network and to identify the specific increase in efficiency, in relation to the methods for communication and knowledge management used.

References

1. Devasirvatham, W., Thiyagarajan, J.D.: Extricating web pages from deep web using DEAIMA architecture. Theoret. Comput. Sci. **931**, 93–103 (2022). https://doi.org/10.1016/j.tcs.2022.07.033
2. Liu, K., Wang, F., Ding, Z., Liang, S., Yu, Z., Zhou, Y.: A review of knowledge graph application scenarios in cyber security (2022). https://doi.org/10.48550/arXiv.2204.04769
3. Xu, G., Hu, W., Qiao, Y., Zhou, Y.: Mapping an innovation ecosystem using network clustering and community identification: a multi-layered framework. Scientometrics **124**(3), 2057–2081 (2020). https://doi.org/10.1007/s11192-020-03543-0

Information Security

Enabling the JSON Web Signature Format to Support Complex and Identity-Oriented Non-web Processes

Michael Hofmeier(✉) and Wolfgang Hommel

Computer Science Department, University of the Bundeswehr Munich,
Werner-Heisenberg-Weg 39, 85577 Neubiberg, Germany
michael.hofmeier@unibw.de

Abstract. This paper examines what rules or extensions have to be applied to the JSON Web Signature format so that it can be used universally in identity-driven non-web processes where identities exchange data, documents or attestations in a decentralized manner but do not know each other. For this purpose, the format and the related process must fulfill certain requirements such as identifiability and support for multiple signatures at possibly different points in time. The German T-prescription was selected as the application scenario, since it involves special requirements for signatures, data protection and data transfer. For this scenario, all the necessary applications and libraries are implemented and the process is run through and analyzed.

Keywords: electronic signatures · json web signatures · public key infrastructure · attestations · identities

1 Introduction

Our work enables a well-known data format that relies on certificates from a Public Key Infrastructure (PKI) in a way that allows for the attestation and verification of information even though the receiving entity knows nothing about the sender.

The targeted format or format modification supports complex non-web processes electronically and with modern syntax. Multiple signatures are to be supported, which can also be added at different times by different identities.

For the conception and testing of the design, the everyday application scenario of the doctor's prescription is used, on which the data concept is developed and tested. This application scenario is described and analyzed in more detail in Sect. 3.

For the intended format, the established JSON Web Signature (JWS) format, is used as a basis and extended and modified accordingly. JWS is based on the JavaScript Object Notation (JSON) and is particularly performant to be parsed in JavaScript environments [4]. A library has also been developed in this research process, with particular attention being paid to the proper validation

U. R. Krieger et al. (Eds.): I4CS 2023, CCIS 1876, pp. 29–47, 2023.
https://doi.org/10.1007/978-3-031-40852-6_2

of all cryptographic processes, as this has not always been the case in the JWS context to date [14]. This and other project content and documentation are provided via a GitHub repository [6].

Prescription of medication by a doctor comes into play here as an exemplary application scenario, or more precisely, the so-called "T-prescriptions" in Germany. T-prescriptions are special prescriptions that may only be used to prescribe medications with the ingredients lenalidomide, pomalidomide and thalidomide. This process was selected because it involves some special requirements in the context of signatures, for instance, multiple signatures, carbon copies, and forwarding anonymized data to authorities. This paper deliberately omits any ongoing digitization processes and establishing standards from the healthcare sector, as it is about the general validation of the format on a complex process, and not about the intention to digitize this explicit process. Nevertheless, the patient should (somehow) be able to receive the prescription as a file or data record and then pass it on to the pharmacist, who then processes it further. This process will be developed in more detail in Sect. 4.

1.1　Research Questions

- RQ1: How must the JWS format be extended or modified to be usable in (half-) automated electronic processes, where the receiver of the data does not know the instances that signed the data (or document)?
- RQ2: What role can a Public Key Infrastructure (PKI) play in this context and how could the combination of JWS (or a derivative) and PKI look like?
- RQ3: Is the derived format extension (or modification) suitable to support data processing, forwarding and validation in a useful way in the outlined scenario?
- RQ4: What are the remaining security risks and which attack vectors are relevant for this scenario?

1.2　Methodology

In this research process, the requirements for the utilized format are first analyzed based on the defined use case. Then, the JWS format is modified by additional rules or extensions to the point where it can meet the requirements.

In the next step, applications are developed for the exemplary use case that implement this format and map the electronic information flow. This is a practical way of testing whether all requirements for data, security and verifiability are met. However, no fully-fledged software is developed here, but input masks and test views that focus on the data of the prescription and the necessary stamps and signatures. Figure 1 shows the individual steps. If optimization potentials or even design errors are identified during implementation, an iterative approach is taken and the design is revised. At the end, the concept and its applications are validated experimentally.

This process thus represents a simple from of design science. Since it concerns a special detail in the overall process of the application, that is, a data exchange

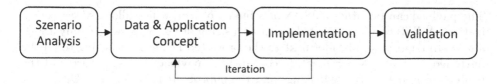

Fig. 1. Technical evaluation method

format, the number of iterations and the maturity of the artifact is sensibly limited to the validation of this aspect. A purely technical evaluation strategy is applied, without human users, since naturalistic strategies are irrelevant for purely technical artifacts or when the planned deployment with users is far in the future [17].

2 Related Work

For the development of the electronic process, it must be determined in which exchange format the verifiable data is to be transferred. Generally formats based on Extensible Markup Language (XML) or JavaScript Object Notation (JSON) are the most commonly used ones, although it is clear from the trend of recent years that XML is slowly being replaced by JSON [15]. Based on these exchange formats, the XML Signature and the JSON Web Signature (JWS) were developed, which allow the transmission of signed data. This section is primarily about these two formats.

2.1 XML Signature

XML Signatures are actually elements of an XML document. They contain information about the signature, such as the algorithm, but also the digital signature itself, and refer to other content elements of the same XML document [2].

Although XML is growing in popularity, XML Signatures have the attractive ability to support multiple signatures [12]. Segments can also be selected via path, though this also makes attack vectors possible. XML Signature Wrapping attacks modify the structure of the original message in some way, so the element that is validated might not be the same as the element that is parsed by the receiver [13]. Many security issues with XML signatures result from incorrect or incomplete validation within the APIs or the libraries used [13], which adds to, or therefore results from, the rather complicated structure compared to JWS.

2.2 JSON Web Signature

The JWS developed by the Internet Engineering Task Force (IETF) is a data structure representing a digitally signed message [7], which consists of a protected header, (sometimes) an unprotected header, a payload and a digital signature.

The payload can be either a JSON or a binary object, which allows direct serialization. A JWS can be presented either as a string or as JSON, where only JSON allows an unprotected header next to the protected header. According to [7] the flattened JWS JSON Serialization contains the payload, the signature and the protected header as Base64 strings and the unprotected header as JSON:

```
{
    "header": { "kid": "..." }
    "protected": "<base64string>",
    "payload": "<base64string>",
    "signature": "<base64string>",
}
```

The complete JWS JSON Serialization (JWS-JS) allows multiple signatures and is composed as follows:

```
{
    "payload":"<base64string>",
    "signatures":[
     {"protected":"<base64string>",
      "header":{ ... },
      "signature":"<base64string>"},
     {"protected":"<base64string>",
      "header": { ... },
      "signature":"<base64string>"}, ...]
}
```

The text representation of the JWS is only available for the JWS Compact Serialization (JWS-CS) and is composed as follows:

```
BASE64URL(UTF8(Header)) + '.'
+ BASE64URL(Payload) + '.'
+ BASE64URL(Signature)
```

A weakness of the JWS-CS shown above is that there can be only one signature for this data set. The JWS-JS allows multiple signatures, but has more complex structure and "...is neither optimized for compactness nor URL-safe" [7].

The following subsections explain the individual components of a JWS.

JWS Payload. The payload is represented as a Base64 string. This can be either a byte array containing a binary/file or a byte array representing a JSON string in UTF-8 encoding.

JWS Signature. The digital signature of the JWS is represented as a Base64 string. The signed data is a composition of the protected header and the payload:

```
BASE64URL(UTF8(Header))
+ '.' + BASE64URL(Payload)
```

According to [7], in the case of JWS-JS with multiple signatures, it is up to the application whether only one or certain signatures or all signatures must be valid during signature verification. This of course provides a lot of room for problematic implementations in libraries.

JWS Header. The JWS header is a JSON object before it is converted to a Base64 string, and is also the most important and complex component of a JWS object. The JavaScript Object Signing and Encryption (JOSE) header definition describes the header parameters for the JWS and the JWT, whereas only the parameters *typ* (Type) and *cty* (Content Type) are defined for the JWT and a number of other properties provide information for the validation of the signature for the JWS [15]. The most important parameters of the JWS are explained in the following:

- kid: The *kid* represents an identifier that the recipient can use to retrieve the public key from a data set known to him, e.g., from a database or from a web service.
- cty: The *cty* parameter is optional and gives information about the media type of the payload.
- typ: The *typ* parameter gives information about the media type of the complete JWS object and is intended for use by applications when different kinds of objects could be present in an application data structure [7].
- alg: The *alg* parameter gives information about the signature algorithm and the Secure Hash Algorithm (SHA) used to create the signature. Valid values include HS256, HS384, HS512, RS256, RS384, RS512, ES256, ES384 and ES512, where, e.g., RS256 stands for Rivest-Shamir-Adleman (RSA) and SHA-256, HS384 for Keyed-Hashing for Message Authentication Code (HMAC) and SHA-384, and ES512 for Elliptic Curve Digital Signature Algorithm (ECDSA) and SHA-512 [8].
- x5u: The *x5u* parameter is optional and provides a URL to the X.509 certificate corresponding to the private key used to create the signature. The certificate(s) available under the URL must be delivered in Privacy Enhanced Mail (PEM) format.
- x5c: The *x5c* parameter is optional and an alternative to the *x5u* parameter. It contains the X.509 certificate(s) as a JSON array of Base64 strings in Distinguished Encoding Rules (DER) encoding, where the first item of the array is the one used for the signature and the following items are the certificates of the certificate authorities (CA).

JWS/JWT in Healthcare Applications [11] has been working on JWS-based adaptive authentication modalities for healthcare applications, introducing additional security mechanisms. For example, timestamps are provided in both the payload and the HTTP request to detect replay attacks. Specifically, they use the JWT format in their proposed authentication modality and rely on additional encryption of the payload.

The *gematik GmbH* is a company founded by the leading organizations in the German healthcare sector to promote and coordinate the introduction, maintenance and further development of the electronic health card and its infrastructure in Germany. In their system-specific concept for e-prescriptions [5], JSON Web Tokens (JWT) are exchanged between the doctor, patient and pharmacist, which can also be provided as a QR code if necessary. The prescription itself is stored on a central resource server and can only be retrieved with the correct token. This is a centralized approach, but shows that JWS or JWT can be an appropriate method. In this work, we set up a non-system-specific and decentralized approach in favor of unification, data protection and the digital sovereignty of the participating identities.

3   Application Scenario Analysis

As mentioned in Sect. 1, the T-prescription as a special form of doctor's prescription is taken as an application scenario.

Physicians may only prescribe drugs containing lenalidomide and thalidomide on a numbered two-part official form issued by the German Federal Institute for Drugs and Medical Devices (BfArM). Medicines containing lenalidomide and thalidomide are used for very rare diseases and are therefore very cost-intensive, which is why high documentation requirements are applied. As with a normal prescription, the original is given to the respective health insurance company. Additionally a carbon copy, on which the patient data are blacked out, is forwarded to the BfArM by the pharmacy on a quarterly basis [10]. Both parts of the T-prescription are shown in Fig. 2.

In order to map this process to an electronic form, the data packets and transfer points as well as the respective sender and receiver must be identified. It is also important to determine who has to sign which data and when, and which data must not be passed on. In the following sections, the process steps are analyzed with regard to these aspects.

3.1   Process

Prescription. The doctor fills in the form with information about the doctor, the patient and the prescribed product. The form gets two signatures, the stamp of the doctor's office and the signature of the prescribing doctor. On the carbon copy of the form, the area where the patient's data is entered is blacked out. Both parts are given to the patient.

Handover to the Pharmacist. The patient hands over the form and carbon copy to the pharmacist and receives the prescribed drugs in return. Depending on the type of insurance, the patient gets back the form stamped and signed by the pharmacist.

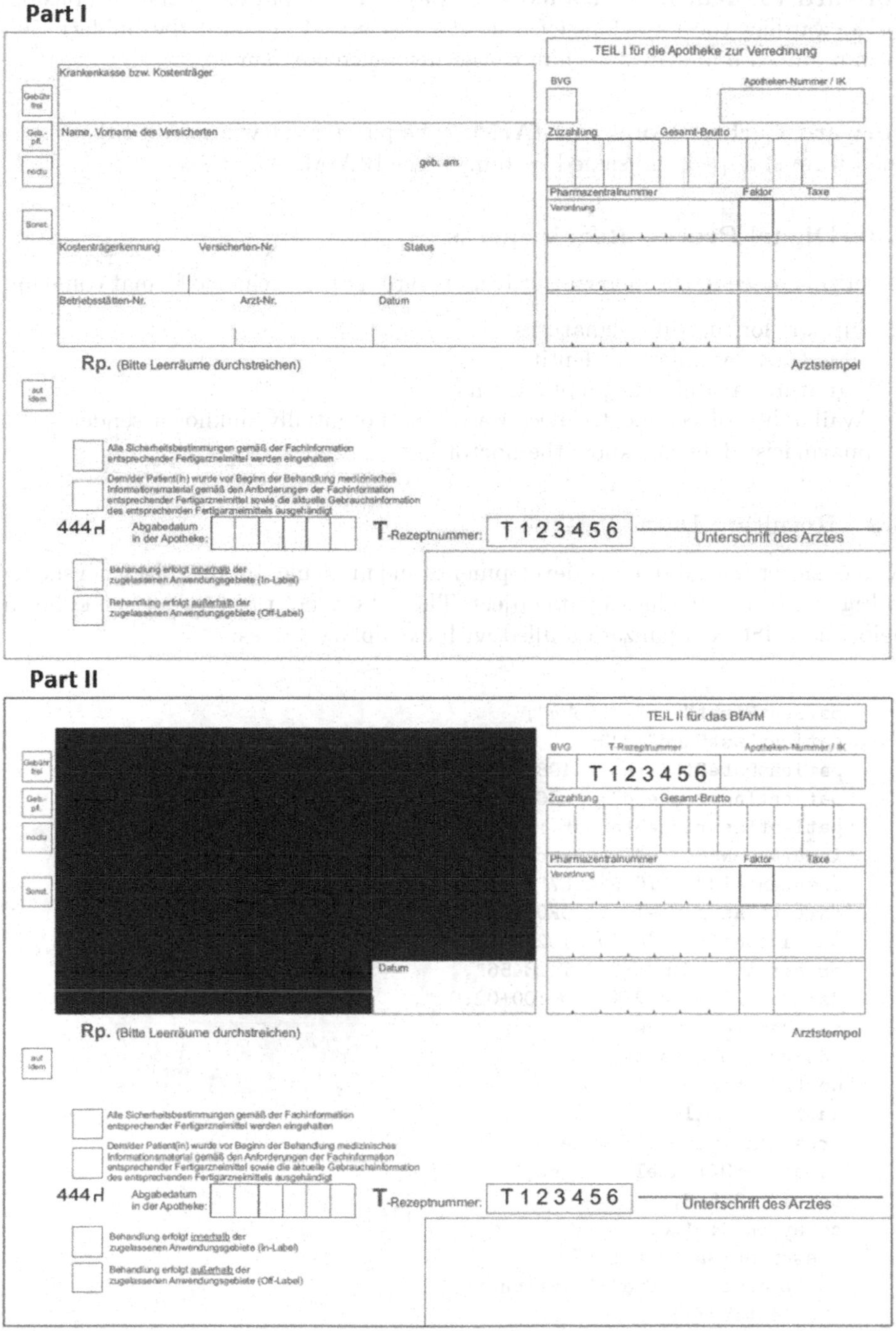

Part I

Krankenkasse bzw. Kostenträger

Gebühr-frei

Geb.-pfl.

noctu

Sonst.

Name, Vorname des Versicherten

geb. am

Kostenträgerkennung   Versicherten-Nr.   Status

Betriebsstätten-Nr.   Arzt-Nr.   Datum

TEIL I für die Apotheke zur Verrechnung

BVG   Apotheken-Nummer / IK

Zuzahlung   Gesamt-Brutto

Pharmazentralnummer   Faktor   Taxe
Verordnung

Rp. (Bitte Leerräume durchstreichen)   Arztstempel

aut idem

Alle Sicherheitsbestimmungen gemäß der Fachinformation entsprechender Fertigarzneimittel werden eingehalten

Dem/der Patient(in) wurde vor Beginn der Behandlung medizinisches Informationsmaterial gemäß den Anforderungen der Fachinformation entsprechender Fertigarzneimittel sowie die aktuelle Gebrauchsinformation des entsprechenden Fertigarzneimittels ausgehändigt

444 ┌┤   Abgabedatum in der Apotheke: T-Rezeptnummer: T 1 2 3 4 5 6   Unterschrift des Arztes

Behandlung erfolgt innerhalb der zugelassenen Anwendungsgebiete (In-Label)

Behandlung erfolgt außerhalb der zugelassenen Anwendungsgebiete (Off-Label)

Part II

TEIL II für das BfArM

BVG   T-Rezeptnummer   Apotheken-Nummer / IK

T 1 2 3 4 5 6

Zuzahlung   Gesamt-Brutto

Pharmazentralnummer   Faktor   Taxe
Verordnung

Datum

Rp. (Bitte Leerräume durchstreichen)   Arztstempel

auf idem

Alle Sicherheitsbestimmungen gemäß der Fachinformation entsprechender Fertigarzneimittel werden eingehalten

Dem/der Patient(in) wurde vor Beginn der Behandlung medizinisches Informationsmaterial gemäß den Anforderungen der Fachinformation entsprechender Fertigarzneimittel sowie die aktuelle Gebrauchsinformation des entsprechenden Fertigarzneimittels ausgehändigt

444 ┌┤   Abgabedatum in der Apotheke: T-Rezeptnummer: T 1 2 3 4 5 6   Unterschrift des Arztes

Behandlung erfolgt innerhalb der zugelassenen Anwendungsgebiete (In-Label)

Behandlung erfolgt außerhalb der zugelassenen Anwendungsgebiete (Off-Label)

Fig. 2. Sample of German T-prescription [3]

Forward to Health Insurance Company. If the patient is not responsible for forwarding the form himself, the pharmacist will forward the unblackened form stamped and signed by him to the insurance company.

Forward Carbon Copy to BfArM. The pharmacist will forward the blackened form stamped and signed by him to the BfArM.

3.2   Digital Process Requirements

From this process, the following criteria regarding the exchange format come up:

- Support for multiple signatures
- Signatures by different identities
- Signatures at different points in time
- Availability of certificates because of the potentially unknown sender - the pharmacist does not know the doctor

3.3   Resulting Data Object

As a basis for the subsequent developments and implementations, the form shown in Fig. 2 is translated into a data object. The data structure of the object is shown below as a JSON serialization filled with exemplary values:

```json
{
    "patientFirstName": "John",
    "patientLastName": "Doe",
    "patientDateOfBirth": "1985/01/01",
    "patientInsuranceId": "ABC1234XYZ",
    "patientInsuranceStatus": "public",
    "insuranceName": "Insurance Corp.",
    "insuranceId": "IC1234567",
    "physiciansOfficeId": "OF0987152467",
    "physiciansId": "DOC0891622",
    "prescriptionNumber": "T123456",
    "date": "2023-04-27T00:00:00+02:00",
    "chargeable": true,
    "chargefree": false,
    "noctu": false,
    "autIdem": false,
    "treatmentInLabel": true,
    "treatmentOffLabel": false,
    "total": 985.3,
    "coPayment": 120,
    "prescriptionItems": [{
        "product": "Example Product 1",
        "factor": 1,
        "fee": 25
    }]
}
```

4   Concept and Format Development

The prescription and the carbon copy are to be created electronically and handed over to the patient as a file or data record. In the superordinate project, in which this research is located, an app for smartphones was developed that serves as a carrier for certificates through which signatures and authentications can be performed. This app is now being extended so that also signed records can be picked up and handed back. The format for these records is derived from JWS in a way that meets the requirements of but is not limited to this process.

4.1   Applications

In this scenario, three applications are developed. Firstly, the app just mentioned, which serves as a pure transmission medium, and secondly, the application for the doctor and the application for the pharmacist (Sect. 5.1). The latter two are implemented as simplified input forms for the desktop and rely on Public Key Infrastructure (PKI) certificates.

Since neither the pharmacist knows the doctor, nor the insurance company the pharmacist, it is not possible to rely on public keys that have already been exchanged, e.g., identified via the *kid*. In order to be able to verify the signatures and stamps and to relate them securely to instances or persons, the use of PKI certificates is a valid approach. The PKI relies on the X.509 certificate standard that binds the identity of the key holder to the holders public key and enables a hierarchic chain of certificate authorities (CA) to validate the certificate [1].

4.2   Data Format

The utilized data format must meet the following criteria, among others, for such a scenario:

- Performant readability of type, content type and description, optimally without deserializing the whole document
- Multiple signatures from different possibly unknown persons at different points in time
- Linking of the signature to a date
- Embedding or linking of the certificate

To meet the requirements we have developed the Certificate-based JSON Web Signature (CJWS), which is divided into three versions. The first version (CJWS1) represents a format that is fully compatible with the JWS compact serialization, but does not yet support all requirements, especially multiple signatures. Nevertheless, this is shortly explained below, since it represents an intermediate step in the development. The second version (CJWS-JS) is a fully compatible JWS as JSON serialization with some disadvantages described afterwards. The third version (CJWS2) is a modification of JWS, which is no longer fully compatible with JWS, but meets all requirements. It is explained finally below and used by the applications in the scenario.

CJWS1. Since this concept is based on a PKI and X.509 certificates, the *x5c* parameter is defined as mandatory. The *alg* parameter specifies the signature algorithm of this certificate and the hash algorithm. The parameter *typ* is set to "cjws1" and another mandatory parameter *dsp* is introduced for the display text/name. The display text is required by the patient's app so that the patient can identify the different records stored in the app. The *cty* parameter is taken here to allow the applications to recognize the purpose of the payload content and to correctly associate and process it. The *day* parameter contains the document's date. The header of the JWS looks like the following for the CJWS1 modification:

```
CJWS1 HEADER:
{
    "typ": "CJWS1",
    "x5c": ["<base64string>"],
    "alg": "RS256",
    "day": "2023/03/31",
    "dsp": "Prescription ...",
    "cty": "german-t-prescription"
}
```

Since this extension is fully compatible with JWS but does not support multiple signatures, the second step is to modify the structure of JWS so that the certificate, the related information, and the signature data are relocated to a separate object that can exist multiple times, similar to the unflattened JWS JSON Serialization. This results in the second version CJWS2, which is described in more detail below.

Advantages:

– Fully compatible with the JWS-CS
– Extractable header without deserializing the whole document

Disadvantages:

– Only usable with a single signature

CJWS-JS. The JWS JSON Serialization allows multiple signatures by introducing a new object for signatures which, in addition to the signature data, has a header and a protected header with possibly optional properties described in Sect. 2.

A CJWS-JS object is a JWS JSON Serialization extended with a strict ruleset regarding header parameters (see Sect. 4.2) and validation. As shown in Sect. 2.2, there is no header on the object itself, only on the subset signatures. For a CJWS-JS the protected signature headers correspond exactly to the header of the CJWS1 where the parameters *typ*, *cty* and *dsp* have the same value for all signatures and can only be stored on the object when a signature is present. A CJWS-JS object is valid if ALL signatures are valid.

Advantages:

- Fully compatible with the JWS-JS

Disadvantages:

- Header information only extractable by serializing the whole document
- Cannot be used without a signature present
- Not URL-safe

CJWS2. Since we want to keep a top level header, we modified the structure in this respect. This modification still allows compact serialization, which is convenient for us when nesting records. Another advantage is the possibility to extract the header from the final string by reading the file or string only until the first "." appears. This, e. g., improves performance for listing multiple objects with their display text.

As mentioned in Sect. 2.2, some libraries might handle signature verification differently or incorrectly due to the vague definition, so some incompatibility might be beneficial. However, in our implementation, all attached signatures must be valid.

The CJWS2 modification introduces a protected header on its top level containing the parameters *typ*, *cty* and *dsp*. The *x5c*, *alg* and *day* parameters are placed directly under the signature object along with the *sig* parameter that stores the signature data as a Base64 string. The signature is computed for the protected header plus the payload plus the *day* parameter (*protectedBase64* + '.' +*payloadBase64* + '.' + *day*).

```
SIGNATURE:
{
    "x5c": ["<base64string>"],
    "alg": "RS256",
    "day": "2023/03/31",
    "sig": ["<base64string>"],
}
```

A CJWS2 then has the following structure:

```
CJWS2:
{
    "protected": "<base64string>",
    "payload": "<base64string>",
    "signatures": ["<base64string>", ...]
}
```

The text representation of the CJWS2 is composed as follows:

```
BASE64URL(UTF8(Header)) + '.'
+ BASE64URL(Payload) + '.'
+ BASE64URL(UTF8(Signature1)) + '.'
+ BASE64URL(UTF8(Signature2)) + ...
```

So with each signature a string is simply appended. The header with the document-related information does not change and can be extracted from the whole string using substring methods. Another advantage is that this object can be transmitted as a string even without a signature if it is not necessary, or added at a later point in time.

As stated above, this structure still allows multiple signatures, e. g., both stamp and signature of the physician, as well as at a later point in time the additional signatures (stamp, signature) of the pharmacist.

Advantages:

– Extractable header without deserializing the whole document
– Support for multiple signatures

Disadvantages:

– Not fully compatible to the JWS standard

Data Protection. Figure 3 shows a comparison of the signature-protected data in CJWS-JS and CJWS2. This also clearly shows the JWS compatible structure of the CJWS-JS and how the general parameters have migrated to the top level header in the CJWS2.

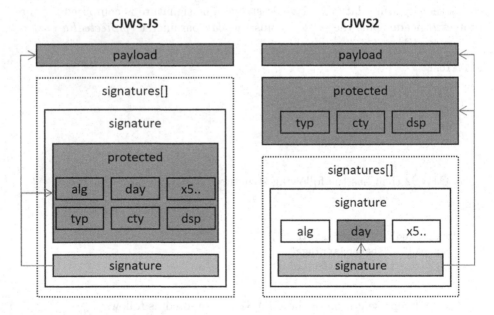

Fig. 3. Data protection in CJWS-JS and CJWS2

5 Implementation

For the implementation of the libraries and applications we have chosen .NET. There are a library for the CJWS classes, a library for the Prescription objects, an application for the doctor and an application for the pharmacy. For the application dedicated to the patient, as already explained, an existing application will be extended. Except for the latter, all libraries or applications are provided in a repository [6].

5.1 Communication

Various protocols were considered for implementing data communication between the specialist applications and the app for the patient. When trying to implement communication via Near Field Communication (NFC), it became apparent that this was not so easy due to the many different formats, hardware support and libraries. As [9] has stated, the mobile device used to communicate with the card reader must be capable of card emulation, and the data size should not exceed 1 KB, which is significantly less than the expected amount of data in our scenario due to the size of the contained certificate and the unknown size of the payload. Bluetooth or Bluetooth Low Energy (BLE) as well as WiFi Direct, on the other hand, fail due to security aspects.

In the end, we introduced a web based data exchange service (DXS) as an additional component, through which the data sets are exchanged as encrypted packets using Advanced Encryption Standard (AES). This approach imposes no special requirements on hardware and software and is outlined in Fig. 4.

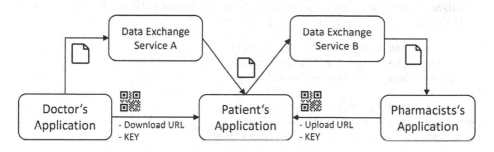

Fig. 4. Web-based communication architecture

The doctor uploads the AES encrypted CJWS to DXS using a valid API key and receives the corresponding download URL in return. The URL and the AES key are converted to a URL using *cjws:* as scheme and presented to the patient via QR code.

The scans the QR code what initiates the download and decryption of the prescription CJWS.

The pharmacist registers a pending upload using a valid API key and receives an upload URL in return. The patient scans a QR code containing the upload URL and the AES key and then selects the CJWS he wants to transmit. This initiates the encrypted upload to the DXS. The pharmacists application then downloads and decrypts the prescription. Since using Hypertext Transfer Protocol Secure (HTTPS), a direct non-interceptable key transmission (camera) and never giving the AES key to the DXS or another party, the personal data is well protected in this approach.

5.2 Data Structure

In the data structure, there are two ways to solve the problem with the carbon copy. One option is to pass two individual objects, one with and one without the patient's personal data. The second option is to put these two (signed) objects into one parent object and serialize it again. Since it is more intuitive for the patient to have one object transmitted and the CJWS2 format allows the absence of signatures, we choose the second option. The payload of the parent CJWS2 then looks like this:

```
{ "prescription": "<CJWS2-string>",
  "carbonCopy": "<CJWS2-string>" }
```

5.3 Class Libraries

During implementation a class library for the prescription objects and a class library for CJWS serialization have been developed. Since the carbon copy is a subset of the prescription, both are derived from the same base class. The serialization library introduces among others the classes *CJWS1*, *CJWS_JS* and *CJWS2*, all sharing the same base class *CJWS*.

```
CJWS cjws = new CJWS2(new CJWS2Header(){
    ContentType = "german-t-prescription",
    DisplayText = "T-Prescription"
});
cjws.SetPayloadObject(prescription);
cjws.Sign(cert, HashAlgorithmName.SHA512);
string prescriptionString = cjws.Serialize();
```

5.4 Data Exchange Service

The DXS was developed as ASP.NET application implementing a single controller with the actions *Register*, *Upload* and *Retrieve*. An uploaded data set is stored in a dictionary for a limited time until it is downloaded by the recipient. The short time slot and the once-only download provide additional security for the already encrypted data. A DXS implemented in this way could be owned by the physician or pharmacist, or it could be a public service. In addition, multiple different services with the same implementation could be used for each transmission. In this implementation, the same service was used for all transmissions.

5.5 Physician's Application

The physician's application was coded as a simple Windows Forms application (Fig. 5). It consists of a simple form with input fields that correspond to the data model of the prescription. After filling out the form, the doctor can generate the prescription and carbon copy with the click of a button, sign it, and present a QR code to the patient for transmission. The application integrates the previously mentioned libraries.

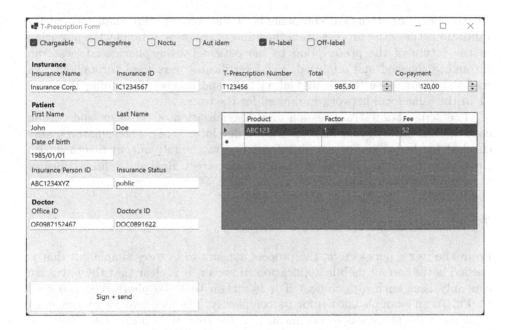

Fig. 5. Screenshot of physician's application

5.6 Pharmacist's Application

The pharmacist's application was also developed as a simple Windows Forms application. It consists of a simple form with text output to display the read data including all information about the signatures. The pharmacist can append their signatures to the included prescription and carbon copy with the click of a button and send on, although the methods for sending are left blank in the sample implementation. The application also integrates the previously mentioned libraries.

5.7 Patient's Application

For the patient, an existing mobile application was extended with the required functions. It was developed using .NET Multi-platform App UI (.NET MAUI).

The QR codes with download or upload URL and key can be scanned for the transmission of the CJWS documents. These documents or data sets such as the recipes can now be stored as CJWS inside the app storage. To list the documents, the first substring (header) of the CJWS1/CJWS2 can be read to output the name and content type and filter by it if necessary.

6   Validation

All the necessary technical components of the concept were implemented for validation. The entire process, from the filling of the prescription by the physician to the return of the prescription to the patient by the pharmacist, was run through, debugged and analyzed. Valid certificates were used throughout. An Android smartphone (Samsung Galaxy S10) and notebooks running Windows 11 in the same local network were used for the tests.

The serialization, transmission and deserialization of the form and carbon copy were monitored and inspected using developer tools. The signatures were checked by the programs and all information was visibly output together with the certificate chain. This information was all correct. Real and valid certificates were used for verification.

7   Conclusion

From the user's perspective, the process appears to be very simple; all that is needed is the correct mobile application. However, it is clear that the physician can only issue such a document if it is certain that the pharmacist can read it. This is an example chosen for its complexity. The fact that all parties must implement the process does not mean that the concept is unsuitable. However, it is necessary to consider implementability for the application of such methods.

Both the libraries and the applications were easily programmable, as .NET comes standard with classes and methods for JSON serialization, cryptography, certificates and network communication.

By using a web-based DXS, QR codes and HTTPS requests, there is no dependency in terms of hardware or operating system, apart from internet connection and camera.

As far as the certificates used are qualified certificates issued by a qualified trust service provider, the handwritten signature or the stamp can be replaced by this according to [16].

The mapped process could have been implemented with CJWS-JS, but was implemented with CJWS2 due to the advantages mentioned above. But basically, both fulfill the minimum requirements for a functional process.

7.1   Answering the Research Questions

Finally, the research questions from Sect. 1.1 can be answered:

RQ1: The JWS format is suitable in its full JSON serialization, but precise specifications/rules must be implemented regarding the header parameters and validation. The certificate related parameters and the parameters *typ*, *cty* and *dsp* are mandatory. In terms of document validation all attached certificates must be valid. For better processing in the applications and to exclude possibly problematic libraries, a slight modification might be advantageous.

RQ2: Since the recipient of the data packets must be able to identify the possibly unknown sender, the use of PKI certificates is a suitable means. PKI certificates are supported by JWS. In the future, these could be replaced by other (decentralized) identity systems that allow the certificates or the public key and the correlated personal data to be retrieved using an identification number, once they have become established.

RQ3: Sect. 6 described the validation of the process. The CJWS-JS format and the CJWS2 format are suitable for transmitting data that must be signed at different times by different people. Both are easy to parse, but only the CJWS2 format allows to extract the header information in a performant way. Since the CJWS-JS is fully compatible to the JWS definition, JWS is suitable to support comparable scenarios, as far as an extended ruleset is implemented.

RQ4: The security risks in terms of data protection in this system are limited to the transmission of data via the DXS. Here, attack vectors that apply to Web services, such as Man in the Middle or Service Impersonation, are possible, but these have no influence on the integrity of the data record itself, since reading and modification are secured by the encryption and signatures. With regard to the data format, the risk lies in the unprotected parameters in the signature. This would allow certificates or algorithm information to be exchanged. However, since these are PKI certificates, this can only make the transmitted document invalid, but not give out false information as valid. To prevent multiple submissions, the pharmacist must register the prescription in a central registry using its number. Also, the *exp* parameter defined in JWS should be included in the library, which specifies an expiration date for the validity of the payload.

7.2 Considerations

This approach relies on indirect transmission of the data packet via the Internet. The reasons for this have been explained, but direct transmission would eliminate some risks. Furthermore, this approach is based on the use and co-delivery of PKI certificates. This could be avoided by introducing central registers or services for retrieving the certificates or by using other standardized techniques to expose the participants certificates like the protocol for DNS-based Authentication of Named Entities (DANE). Then, depending on the used algorithm and key size, the entire data set including signatures might even be small enough to be stored on a rewritable NFC card. This would make an application for the patient superfluous and enable direct transmission.

8   Future Work

Further tasks include implementing and validating the format and transmission methods in other scenarios. If applicable, in addition to the mobile application, other universally usable applications could be developed. Associated security and performance analyses are also worth considering.

These results and implementations should also contribute to implementing digitization projects of identity-driven processes using JSON-based formats. In conjunction with mobile applications such as the one used here, other document types such as vaccination certificates, attendance confirmations or access authorizations could be handled universally. By the decentralization of the communication flows and services, this approach enhances the digital sovereignty of the individual.

It would also be very pleasing if a future version of the JWS JSON Serialization were to get a protected top-level header and a compatible compact serialization, because then this format would be optimally suited for such processes. The compact serialization could use the signature object of the JWS JSON Serialization converted to a Base64 string for this purpose, similar to the CJWS2 but without simplifying the structure.

Acknowledgments. This work originates from the LIONS research project. LIONS is funded by dtec.bw – Digitalization and Technology Research Center of the Bundeswehr, which we gratefully acknowledge. dtec.bw is funded by the European Union – NextGenerationEU.

References

1. Albarqi, A., Alzaid, E., Al Ghamdi, F., Asiri, S., Kar, J., et al.: Public key infrastructure: a survey. J. Inf. Secur. **6**(01), 31 (2014)
2. Bartel, M., Boyer, J., Fox, B., LaMacchia, B., Simon, E.: XML signature syntax and processing version 1.1. Signature **6**(1), 48–49 (2013)
3. Bundesinstitut für Arzneimittel und Medizinprodukte: Bekanntmachung zur Arzneimittelverschreibungsverordnung (AMVV). Online (2016). https://www.bfarm.de/SharedDocs/Bekanntmachungen/DE/Bundesopiumstelle/AMVV/bm-bopst-190716-AMVV-pdf.pdf?__blob=publicationFile
4. Dhalla, H.K.: A performance analysis of native JSON parsers in Java, Python, MS. NET Core, JavaScript, and PHP. In: 2020 16th International Conference on Network and Service Management (CNSM), pp. 1–5. IEEE (2020)
5. gematik: Systemspezifisches Konzept E-Rezept (2020). https://fachportal.gematik.de/fachportal-import/files/gemSysL_eRp_V1.1.0.pdf
6. Hofmeier, M.: CJWS Github repository (2023). https://github.com/LIONS-DLT/cjws
7. Jones, M., Bradley, J., Sakimura, N.: RFC 7515: JSON Web Signature (JWS) (2015)
8. Jones, M.: RFC 7518: JSON web algorithms (JWA) (2015)
9. Karmazín, J., Očenášek, P.: The state of near-field communication (NFC) on the android platform. In: Tryfonas, T. (ed.) HAS 2016. LNCS, vol. 9750, pp. 247–254. Springer, Cham (2016). https://doi.org/10.1007/978-3-319-39381-0_22

10. Kassenärztliche Bundesvereinigung, Bundesärztekammer: Information für ärzte zur verordnung von lenalidomid-und thalidomid-haltigen arzneimitteln. Deutsches Ärzteblatt (2009)
11. Krishnan, V., Sreeja, C., Binu, S., Misbahuddin, M.: A json web signature based adaptive authentication modality for healthcare applications. In: 2022 IEEE International Conference on Public Key Infrastructure and its Applications (PKIA), pp. 1–8. IEEE (2022)
12. Kubbilun, W., Gajek, S., Psarros, M., Schwenk, J.: Trustworthy verification and visualisation of multiple XML-Signatures. In: Dittmann, J., Katzenbeisser, S., Uhl, A. (eds.) CMS 2005. LNCS, vol. 3677, pp. 311–320. Springer, Heidelberg (2005). https://doi.org/10.1007/11552055_41
13. Mainka, C., Jensen, M., Iacono, L.L., Schwenk, J.: XSpRES-robust and effective XML signatures for web services. In: CLOSER, pp. 187–197 (2012)
14. Sheffer, Y., Hardt, D., Jones, M.: RFC 8725: JSON Web Token Best Current Practices (2020)
15. Siriwardena, P., Siriwardena, P.: Message-level security with JSON web signature. In: Advanced API Security: OAuth 2.0 and Beyond, pp. 157–184 (2020)
16. The European Parliament and the Council of the European Union: European Regulation on Electronic Identification and Trust Services for Electronic Transactions in the internal market. Off. J. Eur. Union (2014)
17. Venable, J., Pries-Heje, J., Baskerville, R.: FEDS: a framework for evaluation in design science research. Eur. J. Inf. Syst. **25**, 77–89 (2016)

Bloom Filter-Based Realtime Risk Monitoring of SSH Brute Force Attacks

Günter Fahrnberger[✉] [iD]

University of Hagen, Hagen, North Rhine-Westphalia, Germany
`guenter.fahrnberger@studium.fernuni-hagen.de`

Abstract. Publicly shared hosts on the Internet appeal to well-behaving and mischievous clients in equal measure. Miscreants rapidly enumerate and attempt to capitalize on the hosts' open ports. Specially Command-Line Interfaces (CLIs), such as Secure Shell (SSH), with odds of conquering unlimited permissions on such hosts allure culprits into conducting brute force attacks. Responsible personnel should not unclose SSH ports to the Internet unless inevitable. If opened, installable precautions, like anti-hammering, Intrusion Detection Systems (IDSs), or Intrusion Prevention Systems (IPSs), simply proffer protection with a rash of descriptive attack statistics. Beyond that, pertinent research assists with qualitative pattern-based realtime risk monitoring of SSH brute force attacks. This disquisition appraises such offenses' danger more accurately than preceding methods with the support of a modified Bloom filter and attests the attained superiority over them.

Keywords: Bloom filter · Brute force attack · Monitoring · Risk monitoring · Searchable Encryption Scheme (SES) · Secure Shell (SSH) · Similarity assessment · Supervision · Surveillance

1 Introduction

Once a host offers services over ports opened on a public Internet Protocol (IP) address, it usually does not take long until attackers detect and tamper with them. Malicious motives vary from the quest for thrill over economical espionage to governmental interests. Unless targeted, offenders reconnoiter the public IP address space with network scanners, like Network Mapper (Nmap). Vulnerability scanners (such as Nessus and OpenVAS) conduct such reconnaissance to descry worthwhile attack vectors. Parallel computing helps to scale up reconnoitering capacities. Such an upscaling oftentimes happens involuntarily with the forcible recruitment of captured servers to botnets. Seifert already asserted in 2006 that approximately 500 bot scanners can trawl through the complete IPv4 address range 0.0.0.0/0 in one day [16]. Up to the present, the scanning velocity has been significantly increased. Both ZMap and MASSCAN run on a single node and promise to scan all addresses of 0.0.0.0/0 in 45 min with Gigabit Ethernet or even in 4.5 with ten Gbps [1,8].

U. R. Krieger et al. (Eds.): I4CS 2023, CCIS 1876, pp. 48–67, 2023.
https://doi.org/10.1007/978-3-031-40852-6_3

After the enumeration of all open ports and associated services, hackers can either purposefully exploit known vulnerabilities or try their luck with brute force attacks. The latter obtain their name from iteratively attempting elements of dictionaries or combinations of character sets until success, exhaustion, or cancelation. Brute force attacks can yield swift victories over laxly secured entities or merely waste valuable computing and networking resources. Undefeated targets do not disappoint black hats as their brute force attacks' setup can be deemed to be quick, easy, automatable, and, thus, does not cost them too much effort. It means daily business for them to take flops into account.

Brute forcers can pounce on all services with presumed weak spots and/or credentials. These can be CLIs, databases, or file sharing protocols, e.g. the File Transfer Protocol (FTP) and Samba. Especially CLIs with the chance of adversely taking over underlying operating systems magically attract invasion attempts. That also concerns the contemporary SSH. Its cryptographic capabilities just protect against wiretapping, but cannot innately thwart brute force attacks without further safeguards. For instance, anti-hammering software (also known as login blocker) temporarily or permanently blocks logon attempts from conspicuous sources if there have been too many in a certain period. Experts appreciate fail2ban as a prominent example for such software.

Irrespective of using anti-hammering, system administrators in particular might interest themselves in an overview if and how intensively brute force attacks strain their machines. IDSs and IPSs provide such insights, but miss qualitatively comparing the difference between credentials of abortive login tries and successful logons. The paper about realtime risk monitoring of SSH brute force attacks also ascertains this deficit [12]. It provides a viable solution based on password pattern comparison, but leaves room for improvement regarding risk granularity.

Assuming that an offender knowingly or unwittingly tests all possible passwords with the same pattern as the correct password. For example, let it be *zzzzzz*. Therefore, all attacker's tries consist of exactly six lowercase characters with *aaaaaa* as first, *aaaaab* as second attempt, and so on. The approach at [12] would count all these attempts as evenhandedly dangerous albeit the similarity of each to the true password considerably differs.

Granted that another offense against the same exemplary password occurs with *z*, *zz*, and so forth. Obviously, the sixth attempt with *zzzzzz* succeeds. The method at [12] would not classify the first five attempted passwords as looming risk despite their growing resemblance to the genuine one.

This publication formidably improves the endangerment classification accuracy of the technique at [12] by introducing metrics that assess the similarity of incorrectly entered passwords to real ones. A flanged Condition Monitoring System (CMS) processes these metrics and reports SSH brute force attacks the minute they become too close to functional credentials, i.e. too risky. For this reason, every customary CMS can be modified to appropriately perform realtime risk monitoring of SSH brute force attacks.

Section 2 reflects on academic approaches that could be adapted for metric generation. The data collection in Sect. 3 compiles a novel Bloom filter for password similitude assessment. Section 4 continues with the distillation of Key Performance Indicators (KPIs) for failed logon tries per time unit based upon the generated metrics. The described deployment in Sect. 5 demonstrates the feasibility and plausibility of these newly designed KPIs as well as their refinement compared with those of [12]. Section 6 recapitulates this document and links to promising future work.

2   Related Work

This section spotlights a handpicked variety of publications about likeness determination of character strings by dint of Bloom filters as well as their shortcomings and contributions for realtime risk monitoring of SSH brute force attacks.

Named after the inventor Burton H. Bloom, these filters denote space-efficient data structures that answer set membership queries with some chance of false results [4]. In other words, Bloom filters allow to measure the closeness of a value x to an element y of a set S under a suitable metric.

Manber and Wu utilize an adapted Bloom filter to ensure that users do not set passwords with too much closeness to dictionary words [15]. They motivate their invention with the increasing throughput of password guessing attacks. As long as technical countermeasures do not hamper them, they originate a myriad of attempts in a reasonably short time. Users could be assigned random passwords to deter them from choosing too easily guessable ones. Regrettably, they would not be able to memorize them and jot them down in a possibly accessible place for others. Preferably, an authentication system imposes a strict password policy onto its users, i.e. only allows secure passwords. Manber and Wu recommend (additionally to other rules) rejecting passwords within distance 1 (caused by deletion, insertion, or substitution) to any dictionary word. Thereto, they use exact matching for all derivatives of dictionary elements within distance 1 instead of approximate filtering. Furthermore, they ameliorate the original Bloom filter by utilizing locality. The resultant method also suits spellchecking of large bibliographic files. While Manber and Wu's approach preventatively precludes insecure passwords, Bloom filter-based realtime risk monitoring of SSH brute force attacks in this treatise solves the problem of watching out for login tries with riskily high resemblance.

Kirsch and Mitzenmacher exemplarily point out that candidate matching during a manning process and Deoxyribonucleic Acid (DNA) sequencing benefit from Bloom filters [14]. The authors take advantage of Locality-Sensitive Hash (LSH) functions as a building block to design appropriate data structures. Subsequently, they analyze the performance of a natural scheme under the Hamming metric. It coruscates with space and speed, i.e. provides brisk answers without performing redundant comparisons. Security and, in particular, privacy do not play a role in Kirsch and Mitzenmacher's disquisition because they keep password alikeness completely out of scope.

Goswami et al. complain that treatises (like the aforementioned one of Kirsch and Mitzenmacher) accept False Positives (FPs) and, much worse, False Negatives (FNs) [13]. A False Positive (FP) befalls if a Bloom filter wrongly confirms a set membership. Conversely, a False Negative (FN) bechances once it erroneously denies a contained element in a set. Goswami et al. present a Bloom filter that outputs FNs under no circumstances. It still permits FPs to maintain the space-efficiency of Bloom filters. In the event of a membership confirmation by a Bloom filter, a second, slower, and less space-efficient algorithm can clear up any doubt. Since membership queries most often entail a negative result, such a second, more expensive level rarely needs to be put into operation. Yet again, privacy issues do not have any importance in the scholarly piece of Goswami et al. However, the zero-tolerance of FNs appears to be highly desirable for Bloom filter-based realtime risk monitoring of SSH brute force attacks.

23 years after Manber and Wu's forecited article, Cheng and Rocca revisit the requirement of baffling precarious password choices [7]. To this end, for each entry of a dictionary with popular passwords they calculate umpteen hashes and map them to a sole Bloom filter. This achieves constant time complexity regardless of the volume of processed passwords. The formed Bloom filter most probably does not comprehend the hashes of robust passwords. The scientists test various compositions of amounts of hash functions and Bloom filter sizes for 300,000 password samples in order to minimize the FP rate. They advocate four independent hash functions and a Bloom filter size ten times higher than dictionary extent. Cheng and Rocca's idea augurs well, but does not contribute to improving realtime risk monitoring of SSH brute force attacks.

Aumüller et al. broach the issue of searching for likeness in high-dimensional data sets, by way of example required in data reconciliation, plagiarism detection, and recommender systems [2]. They propose LSH with its sublinear query time as potential panacea, but also allude to its limitations. Hence, they study Distance-Sensitive Hashing (DSH) that substantially extends the capabilities of LSH. DSH proffers a unique framework for finding nearest neighbors, orthogonal vectors, and furthest points as well as for privacy-preserving searches. On the one hand, the DSH applications of Aumüller et al. do not lead to quantitative running time improvements compared to existent solutions. On the other hand, they do not focus on quantifying the alikeness of a received password from a logon try to an authentic one.

The most recently appeared, relevant contribution stems from Beradi et al. [3]. It dedicates itself to detecting and refusing similar passwords and, thereby, discouraging reuse habits. Because expiration policies customarily mandate frequent password changes, affected users tend to adopt or conceive creative ways for merely slight variations. Such a comprehensible behavior ensues from the necessity and volition to remember the multitudinous credentials of daily life. The peril of slightly mutated passwords originates from the practice that villains can readily compute and attempt them via dictionaries of leaked credentials. The similitude of a password stored in hashed format to a successor (in cleartext) cannot be determined. On the contrary, straightforwardly saving old passwords in plaintext for the sake of comparability to new ones undoubtedly bespeaks despicable conduct. For that reason, Beradi et al. obfuscate commonly preferred, old, and active passwords with the aid of a Bloom filter in order to securely render them comparable to fresh ones. The protagonists warn against collisions if too little different hash functions build a Bloom filter. Just as well, they caution against an accelerated probability of FPs in the case of too many chosen hash functions. Generally, they manage the tightrope walk between utility and security. As Manber and Wu's proposal, that of Beradi et al. solely aids to prophylactically impede setting resembling passwords. Above all, it cannot spot exact password matches. In contrast, this paper comes up with Bloom filter-based realtime risk monitoring of SSH brute force attacks. In addition, it applies a Bloom filter with robustness against an unduly amount of used hash functions.

This treatise's forerunner does purposely not appear in this section for two causes [12]. On the one hand, Sect. 1 already delivers sufficient insight and the bibliography at the end a link to the source. On the other hand, it makes no mention of Bloom filters.

Admittedly, there exist more research items about privacy-preserving similarity searching problems and resolutions, e.g. for databases and text documents. Comprehensively citing them would definitely go beyond the scope of this study. Thence, an interested reader may airily find them by seeking after Searchable Encryption Schemes (SESs) in scholarly literature.

3   Data Collection

This section delves into the disclosure and processing of provided cleartext credentials during brute force attacks against an SSH Daemon (SSHD) of an arbitrary Linux operating system. Without additional coding, an SSHD only records login attempts to an authentication log file (such as */var/log/auth.log*) with details as itemized below.

- Timestamp
- Target host name
- SSHD process identifier
- Authentication result
- Entered user name
- Source IP address
- Source Transmission Control Protocol (TCP) port

In opposition to the main interest of this work, such a log file lacks in information about the entered password for the sake of secrecy. Luckily, every contemporary Linux distribution contains the Pluggable Authentication Modules (PAM) as a good framework to unveil plaintext passwords. Changing a PAM configuration fortunately demands superuser privileges and, therewith, restrain ordinary users from revealing foreign passwords.

In summary, this section explains the alteration of six files as stated below.

- /etc/ssh/sshd_config
- /etc/pam.d/sshd
- ~/.google_authenticator
- /root/sshd
- /root/shadow
- /etc/logrotate.d/sshd

/etc/ssh/sshd_config. To record all logon tries, an SSHD must pass each of them to the PAM rather than reject any. This necessitates not to permit or bar any groups or users by commenting out (as the hash characters at the beginning of the upper four lines in the following itemization do) or removing respective entries in the SSHD configuration file */etc/ssh/sshd_config*. Aside from that, SSH access needs to be explicitly granted to the root account as the fifth line shows. The sixth and bottom adjustment delegates the authentication procedure to the PAM.

- # AllowGroups
- # AllowUsers
- # DenyGroups
- # DenyUsers
- PermitRootLogin yes
- UsePAM yes

/etc/pam.d/sshd. The PAM configuration file for SSHD */etc/pam.d/sshd* by default authenticates each local user with their password as single factor whose hash code resides in the shadow file */etc/shadow*. For this purpose, a topical */etc/pam.d/sshd* normally invokes the file */etc/pam.d/common-auth* with common authentication settings for all services (as the middle line of the subsequent listing exhibits). Prior to this invocation of */etc/pam.d/common-auth*, */etc/pam.d/sshd* has to call an executable file */root/sshd* that takes over the recording of an obtained password and creation of its Bloom filter. The uppermost line indicates this addition. An appended, third line after the invocation of */etc/pam.d/common-auth* adds extra security by enforcing Two-Factor-Authentication (2FA) with temporary numbers. Each user must submit their currently valid time-based code as soon as they have entered their right password. For that purpose, each requires a code generator (app) that reads a fresh valid temporary number with six digits every 30 s.

1. auth optional pam_exec.so expose_authtok /root/sshd
2. @include common-auth
3. auth required pam_google_authenticator.so

~/.google_authenticator. In the present case of enforced 2FA, each user has to configure it by executing the file */usr/bin/google-authenticator*. This command displays the initialization string for the code generator (app) and saves it together with a couple of emergency codes to the hidden file ~/.*google_authenticator*, i.e. in the home directory. Alternatively, a skilled user can manually create ~/.*google_authenticator* themselves. The example hereinafter showcases the composition of ~/.*google_authenticator*.

1. FV5CCSJEXKMQWPOJ2FLWKVYJXA
2. "TOTP_AUTH
3. 23442250
4. 31635196
5. 67196172
6. 87069200
7. 87648973

/root/sshd. The executable file */root/sshd* stands out as a merit of this publication. It creates a Bloom filter with 16 bits, another one with 32 bits, and a third one with 64 bits for every gained incorrect cleartext password and compares them with the three corresponding Bloom filters of the correct password. The usage of three sundry Bloom filters in lieu of a sole one enables revealing differences between their degrees of precision. The pick of Bloom filters with 16, 32, and 64 bits follows from the cardinalities of the encoding schemes Base16, Base32, and Base64. The positioning of */root/sshd* in root's home directory protects its secrecy and integrity from accounts without administrative rights. Embedding its unabridged source code at this point would overstretch this disquisition. Instead, the pseudocode in Algorithm 1 imparts the necessary details for comprehension.

After the Bloom filters' initialization in the first line, the loop between lines 2 to 39 iterates over all l characters of the tried plaintext password $PWatt$. Every character influences two bits of each Bloom filter. To let each recurrence of a specific character impact another bit pair in the base16-based (hexadecimal) Bloom filter $b16att$ with high likeliness, the lines 3 and 9 hash the amalgamation of $pwatt_i$ with its position i and the user name $USER$ by means of SHA3-512 respectively SHA3-384 and extract the first character of the hash code. While the utilization of i thwarts recurring hash codes for a $PWatt$, the exploitation of $USER$ impedes identical Bloom filters for users with identic passwords and, on account of this, their facile detecting. The same action takes place for the base32-based Bloom filter $b32att$ in lines 15 and 21 as well as for the base64-based Bloom filter $b64att$ in the lines numbered 27 and 33. The initial Bloom filter's quantity of ones would correlatively rise with an accreting length l [4], converge to an array without zeros and, thereby, increase the likelihood of FPs. Similarly, as mentioned in Sect. 2, too many selected hash functions for a Bloom filter have the same effect by making it prone to FPs due to too little ones [3]. Already a Bloom filter of length $l* $<count of picked hash functions> can merely comprise ones providing that every password character flips a bit from zero to one for each hash function. It goes without saying that a clash of two Bloom filters (one for an attempted and a second for an actual password) without zeros cannot offer any informative value and can be confidently discarded as FP.

Algorithm 1. Creation of Bloom filters

Require: $b16old \in \{0,1\}^{16}$ from */root/shadow* {Import of Bloom filter $b16old$}

Require: $b32old \in \{0,1\}^{32}$ from */root/shadow* {Import of Bloom filter $b32old$}

Require: $b64old \in \{0,1\}^{64}$ from */root/shadow* {Import of Bloom filter $b64old$}

Require: $H(PWcor) \in \Sigma^m | m \in \mathbb{N}$ from */etc/shadow* {Import of password hash $H(PWcor)$}

Require: $PWatt = \{pwatt_1, \cdots, pwatt_l\} \in \Sigma^l | l \in \mathbb{N}$ from standard input {Import of attempted password $PWatt$}

Require: $t(now) \in \mathbb{N}$ from system clock {Import of current Epoch timestamp $t(now)$}

Require: $USER \in \Sigma^*$ from shell environment {Import of attempted user name $USER$}

1:    $H16att = \{\}, H32att = \{\}, H64att = \{\}, b16att = 0000000000000000, b32att = 00000000000000000000000000000000, b64att = 0000000000000000000000000000000000000000000000000000000000000000$ {Initialization of temporary Bloom filters $H16att$, $H32att$, and $H64att$ as well as Bloom filters $b16att$, $b32att$, and $b64att$}

2:    **for all** $i \in \mathbb{N} | 1 \leq i \leq l$ **do** {Iteration over characters of plaintext password}

3:      $h16att = H_{512}(i, pwatt_i, USER)_1$ {Extraction of first base16-character of SHA-512 of character position, character, and user name}

4:      **if** $h16att \in H16att$ **then** {Bloom filter $H16att$ already contains $h16att$}

5:        $H16att = H16att \setminus \{h16att\}$ {Removal of $h16att$ from Bloom filter $H16att$}

6:      **else** {Bloom filter $H16att$ does not already contain $h16att$}

7:        $H16att = H16att \cup \{h16att\}$ {Addition of $h16att$ to Bloom filter $H16att$}

8:      **end if**

9:      $h16att = H_{384}(i, pwatt_i, USER)_1$ {Extraction of first base16-character of SHA-384 of character position, character, and user name}

10:      **if** $h16att \in H16att$ **then** {Bloom filter $H16att$ already contains $h16att$}

11:        $H16att = H16att \setminus \{h16att\}$ {Removal of $h16att$ from Bloom filter $H16att$}

12:      **else** {Bloom filter $H16att$ does not already contain $h16att$}

13:        $H16att = H16att \cup \{h16att\}$ {Addition of $h16att$ to Bloom filter $H16att$}

14:      **end if**

15:      $h32att = H_{512}(i, pwatt_i, USER)_1$ {Extraction of first base32-character of SHA-512 of character position, character, and user name}

16:      **if** $h32att \in H32att$ **then** {Bloom filter $H32att$ already contains $h32att$}

17:        $H32att = H32att \setminus \{h32att\}$ {Removal of $h32att$ from Bloom filter $H32att$}

18:      **else** {Bloom filter $H32att$ does not already contain $h32att$}

19:        $H32att = H32att \cup \{h32att\}$ {Addition of $h32att$ to Bloom filter $H32att$}

20:      **end if**

21:      $h32att = H_{384}(i, pwatt_i, USER)_1$ {Extraction of first base32-character of SHA-384 of character position, character, and user name}

22:      **if** $h32att \in H32att$ **then** {Bloom filter $H32att$ already contains $h32att$}

23:        $H32att = H32att \setminus \{h32att\}$ {Removal of $h32att$ from Bloom filter $H32att$}

24:      **else** {Bloom filter $H32att$ does not already contain $h32att$}

25:        $H32att = H32att \cup \{h32att\}$ {Addition of $h32att$ to Bloom filter $H32att$}

26:      **end if**

27:     $h64att = H_{512}(i, pwatt_i, USER)_1$ {Extraction of first base64-character of SHA-512 of character position, character, and user name}

28:     **if** $h64att \in H64att$ **then** {Bloom filter $H64att$ already contains $h64att$}

29:         $H64att = H64att \setminus \{h64att\}$ {Removal of $h64att$ from Bloom filter $H64att$}

30:     **else** {Bloom filter $H64att$ does not already contain $h64att$}

31:         $H64att = H64att \cup \{h64att\}$ {Addition of $h64att$ to Bloom filter $H64att$}

32:     **end if**

33:     $h64att = H_{384}(i, pwatt_i, USER)_1$ {Extraction of first base64-character of SHA-384 of character position, character, and user name}

34:     **if** $h64att \in H64att$ **then** {Bloom filter $H64att$ already contains $h64att$}

35:         $H64att = H64att \setminus \{h64att\}$ {Removal of $h64att$ from Bloom filter $H64att$}

36:     **else** {Bloom filter $H64att$ does not already contain $h64att$}

37:         $H64att = H64att \cup \{h64att\}$ {Addition of $h64att$ to Bloom filter $H64att$}

38:     **end if**

39: **end for**

40: **for all** $i \in \{0, 1, 2, 3, 4, 5, 6, 7, 8, 9, A, B, C, D, E, F\}$ **do** {Iteration over characters of base16}

41:     **if** $i \in H16att$ **then** {Temporary Bloom filter $H16att$ contains i}

42:         $b16att_i = 1$ {Assembly of Bloom filter $b16att$}

43:     **end if**

44: **end for**

45: **for all** $i \in \{A, B, C, D, E, F, G, H, I, J, K, L, M, N, O, P, Q, R, S, T, U, V, W, X, Y, Z,$

46: $2, 3, 4, 5, 6, 7\}$ **do** {Iteration over characters of base32}

47:     **if** $i \in H32att$ **then** {Temporary Bloom filter $H32att$ contains i}

48:         $b32att_i = 1$ {Assembly of Bloom filter $b32att$}

49:     **end if**

50: **end for**

51: **for all** $i \in \{A, B, C, D, E, F, G, H, I, J, K, L, M, N, O, P, Q, R, S, T, U, V, W, X, Y, Z,$

52: $a, b, c, d, e, f, g, h, i, j, k, l, m, n, o, p, q, r, s, t, u, v, w, x, y, z,$

53: $0, 1, 2, 3, 4, 5, 6, 7, 8, 9, +, /\}$ **do** {Iteration over characters of base64}

54:     **if** $i \in H64att$ **then** {Temporary Bloom filter $H64att$ contains i}

55:         $b64att_i = 1$ {Assembly of Bloom filter $b64att$}

56:     **end if**

57: **end for**

58: **if** $H(PWatt) = H(PWcor)$ **then** {Correct password entered}

59:     $(/etc/shadow \setminus \{USER, b16old, b32old, b64old\}) \cup \{USER, b16att, b32att, b64att\}$ {Update of $/root/shadow$ with current user's name and Bloom filters}

60: **else** {Wrong password entered}

61:     $s16 = 0, s32 = 0, s64 = 0$ {Initialization of similarity counters $s16, s32$, and $s64$}

62:     **for all** $i \in \mathbb{N}|1 \leq i \leq 16$ **do** {Iteration over all 16 bits of Bloom filters $b16att$ and $b16old$}

63:         **if** $b16att_i = b16old_i$ **then** {i^{th} bit of $b16att$ and $b16old$ match}

64:             $s16 = s16 + 1$ {Increment of similarity counter $s16$ by one}

65:         **end if**

66:     **end for**

67:     **for all** $i \in \mathbb{N}|1 \leq i \leq 32$ **do** {Iteration over all 32 bits of Bloom filters $b32att$ and $b32old$}

68:         **if** $b32att_i = b32old_i$ **then** {i^{th} bit of $b32att$ and $b32old$ match}

69:             $s32 = s32 + 1$ {Increment of similarity counter $s32$ by one}

70:         **end if**

71:     **end for**

72:    **for all** $i \in \mathbb{N}|1 \leq i \leq 64$ **do** {Iteration over all 64 bits of Bloom filters
       $b64att$ and $b64old$}
73:       **if** $b64att_i = b64old_i$ **then** {i^{th} bit of $b64att$ and $b64old$ match}
74:          $s64 = s64 + 1$ {Increment of similarity counter $s64$ by one}
75:       **end if**
76:    **end for**
77:    $/root/sshd.log \cup \{t(now), USER, \frac{s16}{16}, \frac{s32}{32}, \frac{s64}{64}, PWatt\}$ {Logging of unsuccessful
       login attempt's Epoch timestamp, user name, similarity indexes, and cleartext
       password to $/root/sshd.log$}
78: **end if**

On this account, Algorithm 1 deviates from the originally proposed Bloom
filter and, thus, introduces a novel derivative. It does not only prepare flips
from zero to one by adding extracted characters of hash codes to the temporary Bloom filter $H16att$ in the lines 7 and 13, to $H32att$ in the lines 19 and
25, and to $H64att$ in the lines 31 and 37. As soon as an already added character recurs for the second time, the instructions in the lines 5, 11, 17, 23, 29,
and 35 undo prepared flips from zero to one by erasing it from all temporary
Bloom filters. This seesaw between addition and erasure of a flip proceeds with
every repetition of an extracted character. In a nutshell, odd occurrences of a
particular extracted character result in its inclusion in a Bloom filter, otherwise
in its absence. A balance between zeros and ones in the (final) Bloom filters
$b16att, b32att$, and $b64att$ ensues.

The loop from line 40 to 44 translates the temporary Bloom filter $H16att$
to the binary array labeled as the Bloom filter $b16att$. For every possible item
of $H16att$ exists a dedicated bit in $b16att$. Line 42 sets the accordant bit in
$b16att$ for each existing character in $H16att$. The loops between line 45 and 50
respectively 51 and 57 repeat this translation from $H32att$ to $b32att$ respectively
from $H64att$ to $b64att$.

A correctly entered password, i.e. $H(PWatt) = H(PWcor)$, entails an
update of the file $/root/shadow$ with the current user's name $USER$ and the
recently compiled Bloom filters $b16att, b32att$, and $b64att$ for $PWatt = PWcor$
in line 59. A sample of $/root/shadow$ follows later on in this section. Every password change exclusively replaces a hash in the file $/etc/shadow$. To perpetuate
sound risk monitoring, a successful login with such a new password must succeed to also refresh $/root/shadow$. In lieu thereof, a modification of the passwd
command can supersede this successional step.

The input of a wrong password leads to the evaluation of three resemblance
metrics between both passwords ($PWatt$ and $PWcor$) in the remainder of Algorithm 1. It begins with the initialization of the three similarity counters $s16, s32$,
and $s64$ in line 61. The loop starting with line 62 and ending with line 66 sifts
through all 16 positions of $b16att$ as well as of $b16old$ and counts their coinciding
bits with the help of $s16$. The amount of matching bits counted by $s16$ conforms
to the number of ones in the output of $b16att$ XNOR $b16old$. Line 67 commences
another loop that evaluates the quantity of congruent bits of $b32att$ and $b32old$

with the variable $s32$ and ends at line 71. The last loop of Algorithm 1 starts in line 72, populates $s64$ with the amount of coherent bits of $b64att$ and $b64old$, and concludes at line 76. Ultimately, line 77 logs Epoch timestamp, $USER$, three similarity indices ($\frac{s16}{16}, \frac{s32}{32}, \frac{s64}{64}$), and $PWatt$ of the miscarried logon try to the log file $/root/sshd.log$. All three similarity indexes reach values between zero and one. The maximum value one seems to represent a properly submitted password at first glance. Attentive readers immediately recognize a one as FP since the submission of a proper password branches out to line 59 and, on that account, cannot hit line 77.

/root/shadow. The file $/root/shadow$ stores the three above-mentioned Bloom filters for the configured password of each user account. As already well-known from $/root/sshd$, its location at root's base directory guards its confidentiality and inviolacy from accounts without administration permission. The row there-inafter gives an example which Bloom filters Algorithm 1 retains in $/root/shadow$ for root with password $abcdef$.

- root 1000010000100111 01000000000100000000100000011001
  001000000000000000000111000000000000000000001000000000000001001000010

As an example, the first Bloom filter $b16att = 1000010000100111$ arises from the (initial characters of the) below-mentioned twelve hash codes.

1. $H_{512}(1aroot) = \mathbf{7}f08f5fd8f185d187d94b07f9f0ca3a8$
   $f63d65d15771620b710a6ea5a7504f7c$
   $b1c3419e8dbc603966547c28d70f55d0$
   $73344df6d1edf51367eba055d29df694 \Rightarrow b16att_7 = 1$
2. $H_{384}(1aroot) = \mathbf{0}ab94bf8362b580ca866ef2c0b5c058c$
   $3d31b966d78dc3413a708d5073ba9bc3$
   $0c9ac97ae4a5815aea242dbad13acf9e \Rightarrow b16att_0 = 1$
3. $H_{512}(2broot) = \mathbf{7}dc8d23d85089b98f7d62da6ee7ab75d$
   $1ed7d871de486f77334668ac1339aa89$
   $130d8d63a068522e24f9cce1e23691b1$
   $1c7c0b97cc9fe82c2de494743910f056 \Rightarrow b16att_7 = 0$
4. $H_{384}(2broot) = \mathbf{5}412d04b42779f1d074e876b8a930b74$
   $a104b655791c9f8ed7560e7eff200a2e$
   $12f084b226c65493a7039f4aba4768d7 \Rightarrow b16att_5 = 1$
5. $H_{512}(3croot) = \mathbf{f}91b0f227951e8ec61a3bef8581b4913$
   $7f99d25d388be0292846391ee00bef58$
   $9df5a52398cc3121e4045d23f0f9dc47$
   $8a65c42d0bf5978cb6e9d681a4db5080 \Rightarrow b16att_f = 1$
6. $H_{384}(3croot) = \mathbf{5}021473f7ae6b23fcc0f1bf6425b4fe0$
   $7b482a263b69dac1053514493a9f415c$
   $626e82e28e094d18d4e18d15dc22cb24 \Rightarrow b16att_5 = 0$
7. $H_{512}(4droot) = \mathbf{a}76342058582688780769d8f866e61f0$
   $ab7e75b285461f5ef7727ec018e5f6d2$
   $33cb45b1a4af4af0a822537072cec1e6$
   $2b46c25796dec3a3c07ea0d3c6157ede \Rightarrow b16att_a = 1$

8. $H_{384}(4droot) = 5a957e7324c5836e8092fc2dbec3120c$
   $6711f1d9f2375ba98bd96b335d88bb4f$
   $e60c337202004c809ec6acbfbb601feb \Rightarrow b16att_5 = 1$
9. $H_{512}(5eroot) = 7537ba88c745ea910fe8739a16628274$
   $f45b7ecdf5234388c55b56d8b8ebeea1$
   $0d14779f02db90458530e03a23d4f6a0$
   $4a938df66dab1967c39dc9db9bcadaa7 \Rightarrow b16att_7 = 1$
10. $H_{384}(5eroot) = e58625679201ae47b99f10a753d36526$
    $48265fb7c86fbeeeb01969e2f7c454eb$
    $9ed5f388d3efc273bb3c3c9ff809f350 \Rightarrow b16att_e = 1$
11. $H_{512}(6froot) = 7423ba59e36e26df46fd34c9b6cfdef5$
    $a31fbce5aec36ab984880f6df5fd6783$
    $0a4ac360d9e9d7256dfda8bcd96670a1$
    $de3369f847224af3c1120bae374ffb9a \Rightarrow b16att_7 = 0$
12. $H_{384}(6froot) = dbd902610a33f872d010a01fe1ea830d$
    $13f232bf845b9bb1029aa4c98e04db70$
    $8b84e536769eabf540c1874a134f7edd \Rightarrow b16att_d = 1$

/etc/logrotate.d/sshd. The size of */root/sshd.log* incessantly increases with every logon failure. This would unnecessarily slow down the Key Performance Indicator (KPI) computation in Sect. 4 more and more if it always scanned the plethora of historical login failures. On account of that, the content as below in the configuration file */etc/logrotate.d/sshd* causes a daily rotation of */root/sshd.log* and a safekeeping period of 366 days that also archives all log files of a leap year entirely.

1. /root/sshd.log
2. {
3. copytruncate
4. daily
5. missingok
6. notifempty
7. rotate 366
8. }

A restart of SSHD activates the explicated changes in this section as prerequisite for KPI calculation.

4   KPI Generation

Because Algorithm 1 computes three autonomous similarity indices for every foundered logon try, the preparation of just as many independent Key Performance Indicators (KPIs) stands to reason. Each KPI shall express the riskiest login failure(s) of the previous time span, i.e. that/those with the highest similitude score.

/root/kpi. In accordance to the requested KPI, Algorithm 2 (implemented by the file */root/kpi*) scans all n similarity figures based on base16, base32, or base64 that Algorithm 1 has logged to */root/sshd.log* during the last time interval. In doing so, the program memorizes the peak, and eventually exits by outputting it. Evaluating the greatest alikeness in place of summating all considered similarity scores makes more sense since one login attempt with a very akin password in the majority of cases poses a sorer threat than multiple tries with less likeness.

Algorithm 2. Creation of KPIs

Require: $base \in \{16, 32, 64\}$ from standard input {Import of requested Bloom filter length $base$}
Require: $n \in \mathbb{N}$ {Import of number of scanned similarity figures n}
Require: $t(now) \in \mathbb{N}$ from system clock {Import of current Epoch timestamp $t(now)$}
Require: $\{t(1), \cdots, t(n)\} \subsetneq \mathbb{N}$ from */root/sshd.log* {Import of n Epoch timestamps}
Require: $\{\frac{s16_1}{16}, \cdots, \frac{s16_n}{16}\} \subsetneq \mathbb{Q}$ from */root/sshd.log* {Import of n base16-based similarity figures}
Require: $\{\frac{s32_1}{32}, \cdots, \frac{s32_n}{32}\} \subsetneq \mathbb{Q}$ from */root/sshd.log* {Import of n base32-based similarity figures}
Require: $\{\frac{s64_1}{64}, \cdots, \frac{s64_n}{64}\} \subsetneq \mathbb{Q}$ from */root/sshd.log* {Import of n base64-based similarity figures}
1: $s = 0$ {Initialization of temporary similarity index maximum}
2: **for all** $i \in \mathbb{N} | 1 \leq i \leq n$ **do** {Iteration over failed logon attempts in */root/sshd.log*}
3:     **if** $60 * (\lfloor \frac{t(now)}{60} \rfloor - 1) \leq t(i) < 60 * \lfloor \frac{t(now)}{60} \rfloor \wedge \frac{sbase_i}{base} > s$ **then** {Unsuccessful login try i happened during recent time span with a similarity index $\frac{sbase_i}{base}$ greater than temporary similarity index maximum s}
4:         $s = \frac{sbase_i}{base}$ {New temporary similarity index maximum s}
5:     **end if**
6: **end for**
7: Output s

/etc/snmp/snmpd.conf. An execution of */root/kpi* merely delivers a snapshot of the demanded KPI instead of its entire history. A CMS lends itself to regularly retrieve KPIs, visualize their histograms, discover and notify anomalies. Aside from alternatives, the Short Network Management Protocol (SNMP) [6] suits the secure and lightweight transmission of KPIs from SNMP-capable nodes to a CMS with so-called Object Identifiers (OIDs). Specifically SNMPv3 (the third version of SNMP) supports the confidential and unaltered transport of OIDs [5]. Because an SNMP Daemon (SNMPD) authenticates incoming SNMPv3-requests on the basis of user names, an operational SNMP account ensures accessibility for a CMS. The excerpt of a sample SNMPD configuration file */etc/snmp/snmpd.conf* hereinafter authorizes the user name nagios to fetch the three KPIs BASE16, BASE32, and BASE64.

- rouser nagios
- exec BASE16 /root/kpi 16
- exec BASE32 /root/kpi 32
- exec BASE64 /root/kpi 64

Each line with keyword exec allocates a leaf of the Object Identifier (OID) sub-tree 1.3.6.1.4.1.2021.8.1.101 to the alluded KPI. The allocation process goes on in sequential order, viz. SNMPD maps 1.3.6.1.4.1.2021.8.1.101.1 to BASE16, 1.3.6.1.4.1.2021.8.1.101.2 to BASE32, and 1.3.6.1.4.1.2021.8.1.101.3 to BASE64.

As soon as an SNMPD operates with the updated */etc/snmp/snmpd.conf*, a CMS may request the three KPIs with the right credentials.

5 Experiment

A few thoughts on the expected metrics deserve consideration at the outset of this section before explicating the conducted experiment.

Firstly, since every similitude score (that Algorithm 1 calculates) reaches a positive fractional value lower than one, also Algorithm 2 can solely return maxima smaller than one as KPIs.

Secondly, an alikeness of zero portends that all bits of a Bloom filter differ from those of another while a likeness of one represents their equality.

Thirdly, unlike the original Bloom filter [4], Algorithm 1 also resets ones to zeros during Bloom filter compilation. On these grounds, the incidence of zeros and ones converges with rising password length l and induces similitude scores of 0.5 even for strikingly unequal passwords. This fact solely renders alikeness indexes between 0.5 and one expressive.

Fourthly, the concurrent employment of several hash functions engenders the change of just as many bits in a Bloom filter per password character. Algorithm 1 uses two (SHA3-512 and SHA3-384), which results in an even number of ones and also of zeros. Accordingly, it solely produces positive fractions with even numerators $s16, s32, s64$ as likeness indices, i.e. $\frac{s16}{16}|s16 \equiv 0$ (mod 2), $\frac{s32}{32}|s32 \equiv 0$ (mod 2), and $\frac{s64}{64}|s64 \equiv 0$ (mod 2). This halves the indexes' resolution in comparison to the usage of simply one hash function.

In general, best practices suggest the use of complex and long passwords. Taking this advice indisputably contributes to security. At the same moment, it degrades the explanatory power of the experiment for Bloom filter-based real-time risk monitoring of SSH brute force attacks. Why? Virtually every attacker would struggle to guess strings that marginally deviate from strong configured passwords. Consequently, the three produced resemblance values of Algorithm 1 and KPIs of Algorithm 2 would fluctuate around 0.5 with rare upturned outliers as FPs. This dilemma between security and presentability can be overcome by configuring a provocatively weak password that grants system access in no case. The superuser account root seems to be an adequate choice. Why? On the one hand, evildoers prefer to launch brute force attacks against it. One the other hand, it should be only accessible via su or sudo over intermediary accounts rather than directly. Loosening security with a simple root password followed by deleting */root/.google_authenticator* smartly does the trick. This guarantees that all root logon attempts fail at any rate, also those with proper passwords. Due to better prospects of success with dictionary in lieu of combinatory brute force attacks, selecting a dictionary entry as password weakens it even more.

The famous text file *rockyou.txt* as outcome of the incident against the former United States (US) company RockYou in 2009 turns out to be a well-established bonanza for picking a deliberately vulnerable password. This repository comprises 14,344,392 distinct cleartext passwords of 32,603,388 marred RockYou customers. It can be effortlessly found with Internet search engines and downloaded from quite a lot of sources. In 2021, the novel file version *rockyou2021.txt* with even 8,459,060,239 leaked passwords emerged on the Internet. Those words consisting of precisely six lowercase characters constitute the second largest subset of *rockyou.txt* with 608,481 words (4.24%) and the biggest of *rockyou2021.txt* with 308,915,776 (3.65%). *abcdef* shapes up as worthy representative of this subset and, on those grounds, becomes the experimental root password.

An SSHD on Ubuntu Linux 22.04 with all heretofore specified configuration adaptions in this document including the impertinently unsophisticated credentials got exposed to the Internet in September 2022. The network topology in Fig. 1 depicts the SSHD's protective embedment in a Demilitarized Zone (DMZ), the deployed protocols SNMP and SSH, and their daemons on Ubuntu Linux 22.04. Once */root/kpi* underwent execution, it evaluated the desired KPI considering all recorded events of the recent full minute. As a consequence of this, a CMS polled a fresh value of each KPI every 60 s with an SNMPv3-request.

Attacker   Internet   Outer DMZ Firewall   SNMPD and SSHD in DMZ   Inner DMZ Firewall   CMS

Fig. 1. Experimental rigging

In favor of comparableness with this paper's predecessor [12], the CMS likewise calculated one fixed threshold (pair), three single dynamic (critical) thresholds, and three dynamical threshold pair selection techniques for each KPI as follows.

- **Fixed approach:** Four differing bits (one character) between both observed Bloom filters pose the (critical) threshold.
- **Three sigma rule without prior outlier removal:** The (critical) threshold lies three standard deviations above the arithmetic mean of an unfiltered KPI history. [9–12]
- **Three sigma rule with prior outlier removal:** The (critical) threshold lies three standard deviations above the arithmetic mean of an outlier-freed KPI history. [10–12]
- **Maximal value:** The (critical) threshold adopts the maximum of an outlier-freed KPI history. [10–12]
- **Tolerant approach:** The maximum of an unfiltered array with dynamical thresholds becomes the critical threshold and the median the warning threshold. [11,12]

- **Balanced approach:** The maximum of an unfiltered array with dynamical thresholds becomes the critical threshold and the minimum the warning threshold. [11,12]
- **Strict approach:** The median of an unfiltered array with dynamical thresholds becomes the critical threshold and the minimum the warning threshold. [11,12]

The CMS computed each of the listed dynamic thresholds by incorporating up to 52 bygone values (dependent on how many it had available) that a KPI had taken during the past 365 calendar days. Rendered more precisely, it utilized those KPI values that it had collected exactly a week ago, exactly two weeks ago, ..., exactly 51 weeks ago, and exactly 52 weeks ago. This approach optimally covers all imaginable attack seasons.

To avoid desensitization by overwhelming floods of notifications induced by short-term peaks, at least ten threshold exceedances at a stretch had to occur to trigger a notification. Apart from other reasons, eligible users might have accidentally entered slightly wrong passwords and boosted the KPIs beyond their thresholds.

All value pairs (each delimits quantity of threshold exceedances and notifications by a slash) in Tables 1, 2, and 3 prove the effectivity of the imposed nine minutes long retention time interval. This becomes manifest in the count of notifications on the right of slashes that clearly undercut the threshold exceedances on the left.

Table 1. Threshold exceedances/notifications of BASE16

	Warning	Critical
Fixed (critical) threshold of 0.75	N/A	103/0
Three sigma rule without prior outlier removal	N/A	2,338/24
Three sigma rule with prior outlier removal	N/A	2,556/17
Maximum value	N/A	3,103/26
Tolerant approach	1,149/58	1,613/71
Balanced approach	1,795/88	1,528/98
Strict approach	679/22	2,666/35

A second glimpse at all three tables discloses an abundance of occurred threshold exceedances and notifications aroused by all methods that dynamically evaluate thresholds. They happened due to the irregular occurrence of SSH brute force attacks. For this cause, none of these algorithms could learn any regularities. It behooves to disregard them now and turn toward the fixed approach.

Table 2. Threshold exceedances/notifications of BASE32

	Warning	Critical
Fixed (critical) threshold of 0.875	N/A	11/0
Three sigma rule without prior outlier removal	N/A	2,797/27
Three sigma rule with prior outlier removal	N/A	2,675/12
Maximum value	N/A	3,308/23
Tolerant approach	1,117/36	1,789/47
Balanced approach	1,636/77	1,731/80
Strict approach	516/18	2,963/38

Table 3. Threshold exceedances/notifications of BASE64

	Warning	Critical
Fixed (critical) threshold of 0.9375	N/A	11/0
Three sigma rule without prior outlier removal	N/A	2,738/26
Three sigma rule with prior outlier removal	N/A	2,585/9
Maximum value	N/A	3,244/28
Tolerant approach	1,139/60	1,819/74
Balanced approach	1,723/107	1,681/116
Strict approach	694/36	2,832/51

Already a discrepancy of one character between genuine and tried password causes up to four discrepant bits between their Bloom filters. It seems to be meaningful to initially determine four nonconforming bits as boundary between hazard and innocuousness.

All three KPIs encountered minutes during the whole examined month each minute with at least one erroneous login attempt whose resemblance score indicated a disparity of four bits or less. BASE32 and BASE64 concurred in the number of eleven such minutes. BASE16 underperformed with 92 threshold exceedances more. Retroactive manual scrutiny identified all of them as FPs. In spite of the eleven (critical) threshold exceedances of BASE32 and BASE64 as well as the 103 ones of BASE16, the CMS did not precipitate any notification. Ten (critical) threshold exceedances in a row would have been needed, but did not happen.

Finally, a comparison with the simultaneously recorded KPI PWDPAT [12] in Table 4 befits. As per Table 4, each of four approaches triggered two critical notifications for at least ten minutes long phases with statistically significant volumes of SSH brute force attacks that had applied the pattern *aaaaaa* of the root password *abcdef*. The passwords of the attacks during both notified phases did not sufficiently resemble *abcdef* to also generate any notification for

Table 4. Threshold exceedances/notifications of PWDPAT

	Warning	Critical
Fixed (critical) threshold of 0.5	N/A	991/2
Three sigma rule without prior outlier removal	N/A	0/0
Three sigma rule with prior outlier removal	N/A	336/2
Maximum value	N/A	425/2
Tolerant approach	319/1	0/0
Balanced approach	445/2	0/0
Strict approach	131/1	312/2

the fixed thresholds of BASE16, BASE32, or BASE64. This upshot proves the superior classification precision of Bloom filter- over pattern-based realtime risk monitoring of SSH brute force attacks for fixed thresholds. The experiment could not show this proof for dynamic threshold culling techniques because of unsteady attack moments. As a side note, the demonstrated method also deals with lateral guessing attacks (password spraying) that test one password against a multitude of accounts rather than oodles of passwords against one account.

6   Conclusion

The antecedent treatise about realtime risk monitoring of SSH brute force attacks does a good job, but at the same time calls for betterment [12]. For that cause, this scholarly piece pursues the idea of investigating their quality by checking Bloom filters of used passwords against those of authentic ones rather than their patterns.

An obligatory literature survey in Sect. 2 sheds light on the origin of Bloom filters. Few published disquisitions apply these data structures to preemptively obviate passwords with too high closeness to formerly utilized ones. Bloom filters have not been employed so far for realtime risk monitoring of SSH brute force attacks.

To produce relief, Sect. 3 describes tailoring the originally suggested Bloom filter in a fashion that ones in its array may also flip back to zeros during its assembling. Moreover, the section reveals all needful settings in a Linux operating system for prudent data collection.

Section 4 explicates the remaining steps on a monitored host to distill one KPI per Bloom filter size and warily convey the resulting KPIs to a CMS. Encrypted conveyance of KPIs and exclusive views on them for superusers in a CMS avert their exploitation for password guessing attacks.

The addressed experiment in Sect. 5 unveils a gimmick how to test the Bloom filter technique under discussion with an intentionally uncomplicated password for the root account without putting it in jeopardy. Afterward, insightful analyses among miscellaneous threshold strategies follow with three major findings.

Firstly, Bloom filter-based realtime risk monitoring of SSH brute force attacks trumps pattern-based with improved preciseness. Secondly, the FP rate negatively correlates with the Bloom filter's quantity of bits. Not for nothing, the amount of fixed threshold exceedances subsided from 103 for BASE16 to eleven for BASE32 and BASE64. Thirdly, brute force attacks nowadays make use of dictionary entries rather than of combinatorial strings because of raised chances of success.

Nevertheless, room for amelioration always remains. Notably Bloom filter-based password pattern resemblance indexing (i.e. amalgamating the antecessor [12] with the recommendation in this contribution) as complemental premonitory risk metric qualifies as prospective development step.

Acknowledgments. Many thanks to Bettina Baumgartner from the University of Vienna for proofreading this paper!

References

1. Adrian, D., Durumeric, Z., Singh, G., Halderman, J.A.: Zippier ZMap: internet-wide scanning at 10 Gbps. In: 8th USENIX Workshop on Offensive Technologies (WOOT 14). USENIX Association, San Diego (2014). https://www.usenix.org/conference/woot14/workshop-program/presentation/adrian
2. Aumüller, M., Christiani, T., Pagh, R., Silvestri, F.: Distance-sensitive hashing. In: Proceedings of the 37th ACM SIGMOD-SIGACT-SIGAI Symposium on Principles of Database Systems, SIGMOD/PODS 2018, pp. 89–104. Association for Computing Machinery, New York (2018). https://doi.org/10.1145/3196959.3196976
3. Berardi, D., Callegati, F., Melis, A., Prandini, M.: Password similarity using probabilistic data structures. J. Cybersecur. Priv. **1**(1), 78–92 (2021). https://doi.org/10.3390/jcp1010005
4. Bloom, B.H.: Space/time trade-offs in hash coding with allowable errors. Commun. ACM **13**(7), 422–426 (1970). https://doi.org/10.1145/362686.362692
5. Blumenthal, U., Wijnen, B.: User-based Security Model (USM) for version 3 of the Simple Network Management Protocol (SNMPv3). RFC 3414 (Internet Standard) (2002). https://doi.org/10.17487/RFC3414
6. Case, J.D., Fedor, M., Schoffstall, M.L., Davin, J.R.: A Simple Network Management Protocol (SNMP). RFC 1157 (Historic) (1990). https://doi.org/10.17487/RFC1157
7. Cheng, N., Rocca, F.: An examination of the bloom filter and its application in preventing weak password choices. Int. J. Comput. Appl. Technol. Res. **6**(4), 190–193 (2016). https://doi.org/10.7753/IJCATR0604.1004
8. Durumeric, Z., Wustrow, E., Halderman, J.A.: ZMap: fast internet-wide scanning and its security applications. In: 22nd USENIX Security Symposium (USENIX Security 2013), pp. 605–620. USENIX Association, Washington, D.C. (2013). https://www.usenix.org/conference/usenixsecurity13/technical-sessions/paper/durumeric
9. Fahrnberger, G.: Reliable condition monitoring of telecommunication services with time-varying load characteristic. In: Negi, A., Bhatnagar, R., Parida, L. (eds.) ICDCIT 2018. LNCS, vol. 10722, pp. 173–188. Springer, Cham (2018). https://doi.org/10.1007/978-3-319-72344-0_14

10. Fahrnberger, G.: Outlier removal for the reliable condition monitoring of telecommunication services. In: 2019 20th International Conference on Parallel and Distributed Computing, Applications and Technologies (PDCAT), pp. 240–246 (2019). https://doi.org/10.1109/PDCAT46702.2019.00052

11. Fahrnberger, G.: Threshold pair selection for the reliable condition monitoring of telecommunication services. In: Krieger, U.R., Eichler, G., Erfurth, C., Fahrnberger, G. (eds.) I4CS 2021. CCIS, vol. 1404, pp. 9–21. Springer, Cham (2021). https://doi.org/10.1007/978-3-030-75004-6_2

12. Fahrnberger, G.: Realtime risk monitoring of SSH brute force attacks. In: Phillipson, F., Eichler, G., Erfurth, C., Fahrnberger, G. (eds.) I4CS 2022. CCIS, vol. 1585, pp. 75–95. Springer Cham (2022). https://doi.org/10.1007/978-3-031-06668-9_8

13. Goswami, M., Pagh, R., Silvestri, F., Sivertsen, J.: Distance sensitive bloom filters without false negatives. In: Proceedings of the 2017 Annual ACM-SIAM Symposium on Discrete Algorithms (SODA), pp. 257–269. Society for Industrial and Applied Mathematics (2017). https://doi.org/10.1137/1.9781611974782.17

14. Kirsch, A., Mitzenmacher, M.: Distance-sensitive bloom filters. In: 2006 Proceedings of the Workshop on Algorithm Engineering and Experiments (ALENEX), pp. 41–50. Society for Industrial and Applied Mathematics (2006). https://doi.org/10.1137/1.9781611972863.4

15. Manber, U., Wu, S.: An algorithm for approximate membership checking with application to password security. Inf. Process. Lett. **50**(4), 191–197 (1994). https://doi.org/10.1016/0020-0190(94)00032-8

16. Seifert, C.: Analyzing malicious SSH login attempts (2006). https://www.symantec.com/connect/articles/analyzing-malicious-ssh-login-attempts

A Complete One-Time Passwords (OTP) Solution Using Microservices: A Theoretical and Practical Approach

Luis E. Almeida[1,2], Brayan A. Fernández[1,2], Daliana Zambrano[1,2],
Anthony I. Almachi[1,2], Hilton B. Pillajo[1,2], and Sang Guun Yoo[1,2,3(✉)] ⓘ

[1] Departamento de Informática y Ciencias de la Computación, Escuela Politécnica Nacional,
Quito, Ecuador
sang.yoo@epn.edu.ec

[2] Smart Lab, Escuela Politécnica Nacional, Quito, Ecuador

[3] Departamento de Ciencias de la Computación, Universidad de las Fuerzas Armadas ESPE,
Sangolquí, Ecuador

Abstract. The objective of this paper is to share the knowledge required for developing a One-Time Password (OTP) system and the practical experience of developing a real one using microservices and different programming languages, remembering that the OTP is the most popular mechanism to carry out a two-factor authentication process. To achieve this purpose, an incremental iterative methodology was used that allowed the prototype to be implemented in different parts. The developed prototype was designed to work in mobile applications with iOS and Android operating systems. In this work, different types of OTP algorithms were used, such as HMAC-based One-Time Password, Time-based One-Time Password and True Random Number Generator. Additionally, for the development of the prototype, various tools and frameworks such as Flask, React Native and Flutter were used, which allowed the development of application components in an agile and efficient manner. The combination of these programming languages and tools resulted in a more efficient and effective implementation of the OTP generator prototype. Once the proposed system was developed, different types of tests were carried out to verify its optimal and efficient functionality.

Keywords: Authentication process · One-Time Passwords · OTP · OTP generators · Two-Factor Authentication · 2FA

1 Introduction

In 1981, Leslie Lamport proposed a secure password authentication method based on a one-way encryption system [1], which allowed users to submit their password to the authentication system securely, even if the communication channel was compromised.

This one-way hashing approach is resistant to encrypted password recovery attacks but has some limitations, e.g., the need to share a secret key between the authentication system and the user; if an attacker manages to obtain the secret key, he/she can crack the

U. R. Krieger et al. (Eds.): I4CS 2023, CCIS 1876, pp. 68–86, 2023.
https://doi.org/10.1007/978-3-031-40852-6_4

stored passwords and compromise the security of a user's account. Therefore, Lamport's method requires careful handling of the secret key to ensure the security of authentication.

Following Lamport's work, further research in the field of password authentication continued, and in 1995, a paper detailing an authentication system based on one-time passwords, called S/Key, was published [2]. S/Key was designed to provide a high level of security in user authentication. The S/Key system is based on the generation of a password that can only be used once. The password is generated from a secret key shared between the user and the server, using a mathematical algorithm. To perform authentication, the server only needs to know the value of the secret key, since the key generation is done on the user's device. However, the security of the S/Key system largely depends on the security of the secret key shared between the user and the server. If the key is compromised, the entire security of the system is compromised [2].

In 1998, a one-time password authentication system, known as One-Time Password (OTP), was introduced to improve user authentication security. This system has been implemented in various applications, including remote access applications and authentication of financial transactions. Based on this work, improvements have been developed such as HMAC-Based One-Time Password (HOTP) [3], which is based on the Hash-based Message Authentication Code (HMAC) algorithm to generate one-time passwords.

An improvement to HOTP is Time-Based One-Time Password (TOTP) [4], which shares the same main idea as HOTP, but uses the current time as input instead of a counter. Time is divided into fixed intervals that are used as counters to generate one-time passwords. Each generated password has a limited duration based on the used time interval. These systems have proven effective in protecting access to online accounts and preventing brute force attacks. However, it is important that users adequately protect the secret keys used in password generation and change these keys regularly to maintain an optimal level of security.

Pseudo-Random Number Generators (PRNG) are algorithms that use a deterministic formula to generate sequences of numbers that appear to be random [5]. This means that, with a given initial seed, the results are predictable and repeatable. Normally, developers needing to generate OTP values make use of PRNG [6]. The problem of PRNG is that it makes use of deterministic algorithms to generate random numbers, which generates periodic and predictable values that can be recreated from the initial seed [6].

To solve this problem, Truly Random Number Generators (TRNG) have been developed, which are based on the entropy of one or several physical sources to generate numbers without any correlation or dependency [5]. Unlike PRNGs, which have a finite number of states and whose outputs can be replicated, TRNGs use different sources of physical entropy to generate bit strings that result in unpredictable values. This makes it extremely difficult to determine how and from where the bits needed to reproduce the output of a generated number are obtained [5]. Works such as [7, 8] have shown that TRNGs are much more secure than PRNGs due to their ability to generate truly random numbers and avoid correlation and dependency of the generated data.

Multi-factor authentication (MFA) is one of several techniques that have been implemented in the field of essential security to prevent unauthorized access to systems, accounts or applications [9]. One of the various ways to apply MFA is the use of one-time passwords (OTP), which provide a high level of security to the user [10]. By using an OTP, you ensure that only the legitimate user who owns the corresponding authentication device can access the protected resource. Furthermore, since the OTP value can only be used once, the risk of someone intercepting and reusing the OTP value to access the protected account or system is eliminated [11].

With this background, in this article, the creation of a One-Time Password (OTP) system prototype for a two-factor authentication system is proposed. The system proposes the implementation of the HOTP and TOTP algorithm and the generation of values through TRNG, to guarantee a random and safe generation of OTP values.

The proposed authentication system is versatile and allows OTP values to be delivered to the user in three different ways, i.e., email, displayed on the screen, and through the Telegram messaging application. The user's choice determines the way he/she receives the OTP code and how the OTP code is generated (i.e., generation algorithm).

Likewise, mobile applications have been developed that allow users to enter the OTP code and validate their access to the account. These mobile apps are secure and allow users to authorize or deny account access after entering the OTP code. The authentication system is secure and efficient, ensuring the protection of online users' personal and financial information, making it suitable for use in a variety of applications.

The system architecture has been designed using microservices to improve communication between OTP value generation services and validation services. In addition, the possibility of adding more OTP value generation options and delivery methods in the future has been considered.

Using TRNG ensures that the generated OTP values are truly random, making it more difficult for attackers to guess the OTP code. Implementing multiple OTP delivery options increases user convenience and reduces reliance on a single communication channel. Overall, the developed OTP system is secure, easy to use, and scalable for future enhancements and expansions.

The present work is structured as follows. Section 2 presents the previous work carried out in the field of generating OTP values, as well as the different algorithms and techniques used. Section 3 explains in detail the methodology used in the development of the work. Section 4 presents the proposed work, including the architecture used and the approach based on increments. Later, the analysis of the tests carried out in the present work are detailed in Sect. 5. Finally, in Sect. 6, the conclusions of the presented work are presented.

2 Related Work

Before proceeding to the development of the proposed OTP system, a systematic review of the literature was carried out, with the aim of fully understanding the available OTP algorithms, as well as their applications and delivery methods. Through this review, it was possible to gather relevant and updated information on the different types of OTP, operation modes, advantages, and disadvantages.

2.1 One-Time Passwords Generation Algorithms

There are multiple algorithms proposed for the generation of One-Time Passwords (OTP). In [12], an innovative model for OTP generation based on the use of a 3 × 3 Vedic multiplier is presented. In this method, the OTP generation process starts by getting the client's login details from the Certification Authority, which are converted to two 8 bits values. These resulting 16 bits are transformed to decimal using binary to decimal conversion (CB2D), resulting in two 3-digit decimal digits that are multiplied together using the 3 × 3 Vedic multiplier, making in this way the OTP code.

It should be noted that the model proposed in [12] presents an important innovation in the generation of OTPs, since it uses an approach based on an ancestral mathematical technique to achieve greater security in the generation of one-time passwords. However, a thorough evaluation of the safety and efficiency of this method is necessary before its implementation.

Other approach is the one presented in [13]. In this work, a solution is proposed to overcome the limitations of the finite OTP system proposed by Lamport i.e., the weaknesses in the length of the finite hash chain, which results in the finite generation of the OTP. To solve this problem, a new hash chain has been designed that allows infinite OTP generation without the need for a shared secret between the parties. Unlike Lamport's system, the new hash chain is made up of multiple short hash chains.

On the other hand, reference [14] describes an efficient two-factor authentication scheme based on negative databases (NDBs). This scheme enables the password changes feature and uses the uncertain properties of negative databases to reduce the frequency of data updates. Furthermore, the scheme is resistant to most attacks, including password guessing attacks and man-in-the-middle attacks.

In article [15], an innovative model for the generation of banking OTP is proposed. This model uses three different inputs that are known by the client, which change randomly, along with an initialization vector (IV), to generate the OTP. The proposed generator is implemented by an Android-based mobile device and the generated OTP is encrypted using the AES-256 encryption algorithm. Once the OTP is generated and encrypted, it is sent to the client through a secure HTTP channel, guaranteeing the protection of the client's personal and financial information. This OTP generation model is highly secure and efficient as it uses multiple inputs to generate the OTP, making it more difficult to guess or forge.

Additionally, in reference [16], a new two-factor authentication method is presented i.e., 2D-2FA, which focuses on improving the efficiency and usability of the Two Factor Authentication (2FA) process. In 2D-2FA, a one-time Personal Identification Number (PIN) is generated on the secondary factor and transferred directly to the server for verification. To evaluate the effectiveness and feasibility of 2D-2FA, a comprehensive security model was defined, and proof of concept was conducted. Additionally, the effectiveness and usability of 2D-2FA was compared to the PIN-2FA method in an in-person usability study. The results of the study showed that 2D-2FA offers higher accuracy and lower delay compared to the PIN-2FA method. It was also found that the usability and user perception of the efficiency, security and accuracy of 2D-2FA are high and comparable to those of the well-known PIN-2FA.

So far, some interesting proposals have been explained, but they do not maintain a specific OTP generation standard. Below are other works that are based on a modality that is more standardized in the generation of OTP codes.

HMAC-Based One-Time Password. HMAC-based One Time Password (HOTP) is a one-time password generation algorithm based on HMAC [3] which was developed to enhance security in two-factor authentication and is still widely used as a standard. Unlike the common OTP which generates a password based on a random value, HOTP uses a sequence of increasing numbers and employs the HMAC algorithm such as HMAC-SHA-1 [17].

The implementation of HOTP involves generating a secret key shared between the authentication server and the user. This key is used for generating OTPs combined with a counter that increments after each use. Since the password generation process is based on HMAC, it ensures that the password is unique and cannot be reproduced without the secret key.

Despite these security measures, HOTP can be vulnerable to brute-force attacks depending on the applied hash algorithm, e.g., in the case of truncated value by HMAC-SHA-1. This situation mandates implementing additional security measures on the authentication server to prevent such attacks.

Time-Based One-Time Password. According to RFC 6238 [4], Time-Based One-Time Password (TOTP) is an authentication mechanism that uses a unique, one-time code which is generated using the current time and a secret key shared between the authentication server and the user's device or application. TOTP is also a variant of the HOTP algorithm, but instead of generating the OTP using a counter, it uses the current time [18].

TOTP is widely used as a two-factor authentication for accessing various systems and services, such as financial applications or games. TOTP uses the HMAC-SHA-1 algorithm for OTP generation, but other algorithms such as HMAC-SHA-256 or HMAC-SHA512 can also be used for enhanced security [19]. The interval for generating a new password is usually set to 30 s, but this value can be adjusted according to the user or system needs. For TOTP generation, a secret key is generated and shared through a secure channel between the client side and the server. The current time is obtained and divided by the time interval to convert it to a string, which is then encoded using a hash algorithm such as SHA-1 or SHA-256. The last digits of the resulting hash are the OTP values, which are usually 6 decimal digits.

True Random Number Generator. True Random Number Generator (TRNG) is a device or program that generates truly random numbers, meaning that those numbers cannot be predicted or repeated [20]. Unlike pseudo-random number generators, which use an algorithm to produce a seemingly random sequence of numbers, TRNGs rely on physical sources of randomness, such as atmospheric noise, thermal noise, radioactivity, or air turbulence [21].

In terms of software, TRNGs are implemented through algorithms that use sources of entropy, such as user activity, mouse movement, or time between keystrokes. These algorithms produce a sequence of truly random numbers that cannot be generated again [21].

TRNGs are very important in cryptographic applications e.g., they are needed to generate cryptographic keys, for authentication (nonces) and for (OTP) generation. They are also used in gaming applications, simulations, and software testing, where a reliable source of randomness is required [22].

3 Methodology

In order to successfully carry out the project, the iterative and incremental development methodology was selected. This methodology is a set of principles that facilitates project management and allows for gradual and iterative development until the desired result is achieved [23]. Figure 1 shows the methodology that has been followed for this work, as well as its different phases.

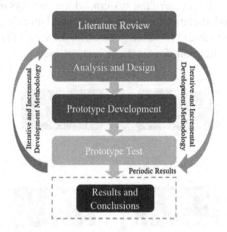

Fig. 1. Stages and methodologies used in this work

As a result of applying this methodology in the present work, a total of four increments with four phases each were carried out. During the analysis phase, the operational characteristics and necessary requirements for the prototype were determined. In the design phase, the solution to the previously established requirements was defined and its implementation was planned. During the development phase, the proposed solution was implemented. Finally, in the testing phase, the implemented solution was evaluated. If errors were detected, they were addressed in the next increment. The iteration of these four stages can be seen graphically in Fig. 2.

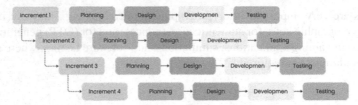

Fig. 2. Increments and phases of the incremental iterative development methodology

4 Proposed Solution

As mentioned previously, the proposed solution was created through increments that increase the different functionalities of the system. But first, the overall architecture of the system was defined to properly coordinate each of the increments.

Figure 3 shows the architecture of the system, which displays the interaction between the application's backend, database, web application, and mobile application. The Backend consists of login services, OTP value generation module, OTP sending module, and OTP validation. The application flow is described below:

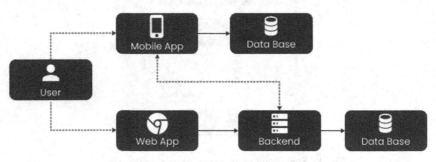

Fig. 3. General architecture of the prototype

1. The user enters their credentials (username and password) in the web application to access the system.
2. The data is sent in encrypted form to the login service, where the existence of the user is checked. If the user exists, step 3 is executed, otherwise, a guide is displayed to set up 2FA.
3. Since the user has correctly entered their credentials and set up 2FA, they are informed that an OTP has been generated and sent, activating the OTP generation and sending services.
4. Once the user receives the OTP, they must enter the 6-digit string into the application. At this point, the mobile application interacts only with the validation service, sending the OTP value along with the necessary data for authentication.
5. If the OTP value is correct, the server grants access to the system.

For the first three increments, we focused on the OTP generation services and the OTP delivery service. In Fig. 4, we can see how the OTP generation algorithms and delivery methods are associated for each one.

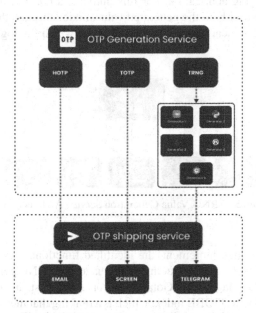

Fig. 4. OTP generation and delivery service

For the fourth increment, the mobile application was developed to connect to the OTP validation service.

Once the general system architecture was designed, the different increments were carried out. In the first increment, a requirements analysis was conducted for TRNG-based OTP generation. Additionally, a microservice-based design was created. In the second increment, an analysis was performed to define the HMAC-based OTP and its development in Python. After the design was defined, the algorithm was developed, and corresponding tests were conducted to validate its proper functioning. In the third increment, an analysis was conducted on TOTP and its implementation using the Python PyOTP library. Finally, in the fourth increment, the design and development of the mobile application were carried out, and respective functionality tests were conducted.

4.1 First Increment

Analysis: The requirements for creating OTP values based on TRNG and transmitting them through the messaging application Telegram were analyzed. As a result, 5 essential requirements were identified, which were defined in the form of user stories. These requirements include: (1) generation of six-digit OTP values; (2) generation of random values for the authentication process; (3) verification of the authenticity of the OTP for the current session; (4) ensuring that the OTP is consumed only once; and (5) rejection of OTP values outside the established time limit.

Design: Based on the requirements defined in the previous step, a microservices architecture was designed (see Fig. 5). These services are responsible for generating OTP values based on physical entropy sources. The generated values are communicated via the Telegram messaging application. For this purpose, a bot was implemented which communicates to the user both the generated value hidden through the Spoiler function, as well as a message indicating the time and IP from which the login attempt is being made.

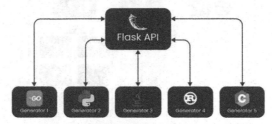

Fig. 5. TRNG Value Generation Service Architecture.

Development: In the first increment, the identified functionalities were developed in each of the previously selected programming languages for TRNG generation implementation. The selected languages were Golang, Python, Java, Rust, and C. These languages were chosen based on the TIOBE index, which is a ranking that measures the popularity of programming languages. Each of the developed codes was deployed in an independent Docker container, and the generated values were communicated through an API developed in Flask. The generated values were sent to the end-user, and in Fig. 6, a message can be observed before and after revealing the generated OTP value. The reason of developing the same functionality in different programming languages was to know their level randomness when generating the OTP.

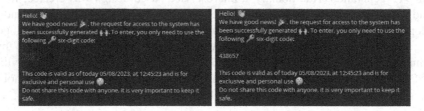

Fig. 6. Comparison of the message before and after revealing confidential information.

Test: Different tests were carried out in order to verify the correct functioning of the main API to generate OTP values. To add an extra layer of randomness when generating OTP values, it was decided to concatenate the value generated by one service with that of another, since each one returns values of three digits. Additionally, it was decided to study the randomness of the values generated by each of the developed services with a goodness-of-fit test, using the statistical technique known as Chi-squared. The Chi test is commonly used in the analysis of random numbers to verify if the generated sequence fits a uniform distribution. Based on the test, it was observed that the language that generated the most random values was C with a test statistic value of 11.67, followed by Golang with 16.6, Java with 20.44, Rust with 20.65, and finally Python with 24.38.

4.2 Second Increment

The technological stack with which the two-factor authentication system was developed was defined, which includes NodeJS, Express, PostgreSQL, and Python. The graphical user interfaces of the web application were developed to allow user interaction. The graphical user interface enables the user to authenticate themselves using their email address, password, and the OTP-generated password, which is sent to the user's email address to verify their identity.

Additionally, an algorithm for generating one-time passwords using an HMAC cryptographic mechanism was developed, which was created to provide a solution to single-factor authentication systems. The following requirements [3] were taken into account to generate this algorithm: (a) generate a shared secret key: this is a character string shared between the server and the client. It is used to generate HOTP codes; (b) calculate the HOTP code: this is done by using an HMAC hash function and a counter that is incremented each time a new HOTP code is requested; (c) verify the HOTP code: the HOTP code is provided to the server, which then uses the shared secret key and the counter to calculate the expected HOTP code and compare it to the provided code, and if they match, the request is authenticated. Figure 7 shows the process of generating HOTP One-Time Passwords.

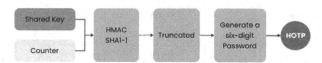

Fig. 7. Password generation process

The algorithm for generating HOTP one-time passwords was developed in the Python programming language, taking into account the following characteristics:

- This algorithm generates 6-decimal digits one-time passwords.
- The generated codes are stored in the PosgreSQL database.
- The HOTP generator function receives the key and the counter number as parameters, while the verifier function receives the key, counter number, and generated password as parameters.
- The generator converts the counter value to a hexadecimal value which is then used along with the secret key for cryptography functions (HMAC, SHA1). The result of the cryptographic function is truncated to maintain the 6-decimal digits requirement.
- The password verifier function verifies if the generated value matches the value sent to the user. If it is correct, the password and the counter value are validated. Otherwise, the value is not validated, and the counter value is not increased.

- The method of delivering the OTP developed in this iteration is the user's email, as this delivery method is fast, easy, and cost-effective to use.

Test: The tests carried out in this iteration was the time performance of the HOTP algorithm. To do this, the time required to generate an OTP code were measured. The process was repeated several times, and the average times were taken to obtain a better estimate of the system's performance.

It is essential to ensure that the HOTP code generation is fast enough to avoid significant delays in the authentication process for users. The time test of HOTP code generation is one of the critical tests to guarantee the optimal performance of the two-factor authentication system. In Table 1, various performed test results are shown. The average for generating a one-time password OTP was 60,512 ms. All tests performed were successful, considering that their time to generate and send varied slightly.

Table 1. Time performance tests

Test Number	Generate OTP [*ms*]
1	61,92
2	60,68
3	58,99
4	61,02
5	63,4
6	57,64
7	52,93
8	51,05
9	81,3
10	56,19
Average	**60,512**

4.3 Third Increment

Analysis: In the third increment of the project, an analysis of the TOTP generator was carried out, taking into account the relevant security aspects for its implementation as indicated in [4]. User stories were also created to identify the key features that the system must have to ensure the security of users' accounts. These user stories were a valuable tool in software development, as they allowed clear and concise definition of user needs and expectations. Each user story focused on specific user requirements and established a clear framework for the team in terms of what features should be implemented and how they should function.

Design: For the generation of TOTP values, the PyOTP library of Python has been used. PyOTP can be used for implementing a two-factor authentication (2FA) or multifactor authentication (MFA) system in web and mobile applications. PyOTP follows the standards defined in RFC 4226 [3] and RFC 6238 [4] regarding security aspects for a secure deployment of the algorithm. The connection with the web application is made through the Flask API implemented in previous increments.

Development: Once the conditions for time-based OTP generation were defined, the PyOTP library was implemented. Endpoints in the API were configured and implemented for consumption by the mobile application to receive OTP values entered by the user, as well as to send the corresponding response of OTP validation. Once the OTP code is received, it is verified to match the value generated by the algorithm. If the received OTP value matches and is within the time limit for input by the client, the validation is considered as successful; otherwise, it is considered as a failed authentication.

Test: For this increment, correct connection and sending of OTP between a client through the API developed in Flask and the OTP generator was verified.

4.4 Fourth Increment

Analysis: Taking into account the general architecture of the authentication system proposed by the authors, the following flowchart was defined to describe the operation that the mobile prototype must fulfill (see Fig. 8), highlighting as main functions that: the mobile prototype must allow the user to register a web application, in such a way that the mobile application can identify the user who wants to authenticate in the different web applications; the mobile application must send the OTP to the correct web application, which contains the correct user session, in order to authenticate it.

For the development of the mobile application, a comparative analysis was carried out among several development frameworks, including Flutter, React Native, Xamarin, Ionic, and Apache Cordova. Based on the fact that the most popular frameworks in the last 5 years according to Google Trends are Flutter and React, these tools were selected to develop the mobile prototypes for the iOS and Android operating systems, respectively. On the other hand, Firestore was used as the database, which is a No-SQL database hosted in the cloud and provided by Firebase. This tool was selected because almost any platform can access this service through an Application Programming Interface (API).

Design: In Figs. 9, 10, and 11, reference images of high- and low-fidelity mockups of the prototype are shown. Low-fidelity mockups are used in early stages of the project, as they help to quickly test and validate concepts and ideas with low cost and simplicity; while high-fidelity mockups represent a more realistic and detailed version of the product and are used to conduct design, navigability, and functionality testing prior to implementation.

Development: When two-factor authentication is activated in the web application, a QR code is generated that contains crucial information for the mobile application to identify both the user and the specific web application. This information includes the name and logo of the web application, the user's email address, and the API to which the mobile prototype must send the OTP. The following describes the functioning of the mobile prototype for the web application registration process and the OTP sending process: (1) The QR code containing information about the web application and the user is displayed to the user upon completing the double factor authentication activation process, (2) the user scans this QR code using the mobile application, (3) the mobile application sends this information to its corresponding database service for storage, (4) the database stores the record of the web application, (5) the database notifies the mobile application about the successful registration of the web application, (6) the mobile application displays the registered web application information on its interface, presenting it in the form of a list.

Test: In [24], different ways to measure the performance of a software product are discussed. One of the metrics mentioned in [24], which was applied to the present work, was the task completion rate for which the software product was designed. This type of metric has a binary format, as the task is either successfully completed or not; there are no intermediate points.

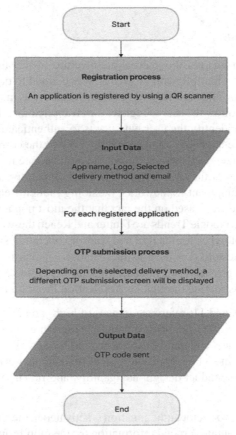

Fig. 8. Flowchart of the registration process and use of the mobile application

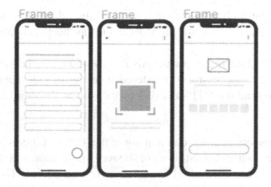

Fig. 9. Low fidelity mockup

Fig. 10. iOS Hifi Mockup

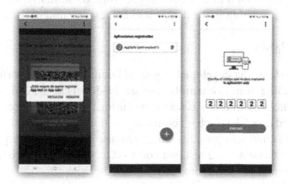

Fig. 11. HiFi Android Mockup

In the case of the mobile application developed in the present work, there are two main tasks for which it was designed:

- Registration of the web application: The user should be able to register a web application in which two-factor authentication has been activated in the mobile application.
- Sending the OTP: Once the user has activated two-factor authentication on the web application and has successfully registered it in the mobile application, the user should be able to send the OTP provided by the web application through the mobile application.

As a result of this test, it was found that out of the 43 test subjects, 4 were not able to carry out the main activities (registration of the web application and sending the OTP). This resulted in a success rate of 91% and an error rate of 9%. The reason of the 4 unsuccessful trials were because those users never had used an OTP system and because the test were carried out without a detailed explanation.

Nielsen's Usability Heuristics: Nielsen's 10 heuristics are based on a set of quite broad usability principles, called "heuristics", that are evaluated by a group of experts in an early stage of the prototype. For these tests, a group of 5 experts specialized in mobile application development and user interface design was selected, in order to identify usability issues on the high-fidelity mockup and correct them before implementation. Additionally, the System Usability Scale (SUS) was applied which was created by John Brooke in 1996. It consists of 10 simple questions that help to understand the usability issues that users face when using a certain system [25]. After applying the aforementioned methodologies, the expert group found the following issues:

- It was noted that the application registration button, which was initially represented with a '+' icon, was not clear for the expert group. So, it was decided to replace it with the "Register" button.
- It was suggested that other frequently asked questions should be included to help the user better understand how the prototype worked. Similarly, this was taken into account and included both in the design and implementation of the final application.

5 Result Analysis

Once the entire system was developed, some additional tests were performed to verify the correct functioning of the system. Below are the details of the executed tests.

Firstly, a goodness-of-fit test was performed using the statistical technique known as Chi-square, denoted by χ^2, which is commonly used in the analysis of random numbers to verify if the generated sequence fits a uniform distribution. The purpose of applying this technique was to obtain the test statistic to determine which program from those displayed in the containers was more random than the others.

Figure 12 shows the histogram of the values generated by a program implemented in Golang. Based on the observation of the histogram, it can be inferred that the values generated by the program are uniformly distributed within the allowed range, which means that each number has the same probability of being generated.

When calculating the test statistic, the values obtained by the programs in different programming languages can be observed in Table 2, which indicates how random each program is.

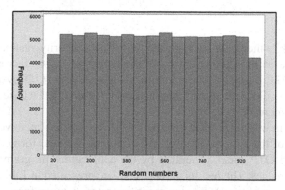

Fig. 12. Histogram of the values generated by Golang

Table 2. Value of the test statistic for each language

Container	Value
Golang	16,5702546
Python	24,3894675
Rust	20,6510416
Java	20,4479638
C	11,6744907

Other performed test was the connection reliability. The API provides a secure means of establishing a connection between different services, such as the validation service and the OTP delivery service. This connection ensures the reliability and protection of the transmitted data through the implementation of encryption techniques. In this aspect, different test were executed to validate the correct performing of the APIs developed in the system.

Additionally, user acceptance tests for different OTP delivery methods were executed. As a result of these tests, the delivery method that had the most acceptance was scanning a QR code containing the OTP information with 65.1%. According to comments made by participants, this was due to the speed at which they could access their accounts. In second place, the SMS delivery method was chosen by the users with 20.9%. Some users claimed that this method was the most familiar one, stating that it was the method used by the banking institution they used. One interesting thing was that no user selected email as his/her preferred delivery method. According to some comments made by participants, this delivery method is inefficient as it requires logging into their email accounts every time they want to authenticate themselves in the applications they want to access.

6 Conclusions

Through this work, a literature study of the OTP-based security system was conducted which could serve as the theoretical basis for proposing a two-factor authentication system based on OTP. Based on the accumulated knowledge, an OTP system architecture was generated using different algorithms such as HOTP and TOTP based on TRNG, and then, it was implemented.

Once the system was developed, different tests were carried out to verify the security and functionality of the system. Firstly, statistical tests were performed to evaluate the randomness of the OTP codes generated by the applications programmed in different programming languages. The results of these tests are presented in Table 2, which shows a detailed comparison of the OTP value repetition rates obtained for each programming language.

It was also verified that the use of privacy functions, such as Telegram's "Spoiler," can be a useful measure to guarantee the privacy and confidentiality of transmitted information. This tool hides sensitive information, preventing third parties from accessing it, and only the authorized recipient can discover its content. Additionally, through a usability analysis conducted on end-users, it was determined that the acceptability percentage of the system was 74.3% average. The range of variation between the highest and lowest acceptability percentages is 9.4%, suggesting that users, regardless of their technical level, felt largely satisfied with the developed system.

It is important to indicate that the implementation of a second factor of authentication is a fundamental technique in cybersecurity to ensure the protection of computer systems. Furthermore, it is crucial to establish strong password policies for users accessing systems to avoid possible vulnerabilities in authentication. The combination of both practices increases the security of the system and minimizes the risk of brute force attacks that could compromise the integrity of the system's data.

Acknowledgments. The authors would like to thank to Corporación Ecuatoriana para el Desarrollo de la Investigación y Academia - CEDIA for the financial support given to this work through its Fondo Divulga.

References

1. Lamport, L.: Password authentication with insecure communication. Commun. ACM **24**(11), 770–772 (1981)
2. Haller, N.: The S/KEY One-Time Password System, RFC1760 (1995)
3. M'Raihi, D., Bellare, M., Hoornaert, F., Naccache, D., Ranen, O.: HOTP: an HMAC-Based One-Time Password Algorithm, RFC4226 (2005)
4. M'Raihi, D., Machani, S., Pei, M., Rydell, J.: TOTP: Time-Based One-Time Password Algorithm, RFC6238 (2011)
5. Manucom, E. M. M., Gerardo, B. D., Medina, R. P.: Security analysis of improved one-time pad cryptography using TRNG key generator. In: 2019 IEEE 5th International Conference on Computer and Communications (ICCC), pp. 1515–1521. IEEE (2019)
6. Ma, S., et al.: An empirical study of SMS one-time password authentication in Android apps. In: Proceedings of the 35th Annual Computer Security Applications Conference, pp. 339–354. ACM (2019)

7. Marghescu, A., Svasta, P., Simion, E.: High speed and secure variable probability Pseudo/True random number generator using FPGA. In; Proceedings of 2015 IEEE 21st International Symposium for Design and Technology in Electronic Packaging (SIITME), pp. 323–328. IEEE (2015)
8. Maksutov, A.A., Goryushkin, P.N., Gerasimov, A.A., Orlov, A.A.: PRNG assessment tests based on neural networks. In: Proceedings of 2018 IEEE Conference of Russian Young Researchers in Electrical and Electronic Engineering (EIConRus), pp. 339–341. IEEE (2018)
9. Tirfe, D., Anand, V.K.: A survey on trends of two-factor authentication. Lect. Notes Networks Syst. **281**, 285–296 (2022)
10. Peeters, C., Patton, C., Munyaka, I.N.S., Olszewski, D., Shrimpton, T., Traynor, P.: SMS OTP security (SOS): hardening SMS-based two factor authentication. In: Proceedings of the 2022 ACM on Asia Conference on Computer and Communications Security, pp. 2–16. ACM (2022)
11. Sarkunavathi, A., Lingeshkumar, S., Muralidharan, L., Vasudevan, P.: A survey on securing OTP using steganography technique. J. Emerg. Technol. Innovative Res. **7**(3), 1120–1126 (2020)
12. Shyry, S.P., Mahithaasree, M., Saranya, M.: Implementation of one time password by 3 * 3 vedic multiplier. In: Proceedings of 2018 International Conference on Computer, Communication, and Signal Processing (ICCCSP), pp. 1–5. IEEE (2018)
13. Park, C.-S.: One-time password based on hash chain without shared secret and re-registration. Comput. Secur. **75**, 138–146 (2018)
14. Liu, R., Wang, X., Wang, C.: An efficient two-factor authentication scheme based on negative databases: experiments and extensions. Appl. Soft Comput. **119**, 108558 (2022)
15. Elganzoury, H.S., Abdelhafez, A.A., Hegazy, A.A.: A new secure one-time password algorithm for mobile applications. In: 2018 35th National Radio Science Conference (NRSC), pp. 249–257. IEEE (2018)
16. Shirvanian, M., Agrawal, S.: 2D-2FA: a new dimension in two-factor authentication. In: Annual Computer Security Applications Conference, pp. 482–496. ACM (2021)
17. Krawczyk, H., Bellare, M., Canetti, R.: HMAC: Keyed-Hashing for Message Authentication, RFC2104 (1997)
18. Sudar, C., Arjun, S.K., Deepthi, L.R.: Time-based one-time password for Wi-Fi authentication and security. In: 2017 International Conference on Advances in Computing, Communications and Informatics (ICACCI), pp. 1212–1216. IEEE (2017)
19. Huseynov, E., Seigneur, J.-M.: Hardware TOTP tokens with time synchronization. In: 2019 IEEE 13th International Conference on Application of Information and Communication Technologies (AICT), pp. 1–4. IEEE (2019)
20. Yu, F., Li, L., Tang, Q., Cai, S., Song, Y., Xu, Q.: A survey on true random number generators based on chaos. Discret. Dyn. Nat. Soc. **2019**(2545123), 1–10 (2019)
21. Bassham, L., et al.: A Statistical Test Suite for Random and Pseudorandom Number Generators for Cryptographic Applications: Special Publication (NIST SP). National Institute of Standards and Technology (2010)
22. Tupparwar, S., Mohankumar, N., A hybrid true random number generator using ring oscillator and digital clock manager. In; 2021 6th International Conference on Inventive Computation Technologies (ICICT), pp. 290–294. IEEE (2021)
23. Mitchell, S. M., Seaman, C. B.: A comparison of software cost, duration, and quality for waterfall vs. iterative and incremental development: a systematic review. In: 2009 3rd International Symposium on Empirical Software Engineering and Measurement, pp. 511–515. IEEE (2009)

24. Suzianti, A., Belahakki, A.: Redesigning user interface of MRT Jakarta's mobile application using usability testing approach. In: 2020 The 6th International Conference on Industrial and Business Engineering, pp. 73–78. ACM (2020)
25. Kaya, A., Ozturk, R., Gumussoy, C.A.: Usability Measurement of Mobile Applications with System Usability Scale (SUS). In: Calisir, F., Cevikcan, E., Akdag, H.C. (eds.) Industrial Engineering in the Big Data Era. LNMIE, pp. 389–400. Springer, Cham (2019). https://doi.org/10.1007/978-3-030-03317-0_32

Environmental Protection

Impact of Speed Limitation on Urban Road Traffic

Mohamed Lamine Benzagouta[1], Hasnaa Aniss[1], Hacène Fouchal[2]([✉]),
and Nour-Eddin El-Faouzi[1]

[1] Université Gustave Eiffel, Champs-sur-Marne, France
mohamed-lamine.benzagouta@ifsttar.fr,
{hasnaa.aniss,nour-eddin.elfaouzi}@univ-eiffel.fr
[2] Université de Reims Champagne-Ardenne, CReSTIC, Reims, France
hacene.fouchal@univ-reims.fr

Abstract. As vehicular communications continue to develop and evolve, data from probe connected vehicles can prove to be useful so to observe traffic dynamics more precisely. Cooperative Awareness Messages (CAM) give us detailed information about the location, velocity and heading of probe vehicles, whereas data from the Green Light Optimal Speed Advisory (GLOSA) give us information about the traffic lights at intersections such as the current phase, time to next phase and the speed advice that allows a driver to avoid a stop at a red light. In this work, we use data that is extracted from a smartphone application that simulates vehicular communications. We match the GLOSA records with the CAMs in order to observe the behavior of vehicles in the segments prior to an intersection. We characterize four different patterns of speed profiles for vehicles in segments with a traffic light intersection.

Keywords: C-ITS · Traffic light · Connected vehicles · Data analysis

1 Introduction

With the aim of improving road safety, comfort, traffic efficiency, energy saving, and the overall road transport experience, modern contributions in both academia and the industry tend to exploit telecommunications to this end. Enabling connected vehicles (CV) to communicate with each other and with other actors on the road such as the infrastructure. Cooperative Intelligent Transport Systems (C-ITS) are systems that allow for such operations to be made.

C-ITS is a system that allows vehicles to connect with each other and with the infrastructure. Its main communication strategy is the Vehicle-to-Everything (V2X) in which, data sharing between the vehicles is done via the Vehicle-to-vehicle (V2V) communication strategy, where vehicles exchange beacon messages such as the CAMs. Whereas communications with the infrastructure are done using the Vehicle-to-Infrastructure (V2I) communication strategy where the vehicles send messages to the infrastructure such as the CAMs [2] and DENMs [3] and receive messages such as the MAPEM, SPATEM and IVIM [4].

U. R. Krieger et al. (Eds.): I4CS 2023, CCIS 1876, pp. 89–102, 2023.
https://doi.org/10.1007/978-3-031-40852-6_5

The C-ITS connectivity is based on two standards of communication, the ETSI's ITS-G5 [6] and the 3GPP's C-V2X [5]. These standards are the most widely used for vehicular communications in Europe. ITS-G5 (and its equivalent DSRC outside of Europe) is based on the IEEE 802.11p or its successor the IEEE 802.11bd and enables short range communications, which are based on adhoc WiFi broadcast links operating on the 5.9 GHz band. The V2I communications are done through the Road Side Units (RSU) which play the role of the infrastructure. Whereas C-V2X relies on cellular networks and allows for long range communications. All communications in C-V2X are scheduled by the eNodeB (or the gNodeB in the case of 5G) which also acts as the infrastructure's access point. The V2V communications are assured by the Sidelink scheme and is also scheduled by the eNodeB.

Green Light Optimized Speed Advisory (GLOSA) is a C-ITS use case. It concerns intersections equipped with a traffic light and indicates to the driver the current phase, time to the next phase and also a speed advice that allows the driver to avoid a stop in the case of a red light. It is based on two C-ITS services [4] which are the Traffic Light Maneuver (TLM) and the Road and Lane Topology (RLT). The TLM sends safety information to vehicles in the nearby intersection, informing them of the real-time state of the traffic light and its future state, as well as the time margin between the two. The message used to this extent is the SPATEM. It is sent periodically to all participants for as long as they are close to the intersection. The RLT sends a digital topology map of the geometry of an area to the nearby vehicles, describing lanes, crosswalks, conflict zones (intersections) and permitted maneuvers. A lane consists of several connected landmarks, and at the connection of these crossing points with a conflict zone, a set of authorized maneuvers is modeled as a connection between the two end points that connect the two lanes with the zone. The message that is used by the RLT is the MAPEM and is transmitted at the same time as a SPATEM when the vehicle approaches an intersection.

In this work, we are interested in intersections equipped with traffic lights. We study the speed profiles of drivers in the road segment prior to the intersection, and classify their behaviors into four repeating patterns. The rest of this paper is structured as follows. Section 2 presents the state of the art and similar works on intersections and probe vehicles data. Section 3 presents briefly the C-ITS as well as its architecture. Section 4 presents the data that was used. Section 5 is dedicated to the analysis of the data and Sect. 6 presents the conclusion.

2   State of the Art

A lot of works focus on traffic estimation from data concerning intersections and probe CVs. In [18] data from traffic lights and CVs was used in order to estimate traffic volume. Based on the position of stop of a CV before traffic lights, the size of the queue is estimated. If another CV comes after it, the upper bound of vehicle arrivals between the two CVs can be calculated based on the trajectory of the second vehicle. They modeled traffic volume in traffic light intersections, then they modeled queue arrivals as a time-dependent Poisson process, the traffic volume parameters are determined using maximum likelihood estimator (MLE) with the Expectation Maximization (EM) algorithm.

Predestination is a method proposed in [13], it aims at predicting the final destination of a trip in progress. The authors gathered data through GPS from 169 drivers doing around 7000 trips. They represented the origin and destination in form of tiles and three probabilistic methods were developed then combined. In the first method a driver's destination is assumed to be belonging to the list of previously visited tiles. The second one considers every possible destination and the last one examines the ground type and assumes the probability of it being a destination (water is unlikely to be a destination for example).

A directional counts at intersections using Floating Car Data (FCD) approach was described in [9] The paper discusses a methodology for compiling directional counts, or traffic flow data at intersections by integrating data from multiple sources, including FCD and section counts. In [8] a statistical method has been used for real time estimation of queue lengths at signalized intersections using probe vehicle location data. The location of the last probe vehicle in the queue is used to estimate its length. They assume that the marginal probability distribution of the queue length is known and they present an analytical formulation that relies on this prior knowledge. The results show that their method can accurately estimate queue lengths.

A stochastic learning framework to estimate the index of a vehicle at signalized intersections has been proposed in [10], multiple experiments have been conducted with data sets from microscopic traffic simulations and field experiments. The framework involves constructing a three layer Bayesian model that models the relation between vehicle indices and the arrival and departure processes. The results showed that the proposed method can accurately estimate vehicle indices at signalized intersections using sample travel times. [12] proposes a method to predict turn directions of drivers at intersections based on past behaviors, likely destinations, and the number of possible destinations by each turn, where it is assumed that drivers tend to take roads that offer them more destination options.

[11] presents a probabilistic method to predict the next road segment a driver will take based on his past traveled segments using GPS data. The experimentation used GPS data from 100 drivers from Seattle area and the results show that the developed Markov model can make predictions that are more accurate than random guessing. In [16], a methodology about testing timed systems is presented and could be used to check if such systems behave properly. [17] a data fusion methodology for traffic flow estimation that combines multiple data sources is proposed. The data sources include FCD from probe vehicles, Detector data, and historic data, and the three are fused using a Kalman filter and then is used to estimate turning volumes at intersections. Another study in [15] gives some ideas on the potentials of connected cars and their limits.

3 C-ITS System

The ETSI standardization institute in Europe defined and standardized a rich communication protocol stack for the C-ITS. The *Facilities* layer where the C-ITS services are implemented plays the role of an interface between the *Network layer (defined as geo-networking layer)* and the *Application* layer (close to the driver and vehicle's sensors). Various messages such as the ones mentioned above are provided by this layer in order to cover a set of C-ITS use cases.

The aim behind sending CAM messages is to give dynamic information about the state of the ego C-ITS station (car, RSU, etc.) in real time (i.e. position, speed, heading, etc.). A C-ITS station sends CAMs to its neighborhood using V2V or V2I communications. Depending on the speed of the vehicle, the frequency of CAM messages varies from 1 s to 100 ms.

The general architecture of the C-ITS V2V is presented on Fig. 1. Each station is supposed to have a set of pseudonym certificates.

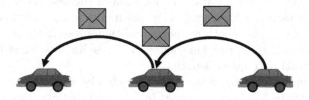

Fig. 1. A general scheme for V2V communication

A vehicle is able to send a message through the network in order to reach its neighbours. The message could reach other vehicles thanks to multi-hop forwarding (Fig. 1).

An RSU plays the same role as a vehicle for the forwarding aspect. In addition to that, the RSU handles all received messages from vehicles in order to run road operator's computations as traffic management, and event recording. In some cases the RSU disseminates events towards other RSUs within the operator's network.

The ETSI has defined an ITS stack where the forwarding mechanism is achieved with the geo-networking protocol [1]. This layer plays the role of the networking layer.

Among different joint initiative projects of European member states aiming at developing and experimenting innovative C-ITS solutions. C-Roads [14] differed from the others (such as SCOOP@F1 and SCOOP@F2 [7]) by its definition of use cases in urban environment and its focus on V2V communications. The project developed new services such as the GLOSA use case.

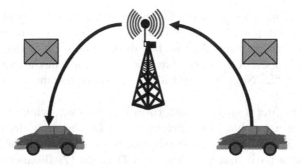

Fig. 2. A general scheme for V2I communication

The C-Roads comprises of a rich architecture combining both short and long range communications as well as other means. As part of the C-Roads architecture, a smart phone application was developed called CoopITS which allows the broadcast of C-ITS messages directly to smartphones using the cellular network. The application was launched in January 2021, and has been functioning since in France and mainly in the region of "la Nouvelle Aquitaine". The application records two types of logs in a server, the first type of logs concerns the actions that are made in the app, such as the display of events and information on the screen. In this type of logs we are mainly interested in the logs of action of the TLM which displays the current phase of nearby traffic lights, and also the time until the next phase and if the lights are red it displays the advice speed to respect in order to avoid a stop. The second type of logs concerns the C-ITS messages, such as the CAM, DENM, SPATEM, MAPEM, and IVIM, the messages are logged in their raw state meaning encoded with ASN.1 uper then decoded and inserted into a database. We are mainly interested in the CAM messages.

4 Smartphone Data

A CAM or Cooperative Awareness Message is a periodical message that is sent by a C-ITS station in broadcast at a frequency of either 100 ms and 1 s in the C-ITS standards depending on the velocity, but its frequency in the CoopITS application is either 1 s and 5 s. A station can be a vehicle, an RSU or a different C-ITS actor. a CAM contains information about the station's state at an instant t such as its StationID which is its identification number in the C-ITS environment, its type (car, motorcycle, RSU, etc.) using the field StationType, its position by means of latitude, longitude and altitude, its heading which is in degrees and represents the angle of the vehicle from true north, and its velocity in m/s. Since the data is generated from a smartphone, the velocity is always positive or equal to zero even if the vehicle is moving backwards.

Each smartphone when using the CoopITS application is attributed a random StationID. The smartphone maintains its StationID for 10 min of operation time, then it is attributed another. And so far, during the time of the study, a total number of 1336573 CAM messages have been recorded in the city of Bordeaux and the region of "La Nouvelle Aquitaine" in France coming from 8667 distinct StationIDs.

We wanted to find a specific pattern in the data set, which is a set of trips of the same trajectory that are likely traversed by the same driver using a car (StationType = 5). Therefore, a search has been applied to the data and we managed to find a path that was traversed 71 times (71 distinct stationIDs) in the same direction in the city of Bordeaux, which represents a total set of 46570 CAM messages. The records belonged likely to the same driver since they all start from the same area and go likely to the same destination.

Figure 3 shows the trajectory that was chosen. The trajectory starts south and goes to the north and was plotted on an OSM map in python using the folium library where each dot represents the position recorded in each CAM message from a single trip (a single StationID).

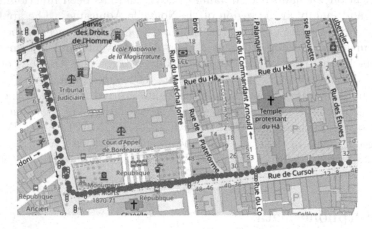

Fig. 3. An example of the trajectory that was extracted from CAM messages, plotted on top of an OSM map

The trajectory was then cut into road segments. A road segment is the portion of the road between two crossings. We then chose a segment where a traffic signal is installed, and where the GPS data are the most precise. The segment that was chosen is shown in Fig. 4. It has a length of 120 m and the shortest recorded travel time of the segment is 6 s.

To determine which CAM points belong to a segment, we created a rectangle out of the segment and checked if the position of the trajectory points fit inside it. Since the data is generated from smartphones, there has been the issue of

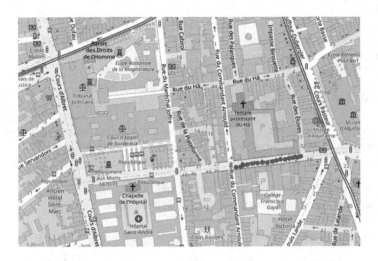

Fig. 4. Trajectory data in the segment that was chosen, plotted on top of an OSM map

GPS precision, certain CAM points were out of bounds of the segment, so we relatively enlarged the sizes of the rectangles knowing before hand that these aberrant data points belong to the segment.

The TLM dataset contains all traffic light signals status notifications that were sent to the smartphones. The smartphones receive notifications about the traffic light status in nearby intersections, as well as the time to the next phase and the speed advice. The speed advice is only present in the case of red light, and it tells the vehicle the speed that it should respect to avoid a stop. Figure 5 represents an example of some TLM records.

log_timestamp	stationID	eventid	currentphase	nextphase	advicetimetonextphase	speedadvice	intersectionid
1627538835910,00	3526965938	8	RED	GREEN	2192	22	219
1627538835912,00	3526965938	8	RED	GREEN	2192	22	219
1627538836909,00	3526965938	8	RED	GREEN	1192	27	219
1627538836910,00	3526965938	8	RED	GREEN	1192	27	219
1627538837909,00	3526965938	8	RED	GREEN	193	32	219
1627538837911,00	3526965938	8	RED	GREEN	193	32	219
1627538838910,00	3526965938	8	GREEN	YELLOW	67192	NULL	219
1627538838913,00	3526965938	8	GREEN	YELLOW	67192	NULL	219
1627538839910,00	3526965938	8	GREEN	YELLOW	66292	NULL	219
1627538839911,00	3526965938	8	GREEN	YELLOW	66292	NULL	219
1627538840910,00	3526965938	8	GREEN	YELLOW	65292	NULL	219
1627538840911,00	3526965938	8	GREEN	YELLOW	65292	NULL	219
1627538841912,00	3526965938	8	GREEN	YELLOW	64291	NULL	219

Fig. 5. An example of some TLM records

A matching between the CAMs and TLMs was then done using the stationID (the TLM user is identified by its StationID). For each CAM message, if a TLM record fits within its time frame with the next CAM message, it was attributed to it. We then observe the behavior of the vehicles along some indicators such as speed variation, redlight status and speed advice over time and distance, which we will present in the next section.

5   Analysis

In this section we present our observations on the trajectory profiles in the chosen segment. We have observed that there exist 4 elemental patterns that are constantly repeating and are summarized as follows:

(a) A free flow driving with a green or yellow light.
(b) A stop in the segment with a green or yellow light.
(c) A free flow driving with a red light.
(d) A stop in the segment with a red light.

These four patterns are elements that constitute the vehicular behavior in the segment, a trajectory in the segment may constitute of one or more of these elemental patterns. The first pattern, which is the free flow at a green light is due to the emptiness of the road before head of the vehicle and until the segment's end, so the vehicle travels without a stop. The second pattern which is the stop at a green light is due to the presence of a queue before the end of the segment so the vehicle has to stop. The third one which is the free flow at a red light is because the vehicle's velocity isn't high enough, it happens in the case where the driver respects the speed advice voluntarily or involuntarily. The fourth one which is the stop at a red light happens when the vehicle's velocity is higher than the speed advice, so it reaches the end of the segment or the beginning of the queue and stops.

Figures 6, 7, 8, and 9 represent the speed profiles of the vehicle in the same road segment matched with the traffic light states. Each dot symbolizes a matched CAM record represented by its velocity in function of time and distance from the start of the segment. Its color represents the state of traffic light it received from the TLM service, where it is either red, green, yellow or blue. Blue means that there is no TLM data for the CAM point. The black dots represent the speed advice the vehicle receives whenever the light is red.

Figure 6 shows the pattern (a), the vehicle entered the segment with an initial velocity of 7.69 m/s which was reported by the smartphone's GPS. The velocity that was reported when leaving the segment was at 10.03 m/s. The vehicle sent all along the segment a total of 13 CAM messages, the measured average velocity from these CAMs was at 9.0 m/s and the time frame between the first and last CAM is 12 s. 120 m which is the segment's length divided by 12 s gives 10 m/s which should be the average velocity. It is not the case due to precision issues in the smartphone's GPS. The vehicle received a green light status all along the segment, and there was no queue at the end of the segment so it traveled it without a stop.

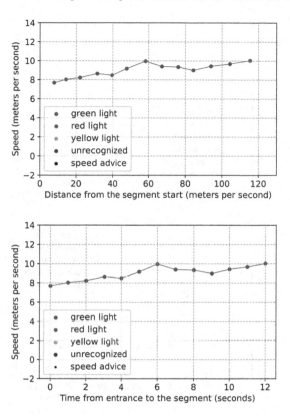

Fig. 6. A trajectory with free flow at a green light (a) velocity in function of the distance (b) velocity in function of time (Color figure online)

Pattern (b) can be observed in Fig. 7, the vehicle entered the segment with a velocity of 8.68 m/s, it reached its top velocity of 11.69 m/s at around second 4 and 58 m from the start of the segment. It left the segment at a velocity of 3.7 m/s. The vehicle arrived at a stop at 103 m from the start of the segment and at 15 s. It spent 33 s to travel the segment and sent an overall of 32 CAM messages. The mean velocity from the CAMs is equal to 3.72 m/s which has an acceptable accuracy. The vehicle encountered a green light all along the segment, yet it stopped 17 m from the end of the segment, this is mostly due to the presence of a queue at the end. The queue was probably generated by the previous red light phase.

Pattern (c) can be observed in Fig. 8, the vehicle sent 26 CAM messages, it entered the segment with a velocity of 6.34 m/s, and left it with a velocity of 6.44 m/s. it lowered its velocity in the middle until it reached 2.22 m/s but doesn't stop. Its average velocity was at 4.57 m/s which has an acceptable accuracy

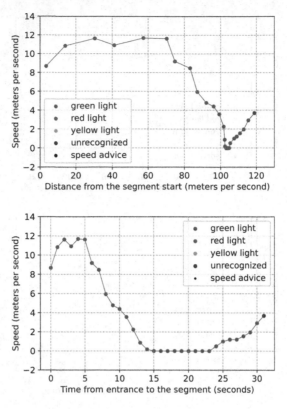

Fig. 7. A trajectory with a stop at a green light (a) velocity in function of the distance (b) velocity in function of time (Color figure online)

since 120 divided by 25 gives 4.8. Since the light is red the vehicle received the speed advice, and overall, the vehicle's velocity was lower than the speed advice, therefore it didn't stop

In Fig. 9 we can observe the last pattern, which is when the vehicle stops at a red light. The vehicle entered the segment at a velocity of 5.36 m/s, and left it at the velocity of 5.26 m/s. It's average velocity was at 3 m/s and it took 34 s to traverse the segment which gives it a calculated average velocity of 3.52 m/s. As with the first case, this is due to the GPS precision. The issue of precision can also be seen at the stop in Fig. 9 (a), which is when the position slightly returns backwards although the velocity was at zero.

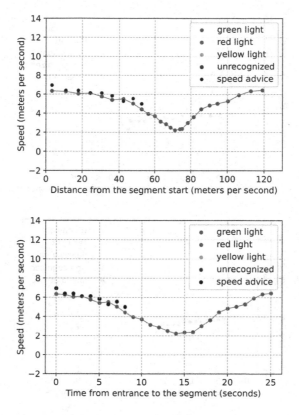

Fig. 8. A trajectory with free flow at a red light (a) velocity in function of the distance (b) velocity in function of time (Color figure online)

In Fig. 10 where the vehicle sent 84 CAM messages, we see a combination of two patterns (d) followed by (b), the vehicle entered the segment at a velocity of 7.84 m/s and stopped at around 46 m from the start of the segment at red light mainly due to the disrespect of the speed advice. After the light turned green it remained still for 20 s then started moving only to stop again at a queue. The queue is probably due to an operation happening at the road crossing. It left the segment at a velocity of 4.51 m/s. The same remark can be done, the vehicle changing its position while at stop and with a null velocity is mainly due to GPS precision.

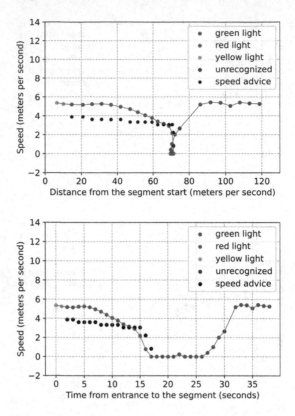

Fig. 9. A trajectory with a stop at a red light (a) velocity in function of the distance (b) velocity in function of time (Color figure online)

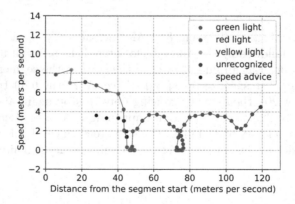

Fig. 10. A trajectory with combined pattern, velocity in function of the distance

6   Conclusion

In this study we used data from the CoopITS application. CoopITS is a C-ITS simulation application deployed in France, where a smartphone plays the role of a C-ITS station. Each action is logged by the application including sending and receiving C-ITS messages. We were concerned with two specific recorded actions by the application, the sending of a CAM message, and the TLM actions. A matching between the CAMs and TLM records has been done and the results were used to investigate the behavior of vehicles in signalized intersections. We chose a segment where a traffic light intersection lies at its end, and we have analyzed the speed profiles of vehicles where we observed and classified four patterns: a free flow with a green light, a stop with a green light due to a queue, a freeflow with a red light due to the respect of the speed advice given by the TLM and last a stop with a red light due to the disrespect of the speed advice.

Acknowledgments. This work was done thanks to CINEA funding for Indid project (Agreement N° INEA/CEF/TRAN/M2018/1788494).

References

1. Etsi en 302 636-4-1; intelligent transport systems (its); vehicular communications; geonetworking; part 4: Geographical addressing and forwarding for point-to-point and point-to-multipoint communications; sub-part 1: Media-independent functionality
2. Etsi en 302 637-2; intelligent transport systems (its); vehicular communications; basic set of applications; part 2: Specification of cooperative awareness basic service
3. Etsi en 302 637-3; intelligent transport systems (its); vehicular communications; basic set of application; part 3: Specifications of decentralized environmental notification basic service
4. Etsi ts 103 301; intelligent transport systems (its); vehicular communications; basic set of applications; facilities layer protocols and communication requirements for infrastructure services, February 2020
5. Etsi ts 136 101; lte; evolved universal terrestrial radio access (e-utra); user equipment (ue) radio transmission and reception (3gpp ts 36.101 version 16.7.0 release 16), February 2020
6. Etsi ts 302 663; intelligent transport systems (its); its-g5 access layer specification for intelligent transport systems operating in the 5 ghz frequency band, February 2020
7. Aniss, H.: Overview of an ITS project: SCOOP@F. In: Mendizabal, J., et al. (eds.) Nets4Cars/Nets4Trains/Nets4Aircraft 2016. LNCS, vol. 9669, pp. 131–135. Springer, Cham (2016). https://doi.org/10.1007/978-3-319-38921-9_14
8. Comert, G., Cetin, M.: Queue length estimation from probe vehicle location and the impacts of sample size. Eur. J. Oper. Res. **197**(1), 196–202 (2009)
9. Fourati, W., Mayerhofer, A., Friedrich, B.: Continuous compilation of directional counts at intersections fusing floating car data and section counts. Transport. Res. Procedia **37**: 235–241 21st EURO Working Group on Transportation Meeting, EWGT 2018, 17–19 September 2018. Braunschweig, Germany (2019)

10. Hao, P., Sun, Z., Ban, X.J., Guo, D., Ji, Q.: Vehicle index estimation for signalized intersections using sample travel times. Transport. Res. Part C: Emerg. Technolog. **36**, 513–529 (2013)
11. Krumm, J.: A Markov model for driver turn prediction, April 2008
12. Krumm, J.: Where will they turn: predicting turn proportions at intersections. Person. Ubiquitous Comput. **14**, 591–599 (2010)
13. Krumm, J., Horvitz, E.: Predestination: inferring destinations from partial trajectories. In: Dourish, P., Friday, A. (eds.) UbiComp 2006. LNCS, vol. 4206, pp. 243–260. Springer, Heidelberg (2006). https://doi.org/10.1007/11853565_15
14. Lokaj, Z., Srotyr, M., Vanis, M., Broz, J.: Technical part of evaluation solution for cooperative vehicles within c-roads cz project. In: 2020 Smart City Symposium Prague (SCSP), pp. 1–5 (2020)
15. Lüke, K.-H., Eichler, G., Erfurth, C.: Potentials and requirements of an integrated solution for a connected car. In: Fahrnberger, G., Eichler, G., Erfurth, C. (eds.) I4CS 2016. CCIS, vol. 648, pp. 211–216. Springer, Cham (2016). https://doi.org/10.1007/978-3-319-49466-1_14
16. Salva, S., Petitjean, E., Fouchal, H.: A simple approach to testing timed systems. In: FATES01 (Formal Approaches for Testing Software), a Satellite Workshop of CONCUR, Aalborg, Denmark (2001)
17. Wolfermann, A., Mehran, B., Kuwahara, M.: Data fusion for traffic flow estimation at intersections, September 2011
18. Zheng, J., Liu, H.X.: Estimating traffic volumes for signalized intersections using connected vehicle data. Transport. Res. Part C: Emerg. Technol. **79**, 347–362 (2017)

Task Planning Support for Arborists and Foresters: Comparing Deep Learning Approaches for Tree Inventory and Tree Vitality Assessment Based on UAV-Data

Jonas Troles[1]([✉])[iD], Richard Nieding[1], Sonia Simons[2], and Ute Schmid[1][iD]

[1] University of Bamberg, Cognitive Systems Group, 96049 Bamberg, Germany
jonas.troles@uni-bamberg.de
[2] TU Berlin, Straße des 17. Juni 135, 10623 Berlin, Germany

Abstract. Climate crisis and correlating prolonged, more intense periods of drought threaten tree health in cities and forests. In consequence, arborists and foresters suffer from increasing workloads and, in the best case, a consistent but often declining workforce. To optimise workflows and increase productivity, we propose a novel open-source end-to-end approach that generates helpful information and improves task planning of those who care for trees in and around cities. Our approach is based on RGB and multispectral UAV data, which is used to create tree inventories of city parks and forests and to deduce tree vitality assessments through statistical indices and Deep Learning. Due to EU restrictions regarding flying drones in urban areas, we will also use multispectral satellite data and fifteen soil moisture sensors to extend our tree vitality-related basis of data. Furthermore, Bamberg already has a georeferenced tree cadastre of around 15,000 solitary trees in the city area, which is also used to generate helpful information. All mentioned data is then joined and visualised in an interactive web application allowing arborists and foresters to generate individual and flexible evaluations, thereby improving daily task planning.

Keywords: Computer vision · UAV data · Human centred AI · Sustainable development · Smart infrastructure

1 Introduction

According to the IPCC report from 2022 [39], the climate crisis is an enormous challenge and already affects the lives of billions of people. One of the many negative impacts of the climate crisis is its threat to whole ecosystems and,

Special thanks to our cooperation partner Smart City Bamberg. The project BaKIM is supported by Kommunal? Digital! funding of the Bavarian Ministry for Digital Affairs. Project funding period: 01.01.2022 - 31.03.2024.

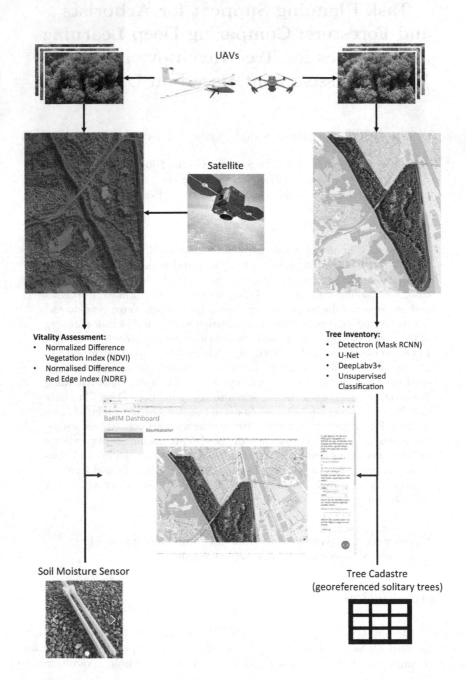

Fig. 1. Overview of the BaKIM pipeline with images from [1, 2, 10, 38]

therefore, the health of trees and forests by rising temperatures and consecutive drought events, as experienced from 2018 to 2020 and in 2022 in Germany [5,14,27]. The consequence is an increasing vulnerability to a variety of pests and increasing tree mortality rates, leading to an increasing frequency and scope of measures arborists and foresters have to take [40]. At least in Bamberg, but presumably in most German cities, this has to be done without an increase in staff in the teams of arborists and foresters because the funding for said departments is seldom increased. On top, they suffer from a shortage of skilled workers.

To tackle these problems, in 2021, a cooperation of *Smart City Bamberg*, Bamberg's lead arborist, Bamberg's lead forester and the *Chair of Cognitive Systems* at the *University of Bamberg* applied for project funding to support Bamberg's arborists and foresters with Deep Learning approaches based on UAV-data (Unmanned Aerial Vehicle). The result is the project *BaKIM*, which aims to generate helpful and flexible information from remote sensing data gathered by UAVs and satellites, as well as data from soil moisture sensors. To generate information from this data, an ensemble of Deep Learning, Machine Learning and statistical methods is used. All information is then visualised in an interactive web application which offers basic Geographic Information System (GIS) functionalities and extends these by easy and fast filtering and plotting. The complete pipeline of BaKIM is illustrated in Fig. 1.

In addition to these goals, it is of great importance for our project to develop a human-centred AI approach as reflected in [48]. BaKIM will not, and does not try to be an autonomous AI approach which replaces the decision-making of arborists and foresters. Quite the contrary, BaKIM will rely on arborists and foresters for: (i) verifying its AI-based decision suggestions, (ii) improving BaKIM, (iii) learning from BaKIM, and (iv) taking responsibility for the final decision as well as for compliance with legislation and ethical standards [43,48].

2 Data Acquisition and Technology

The first and most important data source for BaKIM are two drones which produce high-resolution image data. As EU-regulation [12] forbids the use of UAVs heavier than 250 g over houses and uninvolved people, we decided to additionally use satellite imagery for the health assessment of solitary city trees. To control the assessment of drought stress in trees, 15 soil moisture sensors were installed in the city. In the following, the different data acquisition tools are described.

2.1 Areas of Interest

In BaKIM, we defined several Areas of Interest (AOIs), which we monitor throughout the project and partially sample ground truth labels on a single tree basis to train our different Convolutional Neural Nets (CNNs). See Fig. 2 to get an overview of the size and location of the following AOIs:

- Forest AOIs:
  - Stadtwald AOI: 190 ha, mostly coniferous forest
  - Tretzendorf AOI 1: 60 ha, mixed forest
  - Tretzendorf AOI 2: 45 ha, mixed forest
- Bamberg Hain AOI: 50 ha, park with deciduous forest-like areas
- Bamberg graveyard AOI: 15 ha solitary trees
- Bamberg city AOI: 5,462 ha mostly solitary trees (only satellite imagery)

Fig. 2. All AOIs in and around Bamberg (Top left to bottom right: Tretzendorf AOI 1 (blue), Tretzendorf AOI 2 (green), Bamberg Graveyard AOI (red), Bamberg Hain AOI (orange), Bamberg Stadtwald AOI (yellow)) (Color figure online)

2.2 UAV-Data

Due to the mentioned EU-regulation, we use two different UAVs: One fixed-wing UAV with a take-off weight of up to 5,500g, which we use for forest areas outside of the city and one smaller quadrocopter with a take-off weight of up to 1,050g which we use for the Hain. Both UAVs are shown in Fig. 3.

Trinity F90+: The Trinity F90+ is a fixed-wing UAV with Vertical Take-Off and Landing (VTOL) capability and a flight time of about 90 min. With its 5,500 g take-off weight and 239 cm wingspan, it is a C3 UAV and must be flown in the open A3 category, meaning it must not fly near people and must fly outside urban areas (150 m distance). However, it can carry interchangeable payloads with heavier, more advanced sensors and cover larger areas than smaller UAVs. Therefore, we use it for the three more remote forest AOIs outside of Bamberg.

The first sensor, used for RGB data collection, is a Sony RX1-RII camera with 42.4 MP and a theoretical Ground Sampling Distance (GSD) of 1.55 cm when flying 120 m Above Ground Level (AGL). Our experience shows we get a

(a) Trinity F90+ [38]   (b) DJI M3M [10]

Fig. 3. Both UAVs used for data acquisition in the BaKIM project

GSD of about 1.6–1.9 cm in the finished orthomosaic. The second sensor, used for multispectral (MS) data collection, is a MicaSense Altum-PT with 3.2 MP per MS band and a thermal infrared sensor with a resolution of 320×256 pixels. The resulting GSD is 5.28 cm for the MS bands and 33.5 cm for the thermal band when flying 120 m AGL. Due to supply difficulties, our MicaSense Altum-PT sensor arrived later than expected and was not tested yet.

DJI Mavic 3 Multispectral: To cover RGB and MS data acquisition of the Hain, we use the smaller and lighter quadrocopter DJI Mavic 3 Multispectral (DJI M3M), released in Q1 of 2023. Compared to the Trinity F90+, it does not support swappable payloads and has a much shorter flight time of 43 min at max. In return, with its maximum take-off weight of 1,050 g and a diagonal length of 38 cm, it is a C2 UAV and can be flown in the A2 category where a flight in urban areas and near uninvolved people is possible. The built-in sensor consists of a 20 MP RGB sensor with 2.95 cm GSD at 120 m AGL and a 5 MP multispectral sensor with 5.07 cm GSD at 120 m AGL.

FORTRESS Dataset: To start the training of the different Deep Learning approaches described in Sect. 3 as early as possible, we used the FORTRESS dataset [44]. It consists of 47 ha of very-high-resolution orthomosaics with a GSD of up to 0.6 cm and covers mostly coniferous forest in the southwest of Germany. In total, 16 different classes are labelled in FORTRESS. For a more detailed description of the dataset, see the paper of Schiefer et al. [45].

2.3 Orthomosaic Generation

To get image data where every pixel is georeferenced and the perspective is corrected to a nadir view, the single UAV images need to be processed. For this, different software is available, and we tested two products: *WebODM*[1]

---

[1] https://github.com/OpenDroneMap/WebODM.

which is open source and free software as well as *Agisoft Metashape*[2] which is commercial software. After testing and comparing WebODM and Metashape, we found the orthomosaics produced with Metashape to be of slightly higher quality, showing fewer artefacts. This was especially the case for our images taken with the Trinity F90+, as they lack the very high front overlap necessary for orthomosaic generation. You can find examples of Hain orthomosaics in Figs. 1 and 4.

Image Overlap: Image overlap is the most crucial parameter for orthomosaic generation. Especially when it comes to forests with their small structures (leaves, branches) and the abrupt height changes of the surface (trees, ground). Therefore, a front overlap of 90–95% and a sidelap of 80% is recommended. While the DJI M3M can change its flight speed, the Trinity F90+ must keep an airspeed of 17 m/s to stay airborne. As the maximum shutter speed of the sensors is limited, this results in a maximum front overlap of about 70% for the Sony RX1-RII payload of the Trinity F90+. We partially compensate for this through a sidelap of 90%, but the resulting orthomosaics of the Trinity F90+ still show artefacts in certain points of the forest areas.

2.4   Ground Truth Labelling

Especially for the individual tree crown delineation (ITCD) described in Sect. 3.1, but also for tree species prediction, we need ground truth data on the tree instance level. Therefore, we commissioned a forester to delineate 108 ha of tree crowns in the AOIs Stadtwald, Tretzendorf and Hain. Additionally to the delineation, tree species and a rough vitality assessment is labelled.

2.5   Other Data

Satellite Data: As already mentioned, EU-law heavily restricts flying UAVs in urban areas. Therefore, we will use multispectral satellite imagery taken by the *Airbus pléiades neo* satellite with a GSD of 1.2m. This imagery is tasked for July 2023 and September 2023 and will be used for additional tree health assessment.

Soil Moisture Sensors: To gather ground truth data on drought stress, we decided to use soil moisture sensors provided by *Agvolution*. They track the soil's water content in three different depths and send the data via *mioty* standard to agvolution's server, where they are then processed and made accessible via an API.

Tree Cadastre: Bamberg's arborists have tracked the vitality of most of the solitary trees in the city area for decades and visit every tree at least once a year. This information is stored in the *tree cadastre* and contains, among other things, georeferences, tree species, tree dimension estimations, tree vitality and site information. Unfortunately, the used software does not save a history of this

---

[2] https://www.agisoft.com/.

information per tree location, and no historical backups are available. Therefore, we started to back up the current version every six months to make future time series analysis possible. Figure 4 shows a part of the Hain orthomosaic and tree cadastre information in the form of coloured dots.

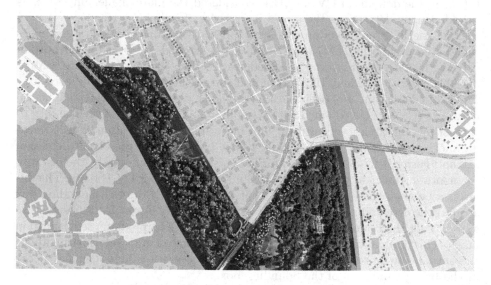

Fig. 4. One possible visualisation of tree cadastre data with the point colour depicting the tree species (Color figure online)

3   Methods of Tree Inventory Generation

While solitary trees in the city of Bamberg are all georeferenced and tracked well, this does not apply to the Hain and the forest areas surrounding Bamberg. The latter are inventoried every 10–20 years by an estimation procedure, and the Hain is partially inventoried because trees near paths are checked regularly. Therefore, according to our forester and arborist, a more frequent and more accurate park and forest inventory procedure supports task planning and allows for a faster reaction to diseases like bark beetle infestation or weather events like storms. To accomplish this, we decided to use high-resolution orthomosaics with a Ground Sampling Distance (GSD) of 1.5 to 2.0 cm per pixel and different Deep Learning and Machine Learning approaches from the Computer Vision domain, which are described in the following sections.

3.1   Single Tree Detection

Single tree detection is divided into two categories: Individual Tree Detection (ITD), which is called *object detection* in the domain of computer vision (CV) and individual tree crown delineation (ITCD), which is called *instance segmentation* in the domain of CV. ITCD is considered the more challenging task, as it additionally determines the crown boundaries of individual trees.

Historically, tree detection was accomplished with unsupervised approaches such as local maxima (LM) [34,37], marker-controlled watershed segmentation (MCWS) [30], region-growing [11], edge detection [49] and template matching [22,28], with LM and MCWS methods being the most commonly used [52]. The rapid development of deep learning methods, especially convolutional neural networks (CNNs), led to much better results in CV tasks due to their ability to extract low and high-level features. This motivated the application of deep learning methods in remote sensing applications. For example, the object detection method Faster R-CNN [50] is used for ITD tasks, and more recently, the instance segmentation method Mask R-CNN [3,20,32,51] is used for ITCD tasks. The difference between these approaches is that Faster R-CNN draws a bounding box around the detected single tree. Mask R-CNN uses the Faster R-CNN structure and extends the bounding box prediction by a branch to predict a segmentation mask. This is advantageous because it provides more accurate information about the actual crown area and avoids or greatly reduces distortions that may occur in the background area of the bounding box.

Both classical and more recent deep learning methods have advantages and disadvantages in processing time and data requirements. The most commonly used classical methods, such as LM and MCWS [52], require a distinct height model to perform their methods. Faster R-CNN and Mask R-CNN, on the other hand, need RGB image data to detect trees. Another disadvantage of classical methods is that they show difficulties in detecting trees in areas where tree crowns overlap strongly [52]. In contrast, Yu [52] has shown that LM and MCWS are less computationally intensive than Mask R-CNN. Another advantage of these classical methods is that they do not require manually labelled data and, therefore, no training phase to detect trees. Faster R-CNN and Mask R-CNN rely on ground truth data and mostly some form of retraining to perform the detection task on new datasets. This makes it clear that the tree detection method should be chosen according to the corresponding forest structure and in accordance with the desired goal.

Due to the higher accuracies of DL approaches in BaKIM, a retrained tree detection model based on the Mask R-CNN *detectree2* implementation is used [3]. Figure 5 shows predictions for a section of the FORTRESS dataset.

3.2   Unsupervised Tree Species Classification

Many UAVs are characterised by relatively low cost and a simple structure. Consequently, the dissemination and usage of UAVs increases, and much high-resolution image data is captured [19,51]. This makes the demand for technologies and solutions that can quickly process this data more urgent. Most, if not

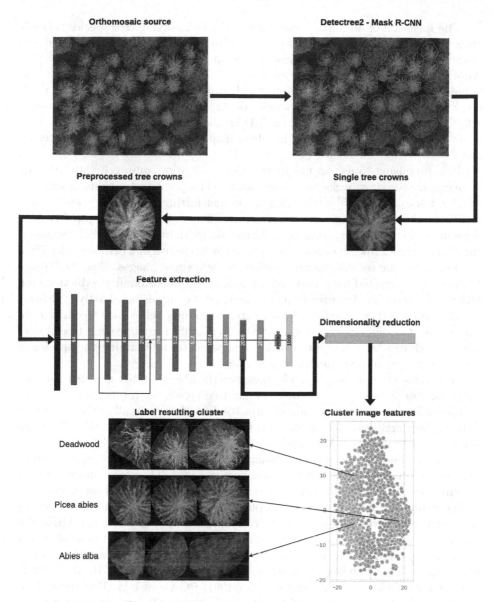

Fig. 5. The pipeline used for the unsupervised classification of single tree crown images

all, current approaches that classify tree species rely heavily on a domain expert to determine tree species for every single tree of the training data in a supervised manner. This cumbersome human labelling process may not keep up with the increasing demand for solutions.

The inclusion of an unsupervised method for classifying tree species is rarely an issue in the literature. Franklin used multispectral data and pixel-based and object-based image analysis to classify tree species in an unsupervised way [15]. Another unsupervised method proposed by Gini et al. also works pixel-based [16]. Schäfer et al. used spectroscopy data to identify tree species via clustering without knowing how many trees per species occur [46]. All these unsupervised methods are based on costly spectral or LiDAR data that may not be available to every practitioner. They are also unable to map a species to a particular detected tree.

It is promising to use an unsupervised classification approach via clustering to overcome the drawbacks mentioned above. The presented pipeline is inspired by the work of [9,18,25] with the goal of transferring their good classification results to the field of single tree classification. The first step in this pipeline is to determine single tree crowns in an orthomosaic, as shown in Fig. 5. Subsequently, small single tree crown images are extracted from the original orthomosaic. Then the preprocessing techniques are applied to these small images. Next, the image features are extracted from these small images. A dimensionality reduction step follows to reduce the features to more meaningful components. Lastly, a clustering algorithm is used, which assigns a corresponding label to each tree image. In this setup, the domain expert only needs to classify the appearing tree classes once, which can be done quite quickly compared to determining the species of every single tree in a particular training set.

A retrained tree detection model based on the Mask R-CNN *detectree2* implementation of [3] was used to detect single tree crowns at the beginning of this pipeline. This model was retrained on a total of 4539 manually delineated tree crowns from orthomosaics: 2262 from the FORTRESS dataset [45], 1651 from the Bamberg Stadtwald AOI, and 626 from the Tretzendorf AOI 1.

This pipeline's preprocessing, dimensionality reduction, and clustering steps can be performed in several ways, as shown in Fig. 6. Therefore, an experiment is conducted to determine and evaluate the best combination of methods. Two different preprocessing steps were applied to the image datasets in this experiment. Once Contrast Limited Adaptive Histogram Equalization (CLAHE) was applied to the images, and once a combination of CLAHE and denoising was applied to the images. Afterwards, the image features were extracted via a forward hook using the following pretrained CNN backbones: VGG16, ResNet152, InceptionV3, EfficientNetV2 and DenseNet201. PCA and UMAP were used for the dimensionality reduction of the image features. The reduced feature vectors were used as input for the cluster algorithms k-means++, mean shift, fuzzy c-means, agglomerative clustering and Ordering Points to Identify the Clustering Structure (OPTICS). Some cluster algorithms such as k-means++, fuzzy c-means (fc-means) and agglomerative clustering require setting the number of clusters in advance, which is difficult. However, in this case, the number of clusters was set to the number of occurring species to obtain more meaningful results. All mentioned methods for each step result in 100 possible combinations.

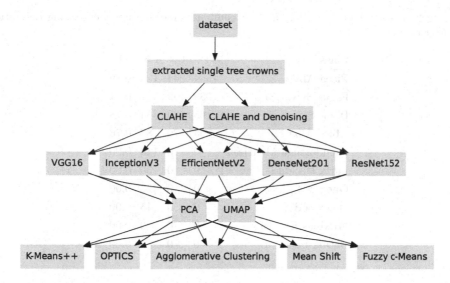

Fig. 6. Scheme representing all possible combinations of methods

Evaluating cluster results is challenging in real-world applications because ground truth labels are often unavailable. In this case, however, ground truth data was available, and therefore cluster algorithms could be evaluated based on the F1-scores. The proposed experiment was performed 30 times, and then the mean F1-scores were calculated from these 30 cumulative values for each possible combination of methods.

Table 1. Five best method combinations from the experiment conducted on the FORTRESS dataset

Preprocess	CNN	DR	Clustering	Species	F1	weighted F1
clahe	densenet	pca	k-means++	4	0.82	0.79
clahe+denoising	densenet	pca	k-means++	4	0.79	0.75
clahe	resnet	umap	fc-means	4	0.75	0.72
clahe	resnet	umap	k-means++	4	0.75	0.72
clahe	resnet	umap	agglo	4	0.75	0.72

Table 2. F1-scores per class for the best combination of methods, clustering the data in four classes

Class	TP	FP	FN	F1
Picea Abies	1534	264	123	0.89
Fagus Sylvatica	589	192	89	0.81
Pinus Sylvestris	165	30	64	0.78
Abies Alba	253	70	87	0.76
Pseudotsuga Menziesii	0	0	113	0.00
Larix Decidua	0	0	30	0.00
Quercus Spec	0	0	23	0.00
deadwood	0	0	15	0.00
Fraxinus Excelsior	0	0	9	0.00
Betula Pendula	0	0	3	0.00

The results of the best-performing combination of methods were evaluated using FORTRESS as an example. The five most frequent tree species after the extraction of 3097 single tree crowns were Picea Abies (53.5%), Fagus Sylvatica (21.9%), Abies Alba (11.0%), Pinus Sylvestris (7.4%) and Pseudotsuga Menziesii (3.6%). Table 1 shows that the best combination is composed of CLAHE, densenet, PCA, and k-means++. The F1-score and weighted F1-score show only slight differences, even though only four of ten classes were clustered. Nevertheless, the large amount of correctly predicted samples from the majority classes has a higher impact on the F1-score than those with a lower sample size. These findings suggest that the proposed pipeline has problems in classifying minority classes. Table 2 shows how only four classes are assigned, which yields high F1-scores for the majority classes, but an F1-score of 0.00 for all unassigned classes.

This unsupervised pipeline demonstrates that tree species can be classified by clustering based on RGB image data alone. However, the inability to detect lower sample classes reduces the practical benefit if a practitioner wants a correct picture of the species distribution. Moreover, it became clear that it is difficult to clearly distinguish the tree crowns of different species because of their similar structure. The results also show that the preprocessing steps are not sufficiently capable of highlighting the particular characteristics of the tree species and that the separation of the clusters needs to be improved in the future.

3.3   Semantic Segmentation of Tree Species

Another way to classify tree species in high-resolution UAV imagery is semantic segmentation. It resembles an ITCD approach that does not distinguish between individual trees but uses less computational resources than, for example, the Mask R-CNN based *detectree2* [3, 45].

In [45], Schiefer et al. explored the viability of using convolutional neural networks (CNNs) for classifying tree species from drone images. They used an adjusted version of U-Net [41], which was originally designed for the segmentation of biomedical images but has found its way into other areas like semantic segmentation of tree species [26]. It is made up of two symmetric paths, the encoder and the decoder. The encoder downsamples the input image to capture contextual information, while the decoder upsamples the encoded feature maps to increase the spatial resolution. One key feature of U-Net is that the decoder also receives skip connections from the encoder. This way, the information learned by the downsampling layers in the encoder is used to reconstruct the input image at its original spatial resolution while preserving fine details and features.

The FORTRESS dataset [44] includes 16 classes. After analysing the share of pixels each class has in the entire dataset, we noticed that the smallest seven classes (*other, Aesculus, Fallopia, Ilex, Fraxinus Excelsior, Larix Decidua* and *Betula Pendula*) combined only makeup 1.3% of the total area covered, while the largest class alone (*Picea Abies*) makes up 38.3%. This substantial imbalance in the dataset was already mentioned in [45], where they tried to mitigate this by using weighted cross-entropy loss. On top of a weighted loss function, we also decided to combine the smallest seven classes into just one class called *other* to adapt to this extreme imbalance in the dataset.

The primary metric we used to evaluate the performance of the models is Intersection over Union (IoU). It measures the accuracy of a prediction as a value between 0 and 1, where 0 means no overlap between the prediction and the ground truth and 1 being an exact match. The overall IoU is calculated as the average of the IoU of each class, weighted by their share in the dataset. The overall IoU reaches around 0.78 after 100 epochs of training. Despite achieving a good overall result, examining the per-class IoU values shows a significant difference in the model's performance across classes that are less represented in the dataset than those that are well-represented. Table 3 shows that classes *Picea Abies, Fagus Sylvatica* and *Abies Alba* make up 75.5% of the dataset and have IoU Test scores of 0.75, 0.73 and 0.76 respectively. While classes *Quercus Spec.* and *Acer Pseudoplatanus* make up 1.9% and have much lower IoU Test scores of 0.11 and 0.39. However, these low representations of some classes will be reduced with the labelled data from the Bamberg AOIs.

As part of future work, we aim to incorporate a post-processing step that was employed in the accuracy assessment of [45]. This involves generating multiple predictions for each pixel using a moving window technique and assigning the final prediction through a majority vote.

We are also currently working on using another CNN for the same task, Deeplabv3+ [8], which is a promising CNN architecture for this task as shown by [13,31,35]. Deeplabv3+ is based on Deeplabv3 [7], which uses atrous convolutions [21] and atrous spatial pyramid pooling (ASPP) [6]. Atrous convolutions are used to retain the same spatial resolution while increasing the feature maps without increasing the parameters or amount of computation. ASPP aggregates features at multiple scales and captures context information from a larger image region.

Table 3. Per class comparison of area-related share and IoU of the validation-set and test-set

class	area-related share	IoU Validation	IoU Test
Picea Abies	38.3%	0.84	0.75
Fagus Sylvatica	26.5%	0.82	0.73
Forest floor	12.6%	0.65	0.54
Abies Alba	10.7%	0.76	0.61
Pinus Sylvestris	4.2%	0.78	0.71
Pseudotsuga Menziesii	3.5%	0.77	0.81
Acer Pseudoplatanus	1.1%	0.46	0.39
Quercus spec	0.8%	0.32	0.11
Deadwood	0.7%	0.30	0.18
other	1.3%	0.27	0.32
weighted average		0.78	0.68

Deeplabv3+ combines Deeplabv3 with an Encoder-Decoder structure like U-Net. It uses a slightly modified version of Deeplabv3 as the encoder. Instead of directly upsampling the encoder output to the original image resolution, the decoder combines them with features from early convolutional layers, analogous to the skip connections used in U-Net. While Deeplabv3+ will most likely outperform U-Net, it also needs more computational resources.

4   Tree Vitality Assessment

Apart from detecting single trees and their species, assessing tree vitality on an instance level is of great importance to arborists and foresters. To accomplish this, we opted for two different kinds of approaches: First, statistical evaluation of multispectral sensor imagery by building indices and second, deep learning methods applied to very-high-resolution imagery to detect dead branches or secondary pests like mistletoes.

4.1   Statistical Indices Derived from Multispectral Data

The usage of multispectral imagery for tree vitality assessment dates back to the 1970s s and has been used since [23, 24, 29, 36, 42, 47]. In BaKIM, we plan to use at least the following two indices:

NDVI: The Normalised Difference Vegetation Index was introduced back in 1974 and is one the most used indices to classify if a pixel shows live green vegetation [42]. It is based on the near-infrared (NIR) band as well as the red band and is calculated as follows:

$$NDVI = \frac{(NIR - Red)}{(NIR + Red)} \tag{1}$$

As all three sensors used in BaKIM capture near-infrared and red bands, we can calculate the NDVI for all AOIs.

NDRE: The Normalised Difference Red Edge index takes the red edge (RE) band as well as the red band into account and represents the chlorophyll content in leaves [4]. In their review of commonly used remote sensing technologies to measure plant water stress, Govender et al. found red edge to be one of the most important bands when investing plant stress [17]. The NDRE index is calculated as follows:

$$NDRE = \frac{(RE - Red)}{(RE + Red)} \tag{2}$$

As all three sensors used in BaKIM capture red edge and red bands, we can calculate the NDRE for all AOIs.

Additionally to the NDVI and NDRE, the thermal band of the *Micasense Altum-PT* sensor theoretically allows us to use further indices that reflect water stress in plants. As the calculation for such indices is often based on additional ground measurements, we still have to see in how far we can implement them in BaKIM [17].

4.2   Deep Learning for Tree Vitality Assessment

A second option for tree vitality assessment from very-high-resolution UAV data is Deep Learning. On the one hand, mistletoe (posing a secondary parasite) can easily be seen in UAV data, and on the other, dead leaves and branches in tree crowns are also visible in UAV data. Therefore, CNNs, as introduced before, can be used to classify mistletoe or the vitality of tree crowns [33]. The only problem is, again, the need for a high amount of training data. Together with an apprentice of the forestry department, we plan to gather ground truth data on mistletoe visible in our UAV data and train an object detection CNN to classify mistletoe. The rough estimation of tree vitality labelled by our commissioned forester, as described in Sect. 2.4, will be used for exploratory tests using image classification CNNs on images of single delineated tree crowns.

5   Interactive Web Application to Visualise Generated Information

Everything described so far is useless if Bamberg's arborists and foresters are not enabled to access the information we generated. To create this access, we chose *dash*[3] to create an interactive web application which visualises all information gathered and generated in BaKIM. The main goal of this web application is to be very flexible so that the arborists and foresters can tailor the underlying data to their needs. This is accomplished by individual filter options and different

---

[3] https://dash.plotly.com/.

views and plots. For the storage and filtering of the data *geopandas*[4] is used, for plotting *plotly*[5] is used, and to visualise the orthomosaics a *mbtileserver*[6] is used. We are currently developing the web application prototype with basic functionalities.

6 Conclusion and Outlook

So far, BaKIM reached important milestones on its way to become a helpful tool based on human-centred AI. The feedback of Bamberg's lead arborist and forester shows that the concept and solutions we are developing promise to be helpful for their daily task planning. Furthermore, the creation of a database of UAV data and predictions, as well as the beginning of tracking the changes made to the tree cadastre, will make time series analysis possible in the future. This will be especially important when it comes to adapting to the climate crisis.

Another benefit of BaKIM is that the infrastructure being built in the project can have multiple uses. For example, the soil moisture sensors installed in Bamberg can also give the arborists live information on the city trees' water deficit. A modified view in the web application could be used to inform Bamberg's citizens about the trees in the city. On top of this, community services like tree watering patronages or an interface to report branches that threaten to fall might be possible in the near future due to BaKIM.

While our tree inventory approaches, with accuracies of about 80%, are not perfect yet, we already plan several changes and improvements which should yield significantly higher accuracies. Nevertheless, even with higher accuracies, BaKIM will by no means be a substitution for the expertise and decision-making competency of the arborists and foresters. Much rather, the higher frequency and detail of information enables them to improve their work and, thereby, the health of trees in and around Bamberg.

References

1. Agvolution: Soil moisture sensor (2023). https://www.agvolution.com/
2. Airbus: pleiades neo (2023). https://www.eoportal.org/satellite-missions/pleiades-neo
3. Ball, J.G.C., et al.: Accurate tropical forest individual tree crown delineation from RGB imagery using mask r-CNN. bioRxiv (2022). https://doi.org/10.1101/2022.07.10.499480
4. Barnes, E., et al.: Coincident detection of crop water stress, nitrogen status and canopy density using ground based multispectral data. In: Proceedings of the Fifth International Conference on Precision Agriculture, Bloomington, MN, USA, vol. 1619, p. 6 (2000)

---

[4] https://geopandas.org/en/stable/.
[5] https://plotly.com/python/.
[6] https://github.com/consbio/mbtileserver.

5. Boeing, F., Rakovec, O., Kumar, R., Samaniego, L., Schrön, M., Hildebrandt, A., Rebmann, C., Thober, S., Müller, S., Zacharias, S., Bogena, H., Schneider, K., Kiese, R., Attinger, S., Marx, A.: High-resolution drought simulations and comparison to soil moisture observations in germany. Hydrology and Earth System Sciences **26**(19), 5137–5161 (2022). 10.5194/hess-26-5137-2022, https://hess.copernicus.org/articles/26/5137/2022/
6. Chen, L.C., Papandreou, G., Kokkinos, I., Murphy, K., Yuille, A.L.: Deeplab: semantic image segmentation with deep convolutional nets, atrous convolution, and fully connected CRFs. IEEE Trans. Pattern Anal. Mach. Intell. **40**(4), 834–848 (2017)
7. Chen, L.C., Papandreou, G., Schroff, F., Adam, H.: Rethinking atrous convolution for semantic image segmentation. arXiv preprint arXiv:1706.05587 (2017)
8. Chen, L.-C., Zhu, Y., Papandreou, G., Schroff, F., Adam, H.: Encoder-decoder with atrous separable convolution for semantic image segmentation. In: Ferrari, V., Hebert, M., Sminchisescu, C., Weiss, Y. (eds.) ECCV 2018. LNCS, vol. 11211, pp. 833–851. Springer, Cham (2018). https://doi.org/10.1007/978-3-030-01234-2_49
9. Cohn, R., Holm, E.: Unsupervised machine learning via transfer learning and k-means clustering to classify materials image data. Integr. Mater. Manuf. Innov. **10**(2), 231–244 (2021). https://doi.org/10.1007/s40192-021-00205-8
10. DJI: M3m (2023). https://ag.dji.com/de/mavic-3-m
11. Erikson, M., Olofsson, K.: Comparison of three individual tree crown detection methods. Mach. Vis. Appl. **16**(4), 258–265 (2005). https://doi.org/10.1007/s00138-005-0180-y
12. European Commission: Easy access rules for unmanned aircraft systems (regulations (eu) 2019/947 and 2019/945) - revision from September 2022 (2022). https://www.easa.europa.eu/en/document-library/easy-access-rules/easy-access-rules-unmanned-aircraft-systems-regulations-eu
13. Ferreira, M.P., et al.: Individual tree detection and species classification of Amazonian palms using UAV images and deep learning. Forest Ecol. Manag. **475**, 118397 (2020)
14. Fischer, J.: Waldzustand 2022. AFZ Der Wald 7/2023(7), 35–36 (2023). https://www.digitalmagazin.de/marken/afz-derwald/hauptheft/2023-7/waldschutz/035_waldzustand-2022
15. Franklin, S.E.: Pixel- and object-based multispectral classification of forest tree species from small unmanned aerial vehicles. J. Unmanned Veh. Syst. **6**(4), 195–211 (2018). https://doi.org/10.1139/juvs-2017-0022
16. Gini, R., Passoni, D., Pinto, L., Sona, G.: Use of unmanned aerial systems for multispectral survey and tree classification: a test in a park area of northern Italy. Eur. J. Remote Sens. **47**(1), 251–269 (2014). https://doi.org/10.5721/eujrs20144716
17. Govender, M., Govender, P., Weiersbye, I., Witkowski, E., Ahmed, F.: Review of commonly used remote sensing and ground-based technologies to measure plant water stress. Water SA **35**(5) (2009)
18. Gradišar, L., Dolenc, M.: Transfer and unsupervised learning: an integrated approach to concrete crack image analysis. Sustainability **15**(4), 3653 (2023). https://doi.org/10.3390/su15043653
19. Hanapi, S.N.H.S., Shukor, S.A.A., Johari, J.: A review on remote sensing-based method for tree detection and delineation. IOP Conf. Ser. Mater. Sci. Eng. **705**(1), 012024 (2019). https://doi.org/10.1088/1757-899x/705/1/012024
20. Hao, Z., et al.: Automated tree-crown and height detection in a young forest plantation using mask region-based convolutional neural network (mask r-CNN). ISPRS J. Photogramm. Remote. Sens. **178**, 112–123 (2021). https://doi.org/10.1016/j.isprsjprs.2021.06.003

21. Holschneider, M., Kronland-Martinet, R., Morlet, J., Tchamitchian, P.: A real-time algorithm for signal analysis with the help of the wavelet transform. In: Combes, J.M., Grossmann, A., Tchamitchian, P. (eds.) Wavelets. Inverse Problems and Theoretical Imaging, pp. 286–297. Springer, Heidelberg (1990). https://doi.org/10.1007/978-3-642-75988-8_28
22. Huo, L., Lindberg, E.: Individual tree detection using template matching of multiple Rasters derived from multispectral airborne laser scanning data. Int. J. Remote Sens. **41**(24), 9525–9544 (2020). https://doi.org/10.1080/01431161.2020.1800127
23. Huo, L., Lindberg, E., Bohlin, J., Persson, H.J.: Assessing the detectability of European spruce bark beetle green attack in multispectral drone images with high spatial-and temporal resolutions. Remote Sens. Environ. **287**, 113484 (2023)
24. Ismail, R., Mutanga, O., Bob, U.: Forest health and vitality: the detection and monitoring of Pinus Patula trees infected by Sirex Noctilio using digital multispectral imagery. Southern Hemisphere Forestry J. **69**(1), 39–47 (2007)
25. Ji, M., et al.: Early detection of cervical cancer by fluorescence lifetime imaging microscopy combined with unsupervised machine learning. Int. J. Mol. Sci. **23**(19), 11476 (2022). https://doi.org/10.3390/ijms231911476
26. Kattenborn, T., Leitloff, J., Schiefer, F., Hinz, S.: Review on convolutional neural networks (CNN) in vegetation remote sensing. ISPRS J. Photogramm. Remote. Sens. **173**, 24–49 (2021)
27. Kehr, R.: Possible effects of drought stress on native broadleaved tree species - assessment in light of the 2018/19 drought. Jahrbuch der Baumpflege **2020**, 103–107 (2020)
28. Larsen, M., Eriksson, M., Descombes, X., Perrin, G., Brandtberg, T., Gougeon, F.A.: Comparison of six individual tree crown detection algorithms evaluated under varying forest conditions. Int. J. Remote Sens. **32**(20), 5827–5852 (2011). https://doi.org/10.1080/01431161.2010.507790
29. Lausch, A., Heurich, M., Gordalla, D., Dobner, H.J., Gwillym-Margianto, S., Salbach, C.: Forecasting potential bark beetle outbreaks based on spruce forest vitality using hyperspectral remote-sensing techniques at different scales. For. Ecol. Manag. **308**, 76–89 (2013)
30. Liao, L., Cao, L., Xie, Y., Luo, J., Wang, G.: Phenotypic traits extraction and genetic characteristics assessment of eucalyptus trials based on UAV-borne LiDAR and RGB images. Remote Sens. **14**(3), 765 (2022). https://doi.org/10.3390/rs14030765
31. Lobo Torres, D., et al.: Applying fully convolutional architectures for semantic segmentation of a single tree species in urban environment on high resolution UAV optical imagery. Sensors **20**(2), 563 (2020)
32. Lucena, F., Breunig, F.M., Kux, H.: The combined use of UAV-based RGB and DEM images for the detection and delineation of orange tree crowns with mask r-CNN: an approach of labeling and unified framework. Future Internet **14**(10), 275 (2022). https://doi.org/10.3390/fi14100275
33. Miraki, M., Sohrabi, H., Fatehi, P., Kneubuehler, M.: Detection of mistletoe infected trees using UAV high spatial resolution images. J. Plant Dis. Prot. **128**, 1679–1689 (2021)
34. Monnet, J.M., Mermin, E., Chanussot, J., Berger, F.: Tree top detection using local maxima filtering: a parameter sensitivity analysis. In: 10th International Conference on LiDAR Applications for Assessing Forest Ecosystems (Silvilaser 2010) (2010)

35. Morales, G., Kemper, G., Sevillano, G., Arteaga, D., Ortega, I., Telles, J.: Automatic segmentation of Mauritia Flexuosa in unmanned aerial vehicle (UAV) imagery using deep learning. Forests **9**(12), 736 (2018)
36. Moran, M., Clarke, T., Inoue, Y., Vidal, A.: Estimating crop water deficit using the relation between surface-air temperature and spectral vegetation index. Remote Sens. Environ. **49**(3), 246–263 (1994)
37. Pitkänen, J.: Individual tree detection in digital aerial images by combining locally adaptive binarization and local maxima methods. Can. J. For. Res. **31**(5), 832–844 (2001). https://doi.org/10.1139/x01-013
38. Quantum Systems: Trinity F90+ (2023). https://quantum-systems.com/trinity-f90/
39. Rama, H.O., et al.: Climate Change 2022: Impacts, Adaptation and Vulnerability Working Group II Contribution to the Sixth Assessment Report of the Intergovernmental Panel on Climate Change. Cambridge University Press, Cambridge (2022). https://doi.org/10.1017/9781009325844
40. Raum, S., Collins, M.C., Urquhart, J., Potter, C., Pauleit, S., Egerer, M.: Die vielfältigen auswirkungen von baumschädlingen und krankheitserregern im urbanen raum. ProBAUM 1/2023, 103 107 (2023)
41. Ronneberger, O., Fischer, P., Brox, T.: U-net: convolutional networks for biomedical image segmentation. In: Navab, N., Hornegger, J., Wells, W.M., Frangi, A.F. (eds.) MICCAI 2015. LNCS, vol. 9351, pp. 234–241. Springer, Cham (2015). https://doi.org/10.1007/978-3-319-24574-4_28
42. Rouse Jr., J.W., Haas, R.H., Deering, D., Schell, J., Harlan, J.C.: Monitoring the vernal advancement and retrogradation (green wave effect) of natural vegetation (1974)
43. Samek, W., Wiegand, T., Müller, K.R.: Explainable artificial intelligence: understanding, visualizing and interpreting deep learning models. arXiv preprint arXiv:1708.08296 (2017)
44. Schiefer, F., Frey, J., Kattenborn, T.: Fortress: forest tree species segmentation in very-high resolution UAV-based orthomosaics (2022). https://doi.org/10.35097/538
45. Schiefer, F., et al.: Mapping forest tree species in high resolution UAV-based RGB-imagery by means of convolutional neural networks. ISPRS J. Photogramm. Remote Sens. **170**, 205–215 (2020)
46. Schäfer, E., Heiskanen, J., Heikinheimo, V., Pellikka, P.: Mapping tree species diversity of a tropical montane forest by unsupervised clustering of airborne imaging spectroscopy data. Ecol. Ind. **64**, 49–58 (2016). https://doi.org/10.1016/j.ecolind.2015.12.026
47. Senoo, T., Honjyo, T.: Assessment of tree stress by airborne multi-spectral scanning data. J. Jpn. Forestry Soc. **70**(2), 45–56 (1988)
48. Waefler, T., Schmid, U.: Explainability is not enough: requirements for human-AI-partnership in complex socio-technical systems. In: Proceedings of the 2nd European Conference on the Impact of Artificial Intelligence and Robotics (ECIAIR 2020), pp. 185–194. ACPIL (2020)
49. Wang, L., Gong, P., Biging, G.S.: Individual tree-crown delineation and treetop detection in high-spatial-resolution aerial imagery. Photogramm. Eng. Remote Sens. **70**(3), 351–357 (2004)
50. Weinstein, B.G., Marconi, S., Aubry-Kientz, M., Vincent, G., Senyondo, H., White, E.P.: DeepForest: a Python package for RGB deep learning tree crown delineation. Methods Ecol. Evol. **11**(12), 1743–1751 (2020). https://doi.org/10.1111/2041-210x.13472

51. Yang, M., et al.: Detecting and mapping tree crowns based on convolutional neural network and google earth images. Int. J. Appl. Earth Obs. Geoinf. **108**, 102764 (2022). https://doi.org/10.1016/j.jag.2022.102764
52. Yu, K., et al.: Comparison of classical methods and mask r-CNN for automatic tree detection and mapping using UAV imagery. Remote Sens. **14**(2), 295 (2022). https://doi.org/10.3390/rs14020295

CarbonEdge: Collaborative Blockchain-Based Monitoring, Reporting, and Verification of Greenhouse Gas Emissions on the Edge

Karl Seidenfad[(✉)], Maximilian Greiner, Jan Biermann, and Ulrike Lechner

Computer Science Department, University of the Bundeswehr München, Munich, Germany

{karl.seidenfad,maximilian.greiner,jan.biermann,ulrike.lechner}@unibw.de

Abstract. Decarbonization calls for efficient and trustworthy monitoring, reporting, and verification (MRV) of greenhouse gas (GHG) emissions. This article proposes a collaborative approach and exemplifies a concrete scenario: the biogas plant scenario. We propose a consortium blockchain as platform and aim to reduce costs and efforts by collaboration and automation in up-scaling GHG management. We present a demonstrator which employs an industry-grade radio frequency identification (RFID) security approach to manage certificate material, a low-code interface for interaction, and the operation of Hyperledger Fabric on industrial edge devices.

Keywords: Blockchain · Business webs · Industrial edge

1 Introduction

Designing community services and going one step forward to innovative, trustworthy digital infrastructures is a crucial issue in one of the major endeavors of this time: decarbonization. "Creating Digital Spirit" is the theme of this year's I4CS conference and our goal with a cutting-edge approach to design blockchain technology for innovative community services to manage greenhouse gas emissions.

The two terms "Decarbonization" and "Net Zero" are associated with the Paris Agreement's goal for the reduction of greenhouse gas (GHG) emissions to limit global warming well below 2 °C (compared to pre-industrial times). The major challenge for increasing ambitions under the Paris Agreement is to hold non-state actors accountable [15,22,35,52]. Carbon markets, such as the European Emissions Trading System (EU ETS), are a well-known tool in this regard, and the EU ETS represents the largest carbon market worldwide [10]. In 2023, the EU ETS will gather approximately 40% of the European GHG emissions (e.g., from the energy and manufacturing industry). In contrast, the remaining

U. R. Krieger et al. (Eds.): I4CS 2023, CCIS 1876, pp. 123–147, 2023.
https://doi.org/10.1007/978-3-031-40852-6_7

60% of emissions are caused by Non-ETS sectors (e.g., agriculture and residential) [12]. Holding non-state actors accountable by a sectoral expansion of the EU ETS is one, albeit an intensely discussed, way to go [6,15,22,29,36,43,52]. This discussion of how to hold-non state actors accountable is fueled by regulations on Environmental Social Governance (ESG) strategies of organizations. The private sector needs to take on more responsibilities. This includes the trustworthiness of GHG emission management. The discussion for holding non-state actors accountable inside the Paris Agreement and the general evaluation of ESG and decarbonization strategies calls for new integration paths on efficient **monitoring, reporting, and verification (MRV)** of GHG emissions.

Our approach is to go to the edge and record greenhouse gas emissions in an integrated way when and where they occur in business activities. This first step was presented at the I4CS conference in 2022 [48]. In this article, we focus on the second element on MRV — by **up-scaling** of MRV for GHG emissions. Upscaling of carbon crediting aims at reducing transaction costs for regular MRV processes and lowering investment risks for implementing emissions mitigation projects [15]. This may be achieved by collectively established baseline emissions, joint reporting automation, or the issue of credits on aggregated reductions across a consortium [36]. This article presents the CarbonEdge technology stack, a technological approach to provide MRV on GHG emissions as a **community service** for the societal important domain of climate action.

A preview of CarbonEdge was presented on the demo track of the 5th IEEE International Conference on Blockchain and Cryptocurrency (ICBC) in Dubai [45]. This article provides technological insides and more features. We systematize our approach of blockchain-driven emissions reporting on the edge [48], and analyze further measures to simplify the design and operation of a consortium blockchain in this regard. The CarbonEdge technology stack represents our findings and provides tooling and infrastructure to automate the deployment of Hyperledger Fabric nodes (preferable on edge-devices). It contains a library of smart contracts to implement MRV tasks, a low-code interface to interact with the network, and an industry-grade radio frequency identification (RFID) security concept. All artifacts are shipped by build automation to deliver ready-to-use application images.

The article is organized as follows. Section 2 presents related work in the fields of blockchain technology and governance, edge computing, and the MRV of GHG emissions. Section 3 presents our scenario-driven and iterative research design. Section 4 lights on the scenario, which defines the scope of our artifact implementation. Section 5 documents the exact implementation of our information system artifacts. Section 6 rigorously evaluates our results, and Sect. 7 summarizes the major findings and gives an outlook to future work.

2   Related Work

The related work of this article consists of blockchain technology and governance, selected projects from practice (e.g., supply chain management and carbon markets), and the use of edge computing. To complete the picture, we light on the foundations for MRV of GHG emissions.

2.1 Blockchain Technology: Selected Applications and Governance

Blockchain technology describes decentralized data management in a peer-to-peer network using an append-only list, the ledger. All nodes in a blockchain network hold a replication of the ledger, and a consensus protocol orchestrates the addition of new ledger entries. The National Institute of Standards and Technology (NIST) defines distributed ledger technologies extensively, especially for blockchain [60].

Blockchain technologies can be distinguished by the right to be part of the consensus or network exposure. Blockchain's network structure can be tailored to suit different scenarios. To do so, it can be differentiated into categories: public (non-permissioned), private (permissioned), and consortium (hybrid) [50]. On the one hand, a public blockchain is accessible by all network users and implemented via a peer-to-peer network, and writing and reading rights are given freely [5]. On the other hand, a private Blockchain provides a closed network that limits participation to a determining part to join, and participants are given a predefined role. Writing and reading rights are bound to these roles [58]. The third category is derived from both prior forms, and the write and read rights are determined by the number of participants [27]. Blockchain technology steps towards technological maturity through the introduction of design patterns [25], taxonomies [21], and a growing number of projects in practice. We exemplify supply chain management (SCM) applications such as IBM's TradeLens [24], BMW's PartChain [31], and SiGREEN by SIEMENS for accounting product carbon footprints along the value-chain on a blockchain [51].

Beyond the popular SCM use case, the discussion about **blockchain-based carbon markets** is vibrant [1,3,10]. Richardson and Xu [39] present the model of a private permissioned blockchain for the EU ETS and discuss potential advantages over existing solutions. Braden [6] evaluates Bitcoin, Ethereum, Hyperledger Fabric, and EOS regarding their applicability to climate policy applications. Schneider et al. [42] compare centralized and decentralized architectures to track international emissions mitigation transfers, and Schletz et al. [41] present a decision framework and architecture to embed the Article 6.2 requirements into a blockchain-based market model.

When it comes to blockchain-based networks or rather consortia, **blockchain governance** is indispensable to fully realize the potential of the technology. A first approach by Beck et al. [4] discusses the dimensions (decision rights, accountabilities, incentives) of IT governance defined by Weill [59] along the blockchain economy and proposes critical questions of these dimensions in the form of a research agenda. Hofman et al. [19] take up Beck's agenda and develop a governance analysis framework that attempts to capture the embeddedness of blockchain solutions. They relate existing power structures (legal, political, environmental, social) to the 5W1H method and describe this as follows: Who? (actors and stakeholders), What? (data, records, logs), Why? (use cases and added values), When? (temporality and change over time), Where? (geography of instantiation), How? (instantiation). Considering the governance within consortia, Yue et al. [62] propose a framework comprising six governance attributes and 13 sub-attributes. These are decision-making processes, accountability and verifiability, privacy and security, trust incentives, and effectiveness. Evidence for the importance of governance for the success of a consortium is provided by Zavolokina et al. [63] in which they present the practical set-up of a blockchain-based car dossier consortium managing car data and seek to improve collaboration between players in terms of management, governance and value creation. In addition to the organizational steps of the consortium establishment, such as the consortium formation, they also describe tensions in terms of the consortium, business value, and governance.

2.2 Edge Computing

Edge computing describes an architecture and paradigm which distributes computing power along the network edge. It contrasts to more centralized approaches such as cloud computing. Edge computing aims at low-latency computation on-site, the reduction of the overall network traffic, and to increase overall equipment effectiveness (OEE). Use cases can be found in areas such as industrial production, autonomous driving, and logistics [49,57]. Yu et al. [61] presents a study of how edge computing improves the performance of IoT networks and structures an edge-computing architecture into three different layers: First, the **front-end** layer consists of end devices, such as sensors and actuators improving the communication among the edge devices and the user interaction. Second, the **near-end** is geographically close to the end user. It consists of cloudlet servers, gateways, and edge devices processing data or executing applications in real-time. Third, the **far-end** layer executes applications with a high demand for computational power.

2.3 Monitoring, Reporting, and Verification of Greenhouse Gas Emissions

Decarbonization is an essential goal of society. In this regard, international carbon markets (e.g., the European Emissions Trading System (EU ETS) [13]) and the evaluation of corporate strategies for Environmental, Social, and Governance (ESG) require a trustworthy data basis. Therefore, the cost-efficient and trustworthy documentation of Greenhouse Gas (GHG) emissions is a central building block of success. Exemplifying the EU ETS: monitoring, reporting, and verification of GHG emissions are part of the annual ETS compliance cycle [14]. The compliance cycle (see Fig. 1) aims to accurately compute internationally tradeable emissions units. Installation owners from specific sectors have to follow the annual compliance cycle, to align with regulations. For this purpose, they **monitor** and **report** their GHG emissions. By an authority, accredited calibration laboratories support installation owners with services such as **verification** of monitoring methods and instrument calibration. Authorities receive reports from installation owners and finalize with their **verification** and, e.g., issue of tradeable emissions certificates for the installation owner.

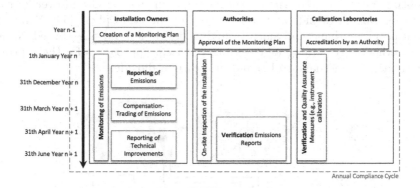

Fig. 1. Example for MRV task scheduling inside the EU ETS compliance cycle

3 Research Design

This article explores the design of an information system for collaborative MRV of GHG emissions. Due to the societal relevance and practical dimension of our information system problem, Brendel et al. [7] recognize the application of the **Design Science** methodology according to Hevner et al. [18] creating information system artifacts that contribute to sustainability and climate action.

Our Design Science project consists of three design iterations. The **first** iteration addressed the use of blockchain technology to bridge between IT and OT in an industrial environment, employs the automation pyramid as the guiding model, and discusses the role of specialized gateways [46]. The **second** iteration demonstrates the feasibility of blockchain-driven emissions reporting by operating a supply chain consortium, which computes the joint product carbon footprint [48]. In this regard, we contributed to Hyperledger Lab's project minifabric by porting minifabric to devices with ARM processors [47].

Our **third** Design Science iteration, which we present in this article, addresses the collaborative automation of MRV on GHG emissions for computing the corporate carbon footprint. The **context** of our Design Science project is shaped by non-state actors [35], which are on duty for the MRV of GHG emissions. They have an interest in cost-efficient processes and compliance with authority regulations. Furthermore, monetizing emissions reductions at carbon markets is a driver of integration. The **Knowledge Base** gathers methods for developing emissions mitigation projects [8], regulatory for MRV of GHG emissions (e.g., inside the EU ETS), and the engineering of blockchain [21,25] and edge computing applications. In this third design iteration, we employ an agile development process for building, testing, and deploying artifacts.

4   Horizontal MRV of GHG: The Biogas Plant Scenario

The scenario concerns methane recovery for generating heat and electricity and preventing landfill gas emissions. Methane is a known GHG and over 25 times efficient as carbon dioxide at trapping heat in the atmosphere [56]. Hence, the prevention of methane emissions is highly desirable, and the United Nations CDM methodology catalog [8] describes practical approaches for the capturing and oxidation of methane to less harmful carbon dioxide.

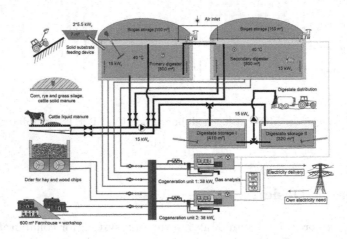

Fig. 2. Architecture of a biogas plant with 76kW cogeneration units according to Ebertseder et al. [9] and referring to ACM0006 - Electricity and heat generation from biomass according to the United Nations CDM methodology catalog [8]

In the scenario, actors produce biogas (e.g., from manure or other biological waste) and operate combined heat and power plants (CHP) (see Fig. 2). The scenario lights on two perspectives of the MRV process - **First**, the reporting of the exact amount of produced biogas units. Since biogas and fossil gas can be transported in the same gas grid, accurate accounting is necessary to allow selective pricing of units and adaptive taxation. **Second**, the combustion of biogas in CHP releases GHG, such as carbon dioxide. To minimize these emissions, the efficient operation of CHP demands monitoring regulatory emissions thresholds and strict quality assurance measures.

4.1   Building an Alliance

The biogas industry is shaped by farms as SMEs, and the operation of corresponding MRV measures demands every single actor to spend efforts for documentation, measuring, and reporting. Our approach of up-scaling the MRV process aims at the reduction of efforts by enabling collaborative automation of MRV tasks between actors inside a jointly hosted infrastructure, following named a consortium.

To design such a consortium of farms, we employ the alliance web according to Tapscott et al. [53]. The business web taxonomy (see Fig. 3) of Tapscott et al. [53] gathers archetypes of networks where actors are collaborating, e.g., to reach a joint goal or following their personal business interests. The business webs differ in the level of control (ranging between hierarchical and self-organizing) and the level of value integration (ranging between low and high).

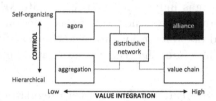

Fig. 3. The b-web typology according Tapscott et al. [53]; the alliance-web is highlighted.

Tapscott et al. [53] characterize the alliance web as a high-value integration without hierarchical control. Actors of the alliance web, e.g., design goods and services or jointly create knowledge and are governed by rules and standards for interaction, actor's behavior, and the determination of value. The alliance web of this scenario follows a horizontal approach [40] of actors (farms) with similar activities, potentially competing in the same business field. Hence, we must deal with a limited amount of trust. However, the actors are interested in cost-efficient MRV processes and regulatory compliance. Finally, for compliance with regulations and due to a lack of expertise in measuring systems, farms must mandate service providers (e.g., calibration laboratories) for calibration and certification of instruments.

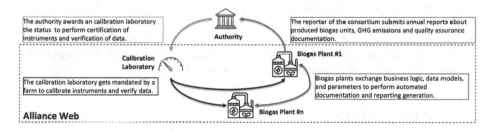

Fig. 4. The stakeholder map of the alliance web in the biogas plant scenario

Note, in the biogas plant scenario, an authority neither becomes an actor inside the alliance web nor has access to the information system. We recognize the setup of an alliance web as a dynamic process, which conflicts with authorities' rather slow response times. Furthermore, an authority typically does not share the same level of interest in cost efficiency as most non-state actors. The stakeholder map in Fig. 4 summarizes our scenario's different types of actors and relationships.

4.2 Features and Processes

As we outlined in the two perspectives of this scenario, actors must track the amount of produced biogas units, and need to operate MRV processes aligned with authority regulations. Furthermore, the focus relies on reducing efforts (e.g., for communication and documentation) to raise the adoption of MRV processes for GHG emissions. Therefore, the scenario aims at designing features for the following domains:

Collaborative Implementation. To align with regulatory and documentation duties, the implementation of internal auditing mechanisms and documentation processes is necessary. The concrete implementation of those mechanisms may differ between sectors but remains rather similar inside a specific domain (e.g., biogas production). We propose the collaborative implementation between actors of the same industry to prevent redundant implementation. Therefore, the biogas scenario actors demand tooling to implement corresponding business logic to align with regulation and securely exchange this business logic with other actors inside the consortium.

Joint Reporting. The idea of actors who jointly report to a single authority has its origin on the concept of scaled-up crediting baselines for GHG emissions [36], as part of a multi-scale approach for mitigating GHG emissions proposed by Elinor Ostrom [34]. The joint reporting aims on reduction of efforts for end-to-end communication between actors and authorities. Therefore, in the scenario, we propose to join numerous actors into a single consortium, which appears from the perspective of an authority as a single reporting entity. For this purpose, we employ an append-only ledger based on Hyperledger Fabric to serve an immutable dataset for compiling joint reporting.

Note, in this article, we elaborate on the perspective of collaborative implementation, and we only discuss possibilities to implement joint reporting. The following section presents the CarbonEdge technology stack and exemplifies the concrete application of the introduced biogas plant scenario.

5 Implementation

To realize a horizontal consortium in MRV of GHG emissions with the features introduced in Sect. 4.2, the CarbonEdge technology stack comprises a layered architecture to connect consortium actors on device-level and serves a codebase and tools to embed MRV-specific processes. Furthermore, CarbonEdge supports industrial-grade devices and protocols and follows a low-code approach to simplify the engineering process and daily operation.

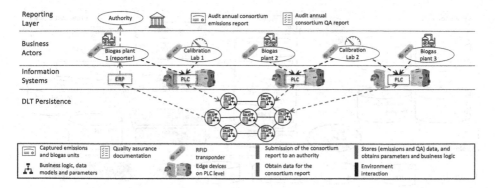

Fig. 5. The biogas consortium with its actors in a layered architecture

5.1 High Level Architecture

The scenario instantiation using CarbonEdge is depicted in Fig. 5. The CarbonEdge technology stack proposes a layered architecture, and employs a Hyperledger Fabric blockchain as its **DLT persistence layer** to allow decentralized logging of data on an append-only ledger. The farmers in the **business actors layer** of Fig. 5 share an interest in cost-efficient processes and compliance with regulations (e.g., reporting produced biogas units). We propose in our design that sharing efforts by collaborative automation of tasks is a strategy to reach the desired cost-efficiency. In the **information systems layer** of Fig. 5, each biogas plant operates an on-site physical edge node. These edge nodes are connected with instruments to obtain sensorical data, and make reading and writing operations on the ledger. Furthermore, actors can interact with the physical node and the whole network thru a low-code interface (see Sect. 5.4). While all biogas plants commit data automatically, one actor is a "reporter." This reporter obtains data from the **DLT persistence layer** and composes a joint audit trail for the public authority inside the **reporting layer**. The following section lights on the architecture of the DLT persistence layer, the actor's roles, and the data distribution.

5.2 Architecture of the Consortium Blockchain

The consortium in our scenario shows a setup of two calibration laboratories and three biogas plants. All plants record produced biogas units and measure emissions, while calibration laboratories are responsible for the certification and partly the maintenance of instruments. Furthermore, one of the biogas plants takes the role of a reporter to exchange data with a governmental authority (see reporting layer of Fig. 5). As stated in Sect. 4.1, actors are potentially competing in the same business field, but have a common interest in efficient MRV processes. We employ a Hyperledger Fabric blockchain as our DLT persistence layer to tackle the potential lack of trust among actors. Therefore, we operate Fabric as a consortium blockchain to provide multiple actors with reading and

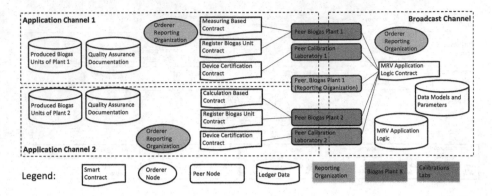

Fig. 6. Channel topology of the biogas scenario

writing operations on the append-only ledger. However, blockchain technology propagates decentralization and full data transparency, which also conflicts with the market competition of actors. Hence, our design must consider additional privacy features inside the consortium. For this purpose, we define dedicated channels and memberships for actors to selectively share data with consortium members. Organizations inside a channel share the exact copy of the ledger and a subset of channel-specific transactions. These transactions are not visible to organizations outside the channel.

The architecture shown in Fig. 6 consists of three channels: A **broadcast channel** for all actors allows the sharing of data models, parameters and MRV application logic for the low-code interface (see Sect. 5.4), and two dedicated **application channels** allow the sharing of data from production and quality assurance measures, between farmers and their calibration laboratory. Furthermore, the reporting organization is also a member of the two application channels and obtains data to generate consortium reporting. To interact with the append-only ledger, each channel provides smart contracts, which embed defined ledger operations. In this regard, we exemplify the smart contracts for logging produced biogas units and the documentation of quality assurance measures inside application channels 1 and 2. While Sect. 5.4 introduces these smart contracts, the following Sect. 5.3 presents the architecture proposal of a CarbonEdge hardware node.

5.3   The CarbonEdge Node Architecture

To run the network setup depicted in Fig. 5, each actor must operate at least one hardware node on site. The CarbonEdge hardware node in the biogas scenario consists of three hardware components (see Fig. 7): First, an industrial grade RFID-reader with a network interface. Second, an edge controller based on the Raspberry Pi Compute Module 3 (CM3) with an ARM64 processor unit, which obtains and processes sensor data. Third, a touch panel to access the low-code

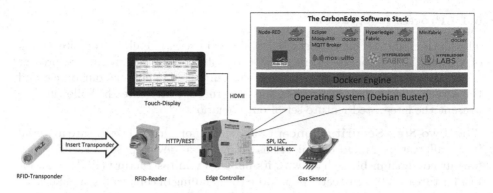

Fig. 7. The hardware components and containerized software stack of CarbonEdge

interface, which runs on the edge controller. A corresponding software stack completes the picture of the CarbonEdge hardware node. We propose a virtualization approach by containerizing our MRV-specific applications as Docker containers to allow a flexible deployment on different hardware devices. The container virtualization of the CarbonEdge node is depicted in Fig. 7. The software stack gathers the following containers:

Node-RED. Node-RED [32] provides a low-code platform for event-based programming of applications using the NodeJS runtime. A node-RED application is called "flow", which can be exported and imported as a JSON data structure between different node-RED installations and devices.

Eclipse Mosquitto. A messaging broker for the Message Queuing Telemetry Transport (MQTT) protocol is provided by Eclipse Mosquitto. MQTT is a IoT messaging protocol with a wide range of adoption. In our scenario, it will be the local messaging bus for sensors, dashboards, and other applications.

Hyperledger Fabric. Hyperledger Fabric is our blockchain framework for the scenario. Hyperledger Fabric comprises dedicated docker containers for Fabric Peers, Orderer, Smart Contracts, and Certification Authorities (CA). Since our edge controller has an ARM64 CPU, we provide own ARM64 compatible Fabric images.

Minifabric. The orchestration of operations, such as standing up or shutting down of Fabric containers, and even the on-boarding of new organizations is done with Minifabric [26]. The Minifabric project implements deployment automation and container orchestration for Hyperledger Fabric (based on Ansible [2]). CarbonEdge contributes to this community project, by providing support for Minifabric on ARM64 based devices.

The following section presents the desired integration of MRV processes using the CarbonEdge hardware node and the containerized software stack of Fig. 7.

5.4 Process Integration

The CarbonEdge technology stack introduced in Sect. 5.3 allows the integration of various MRV processes thru a low-code interface. Furthermore, we present a two-step security concept to harden the CarbonEdge node as our oracle and the attached blockchain network against external security threads. Following, we present the integrated feature-set of our scenario:

The Two-Step Security Concept. The storing of personal certificate material from different users and organizations on one local device poses a security risk for our consortium blockchain with its public key infrastructure (PKI) (e.g., for insider threats [20]). Instead, we propose the handling of certificates on dedicated access dongles combine an industrial-grade RFID access management system and a two-step security concept (see Fig. 8). In the **first step**, the RFID-reader evaluates the local identity of an RFID transponder. For this purpose, the reader is connected to a local user database, which can be hosted inside the reader or remotely in the corporate IT infrastructure. Note this user database belongs only to the local organization. In the **second step**, if the transponder is successfully evaluated and has a valid identity, the reader extracts data from the internal storage of the transponder. In this scenario, we store Hyperledger Fabric-specific certificate material on the transponder. Afterward, the edge controller obtains the certification material via the REST interface of the reader and loads the certificates in its RAM.

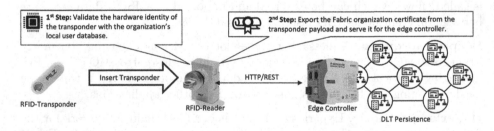

Fig. 8. The two-step security concept of the CarbonEdge node

Tracking of Produced Biogas Units. Serving an accurate history of produced biogas units is a crucial feature of our scenario. For this purpose, we have two potential strategies: First, we could continuously measure the mass flow to compute the corresponding amount of biogas units. Second, we could measure the amount of biomass in the system, estimate a corresponding amount of biogas units, and only selectively use the mass flow measurement to make a plausibility check. The approaches have advantages and disadvantages. While a calculation-based approach is associated with lower efforts for measuring and documentation, a measurement-based approach provides a higher level of accuracy but increases efforts for operation. In our scenario, we prefer a measurement-based approach for biogas units. Therefore, a measurement approach provides by design a higher accuracy, and the usage of CarbonEdge aims to maintain a relatively low level of manual efforts by automation. However, to allow the user a high level of scenario adaption, we consider both approaches in our implementation. Therefore, the node-RED application logic remains rather the same, while only the frequency of flow invocation varies, and the transaction node invokes a different smart contract (see Fig. 9):

Measurement Based Approach. The flow is triggered in a specific time interval to report biogas units using the measurement-based method. Then the flow requests the amount of biogas that have been produced in the period since the last request. In our scenario, we used the MQTT protocol but other protocols, such as, Modbus are suitable too. After the flow has received the measurement data from the sensor, the data is processed and submitted to the blockchain. The transaction will be accepted if the sensor has all the required certifications. Otherwise, an error is raised.

Calculation Based Approach. If the operator of an installation that is subject to biogas production decides to use the calculation-based method the flow is triggered in a specific time interval. If the flow is triggered, a node requests the amount of biomass in the system. Then the amount will be submitted to the blockchain, which uses a smart contract to calculate the potentially produced biogas units. In our scenario, we used a reference model, which specifies the amount of biogas per biomass unit. If the transaction is accepted, a confirmation message will be returned; otherwise, an error will be raised. Note, periodically, the edge node checks the biogas mass flow for the plausibility of the estimation.

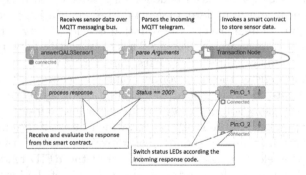

Fig. 9. node-RED flow to embed the (measurement or calculation based) tracking of produced biogas units

Integrated Documentation and Device Certification. The documentation of quality assurance measures and updates on the monitoring method, but also the certification of devices, plays an important role for ensuring trust into the tracking of produced biogas units and measured GHG emissions. The EN14181 standard distinguishes three quality assurance levels (QAL) for the certification, installation, calibration, and validation of automatic measuring systems (AMS), which differ in the interval, relevance to corresponding standards, and responsibilities they address. Note, QAL one (QAL1) only addresses the certification of specific measuring methods, and we assume to employ only certified ones (e.g., mass flow analysis). Hence, CarbonEdge does not consider QAL1-related processes due to missing potential for automation or collaboration (Fig. 10).

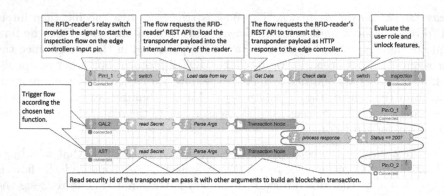

Fig. 10. node-RED flow to embed QAL2 tasks and AST, using the two-step security concept of CarbonEdge

Quality Assurance Level Two (QAL2) and Annual Surveillance Test (AST). Typically, accredited testing and calibration laboratories are responsible for QAL2 tasks and AST. The task frequency may rank up to every three years or due to a major technical update. In general, the certification process of QAL2 and AST are quite similar except the duration of the validity. The validity of the QAL2 is max. three years and the AST has to be certified annually. The certification process requires three steps. **First**, an inspector has to assign himself to the sensor and register the transponder using the security ID, which will be used to authenticate the inspector at the installation of the sensor. **Second**, to trigger the on-site inspection processes the inspector has to insert the previously registered transponder into the RFID reader, which checks if the encoding of the transponder is valid. If the transponder has a proper encoding, the flow will be triggered using the electromagnetic relay switch of the RFID reader. Then the flow checks if the transponder has the required initials of the inspector. Apart from the hard-coded and not changeable security ID, the transponder is read and used for the further process. If the sensor passes the QAL2/AST certification requirements, the flow continues and submits a transaction to the blockchain. This transaction includes the security ID of the transponder, which will be compared to the one presented in step one. If the security IDs are equal, the on-side certification is completed. **Third**, to complete the certification, the inspector has to confirm the certification a second time using his identity, which was used in step one. After that, the certification is valid.

Quality Assurance Level Three. An instrument operator is responsible for the QAL3 compliance, and the task frequency ranks between a few hours up to one year. In order to do so a CarbonEdge node-RED flow is triggered in a specific time interval. After that, the flow requests the drift and precision in zero and the reference point from the sensor and submits the values to the blockchain. A smart contract checks that these values comply with the QAL3 requirements and returns as response success or failure.

Collaborative Implementation of Business Logic. While tracking produced biogas units and documenting quality measures primarily satisfies regulatory duties, CarbonEdge also provides a collaborative implementation of business logic as a meta feature. From the authority perspective, collaboration with non-state actors is secondary but plays a tremendous role for non-state actors in reducing costs by up-scaling. For this purpose, CarbonEdge combines node-RED's JSON-based exchange format for business logic with a corresponding smart contract to exchange node-RED applications between all participants. Actors (e.g., accredited calibration laboratories) develop node-RED flows and submit them as transactions on the consortium blockchain. The stored flow objects are immutable on the ledger and can be obtained by other actors. Assuming a standardized project schema for the consortium (e.g., the CDM method ACM0006), the consortium avoids the redundant implementation by developing business logic once and distributing it over the peer-to-peer network (see Fig. 11). The consortium's business logic may need updates or bug fixes along the project lifecycle. Those changes can be either delivered by biogas plant operators or calibration laboratories.

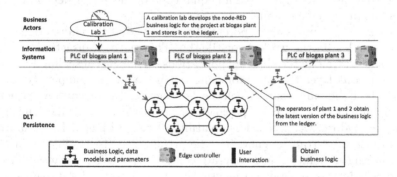

Fig. 11. Deploying business logic for the low-code interface inside the consortium

6   Discussion

In this section, we discuss the technical and organizational aspects of CarbonEdge as our Design Science artifact. We gather considerations on choosing the right blockchain technology, we light on governance aspects for designing a consortium blockchain, and we discuss the value-add of a low-code solution combined with industry-grade hardware.

6.1 Blockchain Design Decisions

Subsequently, we gather essential design aspects for our choice of Hyperledger Fabric in this proposal and discuss Ethereum as a competing technology.

Participation. A consortium shapes an exclusive less-volatile group of actors; the access must be permissioned. The limited amount of trust between the actors matches the concept of a private permissioned blockchain.

Transaction Speed. We expect our consortium to operate the major number of transactions on the machine level (e.g., logging with instruments and sensors), where transaction speeds are typically below one minute according to the ANSI/ISA-95 model of the automation pyramid. A private permissioned blockchain profits from the absence of zero-trust and typically reaches higher transaction speed under comparable conditions.

Transaction Regulation. Monetizing emissions mitigation drives the adoption of MRV. The charge of transaction fees limits this effect, and therefore cost efficiency is pivotal. Hyperledger Fabric offers feeless transactions, but the network's energy consumption still must be considered.

Data Storing and Sharing. Storing data on a blockchain must carefully consider memory consumption and privacy since the data is immutable. We expect the consortium to store the amount of produced biogas units, business logic for the low-code interface, and QA data on the ledger. Hyperledger Fabric offers dedicated channels and private data collections for selective sharing and configuring endorsement policies to manage the transactional power across the actors. Therefore, not all actors may hold an equal copy of the ledger depending on the membership on specific channels.

Note that Ethereum is also a potential candidate, but the transaction speed of the Ethereum leading network is volatile [11]. This makes transaction time a particular issue for time-deterministic applications. Strategies of scaling Ethereum's thruput, such as layer two are promising but increase the complexity of transactions [11]. Ethereum charges volatile transaction fees according to network load and amount of transaction payload. In the absence of this mechanism with Hyperledger Fabric, we expect less volatility of costs. Finally, Ethereum maintains full metadata transparency, but the privacy level is not fine-grain configurable, making it challenging to operate confidential business transactions.

To conclude this section, we mention that a centralized database or cloud solution would also be viable for specific consortia but conflicts with the sovereign self-governance of common goods by a highly decentralized infrastructure. Significantly, the announcement of Google to retire the IoT Core service until August 2023 [16], and the announcement of Microsoft to retire Azure stack Edge [30] until March 2024 strengthens our doubts about sovereignty on centralized solutions with potential vendor lock-in.

6.2 Low-Code and Industry Grade Hardware

This section discusses using a low-code programming interface and industry-grade hardware to connect instruments with our peer-to-peer network. The high demand for software solutions and a general shortage of software developers in various industries shapes the interest in simplifying software development and reducing deployment time. For this purpose, low-code introduces a method to streamline software development and reduce hand-coding efforts by graphical modeling and ready-to-use building blocks. Prinz et al. [38] conduct a literature review on current research objectives of low-code development platforms, and we mention commercial products from the field of robot process automation (RPA) such as, UiPath [54] and Mendix [28].

The Low-Code Integration Pattern. CarbonEdge employs the open-source project node-RED [32] as the low-code software development platform to interact with the edge node and the MRV consortium. We use a recurring integration pattern (see Fig. 12) to embed MRV tasks reproducibly. The design gathers the following elements:

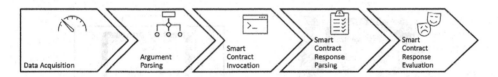

Fig. 12. CarbonEdge's generalized process integration pattern

Data Acquisition. A CarbonEdge hardware node may receive data from integrated instruments over communication protocols such as MQTT or immediately connects to sensors, e.g., thru a two-wire interface (I2C). The low-code application handles data acquisition by incorporating relevant application programming interfaces (API) inside the low-code building blocks (e.g., to interface GPIO pins of our edge controller).

Argument Parsing. Incoming telegrams may be represented by a large bandwidth of data models. To handle incoming telegrams, the low-code application allows flexible customization of the parser. A new software release is unnecessary; the changes are done as a local configuration update by a user with limited programming knowledge.

Smart Contract Invocation. The low-code interface of CarbonEdge holds a function block to invoke smart contracts of the consortium. For this purpose, we hand-over over data (e.g., parsed arguments from incoming sensor data) to the corresponding smart contract.

Smart Contract Response Parsing. To indicate the result of a smart contract operation, smart contracts typically populate a response message. The CarbonEdge low-code interface implements mechanisms to parse response arguments and allows adaptions to changing data models.

Smart Contract Response Evaluation. The response of a smart contract must be evaluated to derive resulting actions. For this purpose, the low-code application may switch optical signals or actuators. Node-RED provides standard libraries to do so.

Industry Grade Hardware. To demonstrate CarbonEdge's concept of dedicated edge nodes and low-code application development in the field, we assemble a mobile demonstrator setup with two nodes using industrial grade, c-rail mounted components (see Fig. 13). The use of c-rail components allows a fast integration into existing racks on-site. The hardware of the edge controller belongs to the RaspberryPi (CM3) product family, which employs an ARM64 processor architecture. The operation with standard components allows a simple replacement with equivalent industrial parts, which prevents vendor lock-in and positively affects the OEE (e.g., by robust housing, standard connectors, comprehensive documentation, and catalog availability). Furthermore, the software stack of CarbonEdge is fully containerized, which allows a simple deployment on any device which fills the minimum requirements, such as the correct hardware architecture.

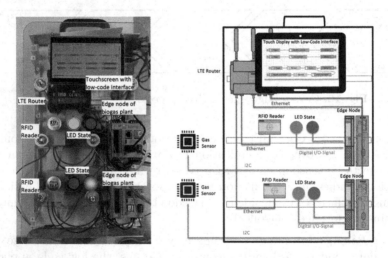

Fig. 13. The mobile setup is equipped with two CarbonEdge nodes, a touch display (left), and the corresponding schematic drawing of the rack (right).

6.3   Aspects of Self-Governance for Communities

The application domain of our proposed solution is shaped by small and medium-sized enterprises (SMEs). Due to the number of actors and the absence of hierarchical control in our alliance web, according to Tapscott et al., [53], our scenario demands a blockchain-specific governance strategy. Jain et al. [23] explore blockchain governance for SME clusters, and references to the "Tragedy of Commons" problem, stated in the dissertation of Hardin [17]. Poux et al. [37] analyze the use of blockchain to support the governance of common pool resources

(CPR) based on Ostrom's design principles of self-governance for communities [33]. In this section, we discuss our governance approach in light of Ostrom's eight design principles and outline whenever an implementation on-chain or off-chain is desired. Note, the term **on-chain** suggests the implementation of business logic as a corresponding smart contract on the blockchain, while an **off-chain** implementation describes a transaction without interacting with the append-only ledger, e.g., an IT process inside an organization, or communication between actors in the physical world:

Clearly Defined Boundaries. The principle addresses the right to withdraw units from CPR. In our scenario, we exemplify two of those CPR: First, biogas plant operators cause emissions by running combined heat and power plants which withdraw corresponding emissions as a CPR. Second, biogas production should be aligned with the actual energy demand of consumers and storage capacities; a control mechanism is necessary to prevent overproduction. Setting a production limit of biogas per hour may act as a virtual CPR. Therefore, we consider an **on-chain** implementation.

Congruence Between Appropriation and Provision Rules and Local Conditions. This principle describes the balance of appropriation and provision according to local conditions (e.g., time, cost, and technology). Our consortium recognizes the aspect of appropriation by aligning thresholds and other parameters to the actual size of a biogas plant. At the same time, our approach to collaborative implementation and using industrial-grade components supports the provision. Both should be balanced by transparent and straightforward metrics measures (e.g., the relation between biomass throughput and generated electricity of each plant). We propose an **on-chain** realization, where issuers maintain personal metrics on the ledger, and calibration laboratories are auditing.

Monitoring. The principle describes the consortium's need for dedicated actors as monitors who are accountable for the behavior of the remaining consortium; to do so, they get extensive monitoring capabilities inside the consortium. In our scenario, the biogas plant 1 according to Fig. 5 is accountable for the consortium and monitors the CPR usage of each issuer **on-chain**.

Graduated Sanctions. Monitoring CPR usage and making specific actors accountable to the consortium allows the operation of graduated sanctions for rule violations. We exemplify an **on-chain** solution where the project organization penalizes negative behavior and incentivize sustainable CPR usage by adjusting the shares on the annual reward from selling certified emissions reductions. Therefore, less consumption of CPR may lead to a higher claim on the yearly remuneration and vice versa. However, CarbonEdge aims at cost-efficient MRV of GHG emissions, and the implementation of graduated sanctions would be out of the scope of the scenario. Still, we outline that CarbonEdge is the foundation to implement those mechanisms for advanced scenarios.

Multiple Layers of Nested Enterprises. This principle gathers governance activities inside layers of nested enterprises. Our proposed consortium explicitly addresses this principle as an **on-chain** solution, where it reports produced biogas units and GHG emissions as a CPR to larger systems (e.g., National Registries, European Transaction Log (EUTL), or International Transaction Log (ITL) [55]). Furthermore, a channel topology allows selective sharing of data and implementation of business relations between consortium members.

The instantiation of CarbonEdge in this scenario considers five of Ostrom's eight design principles on-chain and the following remaining three principles as off-chain processes or excludes them for the MRV use case:

Collective-choice Arrangements. Our proposed consortium explicitly aims at cost-efficient MRV of GHG emissions, and implementing dynamic participation mechanisms would be out of scope. Hence, we propose that participation processes be **off-chain**.

Conflict-resolution Mechanisms. We exemplify one of over 250 possible project methods only from the United Nations CDM [8]. The number of necessary conflict-resolution mechanisms would outweigh the scope of MRV for GHG emissions. Hence, we prefer an **off-chain** solution.

Minimal Recognition of Rights to Organize. The enforcement of rules may be enhanced by legal contracts between consortium actors (e.g., the application of graduated sanctions for exceeding the usage of CPRs). CarbonEdge only serves trustworthy documentation for **off-chain** investigations.

7   Future Work and Conclusion

This article presents the design of CarbonEdge, a toolkit for collaborative MRV of GHG emissions, which employs the edge computing paradigm and blockchain technology. As part of our research design, we introduce the biogas plant scenario. The technological novelty relies on the practical analysis of concrete Industry 4.0 technologies (low-code, edge computing, and RFID) to ease using a blockchain-based solution in an industrial automation environment. For MRV of GHG emissions, security and trustworthiness of data are essential, and the Blockchain, together with secure edge devices, provides collaborative automation of workflows and information security. Tapscott's models of Business Webs inspire our work. We use the Alliance Business Webs as a blueprint for joint interests or competition settings and design our Blockchain accordingly. Business actors with similar value activities may compete on the market but can still benefit from reducing costs through joint GHG emission management. We argue that our ideation of a self-governing consortium addresses a clear research gap on technologically supported governance for up-scaled MRV of GHG emissions. Collaborative automation is a promising candidate to lower transactional costs in the future, but it also demands new integration platforms (e.g., Blockchain for the industrial edge). Guided by Ostrom's eight design principles, we demonstrated the usefulness of our consortium ideation by exemplifying a concrete United Nations CDM method. Our next steps are defined by setting up a realistic installation with an industrial partner to further develop and evaluate our concept in practice. The CarbonEdge source code is available at GitHub [44] and contains the setup documentation. Furthermore, the repository operates an automated build process for ARM64 docker images of CarbonEdge.

Acknowledgements. We acknowledge funding for Project LIONS as part of dtec.bw. dtec.bw is funded by the European Commission under NextGenerationEU.

References

1. Al Kawasmi, E., Arnautovic, E., Svetinovic, D.: Bitcoin-based decentralized carbon emissions trading infrastructure model. Syst. Eng. **18**(2), 115–130 (2015). https://doi.org/10.1002/sys.21291
2. Ansible project contributors: ansible documentation (2023). https://docs.ansible.com/ansible/latest/index.html
3. Baumann, T.: Blockchain and emerging digital technologies for enhancing post-2020 climate markets (2018). https://doi.org/10.13140/RG.2.2.12242.71368
4. Beck, R., Mueller-Bloch, C., King, J.: Governance in the blockchain economy: a framework and research agenda. J. Assoc. Inf. Syst. 19, 1020–1034 (2018). https://doi.org/10.17705/1jais.00518
5. Bozic, N., Pujolle, G., Secci, S.: A tutorial on blockchain and applications to secure network control-planes. In: 2016 3rd Smart Cloud Networks & Systems (SCNS), pp. 1–8. IEEE, December 2016. https://doi.org/10.1109/SCNS.2016.7870552, http://ieeexplore.ieee.org/document/7870552/
6. Braden, S.: Blockchain potentials and limitations for selected climate policy instruments (2019). https://www.giz.de/en/downloads/giz2019-en-blockchain-potentials-for-climate.pdf
7. Brendel, A., Zapadka, P., Kolbe, L.: Design science research in green IS: analyzing the past to guide future research. In: Conference: European Conference on Information Systems (ECIS). Portsmouth (2018). https://aisel.aisnet.org/ecis2018_rp/115
8. Dawson, B., Spannagle, M.: Clean development mechanism methodology booklet (CDM) (2020). https://cdm.unfccc.int/methodologies/documentation/meth_booklet.pdf
9. Ebertseder, F., Kissel, R., Lehner, A., Rivera Gracia, E., Bachmaier, H., Effenberger, M.: Monitoring und Dokumentation von Praxis-Biogasanlagen. Technical Report, Bayerische Landesanstalt für Landwirtschaft (LfL), Freising, Germany (2012). https://www.lfl.bayern.de/mam/cms07/ilt/dateien/langfassung_abschlussbericht_biogas-monitoring_2015.pdf
10. Eckert, J., López, D., Azevedo, C.L., Farooq, B.: A blockchain-based user-centric emission monitoring and trading system for multi-modal mobility. CoRR abs/1908.0, August 2019. http://arxiv.org/abs/1908.05629
11. Ethereum foundation: Ethereum scaling (2022). https://ethereum.org/en/developers/docs/scaling/
12. European commission: questions and answers - the effort sharing regulation and land, forestry and agriculture regulation (2021). https://ec.europa.eu/commission/presscorner/detail/en/qanda_21_3543
13. European commission: EU emissions trading system (EU ETS) (2023). https://climate.ec.europa.eu/eu-action/eu-emissions-trading-system-eu-ets_en

14. European commission: monitoring, reporting and verification of EU ETS emissions (2023). https://climate.ec.europa.eu/eu-action/eu-emissions-trading-system-eu-ets/monitoring-reporting-and-verification-eu-ets-emissions_en

15. Füssler, J., Wunderlich, A., Kreibich, N., Obergassel, W.: Incentives for private sector participation in the article 6.4 mechanism (2019). https://www.dehst.de/SharedDocs/downloads/EN/project-mechanisms/discussion-papers/climate-conference-2019%5C_1.pdf

16. Google cloud: IoT core (2022). https://cloud.google.com/iot-core

17. Hardin, G.: The tragedy of the commons. Science **162**(3859), 1243–1248 (1968). http://www.jstor.org/stable/1724745

18. Hevner, A.R., March, S.T., Park, J., Ram, S.: Design science in information systems research. Des. Sci. IS Res. MIS Q. **28**(1), 75–105 (2004). https://doi.org/10.2307/25148625

19. Hofman, D., DuPont, Q., Walch, A., Beschastnikh, I.: Blockchain governance: de facto (x)or designed? In: Lemieux, V.L., Feng, C. (eds.) Building Decentralized Trust, pp. 21–33. Springer, Cham (2021). https://doi.org/10.1007/978-3-030-54414-0_2

20. Hofmeier, M., Seidenfad, K., Rieb, A., Lechner, U.: Risk factors for malicious insider threats - an analysis of attack scenarios. In: AMCIS 2023 (in press). Panama City (2023). https://aisel.aisnet.org/amcis2023/

21. Hoiss, T., Seidenfad, K., Lechner, U.: Blockchain service operations - a structured approach to operate a blockchain solution. In: 2021 IEEE International Conference on Decentralized Applications and Infrastructures (DAPPS), pp. 11–19. IEEE, August 2021. https://doi.org/10.1109/DAPPS52256.2021.00007, https://ieeexplore.ieee.org/document/9566184/

22. Hsu, A., et al.: Bridging the emissions gap: the role of non-state and subnational actors-pre-release version of a chapter of the forthcoming UN environment emissions gap report 2018. Technical Report, United Nations Environment Programme, Nairobi (2018). https://wedocs.unep.org/bitstream/handle/20.500.11822/26093/NonState_Emissions_Gap.pdf

23. Jain, G., Shrivastava, A., Paul, J., Batra, R.: Blockchain for SME clusters: an ideation using the framework of Ostrom commons governance. Inf. Syst. Front. (2022). https://doi.org/10.1007/s10796-022-10288-z

24. Jensen, T., Hedman, J., Henningsson, S.: How TradeLens delivers business value with blockchain technology. MIS Q. Executive **18**(4), 221–243 (2019)

25. Lamken, D., et al.: Design patterns and framework for blockchain integration in supply chains. In: 2021 IEEE International Conference on Blockchain and Cryptocurrency (ICBC), pp. 1–3. IEEE, May 2021. https://doi.org/10.1109/ICBC51069.2021.9461062, https://ieeexplore.ieee.org/document/9461062/

26. Li, T.: Minifabric: a hyperledger fabric quick start tool (2020). https://www.hyperledger.org/blog/2020/04/29/minifabric-a-hyperledger-fabric-quick-start-tool-with-video-guides

27. Li, Z., Kang, J., Yu, R., Ye, D., Deng, Q., Zhang, Y.: Consortium blockchain for secure energy trading in industrial internet of things. IEEE Trans. Ind. Inf. **14**(8), 3690–3700 (2018). https://doi.org/10.1109/TII.2017.2786307

28. mendix: accelerate enterprise app development (2023). https://www.mendix.com/

29. Michaelowa, A., Brescia, D., Wohlgemuth, N., Galt, H., Espelage, A., Maxinez, L.: CDM method transformation: updating and transforming CDM methods for use in an Article 6 context. Technical Report, University of Zurich, Zurich (2020). https://doi.org/10.5167/uzh-195559

30. Microsoft: the "managed" IoT edge solution on azure stack edge will be retired on March 31, 2024. Transition your IoT edge workloads to an IoT edge solution running on a Linux VM on azure stack edge. (2023). https://azure.microsoft.com/de-de/updates/the-managed-iot-edge-solution-on-azure-stack-edge-will-be-retired-on-march-31-2024-transition-your-iot-edge-workloads-to-an-i/

31. Miehle, D., Henze, D., Seitz, A., Luckow, A., Bruegge, B.: PartChain: a decentralized traceability application for multi-tier supply chain networks in the automotive industry. In: 2019 IEEE International Conference on Decentralized Applications and Infrastructures (DAPPCON), pp. 140–145. IEEE, Newark, CA, USA, April 2019. https://doi.org/10.1109/DAPPCON.2019.00027, https://ieeexplore.ieee.org/document/8783173/

32. OpenJS foundation & contributors: NODE-RED (2013). https://nodered.org

33. Ostrom, E.: Governing the commons: the evolution of institutions for collective action. Political economy of institutions and decisions, Cambridge University Press (1990). https://doi.org/10.1017/CBO9780511807763

34. Ostrom, E.: A multi-scale approach to coping with climate change and other collective action problems. Solutions 1(2), 27–36 (2010). http://thesolutionsjournal.com/print/565

35. Oxford University Press: definition of non-state actor (2021). https://www.lexico.com/definition/non-state_actor

36. Partnership for market readiness (PMR): establishing scaled-up crediting program baselines under the Paris agreement : issues and options (2017). https://openknowledge.worldbank.org/handle/10986/28785

37. Poux, P., de Filippi, P., Ramos, S.: Blockchains for the governance of common goods. In: Proceedings of the 1st International Workshop on Distributed Infrastructure for Common Good, DICG 2020, pp. 7–12. Association for Computing Machinery, New York, NY, USA (2020). https://doi.org/10.1145/3428662.3428793

38. Prinz, N., Rentrop, C., Huber, M.: Low-code development platforms - a literature review. In: The 27th annual Americas Conference on Information Systems (AMCIS), Montréal (2021). https://aisel.aisnet.org/amcis2021/adv_info_systems_general_track/adv_info_systems_general_track/2/

39. Richardson, A., Xu, J.: Carbon trading with blockchain. In: Pardalos, P., Kotsireas, I., Guo, Y., Knottenbelt, W. (eds.) Mathematical Research for Blockchain Economy. SPBE, pp. 105–124. Springer, Cham (2020). https://doi.org/10.1007/978-3-030-53356-4_7

40. Schermuly, L., Schreieck, M., Wiesche, M., Krcmar, H.: Developing an industrial IoT platform - trade-off between horizontal and vertical approaches. In: Wirtschaftsinformatik (WI) (2019). https://aisel.aisnet.org/wi2019/track01/papers/3/

41. Schletz, M., Franke, L., Salomo, S.: Blockchain application for the paris agreement carbon market mechanism-a decision framework and architecture. Sustainability (2020). https://doi.org/10.3390/su12125069

42. Schneider, L., et al.: Robust accounting of international transfers under article 6 of the Paris agreement discussion paper (2017). https://www.dehst.de/SharedDocs/downloads/EN/project-mechanisms/discussion-papers/Differences_and_commonalities_paris_agreement2.pdf?__blob=publicationFile&v=4

43. Schrems, I., Hecker, J., Fiedler, S., Zerzawy, F., Forum Ökologisch-Soziale Marktwirtschaft e.V.: Introduction of an emissions trading system for buildings and road transport in the EU (2021). https://www.umweltbundesamt.de/sites/default/files/medien/479/dokumente/2022_02_08_factsheet_ets_2_final_engl_bf.pdf

44. Seidenfad, K., Biermann, J., Olzem, P.: CarbonEdge Github repository (2023). https://github.com/KSilkThread/carbonedge
45. Seidenfad, K., Greiner, M., Biermann, J., Lechner, U.: CarbonEdge: demonstrating blockchain-based monitoring, reporting and verification of greenhouse gas emissions on the edge. In: 2023 IEEE International Conference on Blockchain and Cryptocurrency (ICBC), Dubai (2023). (in press)
46. Seidenfad, K., Hoiss, T., Lechner, U.: A blockchain to bridge business information systems and industrial automation environments in supply chains. In: Krieger, U.R., Eichler, G., Erfurth, C., Fahrnberger, G. (eds.) I4CS 2021. CCIS, vol. 1404, pp. 22–40. Springer, Cham (2021). https://doi.org/10.1007/978-3-030-75004-6_3
47. Seidenfad, K., Hrestic, R., Wagner, T.: Pull request #322 create RunningOnArm.md on Minifabric from Hyperledger labs (2022). https://github.com/hyperledger-labs/minifabric/pull/322
48. Seidenfad, K., Wagner, T., Hrestic, R., Lechner, U.: Demonstrating feasibility of blockchain-driven carbon accounting - a design study and demonstrator. In: Phillipson, F., Eichler, G., Erfurth, C., Fahrnberger, G. (eds.) Proceedings of the 22nd International Conference on Innovations for Community Services (I4CS 2022). Springer, Delft (2022). https://doi.org/10.1007/978-3-031-06668-9_5
49. Shi, W., Cao, J., Zhang, Q., Li, Y., Xu, L.: Edge computing: vision and challenges. IEEE Internet Things J. **3**(5), 637–646 (2016). https://doi.org/10.1109/JIOT.2016.2579198
50. Shrimali, B., Patel, H.B.: Blockchain state-of-the-art: architecture, use cases, consensus, challenges and opportunities. J. King Saud Univ. Comput. Inf. Sci. **34**(9), 6793–6807 (2022). https://doi.org/10.1016/j.jksuci.2021.08.005, https://www.sciencedirect.com/science/article/pii/S131915782100207X
51. SIEMENS AG: kick off the carbon countdown (2021). https://new.siemens.com/global/en/company/topic-areas/product-carbon-footprint.html
52. Streck, C.: Strengthening the Paris agreement by holding non-state actors accountable: establishing normative links between transnational partnerships and treaty implementation. Trans. Environ. Law (2021). https://doi.org/10.1017/S2047102521000091
53. Tapscott, D., Ticoll, D., Lowy, A.: Digital capital: harnessing the power of business webs. Ubiquity 2000, (May), May 2000. https://doi.org/10.1145/341836.336231
54. UiPath: Build elegant apps for your automations the low-code way (2023). https://www.uipath.com/product/low-code-app-studio?utm_source=google&utm_medium=cpc&utm_campaign=[DACH]_Tier-1_ENG_Brand_T2_Product&utm_term=uipath%20low%20code-p&utm_content=B_Product-Apps&gclid=Cj0KCQjwxYOiBhC9ARIsANiEIfbt3nN1A9Q6ACjS4YXAq_gEj0yM4X_YQCQZJuL_a
55. UNFCCC: data exchange standards for registry systems under the Kyoto protocol. Technical Report, UN (2013). https://unfccc.int/files/kyoto_protocol/registry_systems/application/pdf/des_full_v1.1.10.pdf, https://unfccc.int/sites/default/files/data_exchange_standards_for_registry_systems_under_the_kyoto_protocol.pdf
56. United States environmental protection agency: importance of methane (2023). https://www.epa.gov/gmi/importance-methane#:~:text=Methaneismorethan25,duetohuman-relatedactivities
57. Varghese, B., Wang, N., Barbhuiya, S., Kilpatrick, P., Nikolopoulos, D.S.: Challenges and opportunities in edge computing. In: 2016 IEEE International Conference on Smart Cloud (SmartCloud), pp. 20–26, November 2016. https://doi.org/10.1109/SmartCloud.2016.18

58. Vukolić, M.: Rethinking permissioned blockchains. In: Proceedings of the ACM Workshop on Blockchain, Cryptocurrencies and Contracts, BCC 2017, pp. 3–7. Association for Computing Machinery, New York, NY, USA (2017). https://doi. org/10.1145/3055518.3055526

59. Weill, P.: Don't just lead, govern: how top-performing firms govern IT. MIS Q. Executive **3**, 1–17 (2004)

60. Yaga, D., Mell, P., Roby, N., Scarfone, K.: Blockchain technology overview (2018). https://doi.org/10.6028/NIST.IR.8202,   https://nvlpubs.nist.gov/nistpubs/ir/ 2018/NIST.IR.8202.pdf

61. Yu, W., et al.: A survey on the edge computing for the internet of things. IEEE Access **6**, 6900–6919 (2018). https://doi.org/10.1109/ACCESS.2017.2778504

62. Yue, K.B., Kallempudi, P., Sha, K., Wei, W., Liu, X.: Governance attributes of consortium blockchain applications. In: 27th Americas Conference on Information Systems, Montreal (2021). https://aisel.aisnet.org/amcis2021/strategic_is/ strategic_is/4/

63. Zavolokina, L., Ziolkowski, R., Bauer, I., Schwabe, G.: Management, governance and value creation in a blockchain consortium. MIS Q. Executive (2020). https:// doi.org/10.17705/2msqe.00022

Text Analysis

Support for Fictional Story Writing and Copy Editing

Jörg Roth[(✉)]

Faculty of Computer Science, Nuremberg Institute of Technology, Nuremberg, Germany
Joerg.Roth@th-nuernberg.de

Abstract. Fictional writing is the art of creating stories that are not based on real events or people. In recent years, book projects for smaller communities have become popular, not least due to the success of e-book platforms. In the context of story wringing, copy editing is an important step in the writing process as it ensures the overall quality concerning grammar, spelling and style. Currently, this step usually is executed by costly specialists. This is a problem for writers who are starting their careers. This paper presents a tool platform that simplifies the process of copy editing. Authors can execute first check steps themselves. The amount of further iterations with a commercial lector is reduced or may even be omitted. Our tool is able to apply even complex style rules that are based on deeper grammar analyses of texts.

Keywords: Language models · Fictional story writing · Author support · Copy editing · Grammar analyses

1 Introduction

Fictional story writing is the art of crafting narratives that engage and entertain readers through the use of imagined characters, settings, and events. It allows writers to use their imaginations to produce stories and bring characters and worlds on pages.

More and more people consider fictional writing as a hobby, either for personal enjoyment or to share their work with others. In recent years, the rise of self-publishing platforms has made it easier for hobby authors to share their work with a wider audience [6].

An important step in the publishing process is copy editing. It helps to ensure that the final product is polished and error-free. The process involves correction of errors in grammar, spelling, and punctuation, as well as ensuring a consistent style. It goes far beyond spell-checking of word-processing applications, as it also checks complex style rules. Thus, usually a person (proofreader, lector, editor) with great experience is involved. Usually, this step cannot be carried out by the author itself, for two reasons: first, the author usually concentrates on the content, storyline, figures, and suspense. A typical writing technique is thus to write without too much considering correct grammar and style rules, in order to preserve the flow of ideas. Second, the author usually is too close to his own project, thus often overlooks his own mistakes.

U. R. Krieger et al. (Eds.): I4CS 2023, CCIS 1876, pp. 151–168, 2023.
https://doi.org/10.1007/978-3-031-40852-6_8

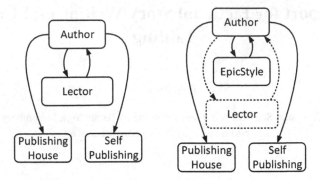

Fig. 1. Workflow without (left) and with a tool (right)

Figure 1 left shows the typical work flow in the publishing process nowadays, even for hobby projects. The document may take several rounds over a lector. This is a costly service that often is paid on page or word basis. In Germany, a common price in 2022 was 6–8 € per standard page (approx. 1,500 letters, 200 words). For, e.g., a typical novel of 400 pages we thus get costs of 2,400 € for a single iteration. In the context of hobby and self-publishing projects this usually does not pay off.

In this paper we suggest tool support to make the process of copy editing more effective (Fig. 1, right). Our tool, called *EpicStyle*, empowers the author to carry out several iterations of proofreading without to involve a third person. Only when this process has been successfully terminated, an external lector may be commissioned. As the tool already ensures a certain degree of text quality, the number of external proof-reading iterations is reduced. Moreover, in hobby projects, authors may self-publish their book without any external service.

The focus of EpicStyle is to provide style comments and correction remarks to given texts. The following list declares, what was *not* the goal of the tool:

- The tool is not designed for text input and layouting. We assume, the author has its favorite tool to enter and edit texts.
- We do not provide additional author tools, often part of writing applications such as character databases or story timelines.
- The tool does not provide any kind of text generation. Only suggestions for word and phrase replacements are integrated.
- The tool does not try to reveal the content of a text. It thus is not able to give hints, e.g., about the tension or soundness of story or vividness or consistency of figures.

In the era of ChatGPT [1] it is essential to provide a tool that preserves the author's writing style, as it is a unique selling proposition strongly related to the writer. Thus, we believe that a tool should not automatically create texts.

The tool currently only supports German language. To make this paper readable, we translated, whenever possible, language-related topics to English. However, this should not indicate English language support of the tool. Moreover, we are aware that some topics cannot adequately be transferred to another language – these are indicated in text.

2   The EpicStyle Tool Environment

2.1   General Architecture and Design Decisions

An important design decision was *not* to integrate any editing capabilities into the tool. Popular tools such as *Papyrus Author* [13] provide multiple services related to authoring tasks such typing/editing, defining layout, but also spell check and thesaurus. The decision to create a tool that *only* supports the revision process was driven by two objectives:

- The development of such a tool was significantly simplified, as we do not have to care about very complex editing functions.
- Users usually have 'their' tool for editing, that they are not willing to change. In particular, if they are experienced authors, it is nearly hopeless to convince to use an other tool.

This decision, however, has certain drawbacks. First, authors have to perform an additional step to get their text into the tool. Second, we have to store the tool state in a separate file structure.

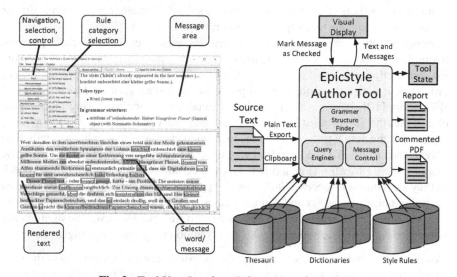

Fig. 2. Tool User Interface (left) and Dataflow (right)

Figure 2 left shows the user interface. The largest part of the screen is occupied by the text. It is rendered by an own rendering engine, thus the layout is not the same as in the source editor.

The actual output is shown in the upper right part of the window: the *style message*. Navigation buttons allow the user to navigate through all messages produced for the text. In addition, the author can click on a certain word, marked to be the anchor of a message. Note that every message must be mapped to a single word in the text, even if it affects a phrase or sentence.

To process a message, the user has three options:

- He decides to ignore this message, either because it was a false positive or he may ignore style critics for artistic reasons. E.g., the tool may mark a repetition of words, but the author did this on purpose.
- He decides to fix the problem in the source. For this, the author must switch to the source editor and change the text.
- If the message is based on a missing dictionary entry, he may create one.

Further tool options are provided to make the process more efficient. E.g., the author may first concentrate on certain style message categories and leaves further messages to later revisions of the text. It was an important goal, not to push an author to a special direction, forced by the tool. Revising texts is a complex task for which each author learned individual habits that should not be changed.

Figure 2 right shows the dataflow. The most convenient way to read the source text is to copy from the text editor to our tool over the clipboard, but also a plain-text export/import may be used.

The tool takes into account three types of additional sources:

- *Thesauri*: for every word in the text, the tool provides synonyms. This is useful, as many style conflicts (e.g., repetitions) can be solved, if another word with a similar meaning is taken. Our tool supports thesauri formats such as [12].
- *Dictionaries*: these are important for two reasons. First, they identify spelling errors. Second: with these, the tool is able to compute grammar structures from texts. Note that our dictionaries must contain *word forms* [3] with all grammar properties, not only lists of correct spellings. We support the dictionary formats *Morphy* [7] and *Wiktionary* [10]. It is a common task to extend the dictionary during the revision phase, thus the author must be able to create own story dictionaries (see below).
- *Style rules*: the actual task of the tool is to provide messages that indicate conflicts to known style rules. We used a hybrid way to detect such conflicts. First, rules can be stored in *style rule files*. E.g., a rule is to avoid certain words outside a direct speech as they are 'common speech'. Such word lists can easily be part of a text file that even an author may change. Second, complex rules are checked programmatically, i.e. by snippets of code. New rules have to be coded by a developer. However, we significantly simplified the expression of such rules in a common programming language.

An important challenge was to manage the *tool state*. The most main part of the state is, which style messages already were checked by the author and marked to be ignored. The problem: as our tool is intentionally not able to change the source file, it must store this information elsewhere. For this, we save a message reference together with a part of the source text that is sufficiently large to identify the respective position in a state database.

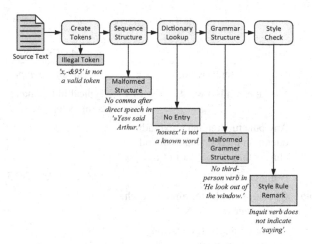

Fig. 3. Input Pipeline

Figure 3 shows the input pipeline. The respective steps are performed, whenever the author pastes a new version of the text into the tool.

First, we retrieve higher-level text structures. For this, we distinguish between *tokens* (e.g., marks, number, quotes, and words) and then compute *sentence structures* (e.g., direct speech, declarative sentence). At these stages, first errors may be detected. E.g., a very common mistake is to confuse quotation marks and commas in the usage of direct speech with *inquit formulas* (also called *dialog tags*, such as '*said Paul*').

Next, dictionaries are applied. Each word token gets *all* possible grammar meanings. Note that in most languages, a single spelling may have multiple meanings depending to the sentence structure.

Using complex grammar rules, the tool detects grammar structures such as objects and predicates. For this, we apply a pattern-based approach (see below). The detection may result in further messages, e.g., if a special tense is not formed correctly.

Finally, we applied style rules. Resulting conflicts usually form the largest part of all messages provided to the author.

2.2 Pre-Processing Input

In order to express high-level style rules, we first have to pre-process the text. From sequences of characters, we first derive tokens. This step reminds of compilers' work.

A first decision was to define meaningful classes of tokens that were of interest for further processing (Table 1). Marks and quotation characters are necessary to retrieve the higher-level structures later. The identification of numbers is required for certain style rules. Two tokens for ellipsis (trailing and mark) seem to be artificial on the first glance. But adding '...' with or without preceding blank means something completely different and is often reason for mistakes. The same applies to the dash.

Table 1. Token types

Type	Meaning	Remarks/Examples
Trailing Ellipsis	'…' that extends a word	'…' in '*sh… happens*'
Trailing Dash	'-' that extends a word	Typical in German for sequences of composites
Mark	Any punctuation mark, excluding quotation marks, also dash and ellipsis that are not part of the word	*., ? … –*
Number	Number, dates	*123 1.1.2023 3.1415*
Quotation Double	Quotation marks for direct speech in different variations	" «» „ "
Quotation Single	Quotation marks for citations in different variations	' ‹ › ‚'
Word	Word, usually with a dictionary entry	*Bamberg word hello has*

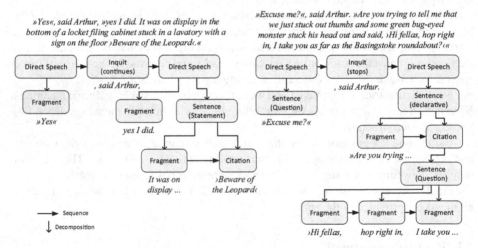

Fig. 4. Example sentence structures

Once the tokens have been indentified, the tool tries to compute the *sentence structure*. Figure 4 shows two examples. Each paragraph is mapped to a tree of primitive structure elements. We again make a selection of those elements that are useful to be distinguished in narrative texts:

- *direct speech* and *inquit formulas* are typical elements to describe dialogs;
- *sentences* (question of declarative) are outside of dialogs ('*The sky was blue.*', '*Where was Paul?*'). The distinction is important as different grammar and style rules have to be applied for questions;
- *fragments* are subordinate clauses, separated by comma;

- *citations* are word sequences, enclosed by single quotes; usually they express cited speech in direct speech or phrases that reference other texts.

Once these structures have been detected, the tool is able to perform an important step: dealing with uppercase/lowercase letters. In German, words may start uppercase (e.g., nouns) or lowercase (e.g., verbs). In many languages, the first word of a sentence always is written in uppercase. Thus, an uppercase word may actually have a lowercase entry in a dictionary. As a consequence, we need a detection of such situations. As starts of sentences may appear also in direct speech and citations, the rules are not trivial, but heavily rely on sentence structures already detected.

We have the following cases:

- Uppercase word and start of sentence: dictionary lookup of the uppercase, but also the lowercase version.
- Lowercase word and start of sentence: give a warning message.
- Not start of a sentence: dictionary lookup of the exact spelling in the text.

Related to this issue are fully capital words (e.g., *'STOP IT'*). Authors may use them to indicate shouting in texts. The respective dictionary entries have to be looked up for both the uppercase and lowercase spellings.

A last pre-processing step was to map intentionally abbreviated words into their actual word form. E.g., *'who's'* is internally mapped to *'who is'* in order to properly perform a grammar analysis. Such a construction often appeared in common speech.

2.3 The Role of the Dictionary and Input of New Words

The word form dictionaries play a major role. It is not only required for spell checking. To find all possible inflections of a word token is inevitable for grammar analyses and style checks. In contrast to other tools (e.g., MS Word [11]), we do not try to perform an analyses without the knowledge of *all* word forms in a sentence. This is because incomplete word forms may only lead to a more or less probable guess rather than a reasonable statement.

Table 2 shows word forms and their occurrence in current dictionaries. Note that until now, only German dictionaries are integrated in the tool. In this paper, examples are not translated literally, but in terms of content. Even though the dictionaries contain nearly 5 million word forms, any new text usually has many missing forms. The reasons are:

- A living language changes constantly, thus society and media permanently create new words that finally find their way to fictional stories. E.g., in 2017, approx. 5000 so called *neologisms* have been collected by the Duden dictionary [4].
- Stories are full of character names (*'Hagrid'*, *' Lord Voldemort'*), usually not known by dictionaries. They at least have to be classified according genus and type (last name, first name).
- Fantasy and science fiction stories are full of new technology, creatures, or magic that result in new names (*'muggel'*, *'babelfish'*). They often are nouns, but also other word forms are affected (*'to disapparate'*, *'hoppy'*). As they are used in the same way as 'real' words in texts, they also must have word form entries.

Table 2. Word Types

Type	Examples	Properties	Stems	Avg. Forms per stem	Total form entries
Adjective	*green biggest*	Participle? Comparative/ Superlative?	26,427	124.5	3,289,554
Noun	*computer tool*	Kasus, Numerus, Genus	78,587	15.1	1,190,211
Verb	*going went been*	Type (full, modal etc.), Person, Tense	9416	29.9	281,308
Name	*Bamberg Einstein*	Kasus, Numerus, Genus, Req. Article?	1436	11.1	15,903
Pronoun	*I his*	Type (poss. Rel., refl. Etc.), Kasus, Numerus, Genus, Person	57	21.8	1243
Adverb	*even slowly*	Type (modal, temporal etc.)	781	1.0	788
Number	*eight thousand*	*none*	442	1.0	442
Verb addition	only in German	*none*	174	1.0	174
Preposition	*between near*	Kasus, Type (modal, temporal etc.)	125	1.0	130
Abbreviation	*UK No PhD*	Salutation?	92		98
Conjunction	*if although*	Adjacent/ Subordinating?	72		84
Interjection	*hey huh*	*none*	59		59
Article	*the a*	Kasus, Numerus, Genus, Definite/ Indefinite?	3		43
Negation	*never no*	*none*	6		6
Total			117,677		4,780,043

- Many languages allow creating new words using *compounds*. Multiple words (usually two) are linked together and provide a more detailed meaning. In German, such compounds are not indicated syntactically, i.e., parts usually are not separated by blank or dashes. Thus, compounds appear as unknown words. They may be formed as nouns, verbs, adjectives adverbs and prepositions.

As the tool provides useful messages on dictionary basis, creating new entries is important part of the revision workflow. Looking at Table 2, for a new stem this can be time-consuming (e.g., 124.5 derived entries for a single adjective stem on average). Fortunately, there exist building rules for certain forms that apply to most stems. E.g., for a German feminine noun, all required forms can be derived from nominative/singular by simply appending certain endings. On the other hand, for masculine nouns, plural is always different, thus had to be entered by the user. In an unlucky case (usually words that are taken from, e.g., French or Latin), up to six forms had to be entered to define all noun forms. Adjectives and verbs are comparable to this.

To simplify the creation of new word form entry, the tool tries to make useful suggestions for unknown words:

- It first tries to guess the word type (e.g., noun). The context in a sentence and uppercase/lowercase writing (in German) may give hints.
- Then attributes are suggested. E.g., some endings in German define the Genus of a noun.
- The user may enter additional properties. E.g., some nouns only occur in singular, or some adjectives do not have Comparative and Superlative.
- Next, the tool applies standard word form rules and creates a suggestion. The user may change individual entries.

Even with good suggestions, this causes more attention by a user compared to tools that just accept a new word as 'written correctly'. However, it ensures a proper analysis.

Looking at compounds: we integrated heuristics to detect compounds, if the parts already have entries. Note that in German, compounds usually have three fractions: first word, additional letters (e.g., 's', 'n', 'e'), second word. E.g., the German word '*Ableitungsregel*' (in English: '*derivation rule*') contains '*Ableitung*' (first word), '*s*' (additional letter), '*Regel*' (second word). The benefit: all word form attributes can be copied from the second word (here '*Regel*'), once a compound has been detected. Thus, in such a case, the user only has to confirm.

2.4 Finding Grammar Structures, the Pattern Language

Finding grammar structures is a difficult task. Depending on the respective language, there are various possibilities to form correct sentences. One of the challenging problems is *ambiguity*. While even a single word form usually has several meanings, it may belong to numerous structures. As a consequence, our approach keeps all possible assignments as long as possible. Only when there is an explicit reason for exclusion, a hypothesis will be removed.

The counterpart to ambiguity is *redundancy*. Redundancy helps algorithms to find structures because word forms are restricted according to their usage in a certain context. To give some examples (for German language):

- Article, adjective, and noun have corresponding Genus, Kasus, and Numerus, if they belong to the same object.

- There exists a fixed mapping between pronouns and Kasus, they request.
- Corresponding subject and predicate have corresponding Numerus and Person.

To express such rules in a compact manner, we introduced a new pattern language. Corresponding expressions are interpreted at runtime. Resulting structures that match the pattern can be accessed from inside the binary of the author tool.

We build the pattern language according to the following mechanisms:

- *Logical expressions*: These may contain any condition among word type (e.g., verb), word attributes (e.g., Genus), word *text* or *stem* using nested logical expressions with *and*, *or*, *not*.
- *Bindings*: To express same attributes among different words, bindings may be included into expressions. They are bound on the first occurrence of the respective attribute and then contain the assigned value in further expressions.
- *Labelings*: the actual result of a matching pattern expression. If a sequence of words matches a pattern, labels can be assigned to individual words of this sequence. E.g., in an object, *article*, *adjective* and *noun* may be labels.
- *Warnings*: A typical mistake of authors is to use wrong word forms in a grammar structure. E.g., in an object, one word may unintentionally have the wrong Kasus. Such sequences do not match the corresponding pattern. However, it would be useful to provide a message such as '*this would be an object, if word xy had Kasus genitive*'. As a consequence, for each pattern expression, the developer may add more rules with relaxed conditions that trigger a warning on misspelling.
- *Jump patterns*: Sometimes, words that belong to a grammar structure do not appear subsequently. E.g., in some German tenses, the auxiliary verbs always appear at the end of a sentence. With jump patterns, we express to skip multiple words that do not belong to the structure. They may define further conditions of jumps, e.g., '*at least one word must be of type xy*'.
- *Named patterns, macros*: To create large patterns, it is useful to base on other patterns. For this, we introduced two mechanisms. *Named patters* are lower-level patterns that may be integrated into conditions. *Macros* are textual replacements for certain conditions that appear multiple times.

Figure 5 shows two examples. Figure 5 top shows a part of the expressions that matches objects in sentences. These lines match word sequences such as '*the green tree*' or '*his car*'. To identify mistakes, the warning patterns indicate the same structure, however, they relax the strong correlation of Genus, Kasus and Numerus. This is performed by parenthesize sub-expressions. The effect of [...] is: all bindings are only evaluated locally, thus outside the brackets, inner bindings are not visible. Thus, these warning patters match to *all* sequences of words with the given types, regardless of correct Genus etc. Note that warning patterns only are evaluated, if the actual pattern does not match, thus they only create warnings, if the strong conditions are not fulfilled.

Figure 5 bottom presents a small section of patterns that detect verb constructions. In German, there exist a huge variety of tenses. Even though, we have six main tenses, they can be set into active or passive, two subjunctive moods, with or without additional auxiliary verb. We get a total of 25 patterns, only for verb constructions.

```
makro ART_PRONOUN =
   Determiner:Article(kas:Kasus=* & num:Numerus=* & gen:Genus=*) |
   Determiner:Pronoun(Type=Poss|Demon|Indef) & kas:Kasus=* & num:Numerus=*)
makro ADJ=Attribute:Adjective(kas:Kasus=* & num:Numerus=* & gen:Genus=*)
makro NOUN =(Noun:Noun(per:Pe3 & kas:Kasus=* & num:Numerus=* & gen:Genus=*)
match: ART_PRONOUN,NOUN | ART_PRONOUN,ADJ,NOUN;
warning: [ART_PRONOUN],SUBST | [ART_PRONOUN],[ADJ],SUBST
           ->'wrong Kasus, Genus or Numerus')


match: Verbconstruct:Verb(per:Pers=* & num:Numerus=* & Mod=Praes & Typ=Aux &
                       Stem=('have' | 'be')),
       JUMP,
       Verbconstruct:Verb(Form=Pa2) |
       ...
```

Fig. 5. Example patterns; object with article and optional adjective (top), verb construction present perfect (bottom)

2.5 Putting all Together, Style Rules

We now have relevant information to express style rules. We decided to formulate style rules mainly programmatically. There is one exception: Word lists that are strongly related to style rules may be stored on separate text files. To give an example: inquit formulas should not describe actions, but request verbs that express '*saying*'. A common mistake of beginners to use other words (e.g., '*laughed*', '*sighed*'). There exist a lot of such legal words, e.g., '*whisper*', '*shout*', '*ask*'. This word list may be extended in the future, thus we store this list in a file and refer to it by a list name. However, the actual detection of conflicts, a developer writes code snippets – usually not longer than a few lines.

To formulate style rules, a developer may take the following conditions into account:

- Is a token inside a certain sentence structure, e.g., inquit formula?
- Is the token of a certain type, e.g., mark, word?
- Is the token exactly a given text, e.g., 'trees', ':', '1'?
- Does the token have a given stem?
- If the token is a word, is it of a specific word type, e.g., verb, article?
- For a specific word type, does it have certain attributes, e.g., noun in plural?
- Is the token part of a specific grammar structure, e.g., predicate?

To simplify the development of respective code, we heavily make use of Lambda expressions [9]. A single call iterates through all token sub-sequences of a given length, meanwhile checking conditions. The result is a list of all sub-sequences that fulfill the required properties. The developer then may

- issue a message for all hits,
- issue a single message, if at least one was in the list or
- just count the hits for statistic purposes.

Numbers 1 to 12 have to be written in letters (e.g., *'eight'*)
```s.findTokens(1,seq->seq[0].isNumberLike(nl->nl.isInt() &&```
```nl.intValue()>=1 && nl.intValue()<=12))```

Special verb combination is correct but unusual in lively texts (in German)
```s.findTokens(2,seq->seq[0].isWord(w->w.hasText("am")) &&```
```seq[1].isVerb(v->v.form==Verb.FORM_INFINITIV))```

Avoid claiming adjectives outside a direct speech
```s.findTokens(1,seq->!seq[0].isInDirectSpeech() &&```
```seq[0].isAdjective(a->CLAIMING_ADJECTIVE_LIST.contains(a.getStem())))```

After "at the beginning" we always have a genitive object (in German)
```s.findTokens(3,seq->seq[0].isWord(w->w.hasTextLowerCase("zu")) &&```
```seq[1].isWord(w->w.hasText("Beginn")) &&```
```!seq[2].isObject(ao-> ao.getKasus()==KASUS_GENITIV))```

A sentence must have subject and predicate ```s.findTokens(1,seq->seq[0].isSubjektPraedikat()).size()>0```

Count 'said' in inquit formulas
```sagteSeqs=s.findTokens(1,seq->seq[0].isInInquit() &&```
```seq[0].w->w.hasText("said"))```

Fig. 6. Example code to detect style rule conflicts

Figure 6 shows some example codes for style rules.

The decision to use program code may be revised in the future, as it is a hurdle for non-developers. However, some rules have a high degree of complexity and thus cannot be implemented with formal languages that have a lower expressiveness. To give an example: one typical mistake of inexperienced authors is to use personal pronouns (e.g., *'her'*, *'it'*), without mentioning a certain person or object with the appropriate Genus before. Or, there may be multiple possible references and the reader cannot be sure about the meaning. To create such warnings, the tool has to iterate through the text and collect objects for a certain number of text lines. Whenever a pronoun appears, this collection is searched. This type of code requires structures like hash tables, branches, loops etc. and thus is difficult to express in a non-programming manner.

Table 3 finally describes the type categories of style rules the tool currently is able to check. The table is constantly extended.

3   Evaluation and Discussion

3.1   Comparison with Other Tools

We compared our EpicStyle tool with other tools in the area. Software that specifically supports a fictional writer still is a marginal phenomenon. Typically, corresponding functions are integrated into a general word processing platform. They usually provide

Table 3. Style Rule Categories (selection)

Category	Meaning, Examples
Input pipeline messages	Illegal token, malformed structure, missing dictionary entry
Grammar problem	A warning occurred during structure finding. E.g., Kasus, Genus, or Numerus of article and noun, or person of verb and object do not match (German grammar)
Inadequate word	A word sounds boring (e.g., *'going'*, *'seeing'*) – there may be a more meaningful word. Or: A word is unusual, e.g., in direct speech. A suggestion for a better word is provided
Inadequate tense	The story should, e.g., entirely be written in past tense, but present tense was used. Or: a tense was used in direct speech that is not very common in real dialogs. Or: passive tense was used, whereas lively writing requires active tenses
Upper/lowercase problem	A word both exists as upper/lowercase (e.g., German *'sie'*, *'Sie'*) and the wrong case was used
'hin', *'her'*	Common word confusion (only German) – these part of words often are used similar, but have a different meaning
'he', *'she'*, *'it'*, *'his'*, *'her'* etc.	Is there an object or person that may be meant be these words? Note that in German, also things and animals may be masculine or feminine
Adverbs	Excessive usage of adverbs is not adequate in lively texts
Claiming adjectives	Certain adjectives that represent a claim should be avoided and should be replaced by sensual adjectives
Comma	Missing or unnecessary commas
Numbers	Some numbers should be written out
Wrong meaning	The meaning of a certain word is not adequate for a context, e.g., no verb that indicates *'saying'* in inquit formulas
Repetitions	A certain word, phrase, or start of sentence appeared too often or already appeared recently
Lengths	A sentence or direct speech was too long

check spelling and grammar, but special support functions for fictional writing, e.g., check of direct speech, narrative tenses are rare or non-existent.

When evaluating other tools, we had to face a problem: it is not obvious, on which mechanisms the analyses functions are built on. We even could not easily detect, what checks actually are made. This was because both the amount of analyses functions and their implementation are a corporate secret. We thus had to rely on black-box tests, i.e. we had to create texts with certain style conflicts to find out, how tools react.

We examined *Microsoft Word* (MS 365] [1] and *LibreOffice* (Version 7.5) [8]. For the latter we activated the so-called *LanguageTool* [5] that provides additional analyses functions for writers. The most popular tool for authors (at least in Germany) is *Papyrus*

Table 4. Detection of Style Conflicts

Style Conflict	Our Tool EpicStyle	LanguageTool	MS Word	Papyrus Author	DeepL Write	ChatGPT
Misspelled verb	+	+	+	+	−	−
Misspelled noun	+	+	+	+	−	−
Misspelled name	+	+	+	+	−	−
Wrong narrative tense	+	−	−	−	−	−
Wrong Kasus (article + noun)	+	+	+	+	+	+
Wrong Kasus (article + adj + noun)	+	+	+	+	+	+
Wrong Kasus (preposition + object)	+	+	+	−	+	+
Wrong Numerus (subject + predicate)	+	−	+	+	+	+
Wrong marks (direct speech + inquit)	+	+	−	−	+	+
Numbers 1–12 not spelled in letters	+	−	−	−	−	v
Personal pronoun without reference	+	−	−	−	−	+
Inquit without a verb indicating 'say'	+	−	−	−	+	−
Usage of claiming adjective	+	−	−	+	−	−

(*continued*)

Table 4. (*continued*)

Style Conflict	Our Tool EpicStyle	LanguageTool	MS Word	Papyrus Author	DeepL Write	ChatGPT
Usage of passive tense	+	–	–	–	+	–
Unusual usage of Future 1 in direct speech	+	–	–	–	–	–
Direct speech was too long	+	–	–	+	–	–
Frequent usage of adverbs	+	–	–	+	–	–
Verb with low expressiveness	+	–	–	+	–	+
Too often the same leading words	+	+	–	–	–	+
Too often the same phrase	+	–	–	+	–	+

Author [13]. It provides a lot of writing functions (typing, layout etc.) but also special services used for book projects, e.g., character database or time lines.

To evaluate the strength of tools based on models created by machine learning approaches, we also checked *DeepL Write* [14]. This tool actually was mainly created to simplify texts; however, also reports style conflicts. The target area of DeepL Write is *not* creative writing and also simplifies, e.g., web content, business texts or manuals. It was not possible to specify the type of text.

We finally checked *ChatGPT* (GPT-3.5) [1]. It is an all-purpose environment to create any texts on demand. To produce a style conflict report, we inserted '*Analyse the following text for stylistic violations. The text was formulated in the narrative form. The text:*' in front of the actual text that should be checked. The result message contained a lot of comments that could not be mapped to a certain text position, but covered the overall text. E.g., one comment was, '*The text has a number of linguistic flaws that result in an unclear and boring narrative.*'. This however is not useful for authors who want to apply certain corrections. ChatGPT also produced several wrong comments, where the respective input sentences were incorrect.

For our evaluation we created a text that contains multiple style conflicts. Table 4 shows the results. Of the traditional tools, each reliably discovered misspellings. DeepL and ChatGPT failed to detect spelling error, as their typical behavior is to 'guess', what new words may mean. This is a big pitfall, as it prevents a systematic detection of typical mistakes in texts.

A second group of conflicts cover wrong Kasus, Numerus, wrong tense, wrong marks and wrong spelling of numbers. Such mistakes occur very often and usually are difficult to detect by the author himself.

Further conflicts address more typical writing faults. They cover statistical problems (longish direct speech), and duplicating words or phrases, usage of boring words and missing references for pronouns.

In comparison, typical grammar faults are mostly detected. Not surprisingly, special analyses for fictional writing are not available in multi-purpose writing environments. Papyrus Author found some of our conflicts, but by far not all. Very surprisingly, even a wrong ordering of marks has been ignored by some tools.

The tools that are based on machine learning models reliably found grammar errors but failed to indicate special style rule conflicts that are only related to fictional writing. As their language models cover all types of texts found in the Internet, they are not specific for this special type of writing. In addition, the output of ChatGPT was difficult to map to the original text, as the environment formulates complete answer text blocks.

Finally, we checked, how other tools deal with unknown words. A typical document check marks new words, suspicious to be a spelling mistake. All tools (also EpicStyle) provide a suggestion of the potential intended word. However, only EpicStyle allows entering a complete dictionary entry, if the word actually was correct. All other tools only allow 'accepting' the spelling as correct. This prevents the tool from recognizing grammar structures in the respective sentence: the author does not have the chance to classify the new word. In addition, derived flexions are still unknown.

3.2 Discussion

We are in the age of large language models [2]. Neural networks claim to contain the ultimate knowledge about a language, learned from millions of documents. EpicStyle, however, is built on a strict symbolic analysis without the usage of any machine learning approach. It detected a lot of style conflicts and may help an author to reduce the number of correction iterations with a lector or commercial correction service. It found more conflicts than other tools, also than tools built on large language models.

It is difficult to predict, how modern developments in the area of artificial intelligence will influence the process of story writing in the future. Presumably, there will be a significant support to automatically produce texts or at least text fragments by language models, relieving authors of tedious formulation work. We thus must ask, if a strong symbolic approach still is appropriate. A first observation: style rules, even though have an artistic facet, are very similar to formal language rules, thus can be formally expressed by explicit conditions. As an example: a rule to avoid a certain phrase, tense or construction in a specific context can easily be expressed in an explicit manner. To learn such a rule from examples would require multiple text examples that are properly tagged by experts. Furthermore, once a large language model identified texts that are not properly written according to that model, it often was not able to explain, what was wrong. We investigated this effect with ChatGPT: it stated that the given text had problems but could not explicitly state, where in the text.

This leads to a further problem: authors have different styles. A conflict for one author maybe an artistic means for another. Thus, a tool should support an author to preserve his or her special writing style. Large language models in contrast take an average of all styles found in texts, even of poorly written documents.

From their nature, machine learning models work with probabilities in a wider meaning. They usually state a degree of having a certain property. This often is a benefit, as even texts with spelling or grammar errors can be interpreted as intended. However, this is a problem, if we focus on such errors.

Finally, we have the problem of unknown words. A language model is trained with texts and all words, these texts contain. However, unknown words (see above) are the typical case, not an exception. Thus, we had to construct a workflow, where we may integrate new words and easily retrain models.

4 Conclusions and Future Work

This paper presented the EpicStyle environment that supports authors in the area of fictional writing. The goal is to significantly reduce the numbers of correction iterations. It strongly relies on word form dictionaries and simplifies the input of new words with all derived forms. An input pipeline detects the coarse structure of texts. A pattern language enables the tool to find grammar structures. Powerful functions allow a developer to easily express style rules with only few lines of codes, taking into account token type, dictionary entries and grammar structures.

Even though the language models based on machine learning approaches currently are not able to detect all style rule conflicts specific for story writing, we expect a high potential in the future. We thus want to combine our tool with these models in the future.

Currently, a developer has to extract style knowledge from writing experts in order to code suitable rules. This is not optimal for two reasons: first, experts and developers think in different mindsets. Usually, lectors or experienced authors know many rules but are not able to easily express them in a structured manner. In addition, corresponding knowledge still is considered as 'secret science', thus experts often are not willing to explicitly tell a reason for a special improvement. Second, to represent this knowledge in programming code and word lists still is a hurdle. We thus want to create another way to express style rules in the future: learning by examples. Whenever an author makes a correction, pairs of old and new versions are stored. If afterwards similar texts occur, the tool creates an adaptive suggestion, based on learned corrections.

References

1. Bishop, L.: A Computer Wrote this Paper: What ChatGPT Means for Education, Research, and Writing, 26 January 2023. https://ssrn.com/abstract=4338981
2. Brants, T., Popat, A.C., Xu, P., Och, F.J., Dean, J.: Large language models in machine translation. In: Proceedings of the 2007 Joint Conference on Empirical Methods in Natural Language Processing and Computational Natural Language Learning, June 2007, Prague, pp. 858–867. Association for Computational Linguistics (2007)
3. Haspelmath, M., Sims, A.D.: Understanding Morphology, 2nd edn. Routledge, London/New York (2010)

4. Klosa, A., Lüngen, H.: New German words: detection and description. In: Proceedings of the XVIII EURALEX International Congress Lexicography in Global Contexts, July 17–21, 2018, Ljubljana (2018)
5. Language Tool. https://languagetool.org/
6. Laquintano, T.: Mass Authorship and the Rise of Self-Publishing, University of Iowa Press (2016)
7. Lezius, W.: Morphy – German morphology, part-of-speech tagging and applications. In: Proceedings of the 9th EURALEX International Congress, August 8–12, Stuttgart, Germany, pp. 619–623 (2000)
8. LibreOffice. https://de.libreoffice.org/
9. Mazinanian, D., Ketkar, A., Tsantalis, N., Dig, D.: Understanding the use of lambda expressions in Java. Proc. ACM Programm. Lang. 1(85), 1–31 (2017)
10. Meyer, C.M.: Wiktionary – The Metalexicographic and the Natural Language Processing Perspective, PhD Thesis, TU Darmstadt (2013)
11. Microsoft Word. https://www.microsoft.com/de-de/microsoft-365/word
12. Naber D.: OpenThesaurus: Building thesaurus with a web community (2004)
13. R.O.M. logicware Soft- und Hardware: Papyrus Author. https://www.papyrus.de
14. DeepL Write. https://www.deepl.com/de/write

AutoNLP: A System for Automated Market Research Using Natural Language Processing and Flow-based Programming

Florian Würmseer[(✉)], Stefan Wallentowitz[iD], and Markus Friedrich[iD]

Hochschule München University of Applied Sciences, 80335 Munich, Germany
{wuermsee,stefan.wallentowitz,markus.friedrich}@hm.edu

Abstract. This paper introduces a novel architecture for an automated market research system that utilizes the Flow-based Programming (FBP) paradigm. The described system allows users to select topics of interest, and then automatically collects website content related to these topics. The system also offers different search modes for searching the collected text corpus, including stem-based and semantic search. These search modes utilize Natural Language Processing (NLP) techniques. The design of the system was developed to meet specific requirements and underwent a thorough assessment. We analyzed the system's runtime efficiency with and without the use of flow-based logic and found scalability issues in the Python library used. Finally, we conducted a user study that evaluated the system's usability, showing that the system can be used without requiring extensive training.

Keywords: Natural Language Processing · Flow-based Programming · Market Research

1 Introduction

Artificial Intelligence (AI) and Machine Learning (ML) is constantly gaining relevance in today's industry. ML can be used to automate tedious, repetitive and mostly digital tasks. Thus, a computer can accomplish those tasks which previously had to be done by a human. This saves time, effort, and money that can be invested in more complex problems instead. Especially in professions that depend on textual research and communication, like market research, the subset of ML, namely Natural Language Processing (NLP), can be helpful. NLP techniques have the ability to build a connection between semantically similar sentences and even whole texts. Semantic search is a key ingredient for automated market research, where products and services of competitors are analyzed and evaluated to gain insights about potential niches.

This research was supported by W.L. Gore & Associates GmbH. Gore is an American technology company that develops a large variety of products in the sectors medicine, filter technology, fabrications, and many other innovative ePTFE based products. Currently, Gore employs just over 12,000 Associates.

This work presents an automated market research system that comprises a web-scraping component to fetch websites using a set of keywords provided by the user. The collected content is indexed for rapid document search and can be queried using two modes: word stem search using a known document ranking algorithm and semantic search relying on a Deep Learning (DL) model. Both use a set of words as input.

Scraping and indexing involve extensive data processing, which necessitates a suitable software architecture. The flow-based programming model offers an intuitive and scalable foundation for data processing. This programming paradigm adapts graph-theory concepts, such as nodes and edges, to describe a process pipeline as a computational graph. Individual nodes represent processing steps, and edges denote connections between these steps. The flow-based approach enables modular, reusable software components and a clear representation of data processing logic.

This paper explores the utilization of the Flow-based Programming paradigm in developing an automated market research tool and puts forward the following research questions:

1. What are the essential design considerations for developing a flow-based software architecture that meets the requirements of automated market research?
2. Can the selected Python library for flow-based programming efficiently process data in terms of execution time?
3. What is the user's perception of their interaction with the system and the functionalities provided by it?

This paper is structured as follows. Section 2 introduces important fundamental concepts needed to understand the main ideas of the paper. The problem statement is detailed in Sect. 3 which also contains resulting functional and non-functional requirements. This is followed by a thorough discussion of the solution concept in Sect. 4. Section 5 describes aspects of the system's implementation. The evaluation of the system is extensively described in Sect. 6. The conclusion in Sect. 7 summarizes the results and describes potential future work.

2   Background

2.1   Natural Language Processing

Natural language processing refers to the ability of computers to comprehend natural language. This includes text classification, translation and natural language generation tasks. Although there are also classic pre-ML algorithms for NLP, DL-based methods are predominant in this research area for a lot of tasks.

An important ML architecture that lately gained a lot of traction is the transformer architecture. A transformer is a specific DL-model that uses so-called attention-mechanisms [22] to express semantic connections between data elements (e.g. tokens in a text). First mainly used for NLP tasks, the concept's usefulness could be proven in related fields like computer vision [8] and audio-processing [23]. Transformers exist in different flavors: Encoders (token sequence to fixed-size vector), decoders (token sequence to predicted next sequence token) and encoder-decoders (sequence to sequence). Encoders can be used e.g. for text-based sentiment analysis whereas decoders have proven to be very powerful auto-regressive text generators [5]. The most obvious use-case for encoder-decoders is automated language translation.

BERT. The Bidirectional Encoder Representations from Transformers (BERT) Model is an architecture that builds on top of transfomers. BERT uses a stack of encoders (depending on the model size conventionally 12 or 16) [7]. The encoders use attention to calculate a semantic score for a sequence of tokens, i.e. text.

SBERT. Siamese BERT (SBERT) is an extension of the BERT architecture that employs two identical pre-trained BERT models. This approach enables additional capabilities that BERT does not support, such as similarity comparison, clustering, and, notably, semantic search – an essential function for our use case [15].

BM25. BM25 is a popular algorithm used in retrieval systems and is present in leading search engines [17]. The core idea of the algorithm is to combine the frequency of a term inside a document with the inverse frequency of that term in all documents of a corpus. Therefore the significance of such terms (usually words inside a query) can be considered in the search.

2.2 Flow-Based Programming

Flow-based Programming (FBP) is a programming paradigm first proposed by Paul Morrison [12]. FBP falls under the category of data-flow programming, a paradigm that aims to model program logic as a directed graph. The directed edges of the graph usually represent the flow of data. FBP extends the concept of data-flow programming by applying solutions to relevant programming problems. The first central point is the formulation of reusable components [12, p.41–53] that increase programming productivity and reduce error rates. These components can be seen as black-boxes. The only thing that should matter when using FBP is what a certain node does, and not how.

While it would be possible to execute each component sequentially (one node at a time), FBP intends to achieve parallelization per default. With an increasing popularity of multiprocessing computers [6] [21], parallelization per default becomes even more valuable. Another advantage of FBP is the minimization of side-effects [11] which increases parallelizability and furthermore makes applications more failure-resistant. FBP-systems often come with a graphical programming language for intuitive computational graph development. Figure 1 shows an example of a FBP data-pipeline. The pipeline displays how data indexing for NLP-based search looks like. The first node, which is also the start node in this pipeline, retrieves some sort of textual data. The edges imply that the data then flows to two different nodes. As stated above, this allows an FBP framework to execute them in parallel since there is no shared data. While one branch is doing data stemming, all others project a chunk of the collected data. After processing, data is collected and stored. In addition to the parallelization, FBP should also make sure that the "Store Data" Node is not being executed before all previous nodes have finished execution.

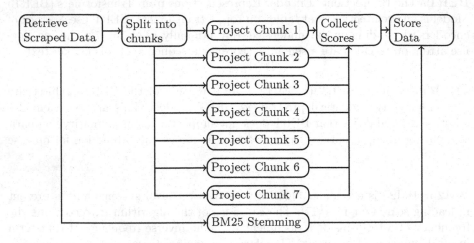

Fig. 1. A data indexing pipeline as an example of FBP-based process logic

3   Problem Statement

This section covers manual market research challenges, the requirements engineering process, and its outcomes.

3.1   Current State: Manual Market Research

While some products and ideas can be used as inspiration, others can open doors for strong partnerships or joint ventures. This awareness can be achieved with market research. Currently, most market research happens manually. Associates within marketing teams use a web browser and a search engine to find websites that could potentially contain information about competitors. The process includes clicking on every plausible search result, skipping advertisement, accepting website cookies and other possible tedious tasks involved in manual web research. Many websites also contain images or videos that block useful written text. Another issue is the internal ranking of websites on commonly used search engines. Whether a website appears first in a given web search depends on many factors such as response time, mobile compatibility, content quality or even included links. The process of optimizing the ranking of a website is known as Search Engine Optimization (SEO). Especially new competitors will most likely not invest in SEO and thus won't be ranked high enough to appear on the first (in most cases) 10 pages of a search. Finding all important competitors and even more so to exclude the possibility of such competitors to exist is a tedious task. Market researchers need to use multiple search terms and inspect up to 20 pages per search term. Depending on the search results this can result in a 12 hours time investment. Since these searches have to be repeated regularly, it is not uncommon to have at least two marketing associates per business division, each spending about 40% of their time on competitor research.[1]

3.2   Requirements Engineering

This section contains functional and non-functional requirements. Requirements engineering and quality assurance followed the processes described in [3]. Each requirement contains a reference, a measurement criteria, an acceptance criteria and a priority. As stakeholders, market researchers, software developers, software architects and DevOps-engineers were identified. Table 1 provides information about the impact of all involved stakeholders. The "influence" and "attitude" range from "+" for positive, "o" for neutral, and "−" for negative. The Identifier (ID) in each table is set for later reference. Table 2 shows derived user groups.

Table 1. Stakeholders and their roles

ID	Description	Internal/ External	Expectation	Influence	Attitude
SH-1	Market research associate specializing in competitor research	Internal	Saving time to utilize skills more efficiently within the organization	+	+
SH-2	Software developer for Data Science	Internal	Reuse functionality of the developed functionality via a Programming Interface	−	+
SH-3	Software Architect	Internal	Reusable stable software architecture design	o	+
SH-4	DevOps-Eningeer	Internal	Good embedding in currently maintained IT-Infrastructure	+	o

---

[1] Data from W.L. Gore & Associates GmbH.

Table 2. User groups

ID	User Group	SH-ID
UG-1	Marketing devision	SH-1
UG-2	Gore Developer Community	SH-2
UG-3	Data Science team	SH-2
UG-4	Emerging Technologies and Innovations team	SH-3
UG-5	InD-DevOps team	SH-4

Functional Requirements. Functional requirements are referenced in Table 3 including a label, description, measurement criteria, priority, user group, and an ID for reference.

Table 3. Functional requirements

ID	Label	Description	Measurement criteria	Priority	UG-ID
F-1	Collect relevant web-resources	As a marketing researcher I would like to enter keywords to collect relevant data from the internet	1–5 keywords and 20 websites per keyword will be collected	High	UG-1
F-2	Web-scraping Application Programming Interface (API)	As a software developer I would like to use a standardized programming interface for web-scraping utilities using a modern search engine to speed up my productivity	API returning 20 scraped websites for up to 5 keywords	High	UG-2, UG-3
F-3	Clean websites	As a marketing researcher I would like to see only valid and well formatted English sentences in my response to further process that information.	Only obtain valid English sentences as plain text	High	UG-1
F-4	Clean websites API	As a software developer I would like to use a standardized programming interface that consumes raw HTML-data and returns valid and well formatted English sentences to further process that information	API only returns valid English sentences as plain text	High	UG-2, UG-3
F-5	Filtering results by word stems	As a marketing researcher I would like to search efficiently in all collected sentences using a keyword to extract specific information	One keyword returns a set of matches containing words from the same word stem	High	UG-1

(*continued*)

Table 3. (*continued*)

ID	Label	Description	Measurement criteria	Priority	UG-ID
F-6	Filtering results by semantics	As a marketing researcher I would like to search efficiently in all collected sentences using semantic comparison to extract specific information	One phrase returns a set of semantically similar matches	Medium	UG-1
F-7	Filtering results API	As a software developer I would like to search efficiently in all collected or provided sentences using semantic or keyword search	API returns a set of similar matches for a provided keyword or phrase	Low	UG-2, UG-3
F-8	Transparency	As a marketing researcher I would like to be aware of the origin website of every search result to further investigate and verify the source	Each match contains the origin URL	High	UG-1
F-9	Search results per user	As a marketing researcher I would like to see my own search results only	Separate context per user	High	UG-1
F-10	Nested Search	As a marketing researcher I would like to search within my set of search results to further restrict search results	Results are reduced by additional keyword	Low	UG-1

Non-Functional Requirements Non-functional requirements are referenced in Table 4 including a label, description, measurement criteria, priority, user group, and an ID for reference.

Table 4. Non-functional requirements

ID	Label	Description	Measurement criteria	Priority	UG-ID
NF-1	Low pricing for storage	All temporary content used for a search should be stored on an affordable and reliable database	Storage cost $\leq$ 5Cent/Gigabyte (GB)	Medium	UG-4
NF-2	Clear outdated data	All data stored during a user search must be deleted once it's no longer needed	Maximum lifetime = 3 days	High	UG-1, UG-4, UG-5
NF-3	Scalable storage	All data stored during a user search must be scalable and accessible from all Gore locations	No manual effort required for extending storage capacity	Medium	UG-4
NF-4	Limited to company use	The application must only be available within Gores Virtual Private Network (VPN)	Application must not be reached from outside the VPN	High	UG-1, UG-4, UG-5

(*continued*)

Table 4. (*continued*)

ID	Label	Description	Measurement criteria	Priority	UG-ID
NF-5	Maximum response time	Every functionality within the application (collecting, indexing, searching) shall respond within a given amount of time	Response time ≤ 40s	High	UG-1, UG-2, UG-3
NF-6	Safe search	The underlying search engine should support a safe-search feature to be compliant with our Code of Conduct (CoC)	No CoC conflicting content is processed	Medium	UG-1, UG-2, UG-3
NF-7	Cross platform	The web-application should be accessible from every Gore-supported device	Accessible via browser	Medium	UG-1
NF-8	High Availability	Both the web-application and the programming interface should be highly available	Availability ≥ 99.9%	Low	UG-1, UG-2, UG-3, UG-4, UG-5
NF-9	Programming Language	Python should be used as programming language to leverage company expertise	Python is used for all AI functionality	High	UG-2, UG-3, UG-4, UG-5
NF-10	Scalability	The application should scale on user count, amount of data and code changes	A mechanism for scaling is in place	High	UG-4, UG-5

4 Concept

4.1 Architecture

The system's functionality is accessible via a Representational State Transfer (REST) service and thus provides strict decoupling between back- and frontend. This allows for different frontend technologies dependent on the supported platforms (NF-7, Table 4). The REST-ful paradigm aims to comply with stateless client-server communication that favors independent requests in order to reduce system complexity. This implies that separate functionality must have separate and independent endpoints. Thus, the proposed backend architecture is split into three different modules: Web-Scraping, Indexing and Search (see Fig. 2). All modules follow the FBP-paradigm for process logic description. For hosting and storage a cloud-based solution was selected (Amazon Web Services (AWS)) in order to avoid self-maintenance and operation. All used AWS services guarantee 99.9% availability [2] (NF-8, Table 4). We chose AWS storage solution Simple Storage Service (S3) with a cost of $0.023 per GB (pricing satisfies requirement NF-1, Table 4). It also provides an option for automated document deletion after a predefined time-frame (NF-2, Table 4). Another advantage is the VPN-integration (NF-4, Table 4).

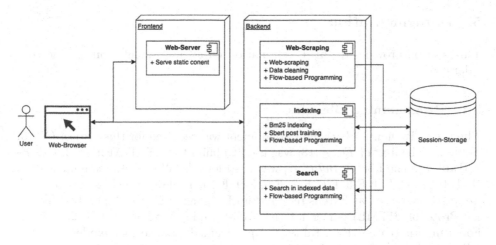

Fig. 2. High-level view on the system's architecture

4.2   Algorithms

The project has specific constraints for the search methods used in the implementation. For word stem search, we utilize the BM25 algorithm, a widely recognized document ranking approach that operates on a set of query words. BM25 ranks words depending on their significance (token frequency and inverse document frequency) but only finds exact matching words. This is much more efficient than matching with the use of wildcards. To enhance our Indexing functionality, we use a stemming algorithm on all searched documents beforehand and store the stem words only. Using the same procedure on the input query, BM25 will now find many more matches as it can now match all words that are based on the same word stem. As every word is mutated during stemming, we need to keep the original data set available in order to back-trace the original sentences. The semantic search relies on SBERT. The two identical bidirectional transformers can map any sentence of arbitrary length to a 768 dimensional space (a convention of the SBERT$_{BASE}$ Model).

By comparing the scraped data and the search query in a high-dimensional space using the cosine similarity score, we can determine the degree of similarity between them. To achieve the best search results, we identify the number of sentences in the document that have a cosine similarity score greater than zero and return them as matches in descending order of their score from one, which is the maximum cosine similarity score, all the way to zero. Any sentences in the document with a score less than or equal to zero are discarded.

5   Implementation

This section provides detailed information on all implementation-specific considerations.

5.1   Programming Libraries

The use of Python for backend development was required for this project (NF-9, Table 4). The library *Flask* [18] was used to build the REST-APIs (F-2, F-4, F-7, Table 3). The library *Boto3* [1] was used for all AWS-related communication (F-1, F-2, F-3, F-4, F-5, F-6, F-7, F-8, F-9, F-10, Table 3). The library *Beautiful-Soup* [16] was used as Extensible Markup Language (XML)/Hyper Text Transfer Protocol (HTML) parser for the Web-Scraping module (F-1, F-2, Table 3. For semantic search (F-6, Table 3), a pre-trained Transformer model from the *SBERT* library [15] was adapted.

The *Rank-BM25* library [4] was used together with the *spaCy* library and the *NLTK* [10] library to achieve keyword scoring (F-5, Table 3). The *Luigi* library was chosen for the FBP-based components because of its proven track record in the industry [20]. Comparing all FBP libraries for Python, *Luigi* was the only one that could satisfy both visualization as well as built in multiprocessing. As *Luigi* comes with its own scheduler and dedicated REST-API it was by far the most advanced library for the use case of this application. The build in multiprocessing together with the visualization of currently running tasks (and possible failures like unavailable websites for the Web-Scraping) turned out to be crucial for the development of the application. The Angular framework was used for frontend development.

5.2   User Interface

The initial search includes additional search terms until a total amount of five is reached (F-1, Table 3). Figure 3 shows an example with three search terms. The user can select with a slider how many websites should be scanned (F-1, Table 3). After the user has entered the search terms, scraped the data via the "Gather" button and indexed the data via the "Process" button, the data can be examined. For exploration the user enters additional terms in a search field and switches between word stem search and semantic search with a toggle (see Fig. 3). In order to allow users to smoothly transition between search results and their sources we included a link to the original website in each search result.

5.3   Data-Flow Pipelines

The implementation of the Web-Scraping, Indexing, and Search modules' processing logic is structured in data-flow pipelines utilizing the *Luigi* framework. In *Luigi*, a processing logic unit that represents a distinct element in the pipeline is called a task.

Figure 4 shows the process pipeline for the Web-Scraping module as an example. The process graph shows dependent tasks: The `Scrape` task (extracts text data from a website) requires the completion of multiple `Clean` tasks (filters website content). Each `Clean` task requires results of a `Fetch` task (retrieves website content) and the `Fetch` task requires a single execution of the `GetUrls` task (collects website URLs). Tasks in Fig. 4 that are not connected directly will be executed in parallel. Figure 5 shows the data-flow pipeline for the Indexing module. The heavy lifting of projecting all scraped sentences to a 768-dimensional embedding space happens in the `ProjectChunk` task. It takes the provided chunk of sentences from the `GetChunk` task and returns a 768-dimensional embedding vector. We leveraged the pre-trained model "msmarco-distilbert-base-tas-b" [9] from the SBERT library [15]. For the BM25 algorithm we use the Snowball stemming algorithm [13,14] included in the NLTK [10] library.

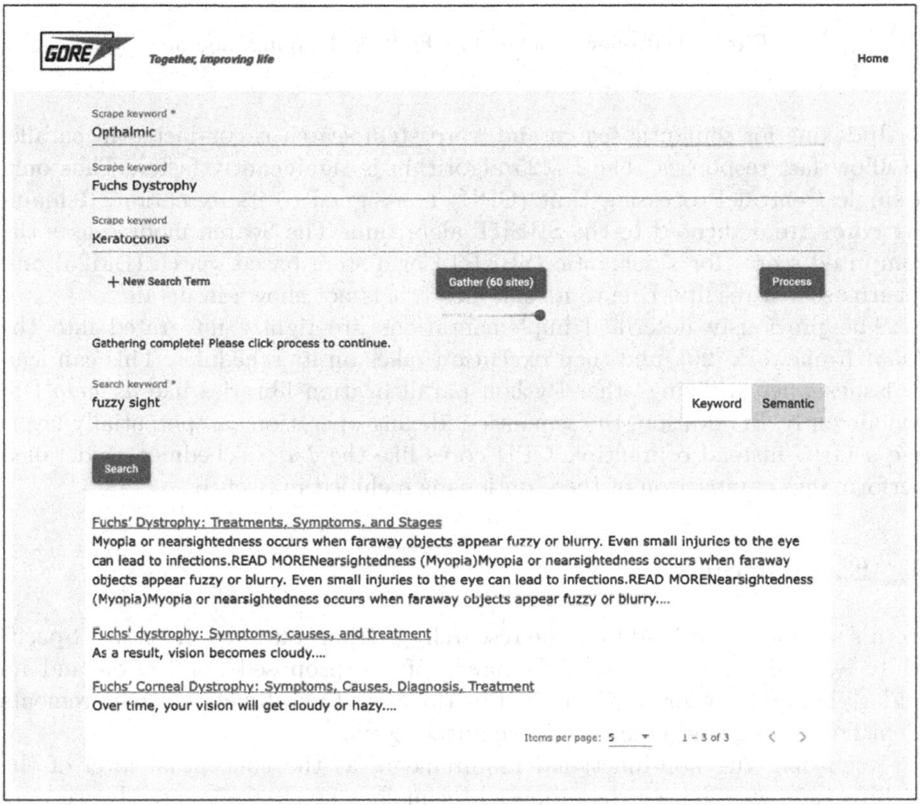

Fig. 3. User Interface (UI) example with three search terms and corresponding search results. The semantic similarity between different terms is noticeable, particularly between the search term "fuzzy sight" and the search result containing "cloudy vision", which have comparable meanings.

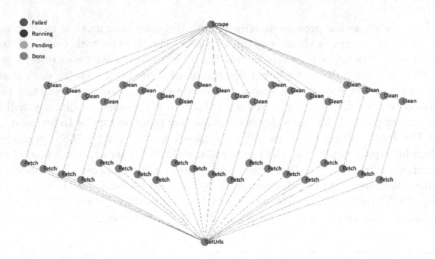

Fig. 4. Data-flow pipeline for the Web-Scraping module

Indexing for semantic search and word stem search is conducted in parallel to allow fast responses. The BM25 algorithm is significantly faster. Thus only a single Central Processing Unit (CPU) is assigned to its execution. Remaining cores are dedicated to the SBERT algorithm. The Search module uses the computed scores for a semantic (SBERT) or a stem based search (BM25) and returns search results. Due to its simplicity, it is not shown in detail.

The previously described implementations are tightly integrated into the *Luigi* framework [20], and their execution relies on its scheduler. This can lead to issues when utilizing other Python parallelization libraries like *asyncio* [19] concurrently. In addition, the semantic indexing operation can potentially leverage a GPU instead of multiple CPU cores like the *Luigi* scheduler. A detailed performance comparison of these options is included in Sect. 6.

6   Evaluation

In this section, we will address the research questions outlined in Sect. 1. Specifically, we will evaluate the performance of the proposed application and its underlying architecture against the functional and non-functional requirements identified during the requirements engineering phase.

Regarding the non-functional requirements at the conceptual level of the architecture, we followed the proposed technology stack. Consequently, we were able to meet requirements NF-1, NF-2, NF-3, NF-4, NF-6, NF-7, NF-8, and

NF-9 (Table 4) through our deployment and programming language choices. In order to verifiy the fulfillment of functional requirements, a user acceptance test was conducted.

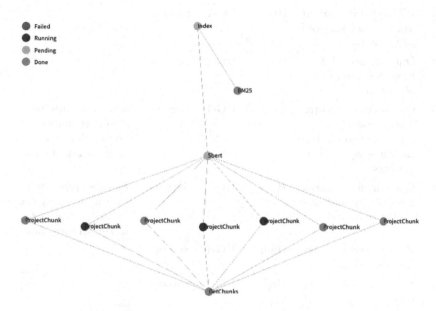

Fig. 5. Data-flow pipeline for the Indexing module. In this instance, the execution of a data-flow was illustrated.

6.1 User Acceptance

During the user acceptance testing phase, the system was evaluated by end-users (user in Table 5) to ensure that all functional requirements were met. The end-users are individuals who are seeking to use the specific feature being tested. Table 5 lists the measurement criteria from Table 3 along with their corresponding IDs and the test outcomes obtained from a group of end-users. The "Comments" column displays any additional remarks provided by the users.

Table 5. User acceptance tests

ID	Measurement criteria	Priority	UG-ID	Test Result	Comments
F-1	1–5 keywords and 20 websites per keyword will be collected	High	UG-1	Success	
F-3	Only obtain valid English sentences in plain text	High	UG-1	Success	
F-5	One keyword returns a set of matches containing words from the same word stem matches	High	UG-1	Success	Some searches did return an empty set as no matches were found in the scraped data.
F-6	One phrase re- turns a set of semantically similar matches	High	UG-1	Success	Some searches did return an empty set as no matches were found in the scraped data.
F-8	Each match contains the origin URL	High	UG-1	Success	
F-9	Separate context per user	High	UG-1	Success	
F-10	Results are reduced by additional keywords	Low	UG-1	Failure	It turned out that in practice the amount of results is manageable and doesn't require further filtering

6.2   Performance

The performance evaluation was conducted to address the second research question and involves comparing two solutions that are identical, with one using FBP through *Luigi* and the other using traditional Python with async and Graphics Processing Unit (GPU) utilities. To compare the worst, average, and best-case scenarios, we profiled both solutions by sending requests with the maximum, medium, and minimum amount of accepted data.

This process was repeated 10 times for each scenario under identical conditions. We used an AWS Elastic Compute Cloud (EC2) instance of type *g3.4xlarge* with an NVIDIA Tesla M60 GPU and 16 CPU cores. The scenarios involve testing each endpoint with and without the use of FBP. Figure 6 presents the average time in seconds for each group along with their corresponding standard deviation, which provides information about the variability of the results.

We can see that using traditional Python multiprocessing functionality performs better than the FBP-based approach and meets the maximum response time requirement (NF-5, Fig. 6). This could be due to the overhead introduced by *Luigi's* custom scheduler. This answers the second research question, even though it is not directly related as we were unable to integrate a GPU in our Elastic Kubernetes Service (EKS)-clusters, so we had to dismiss the reliability requirement stated in NF-10 (Table 4). Moreover, Python async demonstrates superior scalability when processing a growing number of websites. Additionally, the use of a GPU leads to significantly better scalability even with a limited number of websites.

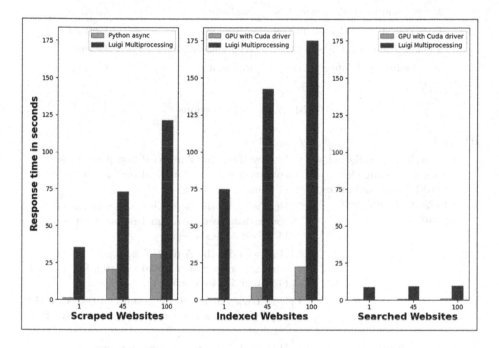

Fig. 6. Average performance comparison

6.3 Usability

To answer the third research question, we conducted a survey to evaluate the overall usability of the application. This survey was administered to a group of interns/apprentices at the organization (Table 6). The aim was to examine whether users could utilize the application effectively and obtain significant search outcomes without any explicit training.

Table 7 displays the list of tasks assigned to each participant along with the corresponding questions they were required to answer during the survey. Possible answers could reach from 1 to 5 including a free text field. Due to space limitations, we do not list all survey responses and only provide a summary discussion of the results. The average rating for Question 1.1 and 1.3 was 4.5, with a standard deviation of 0.5. Question 1.2 and 1.4 received an average rating of $4.1\overline{6}$ and a standard deviation of ≈ 0.69. These results indicate that some topics were more successful than others for most participants.

Table 6. Test group

ID	Field of Study	Degree Type	Semester	Location
1	Management and Informatics	Master	4	USA
2	Economics and Informatics	Master	1	Germany
3	Economics and Informatics	Bachelor	2	Germany
4	Economics and Informatics	Bachelor	2	Germany
5	IT-Managment Assistant	Apprenticeship	6	Germany
6	Computer Science	Bachelor	6	Germany

Table 7. Survey questions

ID	Task	ID	Question
1	Research three different topics once using the AutoNLP app and once using traditional web research.	1.1	How well did the AutoNLP app perform in comparison to your manual research for topic 1? (1 is bad 5 is excellent)
		1.2	How well did the AutoNLP app perform in comparison to your manual research for topic 2? (1 is bad 5 is excellent)
		1.3	How well did the AutoNLP app perform in comparison to your manual research for topic 3? (1 is bad 5 is excellent)
		1.4	How trustworthy are the results on the AutoNLP app? (Did the semantic search query match the results?)
2	Explore all functionality of the app.	2.1	How useful was the representation of the results in the AutoNLP app?
		2.2	How would you rate the user experience of the AutoNLP app?

The comments provided by the participants can be summarized as positive, indicating that they perceived the system as efficient in producing valuable search results and of high quality, often outperforming manual web research. The comments also indicated that the semantic similarity feature was generally accurate but in some cases missed a semantic similarity that could be found through manual research.

The usability section received similar results. Question 2.1 was rated at 4 on average and a standard deviation of ≈ 0.58. The overall user experience was rated at $4.\overline{6}$ on average with a standard deviation of ≈ 0.47. The users commented positively on the usability, stating that the process was smooth and the usage was intuitive without the need for training or explanation of the UI. Additionally, users found that the system's interface was clean and easy to navigate, and preferred it over the user interfaces of common search engines.

One user commented that for large searches, which include around 100 websites, the waiting time of approximately 35 s is too long. This left the user in doubt as to whether something was wrong before the results were finally displayed. Overall, the feedback was very positive and the usability test was successful.

7 Conclusion and Future Work

This paper presented an automated market research system architecture based on the FBP programming paradigm. The system offers various search modes to users, including stem-based and semantic search. The design of the system was developed based on specific requirements and underwent comprehensive evaluation. The evaluation specifically addressed three research questions formulated in Sect. 1. We addressed the first research question by identifying important design considerations for the architecture to meet the requirements, and then evaluated the system's runtime efficiency with and without using FBP (provided by the Python library *Luigi*), as stated in the second research question. Lastly, we conducted a user study to evaluate the system's usability, which answered the third research question by demonstrating that the system could be used without extensive training.

The used FBP library may have problems with scalable multiprocessing, but we still believe that the ease of development provided by this programming paradigm is valuable. We plan to improve the scalability and response times of the system by outsourcing the SBERT module to an autonomous and GPU-supporting AWS service, such as AWS SageMaker, while still using *Luigi* for FBP. The remaining application logic will be deployed via AWS EKS to make it scalable based on the workload.

As part of our efforts to improve the user experience, we plan to display the progress of the data-flow pipeline in the user interface during loading periods, when the user is waiting for the indexing or scraping to complete. By doing so, we aim to provide more transparency and insight into the cause of the waiting periods, which can last up to 40 s. This approach is in response to the feedback we received as part of our user survey.

References

1. Amazon: Boto3 - the aws sdk for python. https://pypi.org/project/boto3/
2. Amazon Web Services, I.: Designed-for availability for select aws services (2023). https://docs.aws.amazon.com/wellarchitected/latest/reliability-pillar/appendix-a-designed-for-availability-for-select-aws-services.html

3. Balzert, H.: Lehrbuch der Softwaretechnik: Basiskonzepte und Requirements Egineering. Spektrum (2009)
4. Brown, D.: Rank-bm25: A two line search engine. https://pypi.org/project/rank-bm25
5. Brown, T.B., et al.: Language models are few-shot learners. CoRR abs/2005.14165 (2020). https://arxiv.org/abs/2005.14165
6. Chowdhary, K.R.: Software-hardware evolution and birth of multicore processors. CoRR abs/2112.06436 (2021). https://arxiv.org/abs/2112.06436
7. Devlin, J., Chang, M., Lee, K., Toutanova, K.: BERT: pre-training of deep bidirectional transformers for language understanding. CoRR abs/1810.04805 (2018). http://arxiv.org/abs/1810.04805
8. Dosovitskiy, A., et al n image is worth 16×16 words: transformers for image recognition at scale. CoRR abs/2010.11929 (2020). https://arxiv.org/abs/2010.11929
9. Hofstätter, S., Lin, S.C., Yang, J.H., Lin, J., Hanbury, A.: Efficiently teaching an effective dense retriever with balanced topic aware sampling. In: Proceedings of SIGIR (2021)
10. Loper, E., Bird, S.: Nltk: The natural language toolkit (2002). https://www.nltk.org/
11. Morrison, J.P.: Flow-based Programming everything flows. https://jpaulm.github.io/fbp
12. Morrison, J.: Flow-based programming: a new approach to application development. J.P. Morrison Enterprises (2010). https://books.google.de/books?id=R06TSQAACAAJ
13. Porter, M.F.: An algorithm for suffix stripping. Program **14**(3), 130–137 (1980)
14. Porter, M.F.: Snowball: a language for stemming algorithms, vol. 11, no. 03, p. 15 (2001), http://snowball.tartarus.org/texts/introduction.html
15. Reimers, N., Gurevych, I.: Sentence-bert: sentence embeddings using siamese bert-networks. CoRR abs/1908.10084 (2019). http://arxiv.org/abs/1908.10084
16. Richardson, L.: Beautiful soup documentation. https://pypi.org/project/beautifulsoup4
17. Robertson, S., Zaragoza, H.: The probabilistic relevance framework: Bm25 and beyond. Found. Trends Inf. Retr. **3**, 333–389 (2009). https://doi.org/10.1561/1500000019
18. Ronacher, A.: Flask. https://pypi.org/project/Flask
19. Guido van Rossum, Yury Selivanov, V.S.: Asynchronous i/o (2013). https://pypi.org/project/asyncio/
20. Spotify: Luigi. https://pypi.org/project/luigi
21. Tröger, P.: The multi-core era - trends and challenges. CoRR abs/0810.5439 (2008). http://arxiv.org/abs/0810.5439
22. Vaswani, A., et al.: Attention is all you need. CoRR abs/1706.03762 (2017). http://arxiv.org/abs/1706.03762
23. Verma, P., Berger, J.: Audio transformers: transformer architectures for large scale audio understanding. adieu convolutions. CoRR abs/2105.00335 (2021). https://arxiv.org/abs/2105.00335

Impact of Data Augmentation on Hate Speech Detection

Hanan A. Batarfi$^{(\boxtimes)}$, Olaa A. Alsaedi, Arwa M. Wali, and Amani T. Jamal

King Abdulaziz University, Jeddah, Kingdom of Saudi Arabia
htarfi@stu.kau.edu.sa, {oaalsaedi,amwali,atjamal}@kau.edu.sa

Abstract. With the increase of social media platforms such as Facebook, Twitter, and YouTube, individuals from diverse cultures and societal backgrounds can communicate and express their viewpoints on several aspects of daily life. However, due to the differences in these cultures, along with the freedom of expression, hateful and offensive speech has increased and spread on these platforms. The detection of hate speech has significantly increased the interest of researchers in natural language processing (NLP). The OSACT5 shared task provides a new dataset that aims to detect the offensive language in addition to identifying the type of hate speech on Arabic social media. However, the available dataset is unbalanced, which leads to low performance, especially in the F1 score. Therefore, in this paper, we focused on overcoming such a problem by augmenting the text data. We fine-tuned and evaluated various pre-trained deep learning models in addition to augmenting the data to achieve the best performance. We observed that data augmentation increases the F1 score. After fine-tuning the QARiB model and augmenting the data we achieved the best F1 score of 0.49.

Keywords: Hate speech detection · Data augmentation · Class imbalance · Text classification

1 Introduction

Social media is a common platform for easy and quick communication between people, expressing their views, and sharing ideas.

People use different social media platforms such as Twitter, Facebook, YouTube, etc. The Arabic language is the formal language talked by two billion people worldwide [1]. In the Arab region, the use of social media platforms is increasing. 90% of the population in some Arab countries use social media, according to the Arab social media report [2].

There is public concern about existing activities in social media resulting from an increase in usage and openness in speech. Such platforms give users the freedom to express their thoughts, opinions, and beliefs, and share information without any constraint or control. However, not all the content posted by people is good and safe. It can be obscene, offensive, or hateful. One of the most offensive speeches that have recently been spread on social media sites is hate speech [3].

U. R. Krieger et al. (Eds.): I4CS 2023, CCIS 1876, pp. 187–199, 2023.
https://doi.org/10.1007/978-3-031-40852-6_10

Hate speech can be defined as "language that attacks or diminishes, that incites violence or hate against groups, based on specific characteristics such as physical appearance, religion, descent, national or ethnic origin, sexual orientation, gender identity or other, and it can occur with different linguistic styles, even in subtle forms or when humor is used" [4]. The diversity of individuals and their context cultures and views can also boost the presence of hate speech [5].

Hate speech can cause significant harm to targeted victims and create a feeling of fear and rejection in their communities. Beyond the physical harm that hate speech causes, it also toxifies public discourse and may create tensions between groups of people. Moreover, it can lead to actual hate crimes [6]. Early detection of content that contains hate speech can attempt to prevent this damage and create online environments that are free of hate and racism.

There are vast amounts of posts and comments sent every second on social media sites that make it difficult to control or trace the content of such a platform. Thus, social media face a challenge in restricting these posts while balancing freedom of speech and expression [7].

In the last decade, because of the growing prevalence of offensive and hateful content on social networking platforms, the systematic detection of hate speech and offensive language has drawn the attention of many researchers. Most social media platforms, such as YouTube, Twitter, and Facebook, have policies against hate speech to prevent any content that targets individuals or groups based on specific characteristics, including gender, religion, ethnicity, race, or nationality [4]. "Although technological progress has been made, the task of filtering hate speech remains predominantly reliant on users' reporting of inappropriate behavior and the monitoring efforts of moderators" should be corrected to "Although technological progress has been made, the task of filtering hate speech remains largely dependent on users reporting inappropriate behavior and the monitoring efforts of moderators" [8]. Controlling a huge amount of content manually on social media is a difficult task. As a result, numerous academic studies on hate speech detection have been conducted, and several workshops and competitions such as HateEval 2019 [9], OffensEval 2020 [10] and OSACT5 [11] have clearly emphasized the importance of this subject.

The Arabic language adds more difficulties for hate speech detection because it is a rich and complex language with different dialects used in every country. Moreover, users of social media often do not follow the rules of grammar and spelling, which further complicates the detection process [12].

There have been some studies on automatically detecting Arabic hate speech, obscene content, and offensive language. The techniques that are employed in these studies use semantic and syntactic features, which are linguistic features utilize to represent the meaning and grammar of words/sentences, and machine learning models that automatically learn from data to make predictions or decisions. Some of these techniques also apply deep learning, which is a type of machine learning models that learns hierarchical representations of data, and most recently, pre-trained models, as deep learning models that are already trained on large datasets and can be used as a starting point for new tasks [13].

The importance of this paper is to address the phenomenon of online hate speech in the Arab region on social media and achieve good performance in fine-grained classification of hate speech to understand the big picture of this phenomenon in social media. Automatic detection of hate speech can reduce harm against individuals and groups and improve the health of online conversations. The majority of previous studies have framed this issue as a binary classification task. However, binary classifications of hate speech are notoriously unreliable [14]. As a result, researchers used a more complex annotation schema to collect higher-quality HS datasets.

In this paper, we used the Arabic dataset provided by the OSCAT5 shared task [15] to improve the performance of fine-grained HS detection by using pre-trained models and data augmentation, which is a technique to increase the size and diversity of training data.

The paper is structured as follows. Section 2 presents related work. A description of the OSACT Fine-Grained Hate Speech Detection Dataset is provided in Sect. 3. Section 4 describes the methodology. In Sect. 5, the results and discussion are presented. Finally, the conclusion is presented in Sect. 6.

2 Related Work

In this section, we discuss previous research that addresses the problem of identifying types of hate speech in Arabic tweets. We categorize papers into deep learning, pre-trained models, and data augmentation.

2.1 Machine and Deep Learning Models

Ousidhoum et al. [16] offered a multilingual dataset for detecting hate speech in Arabic, English, and French on Twitter. The dataset was annotated to five distinct emotion- and toxicity-related aspects: (directness, hostility, target, group, and an annotator's sentiment towards the content. Some data preprocessing techniques were performed on the dataset such as deleting spam tweets, remove emojis and unreadable characters. The deep learning models (biLSTM) perform better than Logistic regression (LR) models with BOW as a feature. For Target Attribute the best Performance achieved for Arabic was F1=56%.

Alsafari et al. [8] the authors have considered the problem of detection of Arabic hate and offensive speech on a dataset from Twitter. They collected 5340 tweets in the Gulf Arabic dialect, and it consists of four classes of hate: nationality, religion, gender, and ethnicity. They performed different machine and Deep learning techniques such as NB, SVM, LR, CNN, LSTM, and GRU to do three different separated classifications tasks, Task 1: classify tweets to (clean or offensive/hate), Task 2: classify tweets to (clean, offensive, or hate), Task 3, classify tweets to (offensive, gender hate, religious hate, ethnicity hate, nationality hate, or clean). For extraction techniques, they used different techniques like (Word/Char-n-grams, Word Embedding, Random Embedding, AraVec (cbow/skip-gram), FastText, and Multilingual Bert (mBert)). For machine learning algorithms, SVM achieved the highest F1-macro for all tasks, Tasks 1 and Task 3 get 85.16%, and 66.86% respectively, with Word/Char-n-grams, while Task 2 getting 73.11% using char-n-grams. For deep neural networks, the highest score was achieved using CNN with mBert over the three prediction tasks, with 87.05%, 78.99%, and 75.51% respectively.

The authors in [17] have considered the problem of Arabic hate speech detection. For this task, a dataset consisting of 11,000 tweets was collected using hashtags. The dataset was labeled into five classes (not hate, racism hate, sexism hate, religious hate, and general hate speech). For text representation, word embedding was used. Different deep learning models such as LTSM, GRU, CNN + GRU, and CNN + LTSM, were used for classification. The highest level of performance was obtained by adding layers of CNN to LTSM with precision, recall, and F1 scores of 72%, 75%, and 73%, respectively.

Alsafari et al. [18] perform additional experiments using different single classifiers of BiLSTM and CNN with word embedding: FastText, AraBert, and MBert. Then different ensemble models of BiLSTMs and CNNs were implemented. The performance of ensemble models outperforms the single models with F1 =91.12% for task1, 84.01% for task2, and 80.23% for task3.

2.2 Pre-trained Models

AlKhamissi and Diab [19] proposed an AraHS model that is an ensemble of models that employs the self-consistency correction method and multitask learning for Arabic Fine-Grained Hate Speech Detection. They used the dataset provided by OSACT5 [15].

Bennessir et al. [20] used a dataset provided by [15] and proposed a model consisting of two layers to detect hate speech on Arabic Twitter: a shared layer containing pretraining models such as AraBERT, MARBERT, and ARBERT, as well as task-specific layers for each subtask, which were fine-tuned through Quasi-recurrent neural networks (QRNN). They showed that Multi-Tasking could get good results in detecting Hate speech by fine-tuning the pre-trained model MARBERT with QRNN.

2.3 Data Augmentation

Data augmentation (DA) is a technique for increasing the variety of training data without collecting new data explicitly. Most solutions enhance existing data with slightly modified copies or create synthetic data, with the objective of utilizing the augmented data as a regularizer to alleviate overfitting in the process of training machine learning models.

In the following, we mention some studies that used data augmentation to increase datasets for offensive and hate speech detection.

Makram et al. [21] overcame the problem of class imbalance in offensive tweet detection and hate speech detection by data augmentation using a contextual word embedding technique (MARBERT).

Alzu'bi et al. [22] used two data Augmentation techniques to increase data in the offensive dataset: Semi-Supervised Learning by fine-tuning AraBERTv0.2-Twitter-base to classify a large collection of tweets extracted from external sources. Also, Contextual Augmentation using AraBERTv0.2-Twitter-base to find a word that has a semantically similar meaning suitable for augmentation.

3 Datasets

We used the dataset provided by [15]. It is about 13k Arabic tweets that vary between Dialectal Arabic (DA) and Modern Standard Arabic (MSA). It is collected using emojis that are frequently used in offensive communications. It is the most comprehensive dataset of annotated Arabic tweets that is impartial toward particular dialects or topics [15]. The dataset was split into three sections: 70% of data was for training, 10% was for development (Dev.), and 20% was for testing. The dataset was labeled for three different tasks: offensiveness detection, hate speech detection, and hate speech type. For hate speech type detection, the dataset was labeled into: Gender, Race, Ideology, Religion, Social Class, Disability, and not hate. On the tweets, some preprocessing steps were applied like replacing URLs with "URL", empty lines with $< LF >$, and the mentions of the user with @USER. The classes in this dataset are very unbalanced, which is one of its limitations. Also, the training set does not contain the Disability class. There are just three tweets that fall under this class, and they are only found in the test and validation dataset. The dataset's statistics are presented in Table 1.

Table 1. Dataset statistics

Type	Train	Development	Test	Total
Normal	5715	865	1654	8234
Offensive	3172	404	877	4453
Gender Hate	456	52	133	641
Race Hate	260	28	78	366
Ideology Hate	144	14	32	190
Social Class Hate	72	10	19	101
Religious Hate	27	4	7	38
Disability Hate	0	1	2	3

4 Methodology

Within this section, we present a discussion of the preprocessing steps applied to the dataset, the Data Augmentation techniques utilized, a general overview of the pre-trained models utilized, and a system overview.

4.1 Dataset Preprocessing

Several preprocessing steps were applied to tweets such as:

- Remove all non-Arabic characters: such as URLs, users' mentions, numbers, $< LF >$, and English letters.
  ex: (RT @USER لاء ان شاء الله تبقى كويسة وتستقرى على حل قريب URL) to (لاء ان شاء الله تبقي كويسه وتستقري علي حل قريب) ("No, God willing, you will be fine and get a solution soon")
- Remove punctuation, emoji. ex: (يوم للنسيان والله 🌷 .) to (يوم للنسيان والله) ("A day to forget, God")
- Remove repetition of characters and extra white space.
  ex: (ليبيبيبيبيه هالانقلاب فجأة عليه) to (ليه هالانقلاب فجاه عليه) ("Why is this coup suddenly on him")
- Normalization of Arabic letters: such replace (أ ، إ ، آ) with (ا), (ة) with (ه), (ى) with (ي).
  ex: (إن بعد العسر يسرآ) to (ان بعد العسر يسرا) ("After hardship, there is ease") (مارحت لمحاضره الصباح) to (مارحت لمحاضرة الصباح) ("I didn't go to the morning lecture") (يكفي الله يرضي عليك) to (يكفي الله يرضى عليك) ("That's enough, may God bless you")

Examples of text before and after the preprocessing step are shown in Table 2.

Table 2. Examples of tweets before and after pre-processing

Before Pre-processing	After Pre-processing	Translation
@USER ردينا ع التطنز 😊 😊	ردينا ع التطنز	we back to mockery
وصارت فطاير البقالات غذاء صحي	وصارت فطاير البقالات غذاء صحي URL	Grocery store pies became a healthy food

4.2 Data Augmentation

We employed two widely-used natural language processing techniques to increase the number of tweets in hate speech classes: back translation and synonym replacement. We excluded the hate disability class from the data augmentation process due to the lack of instances related to disability in the training dataset. Numbers of Train datasets before and after Data Augmentation are shown in Table 3.

Back Translation: The Google Translate API is utilized to translate the text from Arabic to English and then back to Arabic.

Examples of Back Translation:

- **Best cases:**
  The original text is (مو وقت الحراره) ("It's not the time for heat").
  The augmented text is (ليس وقت الحرارة) ("It's not the time for heat").
- **Worst cases:**
  The original text is:

  وين التمر سيد الحلي وملك الفواكه الفاكهه والشوكلاته موجوده والتمر ما شفناه)

  (ليه تزعلوني

  ("Where is the date, the master of sweets and the king of fruits? We have chocolate and fruit, but we haven't seen the date. Why are you making me sad").
  The augmented text is:

  أين التواريخ ، سيد المجوهرات وملك الفواكه والفواكه والشوكولاتة موجودة ،)

  (والتواريخ هي ما رأيناه؟

  ("Where are the dates, the master of jewels and the king of fruits, fruits, and chocolates, and the dates are what we saw?").
  In the given example, the word'date' has two different meanings in English. In the first sentence,'date' refers to a type of fruit, while in the second sentence,'date' refers to a period of time, which alters the meaning of the sentence.

Synonym Replacement: We used an NLPAug Library to do a synonym replacement of text. To find synonyms for words, contextual embeddings like AraBERTv0.2-Twitter-base [23] were used. The percentage of word augmented was 0.2.

Examples of Synonym Replacement:

- **Best cases:**
  The original text is (نحن في زمن كثر فيه الخفيفون و الخفيفات مثيرين للاشمئزاز)
  ("We live in a time where there are many indecent and disgusting men and women").
  The augmented text is
  (للاشمئزاز نحن ف عالم زاد فيه الخفيفون والذين صاروا مثيرين) ("We live in a world
  where there is an increase in indecent and disgusting men and women").
- **Worst cases:**

- Example 1:
  The original text is (خلاص شقيت عجله التنمية وارتحنا) ("enough, I broke the wheel of development, and we rested").
  The augmented text is (كتاب فهمنا به الحياة وارتحنا) ("A book by which we understood life and relaxed").
- Example 2
  The original text is (شذا القرف يلي يكتب) ("What is this shit that writes").
  The augmented text is (شذا الجمال يلي بالسعودية) ("What a beauty in Saudi Arabia").

In these examples, the meaning of the augmented text is very different from the original text.

Table 3. Numbers of Train datasets before and after data augmentation

Class	# Tweets Before DA	# Tweets After DA	% of Augmentation
Not Hate	7634	7634	0%
Gender Hate	437	637	45.8%
Race Hate	251	551	119.5%
Ideology Hate	139	439	215.8%
Social Class Hate	69	469	579.7%
Religious Hate	27	477	1666.6%
Disability Hate	0	0	0%
Total	8557	10207	

4.3   Pre-trained Models

Arabic BERT models performed better than machine-learning models in a variety of natural language processing tasks, which include Arabic text classification [24].

Because the dataset we work on is a collection of tweets for that we selected pre-trained models that were trained using Twitter data with a variety of dialects. To achieve the best results, various pre-trained models were used. Based on [24], the highest-performing models are MARBERT, QARiB, ARBERT, AraBERT, and ArabicBERT.

Following is an overview of the models that were utilized.

- AraBERTv0.2-Twitter-large [23] is a new model for Arabic dialects and tweets, trained on about 60M Arabic tweets. Emojis have been added to the new model's vocabulary, along with common words that were not previously present.
- MARBERTv2 [25] It had been pre-trained on vast amounts of Twitter data, that contains at least 3 Arabic words. 1 billion tweets in both MSA and various Arabic dialects were used to train it. The dataset contains 128GB of text (15.6B tokens), this makes it the largest pretraining corpus of the Arabic models [24]. MARBERTv2's architecture is the same as that of BERT-base [26] with 163M parameters.
- QARiB [27] model is an abbreviation for "QCRI Arabic and Dialectal BERT," developed by the Qatar Computing Research Institute (QCRI) for Arabic natural language processing. Was trained in MSA and different Arabic dialects using 180 million text sentences and 420 million tweets. The Twitter API was used to collect the tweets' data while text data was collected via a combination of Arabic Corpus provided by the Abulkhair [28], OPUS [29], and Arabic GigaWord. The model is a variant of BERT [26] with 110M parameters, 12 attention heads, 768 hidden sizes, and 12 encoder layers.

4.4   System Overview

To fine-tune our BERT-Based Models, we use the Huggingface library [30]. The model was trained with a total of four epochs with a learning rate of 2e-5, and AdamW was used as an optimizer, and a batch size of 16 as recommended by bert authors [26] and cross-entropy for the loss functions. The tokenizer uses 512 maximum-length tokens to encode the input text.

5   Results and Discussion

5.1   Performance Evaluation

To evaluate the model's performance and analyze its effectiveness, we used a variety of metrics. In addition to accuracy, we calculated macro recall, precision, and F1-score. The F1-score is the best evaluation measure to assess the model due to the data imbalance. We also used a confusion matrix.

- Accuracy: This is the proportion of correctly classified tweets, both hate and non-hate, out of the total number of tweets that were classified by the model, regardless of whether they were classified correctly or incorrectly. The equation is as follows:

$$Accuracy = (TP + TN)/(TP + TN + FN + FP) \tag{1}$$

- Recall: This is the percentage of tweets that are successfully classified as hate. The equation for recall is:

$$Recall = (TP)/(TP + FN) \tag{2}$$

- Precision: This metric measures the proportion of correctly classified hate tweets out of the total number of tweets classified as hate. The equation for precision is as follows:

$$Precision = TP/(TP + FP) \qquad (3)$$

- F1 Score: This is a metric for the harmonic mean of recall and precision. The equation for F1-score is as follows:

$$F1Score = 2 * ((Precision * Recall))/((Precision + Recall)) \qquad (4)$$

5.2 Experimental Results

The results of the models before and after Data Augmentation are shown in Table 4. The confusion matrix is shown in Fig. 1.

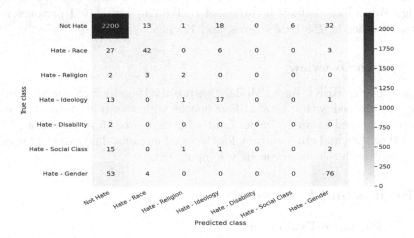

Fig. 1. Confusion matrix

In this work, we used different models - AraBERTv0.2-Twitter-large, MAR-BERTv2, and QARiB - to identify hate speech. The QARiB model produced the best results based on the F1-score. However, due to the data imbalance, the macro-averaged F1 score was low. Most of the tweets were labeled as "Not Hate Speech," with a total of 7,928 out of 8,887. Additionally, there were significant differences in class proportions, particularly in classes of hate speech. Table 4 illustrates that there were only 27 tweets of religious hate speech against 456 tweets of gender hate speech. Furthermore, there were no tweets containing hate speech based on disability in the training data.

To address the issue of imbalanced data, we attempted to use data augmentation techniques, such as back translation and synonym replacement, on the tweets. As a result, the performance of the F1 score increased.

Table 4. Results on the test dataset without data augmentation

Models	Accuracy	Precision	Recall	F1-Score
MARBERTv2	0.92	0.36	0.40	0.38
AraBERT Large-Twitter	0.89	0.13	0.14	0.13
QARiB	0.92	0.44	0.41	0.42
After Data Augmentation				
MARBERTv2	0.92	0.44	0.41	0.42
AraBERT Large-Twitter	0.92	0.50	0.44	0.47
QARiB	0.92	0.55	0.45	0.49

6 Conclusion

Hate speech is a global issue that many organizations and countries are working to combat. With the proliferation of the internet and online social media platforms, the propagation of hate speech has become easier against individuals or groups. The significant increase in harmful content has led researchers to rely on automated techniques to identify and classify such content.

The OSACT-2022 dataset had an imbalance issue that led to a low F1 score. In this paper, we demonstrated how data augmentation techniques could improve the performance of hate speech type detection. We tried three different models and found that the QARiB model produced the best results. The proposed model was evaluated on the dataset provided by [15] for the OSACT-2022 Shared challenges. After data augmentation, the Macro F1-score achieved on the test dataset was 0.49.

In future work, we plan to explore additional techniques, such as random insertion and random swap, to determine the most appropriate technique considering the subtleties of the Arabic language. Additionally, We plan to address the potential loss of meaning that may occur during the back translation process. Furthermore, we plan to investigate the effectiveness of synonym replacement while taking into account the context-sensitive nature of natural languages. These efforts will help us refine our approach and enhance the effectiveness of our model for Arabic language processing tasks.

References

1. Aljarah, I., et al.: Intelligent detection of hate speech in Arabic social network: a machine learning approach. J. Inf. Sci. 0165551520917651 (2020)
2. Salem, F.: Social media and the internet of things towards data-driven policymaking in the arab world: potential, limits and concerns. In: The Arab Social Media Report, p. 7. MBR School of Government, Dubai (2017)
3. Alrehili, A.: Automatic hate speech detection on social media: a brief survey. In: 2019 IEEE/ACS 16th International Conference on Computer Systems and Applications (AICCSA), pp. 1–6. IEEE (2019)

4. Fortuna, P., Nunes, S.: A survey on automatic detection of hate speech in text. ACM Comput. Surv. (CSUR) **51**(4), 1–30 (2018)
5. Watanabe, H., Bouazizi, M., Ohtsuki, T.: Hate speech on twitter: a pragmatic approach to collect hateful and offensive expressions and perform hate speech detection. IEEE Access **6**, 13825–13835 (2018)
6. Müller, K., Schwarz, C.: Fanning the flames of hate: social media and hate crime. In: Report, Competitive Advantage in the Global Economy (CAGE) (2018)
7. Waseem, Z., Hovy, D.: Hateful symbols or hateful people? predictive features for hate speech detection on twitter. In: Proceedings of the NAACL Student Research Workshop, pp. 88–93 (2016)
8. Alsafari, S., Sadaoui, S., Mouhoub, M.: Hate and offensive speech detection on Arabic social media. Online Soc. Netw. Media **19**, 100096 (2020)
9. Basile, V., et al.: Semeval-2019 task 5: multilingual detection of hate speech against immigrants and women in twitter. In: Proceedings of the 13th International Workshop on Semantic Evaluation, pp. 54–63 (2019)
10. Zampieri, M., et al.: Semeval-2020 task 12: multilingual offensive language identification in social media (offenseval 2020). arXiv preprint arXiv:2006.07235 (2020)
11. Mubarak, H., Al-Khalifa, H., Al-Thubaity, A.: Overview of osact5 shared task on Arabic offensive language and hate speech detection. In: Proceedings of the 5th Workshop on Open-Source Arabic Corpora and Processing Tools with Shared Tasks on Qur'an QA and Fine-Grained Hate Speech Detection, pp. 162–166 (2022)
12. Al-Hassan, A., Al-Dossari, H.: Detection of hate speech in social networks: a survey on multilingual corpus. In: 6th International Conference on Computer Science and Information Technology, vol. 10, pp. 10–5121 (2019)
13. Mansur, Z., Omar, N., Tiun, S.: Twitter hate speech detection: a systematic review of methods, taxonomy analysis, challenges, and opportunities. IEEE Access (2023)
14. Sanguinetti, M., Poletto, F., Bosco, C., Patti, V., Stranisci, M.: An Italian twitter corpus of hate speech against immigrants. In: Proceedings of the Eleventh International Conference on Language Resources and Evaluation (LREC 2018) (2018)
15. Mubarak, H., Hassan, S., Absar Chowdhury, S.: Emojis as anchors to detect Arabic offensive language and hate speech. arXiv preprint arXiv:2201.06723 (2022)
16. Ousidhoum, N., Lin, Z., Zhang, H., Song, Y., Yeung, D.-Y.: Multilingual and multi-aspect hate speech analysis. arXiv preprint arXiv:1908.11049 (2019)
17. Al-Hassan, A., Al-Dossari, H.: Detection of hate speech in Arabic tweets using deep learning. Multim. Syst. 1–12 (2021)
18. Alsafari, S., Sadaoui, S., Mouhoub, M.: Deep learning ensembles for hate speech detection. In: 2020 IEEE 32nd International Conference on Tools with Artificial Intelligence (ICTAI), pp. 526–531. IEEE (2020)
19. AlKhamissi, B., Diab, M.: Meta AI at Arabic hate speech 2022: multitask learning with self-correction for hate speech classification. arXiv preprint arXiv:2205.07960 (2022)
20. Bennessir, M.A., Rhouma, M., Haddad, H., Fourati, C.: Icompass at Arabic hate speech 2022: detect hate speech using GRNN and transformers. In: Proceedings of the 5th Workshop on Open-Source Arabic Corpora and Processing Tools with Shared Tasks on Qur'an QA and Fine-Grained Hate Speech Detection, pp. 176–180 (2022)
21. Makram, K., et al.: Chillax-at Arabic hate speech 2022: a hybrid machine learning and transformers based model to detect Arabic offensive and hate speech. In: Proceedings of the 5th Workshop on Open-Source Arabic Corpora and Processing Tools with Shared Tasks on Qur'an QA and Fine-Grained Hate Speech Detection, pp. 194–199 (2022)

22. Alzubi, S., Ferreira, T.C., Pavanelli, L., Al-Badrashiny, M.: Aixplain at Arabic hate speech 2022: an ensemble based approach to detecting offensive tweets. In: Proceedings of the 5th Workshop on Open-Source Arabic Corpora and Processing Tools with Shared Tasks on Qur'an QA and Fine-Grained Hate Speech Detection, pp. 214–217 (2022)

23. Antoun, W., Baly, F., Hajj, H.: Arabert: transformer-based model for Arabic language understanding. In: LREC 2020 Workshop Language Resources and Evaluation Conference 11–16 May 2020, p. 9 (2020)

24. Alammary, A.S.: Bert models for Arabic text classification: a systematic review. Appl. Sci. **12**(11), 5720 (2022)

25. Abdul-Mageed, M., Elmadany, A., Billah Nagoudi, E.M.: Arbert & marbert: deep bidirectional transformers for Arabic. arXiv preprint arXiv:2101.01785 (2020)

26. Devlin, J., Chang, M.-W., Lee, K., Toutanova, K.: Bert: pre-training of deep bidirectional transformers for language understanding. arXiv preprint arXiv:1810.04805 (2018)

27. Abdelali, A., Hassan, S., Mubarak, H., Darwish, K., Samih, Y.: Pre-training bert on Arabic tweets: practical considerations. arXiv preprint arXiv:2102.10684 (2021)

28. El-Khair, I.A.: 1.5 billion words Arabic corpus. arXiv preprint arXiv:1611.04033 (2016)

29. Lison, P., Tiedemann, J.: Opensubtitles 2016: extracting large parallel corpora from movie and tv subtitles (2016)

30. Wolf, T., et al.: Huggingface's transformers: state-of-the-art natural language processing. arXiv preprint arXiv:1910.03771 (2019)

Quantum Computing

Efficient Quantum Solution for the Constrained Tactical Capacity Problem for Distributed Electricity Generation

Stan G. van der Linde[1], Ward van der Schoot[1(✉)], and Frank Phillipson[1,2]

[1] The Netherlands Organisation for Applied Scientific Research,
The Hague, The Netherlands
ward.vanderschoot@tno.nl
[2] Maastricht University, Maastricht, The Netherlands

Abstract. With the transition to sustainable energy sources and devices, the demand for and supply of energy increases ever more. With energy grids struggling to keep up with this increase, we need to ensure that supply and demand are correctly matched. The Tactical Capacity Problem tackles this issue by choosing the optimal location of sustainable power sources to minimise the total energy loss. We extend an existing quantum approach of solving this problem in two ways. Firstly, we extend the problem to include capacity constraints, resulting in the Constrained Tactical Capacity Problem. Secondly, we propose two ways of optimising the performance of the resulting model via variable reduction. These optimisations are supported by numerical results obtained on both classical and quantum solvers.

Keywords: Distributed electricity generation · Tactical planning · Quantum computing · Quantum annealing

1 Introduction

Since the Kyoto Protocol in 1997 [20], governments and citizens have been incentivised to transition to sustainable sources of energy. Whilst this transition was slow at first, it has gained traction recently with many governments, organisations and individuals investing in sustainable power sources such as wind turbines, solar panels, photovoltaic cells, hydro-power stations and heat pumps. At the same time, organisations and individuals are transitioning to devices based on sustainable energy, such as electrical cars and cooking appliances. Altogether, this is posing large requirements on energy grids. With this increase, the call for an appropriate matching between demand and supply is growing louder each day. Current electricity networks are not built for such large amounts of energy, as can for example be seen in the Netherlands [24]. This hinders the full transition to sustainable power usage.

© The Author(s), under exclusive license to Springer Nature Switzerland AG 2023
U. R. Krieger et al. (Eds.): I4CS 2023, CCIS 1876, pp. 203–221, 2023.
https://doi.org/10.1007/978-3-031-40852-6_11

At the same time, these sustainable power sources are less reliable than traditional sources such as gas, oil and coal. This is due to their distributed and irregular nature. As an example, consider the case of solar panels. In sunny weather, solar panels can generate large amounts of power, easily satisfying the needs for a single household. In cloudy weather, however, the amount of power generated is much lower or could even be zero, resulting in large, often non-continuous fluctuations in the power generated per time instance. At the same time, the power generated can fluctuate per location, depending on where the sun has the highest intensity. These fluctuations in both time and location of these power sources often give a mismatch between demand and supply. To circumvent this, energy suppliers have to transfer large amounts of energy from one location to the other. As energy transport is not without losses, this results in large amounts of energy loss.

Various avenues have been explored to reduce this energy loss. Notable examples are adding sufficient storage capacity [10,16], reinforcing existing energy grids [1,6], controlling fluctuations by using smart grids [3,13,14] and managing the behaviour of citizens [5,19,27]. While all of them are valuable, they often fail to tackle this problem at its root, namely the matching of sustainable generators to where demand is highest. Tactical capacity management tries to achieve this exactly. The tactical capacity problem is the problem of choosing the location and type of these distributed generators in such a way that the total energy loss due to transport is minimised. This should take into account both total supply and demand, as well as the capacity of the energy grid.

In 2021, Phillipson and Chiscop [23] proposed an approach for tactical capacity management in the form of a Quadratic Unconstrained Binary Optimisation problem (QUBO), based on work by Croes et al. [2]. This is a general form for problems with binary variables and quadratic objective functions. These problems are known to be hard to solve on classical computers. That is why Phillipson and Chiscop consider a way of solving this QUBO on a new type of computing called quantum computing.

Quantum computing is an emerging computational field in which devices are utilised which are fundamentally different from classical computers. Because these quantum computers are founded on a different field of physics, they offer exponential advantages over classical computers for certain applications and problems. A notable field where quantum computers are expected to have a great advantage, is optimisation. Both the Quantum Approximate Optimisation Algorithm on gate-based quantum computers and quantum annealers are candidates for having advantages over classical algorithms and are active fields of research. Currently, quantum computers are still in development and are not capable to beat state-of-the-art classical solvers. However, quantum annealers are already being used in various practical applications [21,22,28,29] and it is expected that they will significantly outperform classical state-of-the-art at some point in the future. That is why it is important to consider their potential impact now already.

Phillipson and Chiscop show that a quantum annealer can be used to solve the problem of tactical capacity management. They consider the Tactical Capacity Problem for a local energy grid with a certain number of households. In this local grid, different distributed generators can be placed in each household. By considering supply and demand data only, they find allocations of these generators that minimise the total energy loss. They implement their solution on both quantum and classical solvers, showing that a full quantum approach performs worse than high-performing classical solvers such as Gurobi and Localsolver. However, a hybrid quantum-classical solver already outperforms both of them.

We extend this work in a couple of ways. Firstly, we add a capacity constraint to the problem which translates the capacity given by modern energy grids. Specifically, we introduce a capacity constraint to the total energy flowing to or from the local grid. This is becoming more and more relevant with the current energy grids failing to keep up with the increasing supply and demand. The resulting problem is called the *Constrained Tactical Capacity Problem*. Secondly, we show how to encode this constraint into the original QUBO objective function more efficiently than a naive method. We achieve this by carefully considering when certain constraints are of relevance. Lastly, we use a method from [26] to increase the performance of the resulting QUBO formulation even more. We evaluate the performance of the resulting QUBO formulations by solving them on both quantum and classical solvers.

This work is structured as follows. We start with a brief overview of Quantum Annealing and the QUBO formulation in Sect. 2. Afterwards, we present our theoretical results on the QUBO formulation of the Constrained Tactical Capacity Problem in Sect. 3. We implement these theoretical ideas in Sect. 4 by presenting the numerical results of the corresponding experiments. We finish with a discussion and outlook in Sect. 5.

2 Optimisation with Quantum Computing

In the world of quantum computing there exist a variety of fundamentally different computational paradigms. The three main paradigms are Gate-based, Adiabatic and Photonic Quantum Computing. The Quantum Annealing paradigm is closely related to the Adiabatic Quantum Computing paradigm and it is therefore useful to understand the Adiabatic Quantum Computing model first. The "adiabatic" in Adiabatic Quantum Computing is a reference to the adiabatic theorem of quantum mechanics [4]. The adiabatic theorem states that a system, initialised in the ground state, will remain in the ground state if a given perturbation is applied slow enough [8,18]. This principle lies at the heart of the Adiabatic Quantum Computing paradigm. First, a system with a simple Hamiltonian is prepared and initialised in the ground state. Next, the simple Hamiltonian is evolved adiabatically (slowly) to a Hamiltonian whose ground state describes the answer to the posed question. Because the evolution of the Hamiltonian happens adiabatically, the adiabatic theorem guarantees that the state after the evolution is the ground state of the final Hamiltonian.

2.1 Quantum Annealing

When Kadowaki and Nishimori [11] proposed Quantum Annealing, it was not designed with Adiabatic Quantum Computing in mind. Instead Quantum Annealing was a heuristic algorithm for solving discrete optimisation problems using properties of quantum mechanics, inspired by the traditional meta- heuristic Simulated Annealing approach [12]. Even though Quantum Annealing was not proposed with Adiabatic Quantum Computing in mind, it can been seen as a variation of Adiabatic Quantum Computing with two key differences [17]:

1. In the Quantum Annealing paradigm the final Hamiltonian represents a classical discrete optimisation problem (usually an NP-Hard problem).
2. Quantum Annealing does not assume that the entire computation takes places in the ground state, whereas this is required in Adiabatic Quantum Computing.

Since the problem we study in this paper is a discrete optimisation problem, we can turn to Quantum Annealing to find solutions. However, with Quantum Annealing there is no guarantee that the system remains in its ground state throughout the evolution, meaning that there is usually a non-zero probability that the final state is not the ground state. Therefore, a Quantum Annealing computation is always performed multiple times to increase the probability of finding the ground state of the final Hamiltonian.

The classical analogue of quantum annealing is called Simulated Annealing. It lends its name from the annealing process in metallurgy, in which materials are heated and cooled in a controlled manner to change its physical properties. Just like Quantum Annealing, Simulated Annealing can solve QUBOs, but it uses classical resources only. It works by searching the solution space, while slowly decreasing the probability of accepting worse solutions than the current solution. A more interested reader is referred to [9].

2.2 The D-Wave Implementation and QUBOs

To solve a problem with Quantum Annealing, a quantum annealing computer is needed. Different companies offer such quantum computers, with D-Wave being the most notorious of them. D-Wave implements Quantum Annealing by considering final Hamiltonians that can be described by Quadratic Unconstrained Binary Optimisation problems (QUBOs) [25]. The QUBO is defined by the following objective function:

$$E(\boldsymbol{x}) = \sum_{i=1}^{N} Q_{ii}x_i + \sum_{i=1}^{N}\sum_{j=i+1}^{N} Q_{ij}x_i x_j = \boldsymbol{x}^\mathsf{T} Q \boldsymbol{x}, \tag{1}$$

where $\boldsymbol{x} = \begin{bmatrix} x_1 \cdots x_N \end{bmatrix}^\mathsf{T} \in \{0,1\}^N$ is a vector of binary variables and Q_{ij} are real valued constants. Given a QUBO with a particular matrix Q, an associated Hamiltonian is produced. Using Quantum Annealing, the ground state of this Hamiltonian is found, which gives the solution to the QUBO. Therefore, describing a problem in the QUBO formalism yields a formulation suitable for the D-Wave Quantum Annealing hardware.

To solve a QUBO on the D-Wave quantum computers, the problem needs to be mapped to its hardware. This is done by mapping the binary variables of the QUBO to the qubits, which are the physical building blocks of the D-Wave hardware. Currently, quantum annealers have a limited number of qubits, which means that only a limited number of variables can be considered when solving a QUBO. That is why it is important to keep the number of variables in a QUBO formulation as small as possible. Equivalently, we say that the size of the QUBO needs to be small.

2.3 QUBO Formulation Techniques

The QUBO formulation might seem restrictive at first glance, but with standard reformulation techniques [7], many problems can be written as a QUBO, and often in different ways [15]. In this section we will discuss two important techniques that are described in this paper to transform a problem to a QUBO: (1) inclusion of constraints via penalty functions, and (2) binary encoding for integer variables.

Many real-word problems are not without constraints. However, the QUBO does initially not allow for constraints. To overcome this, the constraints are added to the QUBO objective with the use of a penalty function. More specifically, for an equality constraint

$$\sum_i a_i x_i = b, \tag{2}$$

where a_i and b are constants and x_i are binary variables, we can construct the corresponding penalty function:

$$P(\boldsymbol{x}) = \left(\sum_i a_i x_i - b\right)^2. \tag{3}$$

Note that $P(\boldsymbol{x}) = 0$ if and only if the constraint is met. Furthermore, $P(\boldsymbol{x}) > 0$ if the constraint is violated. Hence, if $\lambda P(\boldsymbol{x})$ is added to the objective of the QUBO, where λ is a sufficiently large positive constant, the minimum of the QUBO changes to comply with the constraint.

The second transformation technique from [15] is the binary encoding of integer variables. Many real word problems do not consider binary variables natively. Often, they consider integer variables instead. There are different ways to encode such variables using binary variables, but in this paper we focus on the log encoding of the variables. In the log encoding, for an integer variable $z \in \{0, 1, \ldots, z_{\max}\}$, there are $K = \lfloor \log_2(z_{\max}) \rfloor + 1$ binary variables required.

To use the encoding, we replace an integer variable with the following pseudo-Boolean function:

$$I(\boldsymbol{y}; z_{\max}) = \sum_{i=0}^{K-2} 2^i y_i + y_{K-1}(z_{\max} + 1 - 2^{K-1}), \qquad (4)$$

where $\boldsymbol{y} = [y_1 \cdots y_N]^{\mathsf{T}} \in \{0,1\}^N$ is a vector binary variables. Note that for any $z \in \{0, 1, \ldots, z_{\max}\}$, there exists at least one combination of y_i such that $I(\boldsymbol{y}; z_{\max}) = z$. In addition, for other values of z, no combination of y_i exists such that $I(\boldsymbol{y}; z_{\max}) = z$. Hence, this is a valid binary encoding of the integer z. In this context, the binary encoding is mostly used to reformulate inequality constraints into a QUBO term. For example, an inequality like $0 \leq C \leq b$ is equivalent to C being equal to some integer in $\{0, 1, \ldots, b\}$. Hence, an inequality constraint $\sum_i a_i x_i \leq b$ with all $a_i \geq 0$ can be rewritten as an equality constraint via $\sum_i a_i x_i = I(\boldsymbol{y}; b)$.

3   Distributed Energy Generation

In this paper we extend upon the Tactical Capacity Problem for distributed energy generation described in [23]. This problem describes where different types of distributed electricity generators should be placed within a neighbourhood to minimise energy loss. A high level model is drawn schematically in Fig. 1, showing a neighbourhood of houses, in which every two houses are connected. Each house has its own unique demand and (prospected) generation profile for each potential distributed generator.

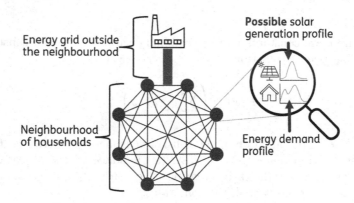

Fig. 1. Setup of the Tactical Capacity Problem. In the lower left, we see a neighbourhood of houses, which is assumed to be fully connected. Each house has a demand profile and a *prospected* energy generation profile. Furthermore, energy can be drawn from or offloaded to the grid outside the neighbourhood.

The neighbourhood is also connected to the energy grid outside the neighbourhood, to which it can draw or to which offload energy. Every time energy is transported there is energy loss. In this model it is assumed that there is no energy loss within a household, a small energy loss if the energy travels within the neighbourhood and a larger energy loss if the energy is drawn from or offloaded to the grid outside the neighbourhood. The Tactical Capacity Problem is to find the optimal locations for certain distributed energy generators, so that the amount of energy loss is minimised. This is done based on the demand and generation profiles.

3.1   Mathematical Formulation

The starting point for our extension is the mathematical description of the Tactical Capacity Problem proposed by Phillipson and Chiscop in [23]. They assume there are M types of possible energy generators, N houses in the neighbourhood and T different time intervals. The tactical capacity problem entails choosing which house gets which sort of generators so that the total energy loss from both energy transportation within the neighbourhood and import to or export from the neighbourhood is minimised over all time periods. We denote x_{ij} for the decision variable:

$$x_{ij} = \begin{cases} 1 & \text{if a generator of type } j \text{ is placed at house } i \text{ ,} \\ 0 & \text{otherwise.} \end{cases} \tag{5}$$

In addition, the problem is governed by a couple of parameters, namely:

1. $s_{ijt} \in \mathbb{Z}^+$: Amount of electricity a generator of type j placed at house i produces in a time period t. Note that these are non-negative integer values.
2. $d_{it} \in \mathbb{Z}^+$: Amount of energy house i demands during time period t. Note that these are non-negative integer values.
3. $p_n \in \mathbb{R}$: Transportation loss fraction from transporting energy within the neighbourhood.
4. $p_s \in \mathbb{R}$: Transportation loss fraction from transporting energy to or from the neighbourhood.

With these variables, the problem of minimising the total energy transportation loss can be written as a QUBO in the following way:

$$\min_{x \in \{0,1\}^{NM}} p_n \sum_{t=1}^{T} \sum_{i=1}^{N} \left(\sum_{j=1}^{M} s_{ijt} x_{ij} - d_{it} \right)^2 + p_s \sum_{t=1}^{T} \left(\sum_{i=1}^{N} \sum_{j=1}^{M} s_{ijt} x_{ij} - d_{it} \right)^2, \tag{6}$$

explained in detail in [23]. In (6), x is a binary vector containing all the decision variables x_{ij}. The objective function of (6) is denoted by $H(x)$.

3.2   Constrained Tactical Capacity Problem

In this work, we expand this problem by adding a constraint to the total energy flowing to or from the neighbourhood, which is a better representation of the real-world scenario. Phillipson and Chiscop show that the total energy flowing to or from the neighbourhood in a certain time period t is equal to $\sum_{i=1}^{N} \sum_{j=1}^{M} s_{ijt} x_{ij} - d_{it}$, with a negative value meaning energy is flowing into the neighbourhood. With the assumption that the wires going out of the neighbourhood have a maximum capacity of C for either incoming or outgoing energy, the following constraint can be obtained

$$\left| \sum_{i=1}^{N} \sum_{j=1}^{M} s_{ijt} x_{ij} - d_{it} \right| \leq C \tag{7}$$

at each time t. If we turn this constraint into a linear (equality) expression in terms of the x_{ij}, we can add it as a quadratic penalty term to the original Tactical Planning QUBO-formulation, hence yielding a QUBO-formulation for the Constrained Tactical Capacity Problem.

To accomplish this, we split up the original constraint into two separate inequalities, namely:

$$\sum_{i=1}^{N} \sum_{j=1}^{M} s_{ijt} x_{ij} - d_{it} \leq C \quad \forall t, \tag{8}$$

$$-\left(\sum_{i=1}^{N} \sum_{j=1}^{M} s_{ijt} x_{ij} - d_{it} \right) \leq C \quad \forall t. \tag{9}$$

These can naively be translated into a quadratic penalty term by consecutively using the binary encoding and inclusion of constraints techniques described in Sect. 2.3. Note, however, that this adds $2\lfloor \log_2(C) \rfloor + 2$ auxiliary variables for each time T.

3.3   Reducing the Number of Constraints

We propose a different solution, which drastically reduces the number of auxiliary variables in most practical scenarios. We do this by first considering whether a constraint can actually be broken or not. From a practical perspective, it makes sense that some constraints will never be violated.

Consider for example (8), which limits the energy production minus demand. In the case that the distributed generators are solar panels, supply will be very low in an early winter morning. At the same time, the energy demand is very high. Hence, this constraint is always met during this time period. A similar argument can be made for (9). During the nighttime the demand is usually very low. Therefore, it is unlikely that the total demand is higher than C.

For some time intervals t, one or both inequalities above will always be true, irrespective of the values x_{ij}. In such a case, we do not have to add any penalty terms to the QUBO. To show this, we first note that the energy production is always non-negative (i.e., $s_{ijt} \geq 0$ for all i, j, t). Hence, we have for each time t that

$$\sum_{i=1}^{N} \sum_{j=1}^{M} s_{ijt} x_{ij} - d_{it} \leq \sum_{i=1}^{N} \sum_{j=1}^{M} s_{ijt} - d_{it}. \tag{10}$$

Hence, we can drop (8) for a certain time interval t when we have $\sum_{i=1}^{N} \sum_{j=1}^{M} s_{ijt} - d_{it} \leq C$. Note furthermore that if $\sum_{i=1}^{N} \sum_{j=1}^{M} s_{ijt} - d_{it} < -C$, then there is no feasible solution. This corresponds to the case where the demand is too large for the grid to handle.

Similarly, we can find cases where we can drop (9). Because the s_{ijt} are non-negative, we have

$$- \left(\sum_{i=1}^{N} \sum_{j=1}^{M} s_{ijt} x_{ij} - d_{it} \right) \leq \sum_{i=1}^{N} d_{it}. \tag{11}$$

Therefore, when $\sum_{i=1}^{N} d_{it} \leq C$ we can drop (9).

In conclusion, the Constrained Tactical Capacity Problem can be written as

$$\min_{\boldsymbol{x} \in \{0,1\}^{NM}} p_n \sum_{i,t} \left(\sum_{j=1}^{M} s_{ijt} x_{ij} - d_{it} \right)^2 + p_s \sum_{t} \left(\sum_{i=1}^{N} \sum_{j=1}^{M} s_{ijt} x_{ij} - d_{it} \right)^2, \tag{12}$$

$$\text{s.t.} \sum_{i=1}^{N} \sum_{j=1}^{M} s_{ijt} x_{ij} - d_{it} \leq C, \text{ when } t \in T_{\text{up}}, \tag{13}$$

$$- \left(\sum_{i=1}^{N} \sum_{j=1}^{M} s_{ijt} x_{ij} - d_{it} \right) \leq C, \text{ when } t \in T_{\text{low}}, \tag{14}$$

where T_{up} is the set of all times such that $\sum_{i=1}^{N} \sum_{j=1}^{M} s_{ijt} - d_{it} > C$ and T_{low} is the set of all times such that $\sum_{i=1}^{N} d_{it} > C$. Note that $T_{\text{up}}, T_{\text{low}} \subset T$ and T_{up} and T_{low} are not necessarily disjoint. This problem can be transformed to a QUBO formulation by adding auxiliary variables in the same way as before.

We wish to include the constraint of (13) and (14) into the objective of the QUBO (12). Using the techniques described in Sect. 2.3, we produced the following corresponding penalty functions:

$$P_{\text{up}}(\boldsymbol{x}, \boldsymbol{y}) = \sum_{t \in T_{\text{up}}} \left(\sum_{i=1}^{N} \sum_{j=1}^{M} s_{ijt} x_{ij} - I(\boldsymbol{y}_t; C + \sum_{i=1}^{N} d_{it}) \right)^2, \tag{15}$$

$$P_{\text{low}}(\boldsymbol{x}, \boldsymbol{z}) = \sum_{t \in T_{\text{low}}} \left(\sum_{i=1}^{N} \sum_{j=1}^{M} s_{ijt}(1 - x_{ij}) - I(z_t, C + \sum_{i=1}^{N} \sum_{j=1}^{M} s_{ijt} - d_{it}) \right)^2. \tag{16}$$

The derivation of (15) and (16) can be found in Appendix A.

Further Reducing the Number of Auxiliary Variables. The number of auxiliary variables used for the constraints can be further reduced by using a technique proposed in [26]. It reduces the number of auxiliary variables by possibly sacrificing some of the solution quality. In this section, we will shortly discuss this trade-off between solution quality and problem size.

Consider a linear constraint

$$\sum_i a_i x_i \le b, \tag{17}$$

where a_i and b are positive integers and x_i are binary decision variables. Following the naive approach as above, this can be turned into a QUBO penalty term by adding $\lfloor \log_2 b \rfloor + 1$ auxiliary variables. The authors of [26] propose a scalar transformation by ρ in the inequality shown in (17) to obtain

$$\sum_i \frac{a_i}{\rho} x \le \frac{b}{\rho}. \tag{18}$$

Note that $\rho = 1$ gives back the original inequality constraint. Again by the same approach as before, this can be transformed into a QUBO penalty constraint by adding $\left\lfloor \log_2 \frac{b}{\rho} \right\rfloor + 1$ auxiliary variables.

With this scalar multiplication, we reduce the number of auxiliary variables by approximately $\log(\rho)$, but this transformation is not "free". The inequality in (18) may contain fractional coefficients. This means that for some possible choices of x, the inequality in (18) holds, while the penalty term in the QUBO does not equal zero, as $a_i x / \rho$ or b/ρ are not necessarily integer valued. This potentially results in some loss of solution quality. The proposers of this technique ran tests to gauge this loss of quality. Even though these tests only ran for specific instances, the loss of performance was quite minimal on average.

For the model proposed in this paper, this would mean that the penalty functions P_{up} and P_{low} could be changed in the following way:

$$P_{\text{up}}(\boldsymbol{x}, \boldsymbol{y}; \rho) = \sum_{t \in T_{\text{up}}} \left(\sum_{i=1}^{N} \sum_{j=1}^{M} \frac{s_{ijt}}{\rho} x_{ij} - I(\boldsymbol{y}_t; \frac{C}{\rho} + \sum_{i=1}^{N} \frac{d_{it}}{\rho}) \right)^2, \tag{19}$$

$$P_{\text{low}}(\boldsymbol{x}, \boldsymbol{z}; \rho) = \sum_{t \in T_{\text{low}}} \left(\sum_{i=1}^{N} \sum_{j=1}^{M} \frac{s_{ijt}}{\rho} (1 - x_{ij}) - I(\boldsymbol{z}_t, \frac{C}{\rho} + \sum_{i=1}^{N} \sum_{j=1}^{M} \frac{s_{ijt} - d_{it}}{\rho}) \right)^2. \tag{20}$$

In the numerical results, instances will be run both with and without this variable reduction, to compare the performance and number of auxiliary variables for both instances.

3.4   Resulting QUBO

Combining the original objective $H(\boldsymbol{x})$ with the penalty functions $P_{\text{up}}(\boldsymbol{x}, \boldsymbol{y}; \rho)$ and $P_{\text{low}}(\boldsymbol{x}, \boldsymbol{z}; \rho)$ produces the following QUBO formulation of the constrained problem:

$$\min_{x,y,z} H(x) + \lambda_{\text{up}} P_{\text{up}}(x, y; \rho) + \lambda_{\text{low}} P_{\text{low}}(x, z; \rho). \tag{21}$$

The hyper-parameters λ_{up}, λ_{low} and ρ are to be chosen suitably.

4 Numerical Results and Discussion

We test our different QUBO formulations by analysing the number of auxiliary variables, as well as measuring the performance of the formulations using both the standard meta-heuristic solver Simulated Annealing and Quantum Annealing.

To analyse the performance of our method, three cases are tested, namely:

1. All constraints are used and no reduction is performed.
2. Unnecessary constraints are removed and no reduction is performed.
3. Unnecessary constraints are removed and a reduction with a factor $\rho = 10$ is performed.

For all the numerical results, the data set from the original publication by Phillipson and Chiscop [23] is used. This data set can be shared upon request. The data set considers the case of $M = 1$ where solar panels are the only available distributed generator. Each household has a unique demand and potential solar generation profile, as shown in Fig. 2. The demand profile was constructed by adding a random deviation from a base pattern shown in Fig. 2a. The solar generation profile was constructed based on a profile for East, South and West facing solar panels, shown in Fig. 2b. For each household a random orientation was given between 0 (East) and 1 (West), and hence 0.5 meaning South.

Results were obtained by running Python code using the packages as listed in Appendix C. The Python source code can be published upon request.

4.1 Analysis of Number of Auxiliary Variables

For each of the QUBO formulations, the number of auxiliary variables is analysed for different numbers of households N. This is done by drafting the QUBOs and dividing the number of auxiliary variables used by the total amount of variables. To draft the QUBO, we need to define the capacity C. We set this value to $C = 5.5N$. This value is chosen empirically so that for each problem size the constraints can be violated, while having a limited amount of feasible solutions. Figure 3 shows the fractions for each of the three cases.

Figure 3 shows that case 1, with no reduction at all, always has a higher fraction of auxiliary variables than case 2 and case 3. This considerable difference between case 1 ad case 2 and 3 shows that the removal of unnecessary constraints has a large effect on the number of auxiliary variables, and hence the QUBO size. Minimising the size of the QUBO is of great importance, because the maximum number of variables that is allowed on current Quantum Annealing hardware is limited. Furthermore, Fig. 3 shows the subsequent reduction with a factor $\rho = 10$ reduces the QUBO size significantly as well, although this effect is smaller than

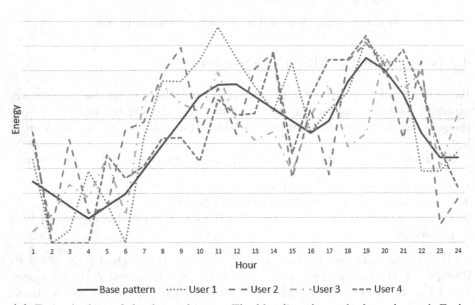

(a) Example data of the demand curve. The blue line shows the base demand. Each user then has a random difference from this base curve.

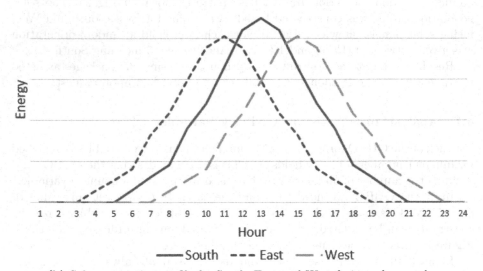

(b) Solar generation profile for South, East and West facing solar panels.

Fig. 2. Example demand and solar generation profiles. These profiles were obtained from [23].

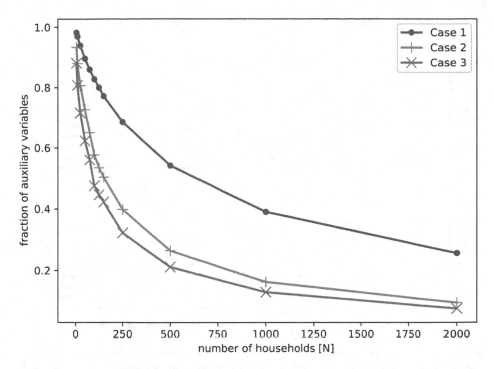

Fig. 3. Fractions of auxiliary variables as a function of the number of households for the three different cases

the sole removal of unnecessary constraints. Hence, we conclude that both our reduction methods are effective at reducing the size of the constructed QUBO, with the first reduction method being the most effective.

4.2 Analysis of Performance

The performance of the different QUBOs is evaluated by solving the QUBOs on Simulated and Quantum Annealing. For both solvers, the total computational time, called End to End (E2E) time for Quantum Annealing, and the solution quality are compared. It should be noted that the presented results do not imply any conclusions of the performance of quantum computers versus classical computers. This is also not the objective of this study. Merely the effect of the reduction method in a classical and a quantum setting are tested. We applied Simulated Annealing and Quantum Annealing with the settings given in Appendix B. The values for the penalty parameters λ_0 and λ_1 can also be found in that section. The results from Simulated Annealing and Quantum Annealing can be found in Fig. 4. It should be noted that the horizontal axes differ between the Simulated Annealing and Quantum Annealing results.

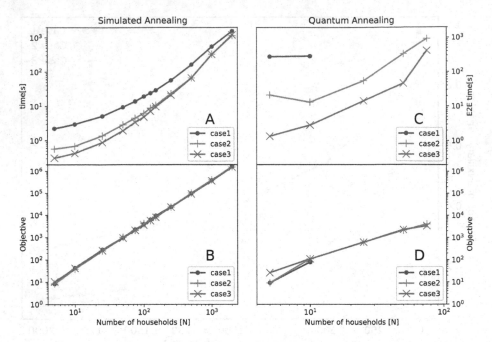

Fig. 4. a) Computation time of the QUBO solved with Simulated Annealing for different N b) Objective value of the QUBO solved with Simulated Annealing for different N c) End to end (E2E) time of the QUBO solved with Quantum Annealing for different N d) Objective value of the QUBO solved with Quantum Annealing for different N

For the quantum setting, the most significant difference can be observed in the in computation time. Note that in both Figs. 4c and 4d the different cases have a different amounts of datapoints. For case 1, we could run problems up to $N = 10$, whereas for case 2 and 3 we could run problems up to $N = 75$. The reason for this difference is based on the QUBO size, with reduced QUBOs allowing for solving problems with a larger number of households on the quantum annealer. The 7.5 times increase of allowed problem size underlines the importance of our reduction methods. Figure 4c shows the E2E time for the different cases. A substantial difference in E2E time between case 1 and the other cases can be observed. Furthermore, the E2E time for case 3 is significantly lower than the E2E time for case 2. This can be explained by the fact that the smaller QUBO produced in case 3 is more easily mapped to the Quantum Annealing hardware. Lastly, Fig. 4d shows that all cases have a similar obtained objective, showing that the reduction methods did not significantly alter the solution quality, as was also shown in [26].

The results for the classical setting are similar to the one observed for the quantum setting. As can be seen in Fig. 4a, the Simulated Annealing computation time for case 2 and case 3 is significantly lower than for case 1, especially for smaller N. This shows that the necessary computation time decreases with a reduced QUBO size. However, in the classical setting, there is only a significant difference in computation time between case 2 and 3 for smaller N and this difference is less pronounced than in the quantum setting. Similar to Quantum Annealing, Fig. 4b shows that for all cases Simulated Annealing gave a similar objective value, which means that the quality of the results was the same for each of the different cases. Hence, the reduction methods also did not alter the solution quality when the problem was solved with a classical solver. From these results we conclude that our reduction method is also effective in the classical case, albeit in a lesser extent.

Theoretically, we expected that the solution quality would differ between the three cases. Specifically, case 1 was expected to perform worse as compared to case 2 since it tries to optimize constraints which are always met. One would expect that classical solvers get stuck in local minima more easily in this case, however this was not observed. Moreover, we would expect to see a difference in solution quality between case 2 and 3, as the reduction to case 3 comes with a potential loss in solution quality. This potential loss in solution quality was not measured using this data set.

5 Discussion

The energy market is shifting towards more decentralised forms of energy generation, like solar and wind energy. This shift increases the opportunity and need to locally match the supply and demand of electricity to negate energy loss over large distances. In this paper we investigate the Constrained Tactical Planning Problem for tactical configurations of distributed electricity generators. This problem extents the Tactical Planning Problem with a capacity constrained of the supply and demand. We show how this problem can be formulated as a Quadratic Unconstrained Binary Optimization problem (QUBO). Furthermore, we show how the QUBO size in terms of number of variables can significantly be reduced in 2 ways; (1) removing unnecessary constraints and (2) reducing the number of auxiliary variables introduced by the inclusion of the constraint into the objective. The effectiveness of these reduction methods was assessed by solving the QUBO for a synthetic data set with both quantum computing (Quantum Annealing) and classical computing (Simulated Annealing).

When using Quantum Annealing to solve the QUBOs, it was observed that both reduction methods lower the end to end time, while having a negligible effect on the solution quality. Hence, both reduction methods are effective at reducing the end to end time. More importantly, there was a considerable difference in the problem size that can be run on current Quantum Annnealing hardware with the different methods. Without any reduction applied, only cases up to $N = 10$ could be run on the Quantum Annealer. However, after removing the unnecessary constraints, this increased to $N = 75$. Therefore, there is a 7.5 times improvement of problem size that could be run on the current Quantum Annealing hardware using these reduction methods, underlining the importance of such reduction methods.

In the classical case with Simulated Annealing, both reduction methods had no significant impact on the solution quality as well. Furthermore, the removal of unnecessary constraints proved to have a significant effect on the computation time. Hence, we conclude that removing unnecessary constraint not only improves the solution found with Quantum Annealing, but also significant improves results found with current classical solvers like Simulated Anealing. On the other hand, the reduction of auxiliary variables only had a significant effect on the smaller problem sizes. For larger problem sizes this reduction method did not seem to alter the computation time. Therefore, we conclude that reducing the number of auxiliary variables is less important for classical solvers.

For further work it would be interesting to investigate how the QUBO formulation and the reduction methods perform on more realistic data sets. During the measurements, we found that our relatively simple data set is somewhat restrictive in measuring the performance of our methods. Depending on the chosen capacity constraint, we noticed that the constraint was either almost always satisfied, or could not be satisfied. Because of this, the impact of adding the capacity constraint to the QUBO was hard to gauge. This suggests that the data set might not have been representative of the difficulty of the problem.

Another avenue for future research would be to see how these reduction methods perform on other classical QUBO solvers, like Gurobi and Local Solver. In addition, these solvers could also be used to see when the quantum approach becomes competitive with these classical solvers which are considered state of the art.

Lastly, it would be interesting to see how these reduction methods perform on entirely different problems. To the best of our knowledge, it is quite uncommon to use heuristics to eliminate certain constraints based on certain knowledge of the problem. Our analysis has showed that these heuristics can be quite impactful, and it would hence be interesting to investigate whether this is also the case for different problems.

A   Derivation of the Penalty Functions

First, the constraint describing the upper bound, as shown in (13), will be transformed into a penalty function. We start by adding the total demand at time interval t to both sides of the equation. Because all s_{ijt} are non-negative, the left hand side is bounded from below by 0. Therefore, (13) is equivalent to

$$0 \leq \sum_{i=1}^{N} \sum_{j=1}^{M} s_{ijt} x_{ij} \leq C + \sum_{i=1}^{N} d_{it} \qquad \text{for all } t \in T_{\text{up}}. \tag{22}$$

Furthermore, s_{ijt} and d_{it} are integer values. Therefore, the inequality constraint in (22) is equivalent to

$$\sum_{i=1}^{N} \sum_{j=1}^{M} s_{ijt} x_{ij} = I(\boldsymbol{y}_t; C + \sum_{i=1}^{N} d_{it}) \qquad \text{for all } t \in T_{\text{up}}, \tag{23}$$

where I is the integer encoding function shown in (4) and $\boldsymbol{y}_t$ is a vector containing auxiliary binary variables. Hence, the penalty function for the upper bound constraint is given by

$$P_{\text{up}}(\boldsymbol{x}, \boldsymbol{y}) = \sum_{t \in T_{\text{up}}} \left(\sum_{i=1}^{N} \sum_{j=1}^{M} s_{ijt} x_{ij} - I(\boldsymbol{y}_t; C + \sum_{i=1}^{N} d_{it}) \right)^2 . \qquad (24)$$

The constraint describing the lower bound, as shown in (14), can be transformed in a penalty function in a similar manner. Note that (13) is equal to

$$\sum_{i=1}^{N} \sum_{j=1}^{M} s_{ijt}(1 - x_{ij}) \leq C + \sum_{i=1}^{N} \sum_{j=1}^{M} s_{ijt} - d_{it}. \qquad (25)$$

Both s_{ijt} and $1 - x_{ij}$ are non-negative. Therefore, (25) is bounded from below by 0, i.e.,

$$0 \leq \sum_{i=1}^{N} \sum_{j=1}^{M} s_{ijt}(1 - x_{ij}) \leq C + \sum_{i=1}^{N} \sum_{j=1}^{M} s_{ijt} - d_{it}. \qquad (26)$$

Similarly to the upper bound constraint, the fact that s_{ijt} and d_{it} are integer values can be used to transform the inequality constraint in (26) to the following equality constraint:

$$\sum_{i=1}^{N} \sum_{j=1}^{M} s_{ijt}(1 - x_{ij}) = I(\boldsymbol{z}_t, C + \sum_{i=1}^{N} \sum_{j=1}^{M} s_{ijt} - d_{it}), \qquad (27)$$

where $\boldsymbol{z}_t$ is a vector containing auxiliary binary variables. Therefore, the penalty function for the lower bound constraint is given by

$$P_{\text{low}}(\boldsymbol{x}, \boldsymbol{z}) = \sum_{t \in T_{\text{low}}} \left(\sum_{i=1}^{N} \sum_{j=1}^{M} s_{ijt}(1 - x_{ij}) - I(\boldsymbol{z}_t, C + \sum_{i=1}^{N} \sum_{j=1}^{M} s_{ijt} - d_{it}) \right)^2 .$$
$$(28)$$

B   Settings for Simulated Annealing and Quantum Annealing runs

For Simulated Annealing we used the D-Wave SimulatedAnnealingSampler with 500 reads, while all other settings were left as default. For Quantum Annealing, we used the D-Wave Advantage system. The number of reads was set to 500 and the annealing time was set to $1000\,\mu s$, while all other settings were left as default. From our experience, these values often yield good results for medium to large problem sizes. With these settings, the total QPU time was approximately $0.6\,s$. Lastly, λ_0 and λ_1 were set to $10N$. An empirical study showed that these values did not have a significant influence on the result. Using these settings the results depicted in Fig. 4 were obtained.

C Python Packages

To generate the results shown in this work, we used the script below. We used Python 3.11 with packages as depicted in Table 1:

Table 1. Packages and versions used

Package Name	Version
dwave-samplers	1.0.0
dwave-system	1.18.0
numpy	1.24.2
pyqubo	1.4.0

References

1. Brinkel, N., Schram, W., AlSkaif, T., Lampropoulos, I., Van Sark, W.: Should we reinforce the grid? Cost and emission optimization of electric vehicle charging under different transformer limits. Appl. Energy **276**, 115285 (2020)
2. Croes, N., Phillipson, F., Schreuder, M.: Tactical congestion management: the optimal mix of decentralised generators in a district. In: CIRED 2012 Workshop: Integration of Renewables into the Distribution Grid, pp. 1–4. IET (2012)
3. Diekerhof, M., et al.: Production and demand management. In: Mathematical Optimization for Efficient and Robust Energy Networks, pp. 3–25. Springer (2021)
4. Farhi, E., Goldstone, J., Gutmann, S., Sipser, M.: Quantum computation by adiabatic evolution. arXiv preprint quant-ph/0001106 (2000)
5. Faruqui, A., Sergici, S., Akaba, L.: Dynamic pricing of electricity for residential customers: the evidence from Michigan. Energ. Effi. **6**, 571–584 (2013). https://doi.org/10.1007/s12053-013-9192-z
6. Gitizadeh, M., Vahed, A.A., Aghaei, J.: Multistage distribution system expansion planning considering distributed generation using hybrid evolutionary algorithms. Appl. Energ. **101**, 655–666 (2012)
7. Glover, F., Kochenberger, G., Du, Yu.: Quantum Bridge analytics i: a tutorial on formulating and using QUBO models. 4OR **17**(4), 335–371 (2019). https://doi.org/10.1007/s10288-019-00424-y
8. Griffiths, D.J., Schroeter, D.F.: Introduction to Quantum Mechanics. Cambridge University Press, Cambridge (2018)
9. Henderson, D., Jacobson, S.H., Johnson, A.W.: The theory and practice of simulated annealing. In: Glover, F., Kochenberger, G.A. (eds.) Handbook of Metaheuristics. International Series in Operations Research & Management Science, vol. 57, pp. 287–319. Springer, Boston (2003). https://doi.org/10.1007/0-306-48056-5_10
10. IET: energy storage system: a potential, "Flexibility Resources" to accelerate the Decarbonisation of smart grid network (2021)
11. Kadowaki, T., Nishimori, H.: Quantum annealing in the transverse ising model. Phys. Rev. E **58**(5), 5355 (1998)

12. Kirkpatrick, S., Gelatt, C.D., Jr., Vecchi, M.P.: Optimization by simulated annealing. Science **220**(4598), 671–680 (1983)
13. Kopanos, G.M., Georgiadis, M.C., Pistikopoulos, E.N.: Energy production planning of a network of micro combined heat and power generators. Appl. Energy **102**, 1522–1534 (2012)
14. Korkas, C.D., Baldi, S., Kosmatopoulos, E.B.: Grid-connected microgrids: demand management via distributed control and human-in-the-loop optimization. In: Advances in Renewable Energies and Power Technologies, pp. 315–344. Elsevier (2018)
15. Lucas, A.: Ising formulations of many NP problems. Frontiers Phys. **2**, 5 (2014)
16. Matthiss, B., Momenifarahani, A., Binder, J.: Storage placement and sizing in a distribution grid with high PV generation. Energies **14**(2), 303 (2021)
17. McGeoch, C.C.: Adiabatic quantum computation and quantum annealing: theory and practice. Synthesis Lectures Quantum Comput. **5**(2), 1–93 (2014)
18. Messiah, A.: Quantum Mechanics: Two Volumes Bound As One. Dover Publications Inc., Mineola (2014)
19. Mutule, A., et al.: Implementing smart city technologies to inspire change in consumer energy behaviour. Energies **14**(14), 4310 (2021)
20. Nations, U.: Kyoto protocol to the united nations framework convention on climate change. 2303 U.N.T.S. 162, United Nations, December 1997
21. Perdomo-Ortiz, A., Dickson, N., Drew-Brook, M., Rose, G., Aspuru-Guzik, A.: Finding low-energy conformations of lattice protein models by quantum annealing. Sci. Rep. **2**(1), 1–7 (2012)
22. Phillipson, F., Bhatia, H.S.: Portfolio optimisation using the d-wave quantum annealer. In: Paszynski, M., Kranzlmüller, D., Krzhizhanovskaya, V.V., Dongarra, J.J., Sloot, P.M.A. (eds.) ICCS 2021. LNCS, vol. 12747, pp. 45–59. Springer, Cham (2021). https://doi.org/10.1007/978-3-030-77980-1_4
23. Phillipson, F., Chiscop, I.: A quantum approach for tactical capacity management of distributed electricity generation. In: Innovations for Community Services. Communications in Computer and Information Science, vol. 1585, pp. 323–333. Springer, Cham (2022). https://doi.org/10.1007/978-3-031-06668-9_23
24. Times, N.: Dutch power grid overloaded in more places; no new connections possible, August 2022. https://nltimes.nl/2022/08/04/dutch-power-grid-overloaded-places-new-connections-possible
25. Venegas-Andraca, S.E., Cruz-Santos, W., McGeoch, C., Lanzagorta, M.: A cross-disciplinary introduction to quantum annealing-based algorithms. Contemp. Phys. **59**(2), 174–197 (2018)
26. Verma, A., Lewis, M.: Variable reduction for quadratic unconstrained binary optimization. arXiv preprint arXiv:2105.07032 (2021)
27. Wolske, K.S., Gillingham, K.T., Schultz, P.W.: Peer influence on household energy behaviours. Nat. Energy **5**(3), 202–212 (2020)
28. Yarkoni, S., Alekseyenko, A., Streif, M., Von Dollen, D., Neukart, F., Bäck, T.: Multi-car paint shop optimization with quantum annealing. In: 2021 IEEE International Conference on Quantum Computing and Engineering (QCE), pp. 35–41. IEEE (2021)
29. Yu, S., Nabil, T.: Applying the hubbard-stratonovich transformation to solve scheduling problems under inequality constraints with quantum annealing. Frontiers Phys. **9**, 730685 (2021)

Quantum Approaches for Medoid Clustering

Thom Sijpesteijn[1] and Frank Phillipson[1,2]([✉]) [ⓘ]

[1] TNO, The Hague, The Netherlands
frank.phillipson@tno.nl
[2] Maastricht University, Maastricht, The Netherlands

Abstract. The k-medoids problem is an important problem in data clustering, which aims to partition a set of data points into k clusters, where each cluster is represented by a medoid, i.e., a data point that is the most centrally located in the cluster. Quantum annealing might be helpful in finding the solution to this problem faster. In this paper we compare three approaches for using the quantum annealer and QUBO-formulations to solve the k-medoids problem. The first approach revolves around a QUBO that encodes the problem as a whole. This approach turns out not to scale well for bigger problem sizes. The QUBO in the second approach comes from the literature and solves only the problem of finding medoids: assigning the datapoints to clusters requires an additional step. The QUBO formulation in the third approach is the same as in the second, but with different penalty parameters. We show that the second and third approaches scale better in terms of complexity than the first approach. However, the original penalty parameters in approach 2 (i.e. those suggested in the literature) do not work well for bigger instances. Taking different parameters makes this approach much better in performance.

Keywords: k-medoids problem · Quantum annealing · Data analytics · QUBO

1 Introduction

The k-medoids problem is a clustering problem similar to k-means, used in data-analytics. The name was coined by Leonard Kaufman and Peter J. Rousseeuw with their PAM algorithm [12]. Both the k-means and k-medoids algorithms are partitional, meaning breaking the data set up into groups, and attempt to minimise the distance between points labeled to be in a cluster and a point designated as the centre of that cluster. In the k-means algorithm, the centre of each outputted cluster is not necessarily one of the input data points. In contrast, k-medoids chooses k actual data points from the given N data points as centres (medoids or exemplars), thereby allowing for greater interpretability of the cluster centres than in k-means. The k-medoids problem is also more able in handling noise in the data.

U. R. Krieger et al. (Eds.): I4CS 2023, CCIS 1876, pp. 222–235, 2023.
https://doi.org/10.1007/978-3-031-40852-6_12

k-medoids has numerous practical applications, such as customer segmentation [21], image segmentation [20], network analysis [10], and bioinformatics [6]. For example, in customer segmentation, k-medoids can be used to group customers with similar purchasing patterns or demographics. In bioinformatics, k-medoids can be used to identify groups of genes that are co-regulated or have similar functions.

In general, k-means problems can be solved by the algorithms from Lloyd [15], Hartigan and Wong [8] and MacQueen [17]. For the first and second of these three, the application to the k-medoids problems is also known [3]. These approaches have in common that both the medoids and the clustering is done iteratively. The approach by Lloyd is known to be quite fast in practice. However, setting theoretical bounds on the running time was hard. Starting from a trivial upper bound of $\mathcal{O}(k^N)$, the work in [1] shows an adjusted version of Lloyd's algorithm that requires $2^{\Omega(\sqrt{N})}$ iterations. The approach by MacQueen only determines the means and has no translation to the k-medoid approach on classical computers.

In recent years, a new computation paradigm has emerged: quantum computing. Already in the current, early stage, quantum computers seem to be useful for optimisation problems such as Medoid Clustering, using Quantum Approximate Optimisation Algorithm (QAOA) [27] or quantum annealing (or adiabatic quantum computing) [19]. Some research has already been conducted into quantum algorithms for (future) gate-based machines, e.g. [14], but the present paper focuses on the quantum annealing paradigm.

Both QAOA and quantum annealing are especially useful for quadratic binary optimisation and would soon be able to compete with traditional quadratic optimisation solvers, using the QUBO (Quadratic Unconstrained Binary Optimisation) or Ising formulation, which are equivalent [16]. We are now in the stage where real life problems are starting to be solved by these solutions, for example in traffic and logistic problems, as shown in [5,9,22,24,25,28].

Their are multiple approaches known in literature for using a QUBO approach for clustering methods, such as k-means, support vector machines (SVM), and distance based clustering, see for examples [2,4,18,26]. In [3] a first approach of solving the k-medoids using quantum computing is presented, where a QUBO formulation is created to solve only the problem of finding the Medoids.

In this paper we investigate a QUBO problem formulation for the entire problem, both finding the medoid and clustering. We compare the performance to a classic approach and to the work of [3]. We also propose a enhancement of the work of [3]. For this, we introduce quantum annealing and the QUBO problem formulation in Sect. 2. Next, in Sect. 3, the mathematical formulation of this Medoid Clustering problem is given and translated into the QUBO problem formulations. We show the performance of these formulations in Sect. 4. In Sect. 5 some discussion and ideas for further research complete this work.

2   Quantum Annealing

Quantum annealing as we know it today started with the work of Kadowaki and Nishimori [11]. The most advanced implementation of this paradigm is the D-Wave quantum annealer. The main idea here is to create an equal superposition over all possible states. Then, a problem-specific magnetic field is slowly turned up in a controlled way, causing the qubits to interact with each other. Now, the qubits tend towards states with the lower energy. In this way, the aim is that the qubits end up in a configuration that optimizes the problem, though there is also a probability of finding a suboptimal solution.

Main input of the D-Wave quantum annealer is an Ising Hamiltonian or its binary equivalent, the QUBO formulation. The QUBO, Quadratic Unconstrained Binary Optimisation problem [7], is expressed by the optimisation problem:

$$\text{QUBO:} \min_{x \in \{0,1\}^n} x^\mathsf{T} Q x, \tag{1}$$

where $x \in \{0, 1\}^n$ are the decision variables and Q is a real-valued $n \times n$ coefficient matrix. QUBO problems belong to the class of NP-hard problems.

To solve the problem that is formulated by the QUBO, it has to be embedded on the hardware. Each variable is translated to one or more (a chain of) qubits. The two most recent machines that are offered by D-Wave, via their LEAP environment, are the D-Wave 2000Q and the D-Wave Advantage. The D-Wave 2000Q has around 2000 qubits in a Chimera architecture, where each qubit is connected with at most 6 other qubits. The D-Wave Advantage, active since 2020, has more that 5000 qubits in the Pegasus architecture, having a connectivity of at most 15. However the number of qubits and their connectivity has grown considerably, they are still of limited size. This means that often the problem can not be embedded on the chip. For this, hybrid black box methods are offered by D-Wave that can handle problems up to one million variables.

For a large number of combinatorial optimisation problems the QUBO representation is already known [7,16]. Many constrained integer programming problems can be transformed easily to a QUBO representation. Assume that we have the problem

$$\min_{x \in \{0,1\}^n} x^\mathsf{T} Q x, \text{ subject to } Ax = b, \tag{2}$$

then we can bring the constraints to the objective value, using a penalty factor λ for a quadratic penalty:

$$\min_{x \in \{0,1\}^n} x^\mathsf{T} Q x + \lambda (Ax - b)^\mathsf{T} (Ax - b)$$

$$\min_{x \in \{0,1\}^n} = x^\mathsf{T} Q x + x^\mathsf{T} R(\lambda) x + \lambda d$$

$$\min_{x \in \{0,1\}^n} = x^\mathsf{T} P(\lambda) x,$$

where matrix R and the constant d follow from matrix calculations. Furthermore, λd is constant and can thus be neglected, as it does not alter the optimal point.

3   Mathematical Formulation

If we have N points that have to be clustered into k clusters, and the distance between points i and j equals d_{ij}, we can define the following problem describing the Medoid Clustering problem.

Define:

$$x_{i,c} = \begin{cases} 1 & \text{if point } i \text{ in cluster } c, \\ 0 & \text{otherwise.} \end{cases}$$

$$y_{i,c} = \begin{cases} 1 & \text{if point } i \text{ is medoid of cluster } c, \\ 0 & \text{otherwise.} \end{cases}$$

The optimisation problem is now:

$$\min \sum_{c=1}^{k} \sum_{i=1}^{N} \sum_{j=1}^{N} x_{i,c} y_{i,c} d_{ij} \tag{3}$$

under the constraints:

$$\sum_{c=1}^{k} x_{i,c} = 1 \qquad i = 1, ..., N \tag{4}$$

$$\sum_{i=1}^{N} y_{i,c} = 1 \qquad c = 1, ..., k \tag{5}$$

$$y_{i,c} \leq x_{i,c} \qquad i = 1, ..., N, c = 1, ..., k. \tag{6}$$

Here, the total distance between the data points and their assigned medoid is minimised in (3). Next, it is assured that each point is assigned to exactly one cluster and that every cluster has exactly one medoid. Finally, (6) makes sure that a medoid can only be defined as the associated datapoint is in the same cluster.

3.1   First QUBO Formulation

In a first, naive, quantum approach we translate the problem defined by (3)–(6) directly to a QUBO formulation, using:

$$v_{(c-1)N+i} = x_{i,k} \qquad i = 1, ..., N, c = 1, ..., k$$
$$v_{Nk+(c-1)N+i} = y_{i,k} \qquad i = 1, ..., N, c = 1, ..., k$$
$$v_l \in \{0, 1\} \qquad l = 1, ..., 2Nk$$

we can rewrite the problem to

$$\min \sum_{c=1}^{k} \sum_{i=1}^{N} \sum_{j=1}^{N} v_{cN+i} v_{(k+c)N+j} d_{ij} \tag{7}$$

under the constraints:

$$\sum_{c=1}^{k} v_{cN+i} = 1 \qquad i = 1, ..., N \tag{8}$$

$$\sum_{i=1}^{N} v_{(k+c)N+i} = 1 \qquad c = 1, ..., k \tag{9}$$

$$v_{(k+c)N+i} \leq v_{cN+i} \qquad i = 1, ..., N, c = 1, ..., k. \tag{10}$$

Considering the last inequality, note that for binary x and y we have:

$$x \leq y \Leftrightarrow x - xy = 0. \tag{11}$$

Using this, we can incorporate the inequality at (10) into the QUBO by defining a penalty of the form:

$$v_{(k+c)N+i} - v_{(k+c)N+i}v_{cN+i} = 0 \qquad i = 1, ..., N, c = 1, ..., k. \tag{12}$$

The resulting QUBO is now

$$\min \sum_{c=1}^{k} \sum_{i=1}^{N} \sum_{j=1}^{N} v_{cN+i}v_{(k+c)N+j}d_{ij} + \alpha \sum_{i=1}^{N} \left(1 - \sum_{c=1}^{k} v_{cN+i}\right)^2 +$$

$$\beta \sum_{i=1}^{k} \left(1 - \sum_{i=1}^{N} v_{(k+c)N+i}\right)^2 + \gamma \sum_{c=1}^{k} \sum_{i=1}^{N} \left(v_{(k+c)N+i} - v_{(k+c)N+i}v_{cN+i}\right) \tag{13}$$

using the penalty parameters (α, β, γ). For α it holds that assigning a point to too many clusters will automatically come at a cost at the original objective function. Not assigning to a cluster gives a benefit of, at most, $\max_j d_{ij}$ for point i. Setting $\alpha = \max_{i,j} d_{ij}$ guarantees (classically) that no benefit is realised in not fulfilling this constraint. For β it also holds that not choosing multiple medoids will be penalised by the original objective function. To prevent the case that no medoid is chosen for a cluster, the penalty should be higher that the expected benefit. This benefit is at most $\max_j \sum_i d_{ij} \leq N \cdot \max_{i,j} d_{ij}$. The last parameter, γ, can be set at zero as the constraint does not seem to be limiting, as breaking this constraint is already expensive in the main objective function. As seen more often, choosing the penalties at the theoretical levels do not work well in quantum annealing due to the scaling of the total problem. We therefore suggest to take: $\alpha = 0.4 \cdot \max_{i,j} d_{ij}$, $\beta = 0.4 \cdot N \cdot \max_{i,j} d_{ij}$ and $\gamma = 0$.

3.2   Second QUBO Formulation

A more sophisticated approach is presented in [3]. The authors combine two problems to come up to a dense formulation to identify the medoids. The step of assigning the data points to the medoids is done separately. The first problem is to identify far apart data points. This is defined as:

$$\max \frac{1}{2} \sum_{i=1}^{N} \sum_{j=1}^{N} z_i z_j \Delta_{ij}, \tag{14}$$

under the constraint:

$$\sum_{c=1}^{N} z_i = k \tag{15}$$

where

$$z_i = \begin{cases} 1 & \text{if point } i \text{ is a medoid,} \\ 0 & \text{otherwise,} \end{cases} \tag{16}$$

and using $\Delta_{ij} = 1 - \exp\left(-\frac{1}{2} d_{ij}\right)$.

This problem can be rewritten in QUBO formulation:

$$\max \sum_{i=1}^{N} \sum_{j=1}^{N} z_i z_j \Delta_{ij} - \gamma \left(\sum_{c=1}^{N} z_i - k\right)^2, \tag{17}$$

which can be transformed to: (see for details [3])

$$\max \sum_{i=1}^{N} \sum_{j=1}^{N} z_i z_j \left(\gamma - \frac{1}{2} \Delta_{ij}\right) - 2\gamma k \sum_{c=1}^{N} z_i. \tag{18}$$

The second problem is to identify central data points. This is defined as:

$$\min \sum_{i=1}^{N} \sum_{j=1}^{N} z_i \Delta_{ij}, \tag{19}$$

under the constraint:

$$\sum_{c=1}^{N} z_i = k, \tag{20}$$

which can be transformed to: (again, see for details [3])

$$\max \sum_{i=1}^{N} \sum_{j=1}^{N} z_i z_j \gamma + \sum_{i=1}^{N} z_i \left(\sum_{j=1}^{N} \Delta_{ij} - 2\gamma k\right). \tag{21}$$

Combining (18) and (21) gives the combined QUBO formulation for this problem:

$$\max \sum_{i=1}^{N} \sum_{j=1}^{N} z_i z_j \left(\gamma - \frac{1}{2} \alpha \Delta_{ij}\right) + \sum_{i=1}^{N} z_i \left(\beta \sum_{j=1}^{N} \Delta_{ij} - 2\gamma k\right) \tag{22}$$

where α and β are trade-off parameters the weigh the contributions of the to underlying models. The authors of [3] suggest to set the weighting parameters to $\alpha = \frac{1}{k}$, $\beta = \frac{1}{N}$ and $\gamma = 2$.

4   Comparison

For the first quantum approach, we previously mentioned our suggestion to scale the parameters α and β with the maximum distance between data points. For the second approach, the authors suggest no such scaling. In particular, the parameter γ is fixed at $\gamma = 2$. As we will discuss in more detail below, a non-scaled definition for γ will lead to issues in certain datasets. Therefore, we also consider an implementation of the second approach where we do scale γ. Concretely, this section will therefore compare the following three algorithms:

- `Algo 1`: use QUBO formulation from (13), with $\alpha = 0.4 \cdot \max_{i,j} d_{ij}$, $\beta = 0.4 \cdot N \cdot \max_{i,j} d_{ij}$ and $\gamma = 0$.

- `Algo 2`: use QUBO formulation from (22), with $\alpha = \frac{1}{k}$, $\beta = \frac{1}{N}$, $\gamma = 2$; then assign each data point to closest medoid.

- `Algo 3`: use QUBO formulation from (22), with $\alpha = \frac{1}{k}$, $\beta = \frac{1}{N}$, $\gamma = 2 \cdot \max_{i,j} d_{ij}$; then assign each data point to closest medoid.

- Control (where relevant): use the standard k-means algorithm provided in the `sklearn` package. This serves as a control in the comparison.

Note that both the QUBO formulations (13) and (22) include penalty parameters α, β, γ, but these are not the same.

In the following, we will conduct a number of simple experiments to compare the efficiency, accuracy and scalability of these algorithms. We use Python to implement the QUBOs and solve them (mostly) using `SimulatedAnnealingSampler` from D-Wave's `neal` package.

4.1   Design and Data Sources of the Experiments

The first experiment investigates how the QUBOs scale as the the number of samples in a dataset increases. We generate a clustering dataset using the `make_blobs` functionality from the `datasets` module in the `sklearn` Python package [23]. Then, we encode the k-medoids problem into a QUBO format using the different approaches, after which we compare the sizes of the QUBOs we acquired.

In the second experiment, we will run a number of tests using D-Wave System's Advantage System quantum annealer to check to what extent datasets generated by `make_blobs` can indeed be solved using the algorithms and solving the QUBOs on an actual quantum annealing device. For the larger third and fourth experiments, we switch to using D-Wave's `SimulatedAnnealer` because it can handle larger sized QUBOs.

The third experiment considers what happens to the accuracy of the algorithms when we increase the number of clusters k. To this end, we again generate a clustering dataset with k clusters using make_blobs. We then temporarily 'forget' the true labellings for this generated dataset and apply the three algorithms specified above. To compare the accuracy, we calculate the adjusted rand score metric for the labels found versus the true labels. Random labellings have an adjusted rand score close to 0.0, while a score of 1.0 describes a perfect match.

The fourth experiment is more realistic in the sense that the datasets are no longer generated as clustering datasets through the use of make_blobs. Instead, we compare the accuracy of the approaches across several toy datasets, in particular the wine, iris and breast_cancer datasets from sklearn [13] with the characteristics given in Table 1.

Table 1. Overview of toy datasets used in Experiment 4

Dataset	# samples N	# classes k	# features
Wine	178	3	13
Iris	150	3	4
Breast cancer	569	2	30

4.2 Results and Findings

Experiment 1: QUBO Size and Complexity. The effect on QUBO size of increasing the number of samples N is given in Table 2. It is clear that the QUBOs for (22) (that is, those used in Algo 2 and 3) are significantly smaller than those for the QUBO (13) in Algo 1. The latter QUBO is more sparse: the percentage of nonzero elements in the matrix is smaller, but the absolute number of nonzero is still bigger. Additional experiments with different values for n_features show that this variable does not affect QUBO size or number of nonzero elements. More precisely, we note that QUBO size for (13) appears to be $2Nk \times 2Nk$, while for (22) we see that the QUBO size equals $N \times N$.

It is important to note at this point that solving the QUBO (13) gives immediate solutions to the k-medoids problem, while solving the QUBO (22) just gives the appropriate medoids. That is, Algo 2 and 3 still need to assign each data point to the right cluster, adding complexity $N \cdot k$.

Experiment 2: In this experiment, we do a number of test clusterings where we solve the QUBOs using D-Wave's Advantage System (DWaveSampler). Table 3 shows the results, where we set number_of_reads=500 and annealing_time=500. These parameter choices did not affect the result much and highly similar results were obtained for other parameter choices.

Table 2. QUBO size for varying number of samples N

N	Algo 1			Algo 2			Algo 3		
	size	nonzero elts	%	size	nonzero elts	%	size	nonzero elts	%
10	80 × 80	680	10.63	10 × 10	55	55.00	10 × 10	55	55.00
20	160 × 160	2560	10.00	20 × 20	210	52.50	20 × 20	210	52.50
40	320 × 320	9920	9.69	40 × 40	820	51.25	40 × 40	820	51.25
80	640 × 640	39040	9.53	80 × 80	3240	50.63	80 × 80	3240	50.63

$k = 4$

N	Algo 1			Algo 2			Algo 3		
	size	nonzero elts	%	size	nonzero elts	%	size	nonzero elts	%
10	120 × 120	1080	7.50	10 × 10	55	55.00	10 × 10	55	55.00
20	240 × 240	3960	6.88	20 × 20	210	52.50	20 × 20	210	52.50
40	480 × 480	15120	6.56	40 × 40	820	51.25	40 × 40	820	51.25
80	960 × 960	59040	6.40	80 × 80	3240	50.63	80 × 80	3240	50.63

$k = 6$

N	Algo 1			Algo 2			Algo 3		
	size	nonzero elts	%	size	nonzero elts	%	size	nonzero elts	%
10	200 × 200	2000	5.00	10 × 10	55	55.00	10 × 10	55	55.00
20	400 × 400	7000	4.38	20 × 20	210	52.50	20 × 20	210	52.50
40	800 × 800	26000	4.06	40 × 40	820	51.25	40 × 40	820	51.25
80	1600 × 1600	100000	3.91	80 × 80	3240	50.63	80 × 80	3240	50.63

$k = 10$

Most notable is the fact that for `Algo 1`, this quantum annealing approach does not work very well. For small problems, e.g., $N = 20$, $k = 4$, the approach has a very low score. For larger problems, the calculation quickly becomes infeasible on the actual quantum device. This is in contrast to `Algo 2` and `Algo 3`, which also work on slightly larger problems. This difference is likely due to the fact that the QUBO formulations scale differently, as evidenced in Experiment 1.

Interestingly, `Algo 2` and `Algo 3` outperform the Control in terms of accuracy, so the QUBO formulation (22) appears to be very accurate. However, the approach using the `SamplerAnnealer` (in particular: finding the right embedding) is relatively slow. In the following Experiments 3 and 4, we will therefore switch to D-Wave's `SimulatedAnnealer`, in order to make larger experiments feasible.

Table 3. Accuracy (`adjusted rand score`) for varying number of samples N and number of clusters k using D-Wave's Advantage System with `number_of_reads=500` and `annealing_time=500`

N	k	Control	Algo 1	Algo 2	Algo 3
20	4	0.58	0.07	1.00	1.00
80	10	0.50	–	0.81	0.62
100	20	0.40	–	0.67	0.68

`n_features = 3`

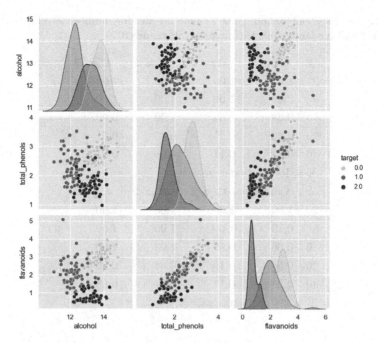

(a) Pairplot of 3 out of 13 features of `wine` dataset. Pairplotting other features gives similar results.

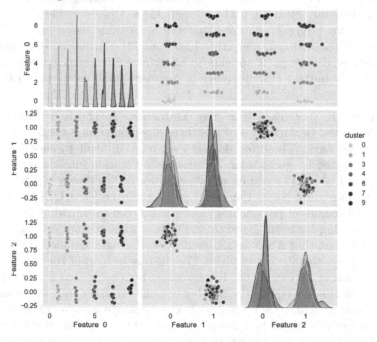

(b) Pairplot of `blobs` dataset with 100 samples, 10 clusters and 3 features.

Fig. 1. Clusters in `blob` datasets are more clearly delineated than in `wine`.

Table 4. Accuracy (`adjusted rand score`) for varying number of clusters k using D-Wave's `SimulatedAnnealer` with `number_of_reads=1000`

k	Control	Algo 1	Algo 2	Algo 3
2	1.00	1.00	1.00	1.00
5	0.49	1.00	1.00	1.00
10	0.48	0.54	1.00	0.90
20	0.40	0.23	0.85	0.71
40	0.21	0.11	0.68	0.63

$N = 100$, `n_features` $= 3$

k	Control	Algo 1	Algo 2	Algo 3
2	1.00	1.00	1.00	1.00
5	0.73	1.00	1.00	1.00
10	0.66	0.59	1.00	1.00
20	0.50	0.19	0.84	0.89
40	0.29	0.11	0.71	0.68

$N = 200$, `n_features` $= 5$

Experiment 3: Accuracy for (small) Generated Datasets. In Table 4, we see the effect on the accuracy of the algorithms for increasing number of clusters k. It is immediately clear that `Algo 2` and `Algo 3` perform better than `Algo 1`. Especially for larger k, we note that the algorithms based on QUBO (22) significantly outperform the algorithm based on (13). Furthermore, we note that the scaling added in `Algo 3` appears to affect performance negatively, as `Algo 2` scores slightly better. The difference is, however, small compared to `Algo 1`.

Experiment 4: Accuracy for Toy Datasets. In the fourth experiment, we investigate the performance of the three algorithms on several toy datasets included in `sklearn`. These toy datasets are more difficult to cluster than the datasets generated by `get_blobs`, because the separation into clusters is not as clear-cut (see Fig. 1). The results of this experiment are shown in Table 5.

Perhaps most notable is the fact that `Algo 2`, i.e., the QUBO (22) with no additional scaling of parameters, does not succeed in providing better-than-random clustering for both the `wine` and `breast_cancer` datasets. More specifically, it turns out that `Algo 2` fails to provide the right number of clusters: in the case of `wine`, the algorithm yields 178 clusters instead of the desired 3, and for `breast_cancer`, it yields 569 clusters instead of the desired 2. In both cases, the number of clusters equals the number of points in the data set, meaning the algorithm simply defines each point as being the single member of its own cluster. We suspect this might be a result of the weighting parameter γ being fixed. Indeed, `Algo 3`, which is identical to `Algo 2` except that it scales the parameter γ, does manage to cluster these datasets reasonably well, especially compared to the other methods.

Table 5. Accuracy (adjusted rand score) for toy data sets using D-Wave's SimulatedAnnealer with number_of_reads=1000

Algorithm	score
Control	0.39
Algo 1	0.33
Algo 2	0.00
Algo 3	0.41

wine dataset

Algorithm	score
Control	0.76
Algo 1	0.79
Algo 2	0.80
Algo 3	0.71

iris dataset

Algorithm	score
Control	0.53
Algo 1	0.46
Algo 2	0.00
Algo 3	0.60

breast_cancer dataset

5 Conclusions and Further Research

In this paper, we discussed three QUBO-based implementations of the k-medoid algorithm: Algo 1 is based on the QUBO formulation of (13) and Algo 2 and Algo 3 are based on (22). The difference between the latter two algorithms concerns the fact that we introduced a scaling for the parameter γ in the Algo 3. No such scaling is used in Algo 2, which fixes $\gamma = 2$.

We compared these algorithms in three experiments. The first experiment compares the QUBO size in the different algorithms. There, we saw that the QUBOs for Algo 2 and Algo 3 have dimension N, while the QUBO for Algo 1 has dimension $2Nk$. However, solving QUBO (22) only yields the medoids, so Algo 2 and Algo 3 get additional complexity Nk for assigning each data point to the appropriate cluster.

In the second experiment, we showed that Algo 2 and Algo 3 outperform Algo 1, both in terms of accuracy and in terms of size they can handle. However, current quantum annealing devices cannot handle larger QUBOs, so even for Algo 2 and 3 the feasible problem size is limited.

The third experiment investigated clustering accuracy as the number of clusters k increases. We saw that Algo 2 performs best, followed closely by Algo 3 and with both significantly outperforming Algo 1.

The final experiment considered the accuracy of the different algorithms when clustering more realistic toy datasets wine, iris and breast_cancer. Here, we noted that Algo 1 and Algo 3 perform similarly, whereas Algo 2 failed to provide a better-than-random clustering for both wine and breast_cancer.

In conclusion, we find that the QUBO (22) is both more efficient and mostly more accurate than the QUBO (13). However, larger datasets might require the penalty parameter γ in QUBO (22) to be scaled in order to find a solution with the correct number of clusters. In particular, we suggested scaling γ with the maximum distance between data points in the set. While this scaling indeed leads to the desired number of clusters, it also affects clustering accuracy negatively.

Future research could be dedicated to optimising the scaling for the parameter γ. The ideal scaling ensures the desired number of clusters is found, with minimal sacrifice of accuracy. Additionally, we note that the formulation in (3) uses the one-hot encoding. Other encoding schemes could be tested, e.g. domain wall encoding, to see how they perform in comparison.

References

1. Arthur, D., Vassilvitskii, S.: How slow is the k-means method? In: Proceedings of the Twenty-Second Annual Symposium on Computational Geometry, pp. 144–153 (2006)
2. Arthur, D., Date, P.: Balanced k-means clustering on an adiabatic quantum computer. Quant. Inf. Process. **20**, 1–30 (2021)
3. Bauckhage, C., Piatkowski, N., Sifa, R., Hecker, D., Wrobel, S.: A QUBO formulation of the k-medoids problem. In: LWDA, pp. 54–63 (2019)
4. Date, P., Arthur, D., Pusey-Nazzaro, L.: Qubo formulations for training machine learning models. Sci. Rep. **11**(1), 10029 (2021)
5. Feld, S., et al.: A hybrid solution method for the capacitated vehicle routing problem using a quantum annealer. Front. ICT **6**, 13 (2019)
6. Geetha, T., Arock, M.: Data clustering using modified k-medoids algorithm. Int. J. Med. Eng. Inf. **4**(2), 109–124 (2012)
7. Glover, F., Kochenberger, G., Hennig, R., Du, Y.: Quantum bridge analytics i: a tutorial on formulating and using qubo models. Ann. Oper. Res. **314**(1), 141–183 (2022)
8. Hartigan, J.A., Wong, M.A.: Algorithm as 136: a k-means clustering algorithm. J. Roy. Stat. Soc. Ser. C (Appl. Stat.) **28**(1), 100–108 (1979)
9. Hussain, H., Javaid, M.B., Khan, F.S., Dalal, A., Khalique, A.: Optimal control of traffic signals using quantum annealing. Quant. Inf. Process. **19**(9), 1–18 (2020)
10. Jie, Z., Li, Y., Liu, R.: Social network group identification based on local attribute community detection. In: 2019 IEEE 3rd Information Technology, Networking, Electronic and Automation Control Conference (ITNEC), pp. 443–447. IEEE (2019)
11. Kadowaki, T., Nishimori, H.: Quantum annealing in the transverse ising model. Phys. Rev. E **58**(5), 5355 (1998)
12. Kaufman, L., Rousseeuw, P.J.: Finding Groups in Data: An Introduction to Cluster Analysis. John Wiley & Sons, Hoboken (2009)
13. Scikit learn: Toy datasets. https://scikit-learn.org/stable/datasets/toy_dataset.html/
14. Li, Y.M., et al.: Quantum k-medoids algorithm using parallel amplitude estimation. Phys. Rev. A **107**, 022421 (2023). https://doi.org/10.1103/PhysRevA.107.022421
15. Lloyd, S.: Least squares quantization in PCM. IEEE Trans. Inf. Theory **28**(2), 129–137 (1982)

16. Lucas, A.: Ising formulations of many NP problems. Front. Phys. **2**, 5 (2014)
17. MacQueen, J.: Classification and analysis of multivariate observations. In: 5th Berkeley Symposium on Mathematical Statistics and Probability, pp. 281–297 (1967)
18. Matsumoto, N., Hamakawa, Y., Tatsumura, K., Kudo, K.: Distance-based clustering using qubo formulations. Sci. Rep. **12**(1), 2669 (2022)
19. McGeoch, C.C.: Adiabatic quantum computation and quantum annealing: theory and practice. Synth. Lect. Quant. Comput. **5**(2), 1–93 (2014)
20. Mehidi, I., Jabri, D., Belkhiat, D.E.C.: Retinal image segmentation using clustering methods: performance analysis. In: IEEE 19th International Multi-Conference on Systems, Signals & Devices (SSD), pp. 1058–1066 (2022)
21. Mufarroha, F.A., Suzanti, I.O., Satoto, B.D., Syarief, M., Yunita, I., et al.: K-means and k-medoids clustering methods for customer segmentation in online retail datasets. In: IEEE 8th Information Technology International Seminar (ITIS), pp. 223–228 (2022)
22. Neukart, F., Compostella, G., Seidel, C., Von Dollen, D., Yarkoni, S., Parney, B.: Traffic flow optimization using a quantum annealer. Front. ICT **4**, 29 (2017)
23. Pedregosa, F., et al.: Scikit-learn: machine learning in python. J. Mach. Learn. Res. **12**, 2825–2830 (2011)
24. Phillipson, F., Bontekoe, T., Chiscop, I.: Energy storage scheduling: a QUBO formulation for quantum computing. In: Krieger, U.R., Eichler, G., Erfurth, C., Fahrnberger, G. (eds.) I4CS 2021. CCIS, vol. 1404, pp. 251–261. Springer, Cham (2021). https://doi.org/10.1007/978-3-030-75004-6_17
25. Phillipson, F., Chiscop, I.: Multimodal container planning: A QUBO formulation and implementation on a quantum annealer. In: Paszynski, M., Kranzlmüller, D., Krzhizhanovskaya, V.V., Dongarra, J.J., Sloot, P.M.A. (eds.) ICCS 2021. LNCS, vol. 12747, pp. 30–44. Springer, Cham (2021). https://doi.org/10.1007/978-3-030-77980-1_3
26. Phillipson, F., Wezeman, R.S., Chiscop, I.: Indoor-outdoor detection in mobile networks using quantum machine learning approaches. Computers **10**(6), 71 (2021)
27. Preskill, J.: Quantum computing in the NISQ era and beyond. Quantum **2**, 79 (2018)
28. Saito, T., Yoshida, A., Kashikawa, T., Kimura, K., Amano, Y.: Combinatorial optimization-based hierarchical management of residential energy systems as virtual power plant. In: 2020 59th Annual Conference of the Society of Instrument and Control Engineers of Japan (SICE), pp. 1833–1839. IEEE (2020)

Quantum Cloud Computing from a User Perspective

Niels M. P Neumann$^{(\boxtimes)}$, Ward van der Schoot, and Thom Sijpesteijn

TNO, The Hague, The Netherlands
{niels.neumann,ward.vanderschoot,thom.sijpesteijn}@tno.nl

Abstract. Quantum computing is a rapidly progressing field: quantum computers are becoming more powerful and an increasing number of functionalities are offered via various quantum platforms and quantum software packages. Current quantum computers can be used almost exclusively via cloud services. It is expected that this will remain the case, at least in the near-term future. For successful adoption of quantum computing by the market, quantum cloud services should be user-centric. To that end, we explore quantum cloud computing from a user perspective. We describe a standardised overview of quantum cloud computing as a whole to create a common language to strengthen research and collaboration on quantum cloud computing. Specifically, we identify different types, information flows and relevant user functionalities of quantum cloud computing, based on their counterparts in classical cloud computing. Combined, this gives an overview of quantum cloud computing for the best user experience, paving the way towards user-centric quantum cloud computing.

Keywords: Quantum computing · Cloud computing · Hybrid computing · User-centric · Vision on quantum cloud computing · functionalities

1 Introduction

Over the last eighty years, the computer has developed significantly.

What started as a large, special-purpose device developed into a general-purpose device of varying size. Computers have become an integral part of our lives and currently they are everywhere.

Recently, a new type of computer, called the quantum computer, has entered the playing field. Quantum devices are developing at a rapid pace and they are likely to establish themselves as the computers of the future. The fundamental laws of quantum mechanics underlie these new computers, allowing them to solve certain problems faster - in some cases even exponentially faster - than classical computers [44]. Because these speedups are problem-specific, quantum computers will not completely replace classical computers and will in fact always be used in conjunction with them.

At the same time, first examples of practical applications of quantum devices have arisen, for example in logistics problems [19,34]. Quantum computers aim

U. R. Krieger et al. (Eds.): I4CS 2023, CCIS 1876, pp. 236–249, 2023.
https://doi.org/10.1007/978-3-031-40852-6_13

to achieve practical advantage over classical devices in various ways, for example through gate-based quantum computing [35], photonic quantum computing [36], quantum annealing [23], and more recently, distributed quantum computing [10].

However, quantum computing also has its own shortcomings. First and foremost, quantum computers outperform classical devices only for some complex problems, so they will likely coexist as a secondary processor, next to classical devices. Next, quantum computers are still under development and it will likely still take years until the promised full-fledged quantum devices are available. In particular, most quantum devices can only operate under strict conditions, such as low temperatures and shielding from outside influences. Because of this, it is unlikely that quantum devices will be available locally in the same sense that classical computers currently are. To ensure quantum computing reaches its maximum potential and applicability, *quantum cloud computers* are required instead. Naturally, accessing quantum computers remotely in a cloud-based setting will come with its own set of challenges.

Over the past couple of years, cloud computing has arisen as the solution for the shortcoming of personal computers in business settings or for computationally heavy tasks. These cloud platforms offer a flexible solution: instead of buying hardware and software, users can rent it from a provider. This flexibility allows users to adapt to current needs, both in terms of size and time. As an example, webshops often see an increase in demand during holiday periods. A cloud platform can flexibly increase the capacity of a server when needed, thereby allowing a webshop to meet the increased traffic. Cloud platforms offer flexibility to users and can lead to lower capital expenses. In contrast, the operational expenses can increase, as users often have to adopt a pay-per-use model [50]. Currently, many different implementations of classical cloud computing exist, such as VPN connections in business settings, or the remote use of a virtual machine.

The first quantum cloud platforms already exist. Different quantum hardware manufacturers provide access to their devices [21,40] through the cloud. Using the available devices often requires using some quantum programming language specific to that platform [26,46,47]. Other quantum cloud platforms act as an intermediate, by providing uniform access to different quantum computers, possibly from various vendors [2,31].

Currently, quantum cloud platforms are mainly used for research purposes, as quantum computing is still in its early stages of development. However, with the rate at which the field is developing, it is expected that business will start using these devices in the near term. To ensure smooth uptake of industry, we must ensure that quantum computing, and particularly quantum cloud computing, becomes user-centric. This can only be done by considering quantum cloud platforms from a user perspective [37].

So far, only a limited amount of research has been conducted on quantum cloud computing from a user perspective. In [24], the impact of quantum computing and cloud computing on one another vis-a-vis user experience is discussed, but the integration with one other platforms is not mentioned. Conversely, in [45] the integration of quantum and cloud computing with its potential advantages for users is theorised, but it is not discussed how this should be achieved. More recently, first descriptions of general implementations of quantum cloud computing were given [13]. In particular, the authors of this work describe how different end users are interested in different access levels of the quantum device.

We extend the literature by describing in more generality how quantum cloud computing could be implemented in a user-centric manner from a functionality point-of-view. We do this by giving a standardised overview of quantum cloud computing based on the best practices in classical cloud computing. With this overview our goal is to create a common language on quantum cloud computing, allowing for better collaboration on its research. In particular, we refrain from aligning current quantum cloud platforms with our identified functionalities, as these platforms are still under heavy development. We do however aim to draw a path towards optimal quantum cloud computing from a user perspective.

This research is performed by using two different methodologies. First, we take classical cloud computing as a starting point and extend it to the quantum case wherever possible. Second, these insights are extended by considering the current state of quantum computing, specifically how it is or will be experienced by users in current and future quantum (cloud) computing.

This work starts by describing already existing classical cloud platforms and gives three commonly used types of services offered by cloud providers in Sect. 2. Then, Sect. 3 describes how to extend these classical services to quantum analogues. Section 4 subsequently gives different interfaces relevant for quantum cloud platforms together with two information flows from the user to a quantum computer. Next, Sect. 5 describes desired functionalities of quantum cloud platforms. Final conclusions and an outlook to future developments are presented in Sect. 6.

2   Classical Cloud Services

2.1   Classical Cloud Platforms

In this section, we give a short overview of classical cloud computing to allow for comparison with quantum cloud computing.

Sharing computational resources as a concept has been around for decades [49]. The first proposals mainly focused on company-internal solutions, also called private clouds. Over the years, the most common type became the public cloud, where a third party offers cloud services. Since the work in [9], which analysed the then upcoming cloud services, many classical cloud platforms emerged offering a wide variety of services.

Cloud computing has become a general-purpose term and typically refers to a flexible solution for storage, computing power, software and networking [38]. Cloud services often provide a flexible alternative to local hardware and software at the end-user side. These cloud services require lower upfront capital expenses, in exchange for higher operational expenses [50].

These operational expenses follow from the contract agreed upon by the cloud service provider and the user. Common examples include a subscription service with monthly fees, pay-as-you-go systems (based on credits) and prepaid use for a several-year period.

An increasing number of parties outsource some or even all of their processes to cloud providers. Examples of cloud services include computational power [4], data storage [5,18] and online text-editors [32].

However, cloud platforms have downsides. The two main ones are security and vendor lock-in. When using cloud platforms, users have only limited influence on the security measures taken to protect their data. If the service provider loses data, for instance due to a hack, sensitive data can become public [48]. Vendor lock-in refers to the difficulty of switching to (similar) services offered by a different provider, for instance due to high costs of adjusting internal processes and software [25].

Cloud services do not offer the solution to all ICT-problems encountered in practice. The adoption of cloud services is generally a trade-off between costs, flexibility and security aspects, which should be carefully analysed for specific use-cases.

2.2   Types of Classical Cloud Services

The services offered by cloud providers are diverse. Yet, they show similarities in the functionalities provided. Based on these similarities, we can group the different services by type. Three common types are [22,30]:

- **Infrastructure as a Service (IaaS)**: Users are provided with the IT-infrastructure, including (virtualised) hardware and storage, and networking. They have to provide, deploy and run software themselves, which gives users a high amount of control. An example of IaaS is an online store outsourcing the website hosting to a cloud service provider. The business still develops, maintains and updates their website, while the cloud service provider takes care of the servers and ensures the business stays online, even during spikes in the web traffic.
- **Platform as a Service (PaaS)**: Users are provided with a platform suitable for running certain applications. Such a platform includes the necessary infrastructure, the operating system and ready-to-use network and storage. Users only have to provide the application to run on the cloud. An example of PaaS is a cloud service provider that offers a pre-configured and maintained virtual machine on which the user can develop software.
- **Software as a Service (SaaS)**: Users are provided with a ready-to-use application or software package. They only have to provide the required inputs for the software. SaaS products can often be used through a website or a specifically developed interface. Examples include online text processors and other office products delivered via the internet.

The key difference between these three services is the extent to which a cloud service provider manages the necessary resources. In IaaS, the cloud service provider manages only the bare essentials and the user retains a wide influence on the configuration. In SaaS, the cloud service provider configures and manages most of the environment and users have little influence on the infrastructure. PaaS is in between both.

The above definitions are useful, but not strict. The different service models may overlap and different types of cloud services, located between these three basic types, exist. For example, the type *Container as a Service* is located between IaaS and PaaS. In this model, users can deploy, manage and modify containers in the cloud. Yet, the distinction in different types helps to group and analyse different cloud services.

3   Quantum Cloud Services

Currently, there are 10–20 different providers of quantum cloud services [3, 16, 21], but this number is growing rapidly. Even though this is still somewhat limited, we can already identify similar types of services as in Sect. 2.2. These types relate to the current state of development of quantum computers and the types of services known from classical cloud platforms.

- **Infrastructure as a Service**: Users are provided with full control over a quantum device, including which operations to apply to which qubit. For academic and research purposes, low-level control over the quantum hardware is useful, such as the ability to execute pulse level instruction in gate-based transmon devices [1].
  As full control over the device could easily break it, users often get access to a fixed set of (parameterised) operations, which are then mapped to the individual qubits. Examples of IaaS include IBM Quantum [21] and Quantum-Inspire [40].
- **Platform as a Service**: Users are provided with higher-level access to quantum computers. The provider assures that hardware-agnostic operations are correctly compiled in hardware-aware operations and mapped to suitable hardware. Software to decompose and map the operations already exists and is part of ongoing research [33, 47].
  Examples of PaaS operations for gate-based quantum backends include single and two-qubit gates and a multi-qubit quantum Fourier transform. Examples of PaaS include Microsoft Azure [31] and D-Wave [15].
- **Software as a Service**: Users are provided with off-the-shelf tools that implement an algorithm to solve their problem. The user, only interested in the end result, is not bothered by the exact (quantum) implementation.
  The first implementations of SaaS products already exist [15]. Here, the software decides for itself how to partition the problem in smaller subproblems and which of them to run on a quantum or classical backend.

Similar to the classical services, these types indicate responsibilities for certain functionalities. Again, overlap between different types of services exists, especially with respect to the currently available quantum cloud platforms: most current PaaS platforms are similar to IaaS platforms. As an example, the services offered by Classiq [11] fall in between PaaS and SaaS.

The identified services work equally well in hybrid and distributed settings. In hybrid settings, quantum and high-performance computers solve a problem together. Distributed algorithms split the operations over multiple devices. IaaS users are given full control over which operations to implement on which devices. For PaaS and SaaS users, the distribution is performed automatically.

4   Interfaces for Quantum Cloud Platforms

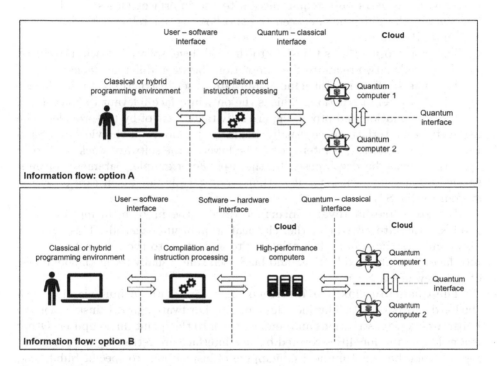

Fig. 1. Overview of the different interfaces for quantum cloud computing. The distinction between these two information flows is not relevant or even noticeable to SaaS and some PaaS users.

An important aspect of the implementation of (quantum) cloud computing is given by *interfaces*. Interfaces are shared boundaries in computing systems across which two or more separate components of the computing stack exchange information. Interfaces help to abstract the information flow between different components and are often used in standardisation settings [17, Fig. 5].

In cloud-based systems, these components naturally arise as user-side (local) and provider-side (cloud or remote). Based on where the separation between local and cloud lies, different interfaces exist. The interfaces hence indicate what potential boundaries are for the user's view depending on the provided service. Generally speaking, the more advanced a user is, the more interfaces they will (need to) access.

Figure 1 gives a schematic overview of two information flows between users and quantum computers, together with possible interfaces. The first information flow corresponds to direct contact from a user to a quantum computer. The second information flow corresponds to a user that performs computations on a remote (high-performance) computer, which interacts with a quantum computer. Notably, the distinction between these information flows is not relevant to all users, as some users only require access to the interfaces closest to the user. Specifically, the difference between the two flows is not relevant to SaaS users and most PaaS users.

The first two interfaces translate to the high-level software stack introduced in [8]. The other two relate to the interactions between different devices.

The **user-software interface** translates user-instructions to hardware-agnostic low-level instructions. This is the only interface relevant to SaaS users, because compilation and processing are fully taken care of by the provider. The user-software interface hence usually forms the boundary of the view of a SaaS user. For PaaS users, this interface will be lower in the software stack, and some operations must be decomposed by the user. For example, parameter optimisation routines in variational algorithms are typically not taken care of by the system for PaaS users.

The **software-hardware interface** divides the problem in multiple subproblems that are solved on either classical or quantum backends. This interface also combines the subproblem solutions to a solution to the full problem. This interface is mainly used by PaaS and IaaS users, and usually forms the boundary of the view of PaaS users.

The **quantum-classical interface** takes care of the communication with the hardware backends. This include compiling hardware-agnostic instructions to hardware-aware instructions and sending them to the quantum computer. Other examples of functionalities covered by this interface are retrieving measurement results from the quantum device, mapping of instructions to specific qubits and applying error correction routines. This interface is only relevant for IaaS users.

The **quantum interface** exchanges information between different quantum computers. This interface is relevant for distributed settings where computations are divided over different quantum backends. This interface should allow interactions between quantum backends, hosted by the same or other parties. The quantum interface is only relevant for IaaS users.

5   Functionalities of Cloud-Based Quantum Platforms

Current quantum cloud platforms offer some functionalities that ease the use of quantum computers, such as decomposing hardware-agnostic instructions to hardware-aware instructions [20, 47] and decomposing a problem in smaller manageable chunks to run separately on a quantum device [16]. However, the total number of functionalities offered is limited.

In this section, we consider different functionalities of quantum cloud services grouped in four different domains: device choice, programming, integration and security. For each of the three cloud service types and each functionality, we indicate what users can expect from the cloud provider regarding the functionality. We identified the different functionalities by considering different usage-scenario's.

The identified functionalities do not aim to impose requirements on current or future quantum cloud platforms, and we do not aim to give an overview of what is currently offered by quantum cloud providers or which functionality should be offered first. Instead, this overview serves as a suggestion towards future developments of these platforms so that a positive user experience is maximised. We believe that some of these functionalities are necessary for quantum computing to be adopted sufficiently well in business processes.

Table 1 gives an overview of the extent to which cloud service providers should arrange functionalities, similar to the one shown in [27].

Table 1. Overview of extent to which a cloud service provider should take care of functionalities ● = fully taken care of; ◐ = somewhat taken care of; ○ = not taken care of

Domain	Functionality	SaaS	PaaS	IaaS
Device choice	Characterisation of quantum devices	◐	◐	●
	Choice in computational device by the user	○	◐	●
	Appropriate device allocation	●	◐	○
Programming	Programming at different complexity levels	○	◐	●
	A hybrid programming environment	●	●	◐
	Automatic quantum operation compiling routines	●	●	○
Integration	Possibility to communicate with other devices	○	●	●
	Integration with classical cloud-services	●	◐	○
Security	Security of computations	◐	◐	◐

5.1 Device Choice

Characterisation of Quantum Devices: This functionality regards listing the relevant properties of quantum devices to allow users to make a conscious choice on which quantum backend to use. Usually, these properties are best summarised by looking at suitable quantum metrics. These metrics can be considered at multiple levels, most notably component-level, system-level and application-level [43]. For gate-based devices, some component-level metrics are the number of qubits, single qubit T1 and T2 times, the read-out fidelity and the fidelity of single and two-qubit gates. Examples of system-level metrics are the quantum volume [14] and the system stability, while the Q-score [29] and the QED-C benchmarks [28] are examples of application-level metrics. Ideally, these metrics should be presented in a uniform manner across different vendors.

Current cloud providers often give a detailed overview of their device in terms of component-level metrics [21,40]. Sometimes, system-level metrics such as the quantum volume are also listed. Application-level metrics are often not shown.

The desired level of detail of the metric depends on the type of service. For SaaS users, only the performance of the device on a certain application matters. For this matter, so an application-oriented performance benchmark [28] is in general sufficient. For PaaS users, system-level metrics, such as the quantum volume [14] are important, but also sometimes component-level metrics such as gate and qubits fidelities. For IaaS metrics, these component-level metrics are the most important.

Choice in Computational Device by the User: This functionality regards the choice of the user in the used computational device. This choice can be based on the characteristics of the available devices or on the available resources. A closely related aspect is simultaneous use of quantum devices in distributed quantum computing, which might become relevant once quantum hardware becomes sufficiently powerful.

Currently, quantum cloud providers give users free choice in which of the available quantum devices to use [16,21,31,40]. Hybrid quantum providers currently offer little choice in which classical device to use for the hybrid computations [15].

Users of SaaS and some users of PaaS will have in general no preference on the hardware backend and hence any sufficiently powerful device can be used. The price, paying method and availability of the device may influence this choice. Users of IaaS typically have a preference for one device over another.

Appropriate Device Allocation: This functionality relates to the previous two and measures whether a quantum cloud provider includes suggestions for a specific device, depending on the given algorithm. Especially with the various number of hardware technologies currently available, it is expected that different devices will excel at different algorithms.

Research on this topic is only just starting [42], hence, this functionality is not yet prevalent. Users are currently free to choose which device they want to use, but there is little guidance as to which device is most suitable for a certain application.

This is a crucial functionality for SaaS users, as they mainly care about running their algorithms in the best way possible. This is also somewhat the case for PaaS users, while this functionality is not really relevant for IaaS users.

5.2   Programming

Programming at Different Complexity Levels: This functionality entails the ability to program quantum algorithms on different levels of complexity.

Examples of these levels of complexity are programming using elementary quantum operations, hardware-agnostic quantum instructions or higher-order routines such as standard circuit implementations.

Current cloud providers provide some variety of complexity levels, as both pulses, single-qubit rotations, basic quantum functions, as well as common quantum functions can be used as basic instructions [16, 21, 40].

This functionality is not relevant for SaaS users, whilst it is very relevant for IaaS users. Depending on the implementation, this functionality might also be relevant for PaaS users.

A Hybrid Programming Environment: This functionality captures the ability for users to program their algorithms in a hybrid programming environment. Ideally, this programming environment is provided by the vendor and users can program the quantum instructions locally in the classical programming language of their choice. However, it is sometimes still desirable for users to be able to install their own code libraries. Quantum subroutines are called within this hybrid programming environment. A more in-depth analysis of hybrid quantum programming is presented in [8]. Results of a quantum subroutine should directly be used as input in the following classical computations.

All current cloud providers currently work in this way, as quantum instructions have to be sent in through classical programs [16, 21, 31, 40].

By definition, this functionality is especially relevant for SaaS and PaaS users. At least the most common programming languages should be supported in this hybrid programming environment.

Automatic Quantum Operation Compiling Routines: This functionality describes the level of compilation from hardware-agnostic to hardware-specific instructions automatically performed by the provider. This compilation can either be done automatically or with (some) input from the users.

All quantum providers currently provide this functionality, as users can implement their algorithms without having to worry about specific compilation [16, 21, 31, 40]. However, some providers do allow some compilation to be done by the user [21].

This is especially relevant for SaaS and PaaS users, for which compilation of instructions is not important. For IaaS users, it might be beneficial if some of the compilation steps can be done manually.

5.3   Integration

Possibility to Communicate with Other Devices: This functionality captures how well different quantum devices can be linked. Linking different quantum devices allows for performing computations between different parties and hence using input from different parties. Additionally, linking quantum devices allows for larger problem instances to be solved. In this way, problems can be broken down into smaller problems that are solved on separate quantum devices, allowing for methods that rely on Divide and Conquer [41].

There is currently no quantum cloud provider which offers communication between different quantum devices.

This functionality is mostly relevant for IaaS and PaaS users. The difference between these two services is the amount control over the communication between different devices. Users of SaaS should only specify if data from various sources is needed and where that data is located.

Integration with Classical Cloud-Services: This functionalities considers the integration with classical cloud platforms. As quantum computers are not expected to replace classical computers. Therefore, a seamless interaction between classical and quantum computers is required. These classical computations can either be performed on a local device or using high-performance computers hosted in the cloud. In this context, it is important to distinguish between hybrid workflows and hybrid algorithms, as indicated in [39].

An important factor in this integration is the communication time between classical and quantum services. This is especially relevant for variational algorithms. For such applications, the compiled circuits are closely related, and hence time can be saved on compilation of the circuit.

Currently, only a limited number of quantum providers offer hybrid services [15]. The few providers that do, often offer hybrid services in a black box manner.

This hybrid quantum-classical setting can be integrated in services offered by SaaS. The software itself should decide which parts are run on a quantum backend and which parts are run classically. For PaaS, these optimisation routines will likely be done by the users themselves. Ideally, the computations are done on a low level in the stack, thereby limiting the need for multiple compilations of very similar quantum circuits. For IaaS users, the integration will mainly be done manually.

5.4   Security

Security of Computations: This functionality relates to the security of the computations. Ideally, users should be able to execute their computations in a secure way, such that no other user can see their computations. The providers themselves however can, in principle, learn all computations performed by a user. This security aspect is as relevant for quantum cloud services as it is for classical cloud services.

With quantum cloud services however, users can resort to blind quantum computing, which shields their operations even from the provider [6,7,12]. This should be implemented such that it gives minimal overhead for the user.

No current quantum cloud provider takes security measures towards shielding user input from the provider. Shielding from other users is implemented.

This functionality is equally relevant for all three types of users.

6   Conclusions and Outlook

To achieve a smooth uptake of quantum computing by industry, we must ensure that quantum computing, and particularly quantum cloud computing, becomes user-centric. Therefore, we considered quantum cloud computing from a user point of view in this work.

We first listed different types of classical cloud services and then identified similar types for quantum cloud platforms. These types help to group the different cloud platforms and to identify different functionalities for each.

To ensure a seamless interaction between different components in quantum cloud platforms, interfaces are necessary. Figure 1 provides a schematic overview of the relevant interfaces. These interfaces also help integrating quantum computing with classical computing, as quantum computers will most likely act as secondary processors, supporting classical computers.

User-centric quantum cloud computing requires various functionalities, only some of which are offered by current quantum cloud providers. We give an overview of desirable functionalities and link them to the different types of services. We believe that some functionalities are vital for quantum cloud platforms to be useful in operational settings.

The defined functionalities, together with the different interfaces, provide a clear path towards quantum cloud platforms that serve different users with different needs in a unified way. With our work, we have taken a step forward towards user-centric quantum cloud computing.

References

1. Alexander, T., et al.: Qiskit pulse: programming quantum computers through the cloud with pulses. Quantum Sci. Technol. 5(4), 044006 (020). https://doi.org/10.1088/2058-9565/aba404
2. Alhambra: The quantum ecosystem that overcomes knowledge barriers (2021). https://www.alhambrait.com/en/products/qpath/
3. Amazon: Amazon braket. https://aws.amazon.com/braket/
4. Amazon Web Services: AWS HPC. https://aws.amazon.com/hpc/
5. Apple Inc.: iCloud. https://icloud.com/
6. Arrighi, P., Salvail, L.: Blind quantum computation. Int. J. Quantum Inf. 04(05), 883–898 (2006). https://doi.org/10.1142/s0219749906002171
7. Barz, S., Kashefi, E., Broadbent, A., Fitzsimons, J.F., Zeilinger, A., Walther, P.: Demonstration of blind quantum computing. Science 335(6066), 303–308 (2012). https://doi.org/10.1126/science.1214707
8. van den Brink, R.F., Neumann, N.M.P., Phillipson, F.: Vision on next level quantum software tooling. In: 11th International Conference on Future Computational Technologies and Applications, pp. 16–23 (2019)
9. Chellappa, R.: Intermediaries in cloud-computing: a new computing paradigm. In: INFORMS Annual Meeting, Dallas, pp. 26–29 (1997)
10. Cicconetti, C., Conti, M., Passarella, A.: Resource allocation in quantum networks for distributed quantum computing. In: 2022 IEEE International Conference on Smart Computing (SMARTCOMP), pp. 124–132 (2022). https://doi.org/10.1109/SMARTCOMP55677.2022.00032

11. Classiq: Designing and implementing quantum algorithms with functional level programming (2023). https://www.classiq.io/docs/functional-level-programming-basics

12. Cojocaru, A., Colisson, L., Kashefi, E., Wallden, P.: On the possibility of classical client blind quantum computing. Cryptography **5**(1), 3 (2021). https://doi.org/10.3390/cryptography5010003

13. Corcoles, A.D., et al.: Challenges and opportunities of near-term quantum computing systems. Proc. IEEE. **108**(8), 1338–1352 (2020). https://doi.org/10.1109/jproc.2019.2954005

14. Cross, A.W., Bishop, L.S., Sheldon, S., Nation, P.D., Gambetta, J.M.: Validating quantum computers using randomized model circuits. Phys. Rev. A **100**, 032328 (2019). https://doi.org/10.1103/PhysRevA.100.032328

15. D-Wave Systems: Hybrid solver for discrete quadratic models (2020). https://www.dwavesys.com/media/ssidd1x3/14-1050a-a_hybrid_solver_for_discrete_quadratic_models.pdf

16. D-Wave Systems: DWave-ocean-SDK (2021). https://github.com/dwavesystems/dwave-ocean-sdk

17. van Deventer, O., et al.: Towards European standards for quantum technologies. EPJ Quantum Technol. **9**(1), 33 (2022). https://doi.org/10.1140/epjqt/s40507-022-00150-1

18. Dropbox: Dropbox. https://www.dropbox.com/

19. Feld, S., et al.: A hybrid solution method for the capacitated vehicle routing problem using a quantum annealer. Front. ICT **6**, 13 (2019)

20. Fingerhuth, M., Babej, T., Wittek, P.: Open source software in quantum computing. PLoS ONE **13**(12), e0208561 (2018). https://doi.org/10.1371/journal.pone.0208561

21. IBM Quantum: IBM Quantum Experience (2021). https://quantum-computing.ibm.com/

22. IDM: Types of cloud services. Medium (2018). https://medium.com/@IDMdatasecurity/types-of-cloud-services-b54e5b574f6

23. Kadowaki, T., Nishimori, H.: Quantum annealing in the transverse Ising model. Phys. Rev. E **58**, 5355–5363 (1998). https://doi.org/10.1103/PhysRevE.58.5355

24. Kaiiali, M., Sezer, S., Khalid, A.: Cloud computing in the quantum era. In: 2019 IEEE Conference on Communications and Network Security (CNS), pp. 1–4 (2019). https://doi.org/10.1109/CNS44998.2019.8952589

25. Kavis, M.: The cloud's lock-in vs. agility trade-off. https://www2.deloitte.com/us/en/pages/consulting/articles/cloud-vendor-lock-in-deloitte-on-cloud-blog.html

26. Khammassi, N., Guerreschi, G.G., Ashraf, I., Hogaboam, J.W., Almudever, C.G., Bertels, K.: cqasm v1.0: Towards a common quantum assembly language (2018)

27. Lanfear, T., Hitchcock, A.M., Berry, D.: Shared responsibility in the cloud - microsoft azure (2022). https://learn.microsoft.com/en-us/azure/security/fundamentals/shared-responsibility

28. Lubinski, T., et al.: Application-oriented performance benchmarks for quantum computing (2021)

29. Martiel, S., Ayral, T., Allouche, C.: Benchmarking quantum coprocessors in an application-centric, hardware-agnostic, and scalable way. IEEE Trans. Quantum Eng. **2**, 1–11 (2021). https://doi.org/10.1109/tqe.2021.3090207

30. Mell, P., Grance, T.: The NIST definition of cloud computing (2011). https://doi.org/10.6028/NIST.SP.800-145

31. Microsoft: Azure quantum. https://azure.microsoft.com/en-us/services/quantum/

32. Microsoft: Office Online. https://www.microsoft.com/en-us/microsoft-365/
33. Möller, M., Schalkers, M.: Libket: A cross-platform programming framework for quantum-accelerated scientific computing. In: Krzhizhanovskaya, V.V., Závodszky, G., Lees, M.H., Dongarra, J.J., Sloot, P.M.A., Brissos, S., Teixeira, J. (eds.) Computational Science - ICCS 2020, pp. 451–464. Springer International Publishing, Cham (2020). https://doi.org/10.1007/978-3-030-50433-5_35
34. Neukart, F., Compostella, G., Seidel, C., Von Dollen, D., Yarkoni, S., Parney, B.: Traffic flow optimization using a quantum annealer. Front. ICT **4**, 29 (2017)
35. Nielsen, M.A., Chuang, I.L.: Quantum Computation and Quantum Information: 10th Anniversary Edition. Cambridge University Press (2010). https://doi.org/10.1017/CBO9780511976667
36. O'Brien, J.L.: Optical quantum computing. Science. **318**(5856), 1567–1570 (2007). http://www.jstor.org/stable/20051746
37. Owen, E.: Quantum cloud computing - Cambridge consultants on how to make it happen (2023). https://www.cambridgeconsultants.com/us/insights/opinion/quantum-cloud-computing
38. PCMag: Cloud computing (2023). https://www.pcmag.com/encyclopedia/term/cloud-computing
39. Phillipson, F., Neumann, N., Wezeman, R.: Classification of hybrid quantum-classical computing (2022). https://doi.org/10.48550/ARXIV.2210.15314
40. QuTech: Quantum inspire home. https://www.quantum-inspire.com/ (2018)
41. Saleem, Z.H., Tomesh, T., Perlin, M.A., Gokhale, P., Suchara, M.: Divide and conquer for combinatorial optimization and distributed quantum computation (2021). https://doi.org/10.48550/ARXIV.2107.07532
42. Salm, M., Barzen, J., Breitenbücher, U., Leymann, F., Weder, B., Wild, K.: The NISQ analyzer: Automating the selection of quantum computers for quantum algorithms. In: Service-Oriented Computing, pp. 66–85. Springer International Publishing (2020). https://doi.org/10.1007/978-3-030-64846-6_5
43. van der Schoot, W.E., Wezeman, R.S., Eendebak, P.T., Neumann, N.M.P., Phillipson, F.: Evaluating three levels of quantum metrics on quantum-inspire hardware. (unpublished)
44. Shor, P.: Algorithms for quantum computation: Discrete logarithms and factoring. In: Proceedings 35th Annual Symposium on Foundations of Computer Science (1994). https://doi.org/10.1109/sfcs.1994.365700
45. Singh, H., Sachdev, A.: The quantum way of cloud computing. In: 2014 International Conference on Reliability Optimization and Information Technology (ICROIT), pp. 397–400 (2014). https://doi.org/10.1109/ICROIT.2014.6798362
46. Smith, R.S., Curtis, M.J., Zeng, W.J.: A practical quantum instruction set architecture (2016)
47. Treinish, M., et al.: Qiskit/qiskit: Qiskit 0.42.1 (2023). https://doi.org/10.5281/zenodo.7757946
48. Vasudevan, T.: Bluebleed leak proves again, not all cloud service providers are secure, https://www.skyhighsecurity.com/en-us/about/newsroom/blogs/industry-perspectives/bluebleed-leak-proves-it-again-you-cannot-assume-cloud-service-providers-are-secure.html
49. White, J.E.: Network Specifications for Remote Job Entry and Remote Job Output Retrieval at UCSB. RFC 105 (1971). https://doi.org/10.17487/RFC0105
50. Wray, J.: Where's the rub: Cloud computing's hidden costs (2014). https://www.forbes.com/sites/centurylink/2014/02/27/wheres-the-rub-cloud-computings-hidden-costs/

Internet of Things

A Feasibility Study of a Lightweight Fog Computing Architecture Integrating Blockchain Technology for Smart E-Health Applications

Mohammad R. H. Mullick, Marcel Großmann, and Udo R. Krieger[✉]

Fakultät WIAI, Otto-Friedrich-Universität, An der Weberei 5, 96047 Bamberg,
Germany
udo.krieger@ieee.org

Abstract. Today, a variety of advanced Internet-of-Things applications like data collection apps for ambient assisted living services supporting elder patients or for the surveillance of smart homes are developed everywhere. Regarding such application scenarios and the requirement to securely disseminate the collected data, we present a fog computing architecture that integrates blockchain technology for privacy aware data sharing. The latter fog-blockchain prototype is based on a private, permissioned blockchain paradigm. We discuss a lightweight implementation of our proposed integrated fog node architecture using Hyperledger Fabric as blockchain with a peer-to-peer network among cheap single-board-computers as basic data collecting peers. Furthermore, we investigate the computing and network performance indices of our prototypical lightweight fog computing architecture.

Keywords: Internet-of-Things · Fog computing · Smart home · Blockchain · Hyperledger fabric

1 Introduction

Nowadays, new advanced Internet-of-Things (IoT) applications are evolving very rapidly and advanced software-defined communication technology like 5G and evolving 6G mobile networks with better network functions virtualization (NFV) techniques are incorporated into the underlying infrastructures of software-defined networks (SDN) for cloud computing, fog computing, and multi-access edge computing (MEC), cf. [1,10,11].

Considering advanced Internet-of-Things applications like data collection apps used for ambient assisted living of patients at their homes or for the surveillance and remote control of heating, ventilation, air condition (called HVAC), washing machines and other entities consuming energy triggered by users' control at their smart homes, one may support an anonymized data collection and the decoupling of personal identities and control functionality by blockchain

© The Author(s), under exclusive license to Springer Nature Switzerland AG 2023
U. R. Krieger et al. (Eds.): I4CS 2023, CCIS 1876, pp. 253–276, 2023.
https://doi.org/10.1007/978-3-031-40852-6_14

technologies, cf. [6,20]. Such privacy protection methods can enable better consumption studies of user communities by service providers. They can also serve the exigency to improve advanced healthcare services or smart energy provisioning at private homes that are raised by current socio-economic developments like aging societies and a period of climate change.

Then the research question naturally arises whether one can incorporate fog computing together with blockchain technology for related IoT-applications and how a resourceful, efficient system design based on an extensible virtualized open source software architecture should look like.

In this paper we investigates the feasibility of using a private, permissioned blockchain concept in a distributed fog computing environment, cf. [13,20,21]. Such a private blockchain aims to work in a controlled setting. It is most suitable for a rapid adoption by IoT-service providers exploiting an SDN/NFV based network environment to interconnect modern IoT devices and cloud, fog, or edge computing systems. On the path between an end device to the cloud every device is maintained by the service provider. Regarding the collection of sensitive personal data in the sketched smart home scenarios like smart ambient assisted living systems, such a private blockchain makes perfect sense to protect the personal data. To study the feasibility and performance aspects of such an integrated architecture we have designed such a lightweight IoT-architecture for the related data collection by personal sensors and implemented it by means of a cheap single-board-computer (SBC). Then the integrated blockchain technology can offer an extensible, immutable, transparent data repository in our fog computing system, cf. [4,10,21]. The latter can be used for securing sensitive smart home applications like the sharing of personal health data that are collected by patients with persistent diseases like diabetes mellitus or arterial hypertension, for instance, or the usage patterns of employed service entities in smart private homes.

We have implemented this distributed architecture by means of Hyperledger Fabric [2] in a test bed of Raspberry Pi SBCs which serve as basic nodes of an underlying peer-to-peer network of this employed permissioned blockchain. Then we have evaluated important performance metrics of our fog computing system by means of a test bed with five SBCs as basic peers of Hyperledger Fabric as its core blockchain component. In the following we discuss our findings regarding this integrated software design and reveal the limits of its implementation by our feasibility study. These technical results may inspire improved fog node architectures and the design of further scalability and feasibility studies in modern smart cities like Bamberg, cf. [17].

The paper is organized as follows. In Sect. 2 we present the foundations of our integrated fog computing system. In Sect. 3 we describe the developed software architecture of the integrated fog-blockchain system and thereafter its implementation in Sect. 4. Then we evaluate some performance metrics of the implemented prototype in Sect. 5. Finally, some conclusions are presented.

2 Foundations of a Fog Computing System Integrating Blockchain Technology

Today, it is a standard edge computing approach to consider the support of advanced IoT-application areas by means of a fog computing architecture shown in Fig. 1, cf. [1,18]. Considering the different IoT-application areas, there are diverse requirements with respect to the underlying architecture of fog nodes and their performance as indicated by Table 1, cf. [1,10].

A fog computing system based on scalable virtualization techniques can process and store a large variety of digital data collected by lightweight clients like sensors in smart homes or in professional healthcare environments like retirement homes. Regarding the next generation of a sharing economy based on the dominance of those digital data, privacy and security issues naturally arise, cf. [14]. The sharing of the collected data by the sensor layer of a hierarchically organized fog computing system can be supported by blockchain technology, cf. [6,20,21].

In particular, healthcare applications have their own unique requirements and challenges such as *security, interoperability, data sharing* and *mobility* support, cf. [14]. In this situation it is necessary to provide access controls, authentication, and non-repudiation of a patient's electronic medical health record or her/his data generated by various medical devices, for instance, sensors collecting the heartbeat rate and the glucose value at various times of the day.

Standard requirements of typical e-health applications in smart homes such as ambient assisted living services which are one focal area of our fog computing architecture with its blockchain functionality often incorporate the following three basic technical design issues:

- In a considered typical IoT-healthcare context *interoperability* turns out to be a major issue. Regarding typical therapeutical scenarios of an affected patient, the patient's healthcare data need to be shared among different doctors or even hospitals. But in a centralized database oriented architecture this may

Table 1. IoT application sectors supported by fog computing and their infrastructural requirements

Application Sectors	Infrastructural Requirements
sharing economy	trustworthy transaction models
insurance/liability	transparency, tamper-proof data management systems
industrial IoT-sector	transparent product lifecycle management
automotive and mobility management	vehicle lifecycle management by tracking the history of a vehicle, verifying the use of various manufacturing elements, etc.
smart city	huge bandwidth, low-latency, privacy, key management
healthcare, education, government	secured identity management, hiding personal information, sharing personal data, only sharing data with intended parties

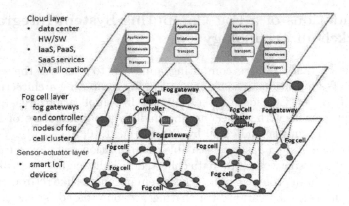

Fig. 1. Hierarchical architecture of a fog computing environment (cf. [21])

be impossible. Furthermore, it also opens up an opportunity for a monopoly regarding a patient's treatment or severe reliability issues.

- *Data sharing* is necessary for a patient to have a unified view of the whole medical data. One may also need to share only some part of the data with some other party. A typical medical diagnostics step may require a patient's thorough medical history over several years depending on her/his age. A centralized solution where data sharing is not possible due to the control by a single entity without securely controlled Internet access may become a bottleneck in such a process, in particular in case of emergency. Therefore, sharing the required personal data is an important factor where a blockchain based solution can substantially improve the medical treatment.

- *Mobility* is becoming another important factor due to the expansion of mobile health applications where various body sensors are collecting personal data continuously, e.g., by means of wearables. Maintaining the privacy of such generated data during the data sharing, consent management, access control, and authentication processes as well as the users' trust in those new technologies constitute key issues of such advanced IoT-scenarios of ambient assisted living and remote e-health services. In this respect various research efforts are currently going on to figure out how blockchain technology can be helpful in a fog computing environment, cf. [4,10,14,18].

A fog computing infrastructure incorporating blockchain functionalities can enable several key features required by these new smart home applications. Here the IoT-environment normally applies a client-server paradigm and the fog computing layer constitutes an intermediary level between the clients and servers. As indicated by Table 2, combining both fog computing and blockchain technology can offer advanced application features like an anonymous sharing of the collected personal sensor data, trustworthy transactions among different parties involved in the considered smart home scenarios and e-health applications, and a secure peer-to-peer communication among all those parties. It can also provide new value-added features like the tracking of the data history, transparency, and a tamper-proof data management, etc., see [20].

Table 2. Key application features offered by an integrated fog-blockchain infrastructure

Application features	IoT	Fog	Fog + Blockchain
Privacy	No	No	Yes
(Pseudo-) anonymous sharing of sensor data	No	No	Yes
Transparency	No	No	Yes
Temper-proof data management	No	No	Yes
Trustworthy transactions	No	No	Yes
Data history tracking	No	No	Yes
Peer-to-peer communication along an overlay network	No	No	Yes
Huge bandwidth	No	Yes	Yes
Low-latency communication	No	Yes	Yes

Regarding the design of an extensible, virtualized, distributed service platform for smart home applications, we have decided for all these reasons to adopt a fog computing approach with an integrated blockchain functionality.

3 Design of a Lightweight Integrated Fog-Blockchain Architecture for Smart E-Health Applications

Considering smart home applications such as e-health apps for ambient assisted living scenarios, the effective integration of blockchain technology into a fog computing environment is a challenging technical issue. First of all, it is necessary to specify the scenarios where the collected sensor data can be shared within the fog-blockchain computing environment. Furthermore, one has to figure out the roles of the stakeholders of such a distributed ledger system.

For this purpose we follow here the fog architecture with its three basic layers depicted in Fig. 1 that we have developed in our previous research on fog gateways, cf. [21]. Regarding this three-layer computing model and its protocol stack, similar design studies and reference architectures already exist with respect to a blockchain integration, see, e.g., that one by Yang et al. [20]. To implement a scalable system it is reasonable to implement virtualized fog gateways on top of cheap SBCs like Raspberry Pi or Arduino systems, cf. [21].

The major problem in setting up such an architecture and its underlying communication network is to meet the required trustworthiness, the tracking, tamper-proof data management, and the privacy, the security, as well as the SLA and QoS related criteria of a considered IoT-application. The latter criteria have to be developed along the three basic dimensions of the *network*, *storage*, and *computation* components in the architecture of the fog gateways, cf. [20]. Regarding a blockchain concept to support the privacy, security, and immutability, one may use the concept of a plain public or a private blockchain, or of a multichain, or the sharding approach, or to use off-chaining or sidechains like Plasma, cf. [4,16,21]. Considering our smart home scenario with personal e-health applications, we can immediately exclude a public blockchain at the edge of an IoT infrastructure and argue that a private, permissioned blockchain has to be chosen to fulfill the functional and non-functional requirements in an optimal way.

Considering the design options with respect to secured smart e-health applications, the use of such a blockchain at the resource constrained IoT-devices is not apparent. In an IoT-application scenario like the healthcare sector where a patient's data may need to be shared amongst multiple parties, e.g., in case of an emergency, a delicate data sharing technique is required for such setting. In this case it is certainly not convenient to handle the issues of smart data processing and the creation of transactions at the edge device with its sensors due to the restricted storage and processing capabilities. Rather than using the edge device itself, one can adapt the blockchain functionality at their logical counterparts within the fog layer, namely the fog gateways. The latter are managing the data collection of the end devices including all their associated sensors. In this case it is a plausible idea to utilize the cloud as a persistent storage of the patient's data. This design can also offer the integration of new machine learning techniques. Regarding the fog computing layer with its distributed gateways and the logical layers of a blockchain, we follow this integrated approach and its related protocol stack shown by Fig. 2.

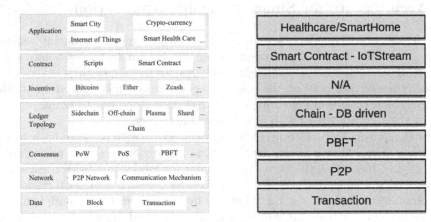

Fig. 2. Functional decomposition of the blockchain stack and its matching with the realized integrated design of our lightweight fog-blockchain prototype (cf. [20])

The fog nodes serve as peers of the peer-to-peer (P2P) network of the blockchain. The consensus protocol of a blockchain and the topology of the distributed ledger platform that is supporting the interaction of the blockchain nodes employing smart contracts can be derived from a given distributed ledger platform, cf. [4, 18, 20]. Our previous research [4, 21] has shown that the Practical Byzantine Fault Tolerance (PBFT) scheme may provide an adequate consensus algorithm for resource constrained fog gateways based on Raspberry Pi SBCs. Therefore, we attempt to incorporate such a scheme to establish the ledger topology among the peers of the realized blockchain.

Deploying a private, permissioned blockchain at the cloud layer gives us the opportunity to share the time stamped and timely ordered data to multiple parties. Regarding the selection of a blockchain platform, we may argue that an open source, enterprise oriented solution where multiple organizations or parties can get involved in both the consensus process and the data sharing process is the right option of the considered smart e-health scenarios. Therefore, we have adopted Hyperledger Fabric [2] as our basic permissioned blockchain. This private blockchain platform is used in our cloud layer for an immutable storage of the collected personal data.

The fog gateways of the fog computing layer will work as the distributed clients of this selected blockchain. It is an advantage of our integrated design that the end devices of the deployed IoT-application with their attached sensors will remain unchanged. Hence, they will not be impacted by underlying design changes in either the fog computing layer or the cloud layer.

In our integrated fog-blockchain approach we also have to look at the network dimension and, in particular, at the peer-to-peer network of the blockchain. The latter is established among the nodes of the blockchain related to the end devices and their controlling fog gateways. The latter nodes incorporate an SDN/NFV functionality, and the employed consensus algorithm of the selected blockchain model, see Figs. 1 to 4. Considering the fog layer, there can be multiple gateways within several sublayers. Regarding the sketched e-health scenario, only a single layer has been studied in the realized fog-blockchain prototype of our feasibility study in Sect. 5.

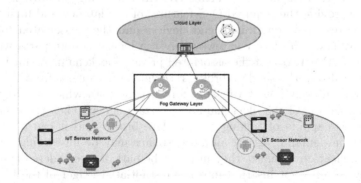

Fig. 3. Overview on the integration of a permissioned blockchain into a fog computing environment of our prototype

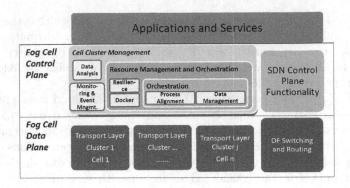

Fig. 4. Prototypical protocol design of a fog gateway (cf. [4])

In general, the application layer of our integrated protocol design can be realized by any IoT-application for smart healthcare, which is backed up by the use of smart contracts. In our approach the latter components are derived from the underlying contract layer of the blockchain platform. As Hyperledger Fabric is a private blockchain, it does not require any incentives in our assumed basic e-health scenario, see Fig. 2.

In conclusion, we adopt to use the blockchain platform Hyperledger Fabric which realizes the topology layer of the distributed ledger instances by a single chain. Its consensus layer uses a PBFT-based solution while the data are processed by means of a transaction from the bottom layer of the chosen protocol model, cf. [2,21]. Considering our overall system architecture, its hierarchical fog computing layer with the associated fog gateways contains an SDN-enabled device layer for real-time data analysis and communication as well as the delivery of service elements to the attached local IoT-devices, see Fig. 4.

We believe that the use of such effective, virtualized fog gateways is a systematic way to provide the required QoS-features of low latency and high throughput for the resource constrained end devices and their associated fog nodes, respectively. Then the latter gateways are the logical counterparts within the established P2P-network of the associated private blockchain. A considered fog gateway will also work as a data broker receiving data streams from the logically attached IoT-end devices. It will only forward the data which are required for a given transaction of the blockchain at a certain epoch. Then the client at the cloud layer is capable of talking to this data broker and it can also create a transaction on demand. As not all data streams may be interesting for a given e-health application scenario, they may not be part of a considered transaction. Then they are also not inserted into the instantiated ledger of the blockchain. In a typical healthcare scenario, involved actors like doctors, for instance, may only be interested to know how often the blood pressure of a particular patient crossed the normal level. Therefore, it makes sense to record only those hashed references as associated information records in the distributed ledger of the realized blockchain.

In summary, we are convinced that this adopted classical three-layer fog computing model in Fig. 1 can provide an efficient technical basis of our integrated fog-blockchain approach. Moreover, it has been designed to satisfy all QoS and SLA requirements of a time-critical IoT-application and can achieve a maximal throughput of processed data requests. The latter features of our prototype have to be validated by adequate experiments in a test bed.

To keep the blockchain architecture as simple and functionally effective as possible, we include here the miner nodes of the private, permissioned blockchain Hyperledger Fabric [2] with their main functionalities. The latter incorporate the verification and validation features and the immutable storage of the collected ledger data at the top-level of our protocol stack given by the cloud layer. We know that Hyperledger Fabric follows the state machine replication approach perceived from a BFT-based consensus mechanism, cf. [19]. It also offers various storage facilities like the ability to use a database, which makes it suitable for various critical IoT-application scenarios. Regarding its application design one can take into account multiple organizations and apply an ordering service.

In Fig. 5 we illustrate the concept of our realized prototype and the interactions among its basic components where we have used only two organizational units for simplicity. Each of these organizations contains two nodes where one of them plays the role of an anchoring peer. The red line indicates a cross-organizational gossiping. The client communication with an anchoring peer and the ordered service are shown in black and green colours, respectively. The blue line indicates a communication relationship between the orderer and the anchoring peer of a transaction.

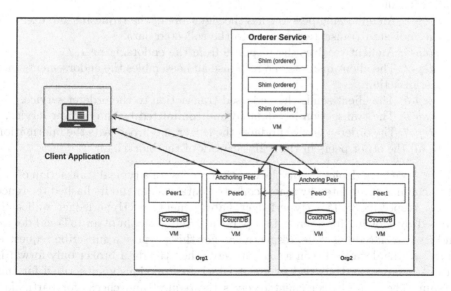

Fig. 5. Overview of the Hyperledger Fabric components among the peers of two different organizations and their interaction in the designed protocol stack of our fog-blockchain prototype (see also [2])

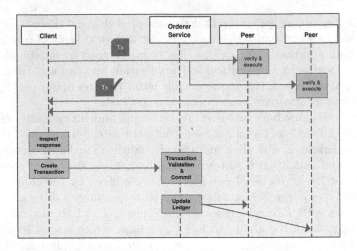

Fig. 6. A sequence diagram of the typical transaction processing steps in Hyperledger Fabric (see also [2])

In Fig. 6 we show the typical steps of a transaction processing of the blockchain following the execute-order-commit pattern which is applied by Hyperledger Fabric [2]. The executed steps of a transaction initiated by the sample of collected personal e-health data records, their analysis and storage are as follows:

– *Step-1:* A client sends a transaction request to the endorsing peers of the blockchain.
– *Step-2:* An endorsing peer verifies the signature of the requestor and executes the indicated transaction related to the collected data.
– *Step-3:* A client receives the response from the endorsing peer.
– *Step-4:* The client inspects the response and assembles the endorsements into a transaction.
– *Step-5:* The client sends the endorsed transaction to the orderer service.
– *Step-6:* The transaction is validated and committed by the orderer service.
– *Step-7:* The orderer service updates the ledger and broadcasts the information to all the other peers in the P2P-network of the blockchain.

In Fig. 7 we have depicted how the creation process of a typical transaction of the blockchain is augmented by a new collected data stream and its hashed reference value, respectively. The Hyperledger Fabric client (or Hyperledger wallet) is started by showing its interest in a particular data stream of an IoT-end device and its associated fog node, respectively. For this purpose a subscribe request is issued to the data broker in a fog gateway. Then the data broker only forwards this stream to the Hyperledger client which has previously subscribed for this stream. The Hyperledger client receives the request and checks for particular, configurable criteria to be met. Then it requests the creation of a corresponding transaction. From this point on every step proceeds as shown in Fig. 6.

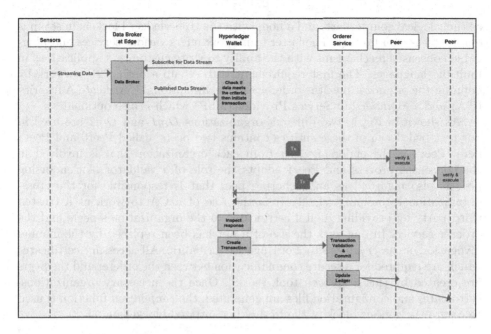

Fig. 7. Workflow of the Hyperledger Fabric starting from an end device with its attached sensors and its associated fog gateway with the data broker functionality directed towards the cloud (see also [2])

Our goal is to provide an effective implementation of this integrated fog-blockchain architecture within a test bed of cheap SBCs and to evaluate its achieved performance with respect to important computing and networking metrics. In this manner we are able to validate the effectiveness and efficiency of our design decisions.

4   Implementation of the Integrated Fog-Blockchain Prototype by the Hyperledger Fabric Platform

We have realized our prototype of the integrated fog-blockchain architecture in a virtualized test bed using appropriate JavaScript elements and related basic Docker images and Docker compose files for all basic elements of our generic software system. By these means we have implemented the sketched integrated fog-blockchain architecture with the help of Hyperledger Fabric, version 2.0, cf. [2]. In our feasibility study we closely follow the well-known Hyperledger Fabric samples and trim it to serve our experimental purposes. In this section we describe the object structures and functions of our implementation in detail to enable the reproducibility of our experimental study.

To conduct related performance experiments in our test bed, the implementation requires to set up a minimalistic network scenario involving end devices. The latter simulate the emission of sensor data. A fog computing gateway is used as their logical counterpart, and a node with the Hyperledger blockchain setup is employed as cloud server. The latter framework offers various services and pluggable consensus mechanisms with the ability to write customized applications in multiple languages. The first requirement is to set up a basic P2P-network by defining the organizations, the orderer service, an optional Certificate Authority (CA) and a Membership Service Provider (MSP) which is also optional.

As shown in Fig. 5, two different organizations *Org1* and *Org2* are used in our test bed. Each of these entities contains two peers, called Peer0 and Peer1 here. Peer0 is the endorsing peer from each organization that is involved in the consensus process and Peer1 adopts the role of a validator. An endorsing peer is also regarded as an anchoring peer that is responsible for the cross-organizational gossiping, cf. [2]. It is the role of a CA to work as a trusted third party by providing digital certificates to the organization's peers and the orderer service. In our tests the use of a CA has been replaced by the manual invocation of the *cryptogen* tool of Hpyerledger Fabric. All necessary certificates which are required for a secure communication between the orderer and the peers are created by this *cryptogen* tool, see [9]. Once the necessary organizations, certificates and configuration files are generated, the *configtxgen* function is used to create the genesis block of the freshly instantiated blockchain, cf. [9].

4.1   Implementing the Peer-to-Peer Network for Hyperledger Fabric

In our implementation a *network.sh* script is used to set up the peer-to-peer network for Hyperledger Fabric. This script *network.sh* is utilized in the script *startFabric.sh* to establish the blockchain's peer-to-peer network, to create channels, to deploy the required chaincode using the script *deployCC.sh* and to test the generated transactions. The script *startFabric.sh* also specifies the employed database and tells the peers which chaincode language is to be used (see *configtxgen* in [9]). The script *envVar.sh* provides the environment variables of the test bed. An overview of all the required scripts and their calling scheme can be seen in Fig. 8.

During the network setup procedure the *network.sh* script creates the necessary Docker containers for the orderer and the involved peer hosts. To run the *orderer service* depicted in Fig. 7, a Docker image for a `hyperledger/fabric-orderer` is used and started by an *orderer* command. Similarly, a Docker image for the needed `hyperledger/fabric-peer` is used to run inside a peer and started by a *peer node start* command. A Docker image for *eclipse-mosquitto* is applied as the MQTT-based *data broker* in our test bed, cf. [1].

4.2   Realizing the Hyperledger Fabric Client

A Hyperledger Fabric client, also known as Hyperledger wallet, has been defined as depicted in Fig. 6. Two scripts *enrollAdmin.js* and *registerUser.js* are used to create the *Administrator* role and the user instances of the blockchain network, see Fig. 9. The *Administrator* of the network is a single built-in peer whereas

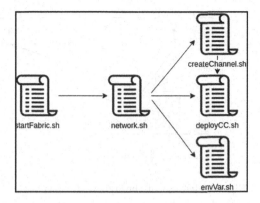

Fig. 8. Created scripts of the fog-blockchain prototype and their interactions in our test bed

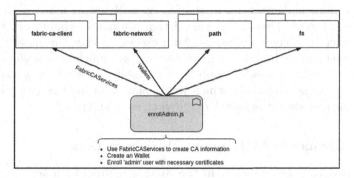

Fig. 9. Overview on the creation script of the admin role

the number of users in a network is configurable. A required *Administrator* id is created by taking all necessary parameters from a specification file *connection-org1.json*, which is generated during the network setup process. This *Administrator* id is used to create the other users of the permissioned blockchain. All the credentials of the users are saved under a *wallet* directory. All the operations in the P2P-network require an *appUser* id from the *wallet*.

The implementation of the Hyperledger client is realized by a JavaScript *pushData.js*. It uses the *fabric-network* module to talk to the fabric network and an *mqtt* server module for its communication with the data broker, cf. [1,2]. Figure 10 shows the imported packages used in *pushData.js*. By standing in the middle it shapes the behaviour of the realized application. It also decides when to create a transaction and which data stream should be kept in the blockchain. In our current test bed implementation the logic for filtering a data stream is hardcoded. It checks the values of the streamed data to see if it passes a certain threshold and only then it pushes the stream to be part of the ledger. It also uses an *appUser* profile before submitting a transaction within the blockchain.

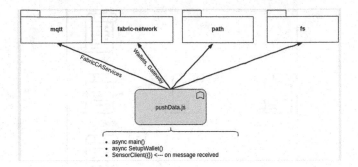

Fig. 10. Design of the hyperledger wallet

At the data stream emission site a *SensorClient* is realized in terms of an *mqtt* client of the data broker service in the fog layer. Hence, it receives all messages from the data broker. Due to its event-driven working mechanism it gets called each time when it receives a message. After executing some threshold checking it calls an asynchronous function *SubmitTransaction* which uses a *globalContract* instance and invokes a *createStream* with necessary parameters. *globalContract* is an instance of the chaincode, which was deployed during the network creation phase. In our test case it is called *IoTStream*, see Fig. 11.

4.3   The Chaincode for Handling the Sensor Data

In a Hyperledger Fabric blockchain the chaincode provides a key functionality. It covers the ability to write a customized application logic using popular programming languages. Basically, it is a container holding multiple smart contracts with a unique identifying name, cf. [2,9]. It allows application developers to concentrate more on developing their business logic rather than concentrating on the complexity of the underlying blockchain network.

In our test bed and its experiments the JavaScript language has been picked for the development of a smart contract and *node.js* has been used as coding framework. In Hyperledger Fabric there are mainly two primary package interfaces for developing smart contracts, namely *fabric-contract-api* and *fabric-shim*, see [15]. The *fabric-contract-api* provides a *Contract* interface and *fabric-shim*, on the other hand, requires to write a smart contract class mainly having two callable functions, namely *Init* and *Invoke*. A defined class needs to be called from *shim.start()*. In our test bed the *fabric-contract-api* has been picked. The developed smart contract is simple and planned to handle data streams by means of a key-value pair where the key is the *timestamp* and the value is the *stream* of the gathered IoT-sensor data set itself.

In our implementation we use the package *fabric-contract-api*, which contains all the contract related functionalities and creates a class called *IoTStream* by extending the class *Contract*. Figure 11 shows the class diagram of the written contract. It depicts an overview of this class diagram that handles the transaction data.

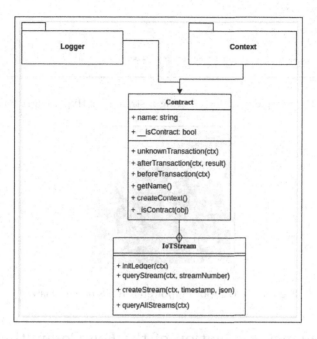

Fig. 11. A smart contract as a key element of an application development based on Hyperledger Fabric

In our experiments the *initLedger* function puts a dummy element into the ledger during the initialization of the smart contract. The class *IoTStream* contains three other functions for creating streams, querying a particular stream and querying all the streams. The prerequisite for creating a stream is to know the timestamp or the range of the timestamp, i.e., start and end epochs.

The listing in Fig. 12, for example, shows the relevant code for creating a stream.

Inside the procedure it calls the *putState* function to store the values. A JSON-string is created from the parameters passed to the function and put as a value to the *putState* function. The *queryStream* takes the timestamp as parameter and returns that specific stream. *queryAllStreams* returns all the streams stored so far. One of the limitations appearing in *putState* is that all the inserted values are stored and must obey a key-value pair style. However, *putState* does not have any support for multi-mapping of the key-value pair so far.

```
1   async createStream(ctx, ctime, desc, value, lat, lng, type, id, unit) {
2     const stream = {
3       desc,
4       docType: 'stream',
5       value,
6       lat,
7       lng,
8       type,
9       id,
10      unit,
11    };
12    await ctx.stub.putState(ctime, Buffer.from(JSON.stringify(stream)));
13  }
```

Fig. 12. Sample code for creating a stream for Hyperledger Fabric

Fig. 13. A Hypriot empowered RPi3 based cluster

5   Performance Evaluation of the Fog Computing System with Its Integrated Blockchain Functionality

In our prototype fog gateways with the Hyperledger Fabric blockchain have been realized by cheap Raspberyy Pi SBCs. To analyze the efficiency and limitations of this implemented fog-blockchain architecture, at least three different entities have to be considered during an evaluation of the resulting performance indices, namely end devices, fog gateways and blockchain peers. To simulate an end device, first a script is used to generate sensor data. Typically, IoT-end devices of smart home applications are known to communicate using MQTT, cf. [1]. Our experimental test system simulates the end devices' behaviour at various speeds to create the transaction load of the blockchain within our virtualized fog computing environment. A cluster of Raspberry Pis (RPis) based on the HypriotOS [7] operating system is used as fog gateways with virtualized functionalities. The test bed server has been powered by a x86_64 based Quad Core machine enabling hyperthreading (HT) to host the Hyperledger Fabric blockchain. Various configuration details of our test bed are outlined in Table 3.

Figure 13 shows the fog gateway that has been used in the experiments of the test bed. The RPi cluster is made of five RPis. They use ARM processors which are very suitable for a lightweight fog gateway. The RPis are also known for their low power consumption. Each of these used fog gateways has a 64 bit

Table 3. Hardware and software specification of the test environment

Properties	Fog Gateway	Server
OS	Hypriot	Ubuntu
CPU	ARMv7 rev4@1.4 GHz	x86_64@1.6 GHz
Docker	18	18.06.3-ce
Kernel	4.14.34	5.4.0-rc5
Core	Quad Core	Quad Core + HT

Quad Core ARM processor with a clock speed of 1.4 GHz. Our prototypical fog gateway is running HypriotOS as kernel, cf. [7]. The latter is a GNU/Linux based operating system derived from Debian which allows it to run containerized applications. HypriotOS based RPi computers appear as a prime candidate of a cheap fog node as they make the cluster effective regarding a smooth application deployment. They can also offer suitable monitoring capabilities.

On the other hand, the server system used in our test bed is backed by an Intel based 64-bit processor with 16 GB memory running Ubuntu 18.06 as operating system. An enterprise grade server would come with different grades of processors. But regarding the experiments of our feasibility study, we only try to understand the suitability of our design settings. We shall illustrate that the performance results inferred from our experiments can be multiplicatively applied to more powerful servers.

To set up a peer-to-peer test network of the blockchain all the involved devices have been connected within a single communication network. Each data generator of a sensor and its fog gateway are connected via a hub over a Gigabit Ethernet interface. The server hosting Hyperledger Fabric has been connected to this network via a rather slow wireless interface. In a real world environment it is expected that a sensor network is connected directly to the fog gateway without an intermediary and by a relatively low latency connection compared to the more powerful connection from a fog gateway towards the cloud.

To properly utilize the fog computing gateway, an overlay network has been created within the blockchain topology of Hyperledger Fabric using *Docker Swarm*, cf. [5]. Running Docker in swarm mode requires a declaration of a *manager* node and some *worker* nodes. The *manager* node is responsible for distributing the transaction load of the blockchain amongst all *worker* nodes. In our test bed five client instances were used to generate sensor data streams. Each client's transaction requests were load balanced via the *swarm manager* node amongst all the available worker nodes. Likewise, at the server end five instances of a Hyperledger client were created and each of them started to receive transaction requests from all of these cluster nodes. The clients were generating data at an overall rate of 100 packets/second where each instance generated data at a rate of 20 packets/second.

Based on this described setup of the fog-blockchain prototype within our simple test bed, CPU usages were measured at the fog gateway nodes. A snapshot of these CPU usages during the experimental evaluation can be seen in Fig. 14. The experiments are showing how the block creation timeout value impacts on the CPU usage of a gateway. The CPU usage has been scaled in a window of 0.0 to 1.0. The greater the timeout value is, the more visible are the CPU usage spikes due to the time difference regarding the creation of transactions. The oscillation of the CPU utilization indicates that the CPU of a gateway is not utilized to its fullest level. Being in a container environment within an operating system based on a Linux kernel, which only allocates a portion of the adjustable CPU capacity to the containers, it can only utilize a part of the whole physical CPU capacity. Therefore, the interpretation of the evaluation is a relative measure. Moreover, the peers running inside a deployed Docker container are not CPU intensive. Thus, the transaction requests were not utilizing the CPU to its fullest level. Apart of that, the results also depend upon the synchronization characteristics of the containerization environment which requires that they may also wait for resources other than the physical CPU such as the memory and I/O capacities.

In our performance experiments the CPU usages have been gathered from the *sysfs* interface of our fog computing system. *sysfs* is a RAM-based filesystem which is used to export low level details regarding various system resource usages for user space applications as well as debugging. Reading data from *sysfs* has very low overhead compared to running system monitoring software like cAdvisor [3]. *sysfs* also allows us to pick up only the necessary information. In our case only memory and CPU usages of a fog gateway were needed. To gather these memory and CPU usage values a simple bash script has been used. This script sleeps for 1 s, then wakes up and dumps the CPU usages from `/sys/fs/cgroup/cpu/cpuacct/cpuacct.usage` into a file. The CPU usage values exposed via *sysfs* are recorded on a nanosecond scale. The formula used to obtain the CPU utilization is given by $v1-v0/(1000000000*cpunr)$. Here $v0$ and $v1$ are the values read at time $t0$ and $t1$, whereas $cpunr$ is the number of used CPUs within the physical system of a fog node. Similarly, the memory usage values were taken from `/sys/fs/cgroup/memory/memory.usage_in_bytes`.

Let us look at a typical experiment within our fog-blockchain test bed. Applying a block timeout of 2 s for a block creation step during the runtime of 365 seconds, 13000 transactions were created and amongst them 7500 were successful. The maximum limit was 10 messages per generated block of the blockchain. All the transactions were write-only transactions. In this setting it was possible to handle approximately 20 transactions per second on a RPI fog gateway. A failure in transaction handling indicates a timeout event received from the peers before a commit event of the blockchain. When the timeout value is 5 s, is has been possible to process all the transactions. In order to achieve this outcome, changes by increasing the key parameters *maximum message count* and *preferred max size* of our transactions were executed.

Table 4 shows the key configuration options for each timeout value. A lower block timeout value provides low latency, but it may not scale well. To achieve scalability, an increasing timeout value is necessary. This strategy is a trade-off between latency and scalability within a RPi fog gateway which needs to be addressed based on the requirements of a smart home application.

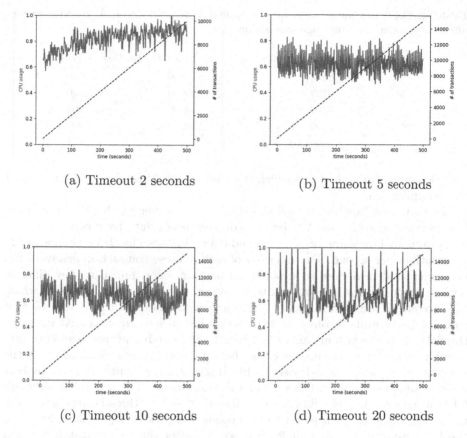

(a) Timeout 2 seconds

(b) Timeout 5 seconds

(c) Timeout 10 seconds

(d) Timeout 20 seconds

Fig. 14. CPU usages with different timeout values over 500 s with the same amount of load

Our experiments show that other factors to achieve an adequate throughput of approved transactions in Hyperledger Fabric are determined by the size of a block and the state management. The size of a block depends upon the application logic, the timeout value and the limit regarding the number of transaction messages which can be incorporated into a block of the blockchain. To achieve a satisfactory throughput, necessary changes can be made to these parameters which depend upon the application requirements. Our experiments only deal with a few variations in the timeout and the message limit size.

Regarding the state management two primary databases are used in Hyperledger Fabric, namely *LevelDB* and *CouchDB*, cf. [9]. Although, LevelDB is well known for an adequate throughput, the performance of CouchDB has been increased since the deployment of Fabric version 2.0. Thus, we have used CouchDB for the state management and Hyperledger Fabric version 2.0 has been applied during the evaluation phase of our settings. Moreover, CouchDB

Table 4. Configuration options for the transactions per second (TPS) with various timeout (seconds) and message size parameters

Timeout (sec)	Preferred Max. Size (KB)	Max. Message Count	TPS
2	512	10	20
5	8192	10000	200
10	8192	10000	200
20	8192	10000	200

provides better query features which is an important aspect for developing smart home applications.

To figure out how much load the Hyperledger server can handle, a separate load generation technique has been used. The sensor data have been generated in a gradually increasing order, each end device instance has been generating 20 transactions per second. The intensity of each of these transaction instances has been increased in a close to exponential back-off algorithm. But they differ in terms of choosing the inter-arrival time between two transaction instances which was driven by the load intensity. The number of instances can have a highest value of thirty units. From each transaction instance to create a next instance, the delay between two instances is driven by the number of instances currently running. After the first instance and before creating the second instance the delay is one second. The delay slot is like $[1, 2, 3, 4, ..., N]$ where N is the highest number of transaction instances. For this experiment N is set to 30, although CPU usages reached the limit even before that and 30 threads were not really used. The delay is given in terms of seconds and picked sequentially. So, after the first instance, it will wait for one second, after the second instance it will wait for two seconds and so on until it reaches its limit. In this way it would be possible to find out the amount of transaction load which is required to fully utilize the CPU. To generate the load in this way, the sensor data generator script *mqttgen.py* has been modified to enable a multi-threading, which is configurable via the configuration file *config.json*. Figure 15 shows the CPU usages during the runtime of this transaction load. Hyperledger Fabric was configured with a timeout of 5 s. The load was generated in a gradually increasing order and the transaction rate per second has been indicated by the blue line. It is shown that it took 80 s to reach this peak utilization.

Figure 16 shows the corresponding memory usage of the server in the test bed. The blue line indicates the transaction rate per second. The server ran out of memory during this operation and the Out-of-Memory (OOM) [8] manager got into an action to rescue the situation. This outcome is indicated by a drop in the memory usage graph.

Figure 17 shows the default network usage statistics in terms of the number of kilobytes sent and received over the bridged P2P-network of the blockchain. Here cAdvisor [3] has been used to collect the network statistics.

These experiments can only indicate the feasibility of our proposed system design. More extensive validations of the integrated fog-blockchain architecture

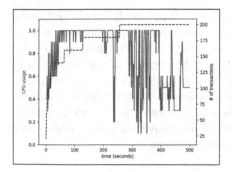 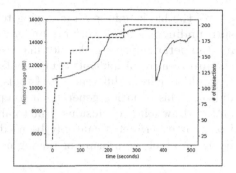

Fig. 15. The time it took for the server to get to its peak usage scenario in the experimental setup is shown.

Fig. 16. Memory usages (in megabytes) snapshot during the evaluation phase

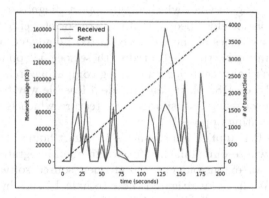

Fig. 17. Network usages (in kilobytes) during the evaluation phase with default timeout 2 s

with real-life smart home and e-health applications are required to assess the efficiency and scalability aspects of our design decisions in more realistic scenarios.

5.1 Limitations of Our Experiments

Measuring the relevant performance indices of a blockchain framework in a fog computing environment is challenging, cf. [21]. The first problem is to simulate the fog computing infrastructure properly. In such a scenario typically multiple entities are involved and they are connected to each other via different types of network connectivity. In a real world this connectivity variation can be very diverse. Measuring the system performance based on CPU and memory usages is only one part of the whole performance analysis setting. The delay along the used diverse communication channels will also severely impact on the performance measurements of a blockchain, cf. [12].

As the blockchain is an emerging technology, all the applications and tools surrounding this framework are under rapid development. The tools for measuring the performance are also not mature enough right now. Furthermore, due to the involvement of multiple components over a P2P-network of varying latency, it would require a different set of tools for analyzing the network performance indices. This situation generates a complex scenario to collect reliable numbers and to draw solid conclusions. Due to all these limitations, the results excerpted from our experiments can only be used for an indicative purpose, rather than being an absolute measure of the fog node performance.

6   Conclusions

Nowadays, new advanced Internet-of-Things applications are required to support the effective processing of smart home data, e.g., arising from HVAC applications, cf. [1]. Other examples are given by smart e-health applications like ambient assisted living services which may support diagnostic and therapeutic healthcare protocols for elder people in a modern society, cf. [10]. To cope with privacy and security issues of these data collected by advanced sensors in such an advanced IoT-infrastructure dedicated to these specific application areas, the integration of blockchain technology into a fog computing architecture has been considered recently, cf. [18,20]. It can provide a feasible way to realize a secure distributed data processing and storage architecture which is required by this advanced fog computing approach.

Regarding the IoT-application scenarios for smart homes, the basic research question arises how a resourceful, efficient design of an integrated fog-blockchain system based on an extensible virtualized open source software architecture should look like. We have investigated these technical issues by means of a feasibility study and developed a lightweight software architecture. It integrates a set of fog gateways and the blockchain technology, cf. [4]. We have implemented this distributed architecture by means of Hyperledger Fabric [2] in a test bed of cheap Raspberry Pi SBCs as basic fog nodes of an underlying peer-to-peer network in such a private, permissioned blockchain. The key issue whether these fog nodes with their virtualized functions based on a Docker orchestration framework can meet the required computing and networking goals has been addressed in terms of a series of performance tests within our test bed. Our experiments have revealed the feasibility of the proposed software architecture as well as its benefits regarding potential smart home and smart e-health applications. However, theses tests have also illustrated the intrinsic performance limitations of the developed fog-blockchain architecture if simple SBC systems like Raspberry Pis are used for the implementation.

Further performance studies are needed to evaluate the full potential of the developed fog-blockchain approach for the secure provisioning of required e-health data, for instance, to collect the blood pressure and glycose values of elder patients with diabetes mellitus at their homes or for new healthcare services in smart cities. Moreover, the scalability and efficiency of the adopted three-layer architecture should be investigated more carefully by several performance experiments within an extended real-life test bed. Furthermore, the adoption of new federated learning techniques to analyze the collected data at the fog or cloud layer and to trigger immediate actions if needed may be an interesting extension of our distributed edge computing system. These technical issues shall become a subject of our future research.

Acknowledgment. This feasibility study was done while Mr. Mullick was working in the Computer Networks group at the University of Bamberg. The other authors are very much indebted to his efforts in implementing a first prototype of the integrated fog-blockchain architecture with Hyperledger Fabric.

References

1. Al-Fuqaha, A., et al.: Internet of Things: A Survey on Enabling Technologies, Protocols, and Applications. IEEE Commun. Surv. Tutorials **17**(4), 2347–2376, Fourth Quarter (2015)
2. Androulaki, E., et al.: Hyperledger fabric: A distributed operating system for permissioned blockchains. In: Proceedings of the Thirteenth EuroSys Conference, ser. EuroSys '18, New York, NY, USA, pp. 30:1–30:15, ACM (2018)
3. cAdvisor (Container Advisor). https://hub.docker.com/r/google/cadvisor/
4. Cech, H.L., Großmann, M., Krieger, U.R.: A Fog Computing Architecture to Share Sensor Data by Means of Blockchain Functionality. In: IEEE International Conference on Fog Computing (ICFC) 2019, pp. 31–40 (2019)
5. Docker Engine: Swarm mode overview. (2023). https://docs.docker.com/engine/swarm/
6. Fernández-Caramés, T.M., Fraga-Lamas, P.: A review on the use of blockchain for the internet of things. IEEE Access **6**, 32979–33001 (2018)
7. Fichtner, G., et al.: HypriotOS. https://blog.hypriot.com/
8. Gorman, M.: Understanding the Linux Virtual Memory Manager, Chapter 13 Out Of Memory Management. https://www.kernel.org/doc/gorman/html/understand/understand016.html
9. Hyperledger: Hyperledger-Fabric - A Blockchain Platform for the Enterprise, (2023). https://hyperledger-fabric.readthedocs.io/en/release-2.5/
10. Islam, S.M.R., Kwak, D., Kabir, M.H., Hossain, M., Kwak, K.S.: The internet of things for health care: a comprehensive survey. IEEE Access **3**, 678–708 (2015)
11. Kreutz, D., et al.: Software-Defined Networking: A Comprehensive Survey. In: Proceedings of the IEEE, vol. 103, no. 1, pp. 14–76, January (2015)
12. Krieger, U.R., Ziegler, M.H., Cech, H.L.: Performance modeling of the consensus mechanism in a permissioned blockchain. In: Gaj, P., Sawicki, M., Kwiecień, A. (eds.) CN 2019. CCIS, vol. 1039, pp. 3–17. Springer, Cham (2019). https://doi.org/10.1007/978-3-030-21952-9_1
13. Li, C., Zhang, L.: A blockchain based new secure multi-layer network model for internet of things. In: IEEE International Congress on Internet of Things (ICIOT) 2017, pp. 33–41, June (2017)
14. McGhin, T., Choo, K.-K.R., Liu, C.Z., He, D.: Blockchain in healthcare applications: research challenges and opportunities. J. Netw. Comput. Appl. **135**, 62–75 (2019)
15. npm.community, fabric-contract-api, (2020). https://www.npmjs.com/package/fabric-contract-api

16. Poon, J., Buterin, V.: Plasma: Scalable Autonomous Smart Contracts, (2017). https://plasma.io/plasma.pdf
17. Stadt Bamberg, Stabsstelle Smart City, 96047 Bamberg, Germany. https://smartcity.bamberg.de/ueber-das-programm-smart-city-bamberg/
18. Tuli, S., Mahmud, R., Tuli, S., Buyya, R.: Fogbus: a blockchain-based lightweight framework for edge and fog computing. J. Syst. Softw. **154**, 22–36 (2019)
19. Vukolić, M.: The quest for scalable blockchain fabric: proof-of-work vs. BFT replication. In: Camenisch, J., Kesdoğan, D. (eds.) Open Problems in Network Security, pp. 112–125. Springer International Publishing, Cham (2016)
20. Yang, R., Yu, F. R., Si, P., Yang, Z., Zhang, Y.: Integrated Blockchain and Edge Computing Systems: A Survey, Some Research Issues and Challenges. IEEE Commun. Surv. Tutorials, **21**(2), 1508–1532, Secondquarter (2019)
21. Ziegler, M.H., Großmann, M., Krieger, U.R.: Integration of Fog Computing and Blockchain Technology Using the Plasma Framework. In: IEEE International Conference on Blockchain and Cryptocurrency (ICBC) 2019, pp. 120–123 (2019)

Towards Designing a User-Centered Local Community Platform to Foster Social Cohesion in a Multi-Generational Smart Community

Sabrina Hölzer[(⊠)], Lucie Honner, Wesley Preßler, Antonio Schulz, and Christian Erfurth

University of Applied Sciences Jena, Jena, Germany
`Sabrina.hoelzer@eah-jena.com`

Abstract. In recent years, the emergence of smart cities and other related initiatives has prompted a growing interest in the role of digitalization in the housing sector. Housing cooperatives are increasingly exploring new and innovative concepts of community living and social connectedness within neighborhoods. In the context of the research project "Multi-Generation Smart Community" (mGeSCo) we are investigating and testing digitization in various dimensions using a living lab approach in the "Smart Quarter" Jena-Lobeda, which is currently home to 228 residents. In cooperation with different stakeholders, network partners and residents, interdisciplinary solutions are being developed and explored in the dimensions of work, living, housing and caring. The neighborhood residents can obtain benefits from a diverse range of digital amenities. In order to enhance acceptance and effectiveness while improving the well-being of the community, both analog and digital methods of participation and communication are being integrated. For example, a community platform designed for a neighborhood can improve well-being by fostering community, social support, trust, engagement, and comfort with smart technology in homes. The paper aims to provide insights in the designing process, information on challenges and peculiarities of the neighborhood, as well as to form a preliminary approach for a user-centered design of a neighborhood platform. While the overall conceptualization will involve additional aspects (such as user experience, interface design, communication and content strategy, analytics, and security), the initial step will focus solely on user needs and the associated features and functions of the platform.

Keywords: Smart community · Smart community services · Smart home · Social cohesion · Multi-generational · User-centered design · Community participation · Sustainable urban development · Living and aging in place

1 Introduction

In recent years, the emergence of smart cities and other related projects and initiatives has prompted a growing interest in the role of digitalization in the housing sector. Housing cooperatives are increasingly exploring new and innovative concepts of community living and social connectedness within neighborhoods. The rapid advancements

© The Author(s), under exclusive license to Springer Nature Switzerland AG 2023
U. R. Krieger et al. (Eds.): I4CS 2023, CCIS 1876, pp. 277–291, 2023.
https://doi.org/10.1007/978-3-031-40852-6_15

in technology have transformed many aspects of our lives, making them easier and more efficient. Smart communities, which integrate technology, sustainability, and community participation, have emerged as a new paradigm for urban living. Especially today, where living and aging in place has become increasingly important, creating, and maintaining a healthy local community or neighborhood is crucial. As people age, they may become more reliant on their immediate environment for support and social interaction. This underscores the need for a user-centered local community platform that can promote social cohesion, support healthy aging in place, and consider the specificities of a local multi-generational smart community or neighborhood. Despite the increasing prevalence and targeted promotion of community platforms and other digital media that are designed to foster social cohesion and engagement within local communities, there is a paucity of empirical research on the actual use and impact of these platforms in specific social contexts. Similarly, due to the existence of numerous platforms with different focuses, there are also a variety of features, making it difficult to determine which platform is precisely suitable. This highlights the need for further investigation into the potential benefits and challenges of user-centered local community platforms and underscores the relevance of the present paper, which seeks to introduce a specific platform designed to address the unique needs and interests of a particular local community.

This working paper aims to describe the motivation, goals, research questions, and methodology for introducing a specific community platform as part of the Multi-Generation Smart Community (mGeSCo) project. The mGeSCo project is an interdisciplinary research and development project that aims to create a model for a sustainable and livable smart community that promotes social cohesion and healthy living and aging in place. The proposed community platform is a key component of this model, and will be designed to support local community engagement, facilitate social interaction, and promote a sense of belonging and ownership among its residents. This paper outlines the research questions that guides the development of the platform, describes the methodology that will be used to gather data and insights from residents, and highlights the potential benefits of the platform for promoting social cohesion.

While the overall research questions of the project include an overall inquiry into the effectiveness of digital tools in facilitating new work environments, social participation, active aging, and place-based living within a heterogeneous neighborhood model. The paper specifically focuses on exploring the features necessary for designing a platform that fosters a sense of community. Therefore, the following inquiry is the guiding research question:

RQ: What are the necessary features to design a platform that fosters social cohesion in a local community?

The research question will be addressed by examining the theoretical framework, analyzing a practical project, identifying key elements or features by analyzing the features of existing platforms, which were evaluated using a frequency distribution. Furthermore, aligning needs and features will be done using the Use and Gratification Theory. However, additional investigations and validations are required to support the hypotheses. Subsequent steps to be taken will be explained in detail.

2 Fundamentals and Related Work

2.1 Definitions and Concepts

Neighborhood. For the definition of the used term in this paper, it is necessary to understand that one can use the term »neighborhood« interchangeably in English, although in German they have completely different scientific backgrounds and thus different meanings. The term neighborhood in the means of the German word »Quartier« explains "a geographic place [or a physical entity [1]] where people with common interests and values live in close proximity and interact on a regular basis" [2]. Neighborhood by the means of the German Word of »Nachbarschaft« means a social entity that can influence a wide range of social processes, from individual well-being to community-level outcomes such as crime rates and civic engagement. Neighborhoods can be characterized by factors such as population density, socioeconomic status, and racial and ethnic diversity, among others. A physical space or geographic area with defined boundaries.

Neighborhood and Community Platforms. Neighborhood and community platforms are currently lacking a clear definition, with various approaches focusing on individual requirements and circumstances. For example, Schreiber et al. [3] define neighborhood platforms based on spatial distance, while Vogel et al. [4] describe online neighborhood social networks as a sub-class of online social networks that allow local community members to interact, share information, and participate in volunteering activities. Despite a growing range of digital platforms aimed at promoting communication and participation at the neighborhood or community level, they have not been extensively studied. Research has shown a focus on platforms designed to promote participation among a specific target group or wider neighborhood, with fewer platforms specifically targeting local, site-based neighborhoods with multigenerational residents living in a technologically enhanced residential setting.

Platforms can range from volunteer-run neighborhood blogs and local discussion groups on social media (e.g., Facebook or WhatsApp), to local regional-based initiatives (e.g., Quartiersleben Neuhegi or Meine Nachbarn Hamburg) [5, 6] or target-based networks (e.g., Unser Quartier, Digitale Dörfer or Crossiety) [7–9]. Country-specific networks include fürenand.ch and hoplr.com, while there are also commercially managed online platforms specifically designed for neighborhood communities, such as nebenan.de or nextdoor.com. Vogel et al. [10] propose a taxonomy and archetype framework for classifying online neighborhood social networks, with a focus on promoting social connections. However, neighborhood-specific requirements such as smart home devices and services could be integrated into platform design to create unique features tailored to the living situation.

Some neighborhood platforms, such as Animus, Casavi, and Allthings [15–17], focus on property management but also include features for resident networking and communication, including messaging, directories, event calendars, and feedback/rating functions. However, a strong emphasis on property management may neglect other essential functions for neighborhood development, such as addressing resident needs and promoting interaction between residents and the local community.

Newer concepts like Mobile Quarter Applications (MQAs) are mobile applications designed to simplify daily living, promote climate consciousness, and sustainability.

However, their focus tends to be on promoting communal energy conservation, with a target audience consisting mostly of individuals under the age of 50 [14].

There are various approaches to digital neighborhood platforms, and it is crucial to identify the features that promote residents' well-being and foster social cohesion while balancing local characteristics and living conditions. The importance of promoting not only well-being but also social cohesion is explained further. Proper investigation and analysis of existing platforms and their features that meets the unique needs of the community are necessary to design a neighborhood platform.

2.2 Digital Platforms and Social Cohesion in Local Communities

Digital platforms have the potential to create social cohesion. Research by Hampton & Wellman [15] has shown that digital technology can provide a space for individuals to connect with others who share similar interests and values, regardless of geographic location. Additionally, digital platforms can facilitate the exchange of information and resources, which can foster a sense of interdependence and cooperation among users [16].

On the other Hand, there are concerns that digital platforms may hinder social cohesion. For example, Putnam [2] argues that the use of digital technology can lead to a decline in face-to-face interactions and weaken social bonds. Others point to the potential for digital platforms to reinforce existing social hierarchies and perpetuate inequality [17]. Social cohesion can be formed through digital technology in various manner. Digital platforms can provide a space for individuals to share their experiences and perspectives, which can foster empathy and understanding among users [16]. Additionally, digital platforms can provide means for individuals to participate in collective action, such as social movements and advocacy campaigns, this can lead to a sense of shared purpose and community [18].

However, the potential for digital platforms to create social cohesion is not guaranteed. Factors like platform design, user behavior, and social context can significantly influence the extent to which digital platforms foster social cohesion [19].

Furthermore, the impact of digital platforms on social cohesion is likely to vary across different populations and social contexts. Therefore, it is crucial to comprehend the users' needs and implement a platform accordingly. Building on the concept of community platforms and social cohesion, this paper draws on the Use and Gratification Theory to examine the needs, uses, and adaptations of user-centered local community platforms.

2.3 User-Centered Design Principles and Methods

The use and adoption of technology is a complex process that depends on various factors. To better understand these factors, various theories and models have been developed over time. For several decades, research on media use and effects has relied on the Uses-and-Gratifications approach and has revived it in the context of new media [20]. In this context, the Uses and Gratifications Theory emphasizes that people actively choose media to satisfy their needs and interests based on social, cultural, and personal factors.

People do not just use media passively; they consciously choose which media they want to use and what needs they want to meet with them. This theory can help to understand how users perceive new technologies and how they use their experiences and skills to integrate the technology into their everyday lives [21].

The basis of the Uses and Gratifications theory is formed by psychological and social needs that generate certain expectations towards the media. This, in turn, results in specific usage motives that are ultimately decisive in the selection of certain media offerings. If the expectations are met and the desired gratifications are obtained, the likelihood of selecting the same media offering in the future increases [20]. Katz et al. [22] identified five fundamental needs, based on social roles and psychological dispositions, that are strengthened through media use:

- cognitive (in terms of information, knowledge and understanding),
- affective (in terms of aesthetic, emotional experiences),
- personal-integrative (in terms of credibility, trust, stability, and status),
- social-integrative (in terms of contact with family, friends, and the world), and
- escapist (tension relieving) needs.

Each medium has a unique combination of content, attributes, and contexts that can contribute to fulfilling these needs. The question is which combinations of media attributes are best suited to fulfilling specific needs [20]. Continual examination of these needs and their manifestations in users' behavior is necessary due to the evolution of technology and the emergence of new media platforms. By exploring these needs, researchers can determine how media can best satisfy users and improve their experiences [23].

3 Case Analysis: Smart Quarter Jena-Lobeda

3.1 Overview of the Local Community and Characteristics

The Smart Quarter is located in Jena, Germany, and is a small community consisting of three residential complexes. The focus of the neighborhood revolves around this area, as well as the implementation of specific measures and initiatives. It is characterized by a number of special features, which will be discussed in more detail below. First and foremost is the overarching vision of the neighborhood, which aims to create a sustainable, future-oriented, and technologically developed residential area in which the needs of residents are paramount. In addition, social and environmental factors are considered.

In exploring the Smart Quarter Jena-Lobeda, there are four main research dimensions that guide the development and understanding of this innovative living environment: Housing, Living, Caring, and Working. The Housing dimension focuses on integrating smart home technologies into the residential spaces. A select group of tenants were given a suite of Smart Home gadgets to test over one to two months. The implementation and utility of these gadgets were assessed through three subsequent interviews, which evaluated their impact on the tenants' daily lives and the frequency of their use. These insights are crucial in understanding how smart technologies can enhance residential living and the parameters of their acceptance among users. In the Caring dimension, the focus is on promoting health and fitness through technology. A set of smart gadgets, including

Smartwatches, a smart bodyweight scale, and an activity tracker, were distributed to residents. Similar to the methodology used in the Housing dimension, the research process involved giving these devices to residents for testing and subsequently evaluating their experiences and acceptance of the technology through interviews. The Working dimension presumably explores the intersection of technology, work, and residential living in the Smart Quarter, potentially examining topics such as remote work capabilities, co-working spaces, or digital skills training. The final dimension of the research is centered on the Living dimension, which has been given significant importance in this paper. The Living dimension is dedicated to creating a sense of community by utilizing a community platform. Across all these dimensions, the acceptance of technology and the digital literacy of residents are evaluated, providing important insights into the role of technology in modern living environments.

Within the quarter complex, which comprises three construction phases, approximately 228 people live in 200 apartments. Demographically, the neighborhood residents are made up of a wide variety of population groups, including families, seniors, and students. Living in the Smart Quarter is characterized by a wide range of offerings and services, including smart devices and smart services. The Smart Quarter is equipped with built-in smart features such as heating control and shutter control through a wall-mounted tablet. For any technological queries or issues, a community manager is readily available to support the residents. These built-in features and support systems further strengthen the integration of smart technologies into the residents' daily lives, enhancing the overall living experience within the Smart Quarter. Furthermore, the residents can take advantage of various third-party services, including car-sharing, e-receipts, energy monitoring, parcel services, and smart washing. This indicates the complexity of the environment in which the residents live (see Fig. 1).

Fig. 1. Overview of the Smart Quarter Living Environment (own representation)

Another important factor or group within the Smart Neighborhood are the stakeholders, including residents, businesses, academic institutions, and the public utilities. Each of these groups play an important role in supporting the continued success of the neighborhood and contribute to the development and implementation of innovative solutions. Funding for the Smart Quarters comes from a variety of sources, including public funding and grant programs. The use of cutting-edge technologies is a major contributor to value creation for residents. Smart grids, the use of renewable energy and the integration of smart home technologies are prominent examples. The Smart Quarter Jena-Lobeda represents a prime example of contemporary, needs-oriented urban development. The above factors, including the unique characteristics of the residential neighborhood and its framework, form the basis for exploring the potential benefits that digital solutions could offer to the area's multigenerational population.

3.2 Identification of Key Challenges

After elucidating the characteristics of the smart neighborhood, three key challenges have been identified as a result.

Information Overload and Interoperability. The presence of numerous smart living offers, smart services, and ongoing research projects in the smart neighborhood can lead to an overwhelming amount of requests and information. This includes difficulty in reaching and engaging with residents through analog media, and the need for community management to identify effective channels and features that align with the needs of residents. Additionally, residents may struggle with the interoperability of various devices and the lack of a grounded knowledge base on how these devices operate. The platform could serve as a helpful tool to address this issue.

New Occupancy. Another challenge facing the neighborhood from the project is new occupancy. As Schreiber and Göppert [3] have pointed out, an online local neighborhood platform can facilitate initial contact between neighbors and thus make it easier to establish offline social relationships. By providing a platform for residents to communicate, share information about needs, activities, and events, these platforms can create a sense of connectedness and reduce barriers to local engagement in community activities. Urban neighborhoods are characterized by hybrid forms of community engagement, where there is a constant alternation or transition between online and face-to-face interactions. In general, neighborhood platforms can be particularly helpful in fostering networking in newly emerging neighborhoods and communities, as newcomers who have not yet established networks in their local area are increasingly taking advantage of such platforms [3, 24].

Expectation in Communication. Communication and networking through digital media, such as large networks like Facebook or messengers like WhatsApp, have become normality for many people. On the other hand, residents continue to receive information about new developments through traditional methods such as notices on stairwells, even though residents themselves increasingly use new devices such as smartphones or tablets. This change in usage also leads to a change in expectations. Even in smart neighborhoods where smart home devices are already installed, communication tends to be analogue, via printed materials such as magazines. Neighborhood platforms can also help to address this issue and support improved communication. By utilizing digital channels such as mobile apps, email newsletters, and social media, these platforms can provide residents with quick and convenient access to important information and updates. Additionally, they can facilitate greater interaction and engagement among residents, fostering a sense of community and promoting a more collaborative and supportive living environment [25].

These challenges underscore the importance of community management and the use of a community platform as a means of addressing them. The project aims to support the formation of a community while considering the actual conditions of the neighborhood. To achieve this, the platform must represent the real structures of the neighborhood and promote a sense of well-being among residents. The platform must also be inclusive, catering to the needs and requirements of all potential users without excluding any particular group. Early involvement of users is crucial, and a participatory approach should be adopted to increase acceptance and make early citizen involvement possible [26].

Before delving into the discussion of the participation process in the upcoming section, the next section will thoroughly examine potential platform features in light of user needs. This analysis aims to identify and evaluate the features that have the potential to effectively address the diverse range of user needs. Through the alignment of platform features with the identified needs, an evaluation can be conducted to assess the platform's capacity to effectively address and meet the requirements of its users.

4   User-Centered Design Process

4.1   Platform Features and User Needs

In order to address the needs of potential users and promote a sense of community through the utilization of a community platform, it is crucial to identify the key features that would facilitate these goals. In this section, selected neighborhood platforms were examined to analyze their features and assess their alignment with the needs identified in the Use and Gratification Theory. Through this exploration of platform features, valuable insights can be gained on potential adaptations or enhancements that could better cater to the needs of prospective users within the Smart Quarter Jena-Lobeda context.

To identify important features, a comparative analysis was conducted on approximately 10 different platforms as well as research prototypes. The analysis revealed that the following features appear to be important for the use of platforms in neighborhood development projects. Features that emerged as the common denominators across these platforms are:

- Profile Creation: The ability for residents to create their own profiles and share their interests, skills, and needs with others in the neighborhood.
- Event Calendar: A feature that displays events in the neighborhood and informs residents about upcoming activities. This can range from community events such as festivals and markets to housing needs such as workshops for home repairs.
- News: A feature that provides residents with a news page that aggregates news relevant to the neighborhood or community.

- Group Functionalities: A feature that allows residents to form and organize groups based on common interests or goals within the neighborhood, such as gardening or child/parents' groups.
- Digital Bulletin Boards: A feature that provides a platform for residents to post and share information with others in the community, such as upcoming events, recommendations, questions or community announcements.
- Resource Reservation and Calendar: A function that allows residents to reserve and schedule the use of shared resources, such as community spaces or tools, and view availability through a shared calendar.
- Community Directory: A list of people, groups, and organizations in the neighborhood that could be useful for residents. This can include local businesses, neighborhood helpers, schools and daycares, or even groups for hobbies or interests such as yoga or cooking.
- Chat or Messaging Function: allows residents to communicate with each other through the platform, either privately or in group chats.
- Online Marketplace: A platform where residents can sell, buy, or exchange local products and services. This could range from secondhand items to handmade goods and local food.
- Sharing Function: A feature that allows residents to lend or share items and resources with each other, such as tools, sports equipment, kitchen appliances, or even cars. This can help to make resources in the neighborhood more efficiently used, while also strengthening neighborhood relationships.
- Knowledge Base/Smart Home Features: Smart neighborhoods could offer features for exchanging information and resources for smart home technologies. Residents can learn about new developments, security measures, and energy efficiency, as well as share their own experiences and tips.
- Emergency and Safety Alerts: A feature that quickly and effectively notifies residents in emergency situations such as natural disasters, accidents, or criminal activities. This feature could also include a public forum for neighborhood emergencies and a way to request help and support.
- Feedback and Review Function: A way for residents to provide feedback and reviews to evaluate the neighborhood and its facilities. This could help identify issues and suggest improvements.
- Polls and Voting: A feature that allows residents to give their opinions and vote on issues that affect the neighborhood, such as decisions on public spending or planning of urban development projects.
- Service Booking: A feature that allows residents to find and book local services such as cleaning, maintenance, or household assistance.
- Games and Entertainment: A feature that provides residents with games and entertainment options within the community platform. This could include virtual games, quizzes, and puzzles as well as access to streaming services for movies and TV shows. The feature could also allow residents to organize and participate in community events, such as game nights or movie screenings.
- Public Transportation Information: A feature that allows residents to receive real-time information about public transportation options near the neighborhood, such as schedules, delays, and departure times. This feature could also display connections

and routes to other neighborhoods or destinations in the city, helping travelers plan and optimize their journeys

To understand the frequencies of the features, Fig. 2 illustrates the percentage distribution of the included features.

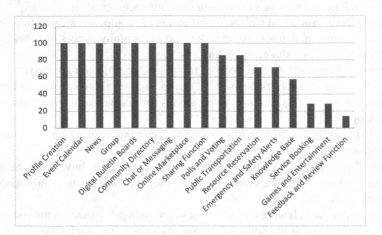

Fig. 2. Percentage distribution of the included features (own representation)

It is notable that the features Profile Creation, Event Calendar, News, Groups, Digital Bulletin Board, Community Directory, Chat, Online Marketplace, and Sharing Function were available in every examined platform. Therefore, special importance should be placed on these functions when selecting or designing a platform. On the other hand, Service Bookings, Games and Entertainment, and Feedback and Review Functions were not as commonly found. However, these features could become important, especially in terms of well-being and overall integration within the community.

To enhance understanding and establish a foundation for subsequent evaluation, the first step involves examining which user needs can be associated with specific platform features. Figure 3 presents a first approach in understanding the relationship between user needs and platform features. In the subsequent investigations, it will be crucial to examine whether the identified needs resonate with the residents in the smart neighborhood and whether the existing platform features adequately address these needs. Furthermore, the evaluation will explore the possibility of additional or alternative features that could potentially fulfill these needs, as well as assess whether there are any features that cater to different needs. The goal is to determine which features are most effective in meeting the residents' needs and enhancing their experience.

To explore the impact of platform features on the formation of a community and social cohesion, it is essential to conduct user-centered research to identify and comprehend these needs. The future research process will provide valuable insights into the extent to which user needs and platform features influence the development of a sense of community and social cohesion. By investigating the relationships between these factors, the team can gain a better understanding of the role that platform features play in

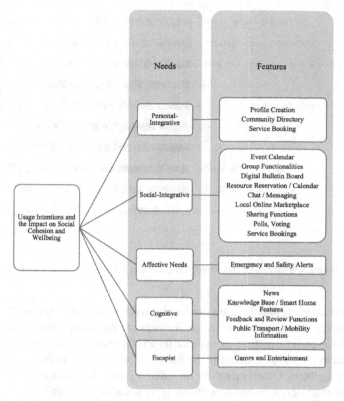

Fig. 3. Integration of Use and Gratification Theory and platform features

fostering community building and strengthening social bonds. This knowledge will contribute to the design and implementation of effective platforms that promote community engagement and enhance social cohesion in smart neighborhoods.

4.2 Exploring User Needs and Stakeholder Engagement

To identify the relevant functions in the diverse neighborhood of the Smart Quarter Jena-Lobeda and align the offer with the needs analysis, several steps are planned. One of the steps is the conduction of surveys among the residents of the neighborhood. These surveys will gather information on the needs and preferences of the residents, as well as their opinions on the existing services and functions in the neighborhood. This information will be valuable in determining which features are most relevant and necessary for the community. This valuable data will also provide insights into the existing level of social cohesion among the residents and assist in identifying the key features which are essential for fostering a stronger sense of community.

A survey was conducted among 228 residents in May/June 2023 (N = 228). While the analysis is still ongoing, there are no final results yet. However, initial evaluations reveal indications of desired features as depicted in Fig. 4.

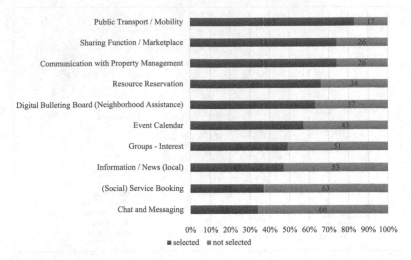

Fig. 4. Preliminary analysis of the survey on platform features n = 39 (own representation)

The results indicate that there are similarities with existing features on other platforms and also provide an indication of which features are most important. While there is a strong emphasis on information about mobility and the exchange or sale of goods, contact with the landlord is also important. In fact, it is even more important than directly contacting neighbors. Other mentions included a desire for increased connectivity of smart home/smart services and a platform representation through the home tablet. As mentioned, these are just preliminary analyses that need to be further understood in order to draw definitive conclusions which is why the team plans to conduct separate workshops consisting of representatives from residents and institutional stakeholders (focus groups) to further develop the platform and platform integration. The aim of the workshop with institutional stakeholders is to gain their (active) support for and identification with the platform. Meanwhile, the workshop with residents will focus on understanding their daily routines, the challenges they face, and the needs that arise from them. Through this, the team aims to identify how the platform can alleviate these needs and improve the residents' daily lives. The feedback gathered from both workshops will be used to refine the platform prototype or selected existing solution and will be tested by the residents of the Smart Quarter. This testing phase will be accompanied by qualitative interviews to evaluate the effectiveness of the platform and to identify areas for further improvement.

Another step is conducting interviews with representatives of local organizations and businesses. Through these interviews, the team will gain insights into what functions these organizations and businesses can offer and what needs they see among the residents of the neighborhood. These interviews will help to identify potential partners for implementing new services and functions in the neighborhood.

Through these various steps, the team hopes to identify the most relevant and necessary features for the neighborhood and to align the existing services with the needs and preferences of the multigenerational community.

5 Discussion and Conclusion

In the development of a community platform for smart neighborhoods, it is crucial to consider not only the features but also the underlying framework conditions. This encompasses various aspects such as stakeholders, marketing strategies, resource allocation, funding mechanisms, and the formulation of effective strategies and goals for implementation. Additionally, the existence of alternative platforms should be taken into account when deciding whether to develop the platform internally or to leverage existing solutions.

Engaging residents and addressing socioeconomic diversity is one of the primary challenges in establishing an active community platform. One contributing factor is the lack of an integrated community management system with various events and activities. This poses difficulties in reaching out to the residents, fostering their participation, and reaching a critical mass. Addressing this challenge requires active collaboration with the relevant stakeholders and joint efforts to engage with the community effectively. Another important aspect to consider before conducting a deeper evaluation and selection or development of the platform is the financial risk involved. At the beginning, funding for neighborhood platforms is often obtained through grants and other forms of financial support. However, to ensure the long-term sustainability of these platforms, it is important to have a clear plan for ongoing funding and support.

Neighborhoods differ and there is, until now, no universal way of neighborhood development due to varying socio-demographic, economic, and social structures. The composition of a group, such as older residents, can also impact the process. Identifying these neighborhood-specific factors is crucial as it influences development and participation processes in terms of action areas and engagement forms. By drawing on the Use and Gratification Theory, this paper has emphasized the significance of understanding users' needs and motivations to design an effective platform. The theory highlights that individuals actively choose media and technology to satisfy their cognitive, affective, personal-integrative, social-integrative, and escapist needs. By aligning these needs with the features of the platform, it becomes possible to create a platform that caters to the unique requirements of the local community. However, several challenges and considerations need to be addressed in the design and implementation of the platform. These include information overload and interoperability issues, ensuring user-friendly interfaces and accessibility for all residents, and the integration of third-party services and stakeholders. By addressing these challenges, the platform can create a sense of community, facilitate social interaction, and promote a sense of belonging and ownership among residents.

In conclusion, a user-centered local community platform has the potential to significantly enhance social cohesion in a multi-generational smart community. By understanding the unique needs of the community, aligning them with the features of the platform, and addressing the challenges and considerations, it is possible to design a platform that fosters social cohesion, supports healthy aging in place, and promotes a vibrant and connected local community while considering the specific characteristics of the neighborhood. The findings from this research will contribute to the design and improvement of community platforms, enhancing the sense of belonging and connectedness among residents. Furthermore, the exploration of social cohesion within the neighborhood highlights the importance of considering the unique characteristics and dynamics of the community when implementing technological solutions. By integrating user-centered approaches and continuously assessing the impact of platform features, stakeholders can ensure that community platforms effectively support the formation of strong and inclusive communities.

This research presents opportunities for further investigation and provides valuable insights for future smart neighborhood initiatives. While additional research and validation are required to refine platform design and implementation, the potential benefits for the community are promising.

References

1. Sampson, R.J., Raudenbush, S.W., Earls, F.: Neighborhoods and violent crime: a multilevel study of collective efficacy. Science **277**, 918–924 (1997). https://doi.org/10.1126/science.277.5328.918
2. Oberle, M.: Robert D. Putnam: Bowling Alone. The Collapse and Revival of American Community, New York: Simon and Schuster 2000, 541 S. In: Salzborn, S. (ed.) Klassiker der Sozialwissenschaften, pp. 408–411. Springer, Wiesbaden (2016). https://doi.org/10.1007/978-3-658-13213-2_95
3. Schreiber, F., Göppert, H.: Wandel von Nachbarschaft in Zeitendigitaler Vernetzung: Endbericht. vhw - Bundesverband für Wohnen und Stadtentwicklung e.V, Berlin (2018)
4. Vogel, P., von Mandelsloh, F., Grotherr, C., Gaidys, U., Böhmann, T.: Design and evaluation of an online neighborhood social network for fostering social connectedness and participation: lessons from two urban neighborhoods. In: 41st Proceedings of the International Conference on Information Systems (ICIS), pp. 1–17. Association for Information Systems, India (2020)
5. Quartierleben Neuhegi. https://neuhegi.mopage.ch. Accessed 25 Apr 2023
6. Meine Nachbarn Hamburg. https://www.meinenachbarn.hamburg. Accessed 25 Apr 2023
7. Unser Quartier. https://unser-quartier.de. Accessed 24 Apr 2023
8. Digitale Dörfer. https://www.digitale-doerfer.de. Accessed 25 Apr 2023
9. Crossiety. https://www.crossiety.ch. Accessed 25 Apr 2023
10. Vogel, P., Grotherr, C., Kurtz, C., Böhmann, T.: Conceptualizing design parameters of online neighborhood social networks. In: Proceedings der 15. Internationalen Tagung Wirtschaftsinformatik 2020. GITO Verlag, Berlin (2020)
11. Animus. https://animus.de. Accessed 26 Apr 2023
12. Casavi. https://casavi.com/de/. Accessed 24 Apr 2023
13. Allthings. https://unser-quartier.de. Accessed 24 Apr 2023
14. Bonenberger, L., Graf-Drasch, V., Meindl, O.: Handlungsempfehlungen für die Gestaltung mobiler Apps in smarten und nachhaltigen Quartieren. HMD. **58**, 1163–1179 (2021). https://doi.org/10.1365/s40702-021-00769-1
15. Hampton, K., Wellman, B.: Neighboring in netville: how the internet supports community and social capital in a wired suburb. City Community **2**, 277–311 (2003). https://doi.org/10.1046/j.1535-6841.2003.00057.x
16. Bellogín, A., Castells, P.: A performance prediction approach to enhance collaborative filtering performance. In: Gurrin, C., et al. (eds.) ECIR 2010. LNCS, vol. 5993, pp. 382–393. Springer, Heidelberg (2010). https://doi.org/10.1007/978-3-642-12275-0_34
17. Boyd, D.: It's Complicated: The Social Lives of Networked Teens. Yale University Press, New Haven London (2014)
18. Earl, J., Kimport, K.: Digitally Enabled Social Change Activism in the Internet Age. MIT Press, Cambridge (2014)

19. Hampton, W.H., Unger, A., Von Der Heide, R.J., Olson, I.R.: Neural connections foster social connections: a diffusion-weighted imaging study of social networks. Soc. Cogn. Affect. Neurosci. **11**, 721–727 (2016). https://doi.org/10.1093/scan/nsv153

20. Stark, B., Schneiders, P.: Uses and Gratifications Research: von Elihu Katz, Jay G. Blumler, und Michael Gurevitch (1973). In: Spiller, R., Rudeloff, C., Döbler, T. (eds.) Schlüsselwerke: Theorien (in) der Kommunikationswissenschaft, pp. 47–67. Springer, Wiesbaden (2022). https://doi.org/10.1007/978-3-658-37354-2_4

21. Katz, E., Blumler, J.G., Gurevitch, M.: Uses and gratifications research. Publ. Opin. Q. **37**, 509 (1973). https://doi.org/10.1086/268109

22. Katz, E., Haas, H., Gurevitch, M.: On the use of the mass media for important things. Am. Sociol. Rev. **38**, 164 (1973). https://doi.org/10.2307/2094393

23. Kasirye, F.: The importance of needs in uses and gratification theory (2022). https://doi.org/10.31124/advance.14681667

24. Witten, K., Kearns, R., Opit, S., Fergusson, E.: Facebook as soft infrastructure: producing and performing community in a mixed tenure housing development. Hous. Stud. **36**, 1345–1363 (2021). https://doi.org/10.1080/02673037.2020.1769035

25. Schultze, A.: Die Digitalisierung in der Wohnungswirtschaft – Aktuelle Trends und zukünftige Herausforderungen. In: Hildebrandt, A., Landhäußer, W. (eds.) CSR und Digitalisierung, pp. 101–115. Springer, Heidelberg (2021). https://doi.org/10.1007/978-3-662-61836-3_7

26. Schmidt, G.: Urban governance, zivilgesellschaftliche Partizipation und lokale Demokratie: Ein Transformationsprozess auf halber Strecke. In: Schmidt, G. (ed.) Urban Governance zwischen Inklusion und Effektivität, pp. 223–246. Springer, Wiesbaden (2014). https://doi.org/10.1007/978-3-658-04371-1_6

Efficient Internet of Things Surveillance Systems in Edge Computing Environments
Accessible via Web Based Video Transmissions from Low-Cost Hardware

Marcel Großmann[✉], Lukas Klinger, Vanessa Krolikowsky, and Chandan Sarkar

Fakultät WIAI, Otto-Friedrich-Universität,
An der Weberei 5, 96047 Bamberg, Germany
`marcel.grossmann@uni-bamberg.de`

Abstract. Video surveillance plays an important role in society, even though current systems are expensive, proprietary, and lack the portability to be useful in small-scale scenarios. In contrast, cheap Single Board Computers (SBCs) are easily deployed and integrated into existing Internet of Things networks, where sensor nodes can trigger various actors. Besides proprietary video transmission tools, the WebRTC framework enables access to Peer-to-Peer communications by all commonly available web browsers. By connecting these two paradigms, sensor nodes can detect predefined events and notify users with an announcement of an easily accessible video stream recorded by a cost efficient camera node.

We are exploiting the video streaming capabilities of a popular SBC model, the Raspberry Pi, and evaluate the expected Quality of Experience in combination with the stream's resource utilization on the source node. The trial framework is made publicly available to conduct measurements on any upcoming hardware platform. Finally, we provide a prototype of a sensor-triggered video surveillance system based on container virtualization. Any user interacts with it by a state-of-the-art browser and every system administrator easily initiates the open-sourced system by running our micro-service stack.

Keywords: Video streaming · Resource evaluation · WebRTC · Surveillance system · Virtualization · Fog computing

1 Introduction

In current years Internet of Things (IoT) continues to be a growing trend in computing and innovation. The ubiquity of smart devices increases, which in turn causes an increase in network traffic, bandwidth, and security concerns. In order to counter these issues at the edge of the network, computing gets consistent promotion and the paradigm of *data follows computation* prevails. We discover a wide range of application areas where IoT brings innovative solutions. Smart devices monitor home and office environments in order to save energy, enhance security and surveillance, or simply improve the quality of live. The

U. R. Krieger et al. (Eds.): I4CS 2023, CCIS 1876, pp. 292–311, 2023.
https://doi.org/10.1007/978-3-031-40852-6_16

health care sector tries to help the weak and elderly population with solutions like fall detection due to weakness with the help of wearable sensors and analysis of body movement patterns or remotely monitoring health conditions and suggesting medications. Availability of precise location data for human beings and non-human assets enables development of cutting-edge location-based services, which accommodates for a myriad of possibilities, e.g., location-aware augmented reality video games, smart transport systems or even predicting possible drastic changes in weather conditions based on a given location. Thus, one potential capability results in a multitude of possibilities.

Telemedicine is defined by the diagnosis and prescription of medicine to patients over telecommunication technologies, which allows doctors to remotely assist people in need across the geographical barrier. Although, telemedicine is not a new concept as a whole it comes with certain inherent constraints. Popular telemedicine solutions used by large hospitals and health care centers are proprietary and not always easy to use for everyone. They use dedicated video cameras or microphones or sometimes may require applications to be installed on the computers. From the consumer perspective availing these services is not always affordable. In order to counter these limitations Antunes et al. [18] suggested an easy to implement browser-based web application with the help of WebRTC. According to their solution, both parties, who are engaged in a session, must fulfill their requirements of a web browser, a web camera, and a microphone. The application uses a core module, which is responsible for connecting two peers and maintaining the session along with an identification of logged-in users. The implementation was tested with varying scenarios of communication between domestic users and medical professionals with promising outcomes.

Sulema and Rozinaj [26] proposed an innovative idea of a three-dimensional video conferencing system based on WebRTC, where they studied that being face-to-face in person is the most effective way of communication. While that is not possible in a remote fashion, implementing three-dimensional imaging could offer that benefit. Besides, it is observed that consumers are more comfortable communicating with higher resolutions and bigger interfaces compared to their smaller counterparts, e.g., smartphones. In order to ensure accurate processing of image data from all four viewpoints Sulema and Rozinaj [26] suggest the use of a media server, e.g., Kurento [8]. Kurento integrates WebRTC along with an advanced computer vision API in order to offer transmission, processing, augmented reality, and various other facilities in order to simplify media-oriented application development.

Over a careful analysis of the listed specimens, we came across some constraints of those implementations. The telemedicine solution is inherently browser dependent. In order to engage in interactive bi-directional communication, both parties need to invoke a web browser, which supports WebRTC [19]. Three-dimensional video conferencing relies on a media server for a heavy load of image processing computation and the solution is focused on some conceptual use cases.

While these implementations serve their specific purposes, none of them features a framework standardization in the context of IoT [17]. In spite of being distributed applications, they do not feature any specific design pattern. Our focus is to embed the physical objects with lightweight sensor modules in order to transform these objects into sources for collecting data. Therefore, these IoT objects must function with limited computing power. The IoT solution for video streaming must not create any resource bottleneck in such devices. Furthermore, the video stream is meant to be consumed with the help of web browsers or smart devices like phones or tablet computers. We want to avoid the installation or heavy load of configuration at the consumer end and seek for a lightweight solution for video streaming, which allows fast prototyping and avoids the overhead of configuration on the consumer's side. We need to feature an appropriate distributed system design pattern and a service-oriented approach to boost scalability and maintainability.

Therefore, in this study we set our goal to build a conceptual foundation of a video surveillance system for the IoT along with its constraints. Beginning with an evaluation of video streaming performance on SBCs with different settings, we try to evaluate, which combination suites best for a standardization of an application framework with the help of WebRTC. We adapt to an appropriate architectural design pattern in order to create a fast, efficient, browser-independent, maintainable, scalable, and distributed IoT prototypical solution. Finally, we evaluate our approach based on the objective and the outcome.

2   Foundation

2.1   Virtualization on a Single Board Computer

A standard framework for IoT solutions faces the heterogeneity of underlying hardware and software, which need to be abstracted away in order to support easy manageability. Therefore, virtualization offers attributes like availability, isolation, and security. Despite these benefits, virtualization often suffers from some performance bottlenecks as conferred by Regola and Ducom [24]. For our purpose, we need a lightweight solution to spin up the application components faster in an environment with constrained resources. Recent developments of Linux container technology work as a lightweight alternative for traditional hypervisor-based virtualization methods [27]. Linux container technology allows us to distribute the physical machine resources among multiple isolated contexts of processes. Therefore, container-based lightweight virtualization operates with abstraction at the level of system processes while hypervisor-based virtualization offers it at the level of hardware with guest operating systems [27]. Each container appears as an independent tree of system processes. Figure 1 depicts the contrast between hypervisor-based and container-based virtualization techniques.

The isolation of processes in Linux container-based virtualization is achieved by using the Kernel namespaces while the resource management is dealt by Linux' control groups mechanisms. Each container runs within the scope of its namespace and its access is limited to it. Control groups allow the Docker [5] engine to share the computational resources to containers and enforce necessary

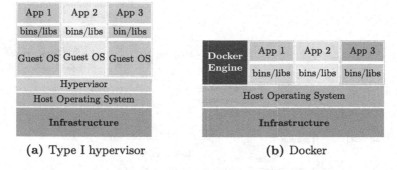

(a) Type I hypervisor   **(b)** Docker

Fig. 1. Comparison of hypervisor-based vs. container-based virtualization techniques

constraints. With the help of registries, the ephemeral basis for containers called Docker images can be distributed among the community. A container is the running instance of an image, where a writeable layer is added on top of the image's file system.

Unfortunately, the Kernel dependency of container virtualization needs a generation of separate images, which are suitable for different architectures in order to be used on, e.g., both, commodity computers with 64-bit CPUs and Raspberry Pis (RPis) with the 64-bit ARM architecture. However, with the help of the Quick Emulator (QEMU) [10] and the tool docker buildx, they can be build on commodity hardware. At the end of such a build process, different images exist, which are identified by a unique hash value and are finally linked together by a Docker manifest to be resolvable under a common name that is independent from the underlying architecture. To ease the development, automation can be realized with Continuous Integration (CI) tools, where developers upload changes to a Git repository and new images are automatically generated and pushed to a registry for Docker images [cf. 20]. After the publication of the multi-architecture description within its images on a registry, a Docker engine resolves its needed image by pulling the manifest and choosing the image's hash value based on the machine's architecture. For this publication, we chose *Github* to publish our code and integrated *Github actions* as CI tool to deliver multi-architecture images to the registry *ghcr.io* as depicted in Fig. 2.

Finally, networking plays the most crucial part for our prototype and any IoT solution. Docker allows handling the networking in a platform-independent manner, where it provides the customization options for networks in the form of drivers. Apart from these defined network drivers, Docker is flexible enough to allow third-party network plug-ins.

2.2   Peer-to-Peer Transmissions in WebRTC

In WebRTC the *RTCQUICTransport* interface encapsulates the browser-based Real-Time Communication (RTC) and associated configurations by using QUIC as transport protocol. It is comparable to the *RTCPeerConnection* interface of

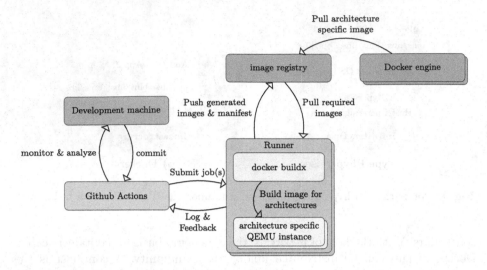

Fig. 2. CI workflow for Github actions to build multi-architecture Docker images

the traditional specification of WebRTC and can be instantiated with the *RTCIceTransport* and a sequence of *RTCCertificate* objects. The *RTCIceTransport* object encapsulates the information about the Interactive Connection Establishment (ICE) transport layer, which deals with the transmission and reception of data and exposes invaluable information about the state of a Peer-to-Peer (P2P) connection at any given point in time. With this specification, the handshaking between two separate peers engaged in communication takes place with the help of an ICE specification.

Loreto and Romano [22] described the need of exchanging the network reachability information between the engaging parties in order to establish data streams between them. This process of exchanging the network reachability information is encapsulated by the ICE framework. Essentially, ICE helps the peers to discover each other's presence in the network before establishing the communication. Local ICE agents are responsible to gather information about local Internet Protocol (IP) addresses and port numbers, to check connectivity between potential peers, and to send keep-alive messages. After the establishment of a local session description, the local ICE agent gathers information about the local IP addresses for potential peers, which are normally located behind Network Address Translations (NATs). Once the callee is selected, the ICE agent queries its public IP address and reachable port number from a Session Traversal Utilities for NAT (STUN) server. A Traversal Using Relays around NAT (TURN) server provides a fall-back strategy if the connection establishment with the intervention of a STUN server fails.

2.3   Internet of Things in the Fog and Edge Computing Paradigm

The idea of digitally capturing *everything* is a central one for the IoT. It can be done with wildly heterogeneous and cost efficient arrays of sensors available today. When it comes to the interpretation and attribution of semantic values to the plethora of raw data though, most IoT devices are not equipped to realistically fulfill the specific task. This shortcoming is due to the fact that those devices are heavily constrained in their locally available resources. Inferring knowledge from the immense amount of raw data is a compute heavy task that, depending on the application scenario, can require hard real-timeliness [23]. Finally, the generated high volume of data has to be transmitted to the cloud provider and results need to be sent back. This reserves a sizable portion of the available bandwidth, which could be used for other purposes. To avoid those issues, Fog and Edge Computing (FEC) concepts came to the picture. So what is FEC? The main idea of FEC is to bring the data processing near to the end users. Fog Computing (FC) and Edge Computing (EC) have many similarities, but they are not the same; the main difference is the placement of the business logic. In EC infrastructures, business logic or data processing is placed at the network edge, whereas FC describes the placement on any device from the cloud to the edge environments [21]. In many ways, FC and EC work together to achieve the desired result [25]. Low latency applications profit from FEC since data processing can be located near to respective devices. We can categorize the business model of FEC similar to Cloud Computing (CC) in the form of Everything as a Service (XaaS), where the range of services is lower than in traditional CC as more restrictions need to be concerned.

For our prototype, a SBC provides the service for streaming a live video from a camera, which may be started based on sensor readings. The same device or even a different one hosts a WebRTC service, which enables end users to connect to the video stream. Those devices constitute the edge of our architecture and combine the IoT with the FEC paradigm. Furthermore, we also need cloud services for ICE as described in Sect. 2.2, which allows mobile devices to connect to our WebRTC service.

3   Video Transmissions on Single Board Computers

3.1   Evaluation Framework for Video Streaming

First of all, testing the capabilities to deliver video streaming to different SBC models is necessary. To evaluate our testing framework, we use a simple setup, where a camera is attached to the RPi and streams a video to the client, which resides in the same network, as shown in Fig. 3. Therefore, every popular streaming framework is packaged into a container and is monitored by *cadvisor* [3]. We set up publicly available multi-architecture images for FFmpeg [6], GStreamer [7], and VLC [15] on Github [13], which are built in the fashion of Fig. 2. Moreover, we provide a script, which runs on the receiver, executes the configured trials and collects both, the resource usage data and the received video.

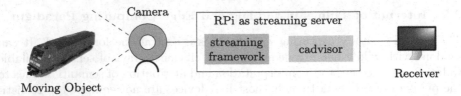

Fig. 3. The video streaming configuration for the ten minute video trials capturing a locomotive as moving object

For our trial framework we focused on the most commonly available video codecs, which we shortly describe:

- H.264/MPEG-4 AVC is a popular codec used in applications such as Blu-ray discs, video streaming, and video conferencing. With its high compression efficiency and device compatibility, it is suited to a wide range of devices.
- H.265/HEVC is a newer codec that offers even better compression efficiency than H.264/MPEG-4 AVC. Compatibility is not as high as H.264/MPEG-4 AVC, but adoption is slowly increasing.
- VP8 was invented as part of the H.264 video codec by Google. It is a free and open source codec and offers a high compression efficiency.
- VP9 is a free and open source codec developed by Google and the successor of VP8. It offers high compression efficiency and is compatible with a wide range of devices.

We performed the evaluation on two RPis, the RPi 3 (v1.2) with 1 GB of memory and the RPi 4 with 8 GB. On both RPis we used a Debian 12 (Bookworm) image [4] and installed the Docker environment on them. The video streams for each codec and each framework ran for ten minutes and the cAdvisor [3] statistics were gathered for each container. For comparable results, we chose a resolution of 640 × 480 pixels and a framerate of 30 frames per second (fps). As shown in Fig. 3 we used a model railway for the video streams to be encoded by the RPi and capture a moving locomotive.

3.2   Evaluation of the Resource Utilization on the Raspberry Pis

In Fig. 4 we use boxplots, which show the statistical summary of the resource consumption for the video transmission time. In Fig. 4a the CPU utilization shows that the RPi 3 struggles a lot for different codecs to perform a stable encoding for the selected resolution of 640 × 480 pixels, which can be recognized by huge variations in the boxplots. Every time the RPi 3's CPU, or at least one core of it, is overloaded, it drops frames to reduce the workload and starts to encode again, which at some point leads to exhaustion again. Besides, the H.264 and VP9 codec recognize beforehand with which rate the encoding is possible. In contrast, the RPi 4 performs quite good as shown in Fig. 4b and produces a video stream for almost all combinations. The memory usage evaluation of Figs. 4c and 4d discloses that the VLC framework has the highest footprint,

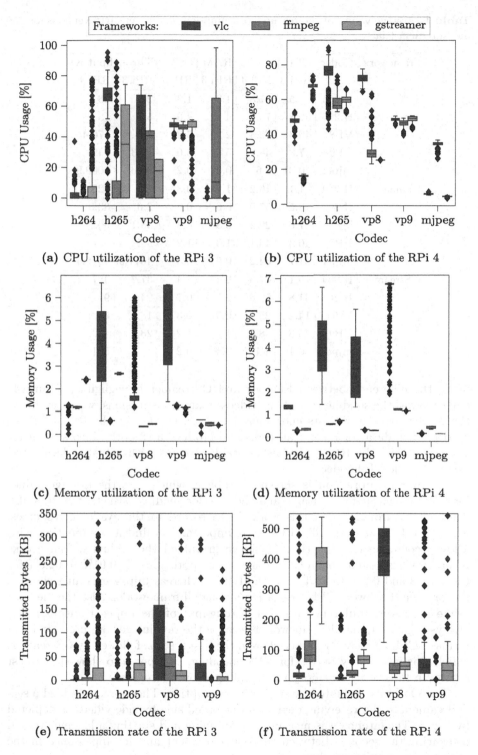

Fig. 4. Evaluation of the resource consumption for ten minute video streaming using different video codecs on three available encoding frameworks

Table 1. Average values of the resource consumption on different RPi versions for our measurement trials

Framework	Codec	CPU [%]		RAM [%]		Throughput KB/s	
		RPi 3	RPi 4	RPi 3	RPi 4	RPi 3	RPi 4
VLC	H.264	2.5	47.8	1.3	1.3	2.6	33
	H.265	62.8	75.1	4	4.0	5.4	13.5
	VP8	40.3	72.3	2	3.2	143.8	570.4
	VP9	47.8	48.4	5	6.6	16.3	249
	mjpeg	0.01	0.6	0.6	0.2	39.6	5009.9
FFmpeg	H.264	1.1	16.2	1.2	0.3	5.7	125.3
	H.265	8.5	57.9	0.6	0.6	2.6	33.3
	VP8	27.6	29.4	0.3	0.3	38.1	50.2
	VP9	46.3	46.1	1.3	1.2	3.4	6.8
	mjpeg	31.7	34.2	0.5	0.4	4617.9	4628.4
GStreamer	H.264	9.1	67.8	2.4	0.4	37.7	487
	H.265	31.8	59.6	2.7	0.7	24	91
	VP8	14.2	25	0.5	0.3	18.4	63.2
	VP9	45.8	48.6	1.2	1.2	23.4	43.2
	mjpeg	0.1	4.4	0.4	0.2	—	5019.3

while the difference between FFmpeg and GStreamer is negligible. Figures 4e and 4f reveal the sending rate of the video stream transmissions, where we hided the mjpeg codec due to its enormous data rate. Obviously, the RPi 3 fails to send enough data for almost all codecs to produce a smooth video stream for our trial, while the RPi 4 establishes stable streams with valuable data rates, except for the VP9 codec.

An overall impression is shown in Table 1, which lists the average values for CPU usage, memory usage, and the rate for sending packets, which is also denoted as throughput in this work. With regard to the available resources, which are limited by small SBCs, it is important to find a combination with a low resource usage footprint. As shown in Table 1 the evaluated frameworks reveal obvious deviations in CPU usage from approximately 0.01% to 62.8% for the RPi 3 and 0.6% to 75.1% for the RPi 4, whereas mjpeg encoding shows a low or even the lowest CPU utilization among all frameworks. Also the memory usage reveals a similar picture. The throughput of the mjpeg transmission is always higher among all frameworks because the raw images are used for it. In terms of CPU efficiency FFmpeg showed the best results, followed by GStreamer, which was marginally better for VP8 encoding. FFmpeg also showed the best results in the average memory usage, followed by GStreamer.

The QoE was evaluated by subjective perception. Therefore, we added a second camera to the receiving device and recorded side-by-side videos as depicted by Fig. 5. The latency was measured by stopping and starting a locomotive and measuring the seconds between the real movement and its appearance in the stream. The results are shown in Table 2.

Fig. 5. A video stream record example for VP9 encoded by GStreamer for evaluating the Quality of Experience (QoE). On the left side the stream of the RPi 4 is recorded, while the right one shows the live video from a second camera attached to the receiving device.

Table 2. QoE evaluation of the received video streams Quality: ++ (very good), + (good), o (medium), - (bad), – (very bad) Latency: ++ (<1 s), + (1–3 s), o (3–6 s), - (6–9 s), – (>9 s)

Framework	Codec	Quality		Latency	
		RPi 3	RPi 4	RPi 3	RPi 4
VLC	H.264	–	++	–	+
	H.265	–	+	–	-
	VP8	o	o	–	o
	VP9	–	–	–	–
	mjpeg	–	–	–	+
FFmpeg	H.264	o	++	–	++
	H.265	-	++	–	++
	VP8	+	++	o	++
	VP9	–	–	–	–
	mjpeg	o	++	–	–
GStreamer	H.264	o	++	–	++
	H.265	–	+	–	+
	VP8	–	+	–	+
	VP9	–	-	–	–
	mjpeg	—	++	—	++

If the latency occurred to be less than a second, the latency was rated with ++. For GStreamer, mjpeg encoding delivered no results for the RPi 3, as it was not possible to play the stream with any player.

In general, most of the frameworks accomplished to stream an acceptable video on the RPi 4 for the given purpose of video surveillance. But in terms of quality and especially latency, several framework and codec combinations surpass others. While a latency of 3–9 s, e.g. for VLC, seems more than acceptable, the end user would welcome the possibility of a nearly live transmission like FFmpeg with H.264, H.265, or VP8, or GStreamer with H.264 with regard to the expected latency of the Internet. In terms of image quality, FFmpeg in general and GStreamer with H.264 showed the best results and overall very smooth motion.

Unfortunately, we only configured a fixed resolution (640 × 480) and framerate of 30 fps for all frameworks and codec combinations such that the RPi 3 occurs to be a bad choice for video surveillance. Nevertheless, different settings for each framework could render a better result on the RPi 3 and increase its suitability. They can be easily found by adjusting the resolution and framerate values with our trial framework and analyzing the resulting video stream.

To summarize, the best codec to use on the RPi 4 with any framework is H.264. Since WebRTC only supports H.264 or VP8 encoding, only VLC, FFmpeg and GStreamer without mjpeg encoding can be considered. As mentioned before, it is important for an IOT solution to find a technique with a reasonable balance between resource consumption and video quality. Despite the good quality, almost all codecs show a higher demand on resources for VLC in contrast to FFmpeg with H.264 or VP8 and GStreamer with VP8. Therefore, the latter are all good candidates for the purpose of video surveillance.

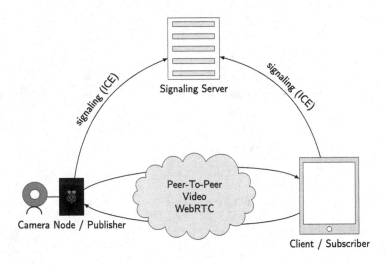

Fig. 6. Architecture of a P2P system, where a RPi publishes a video over WebRTC to a connected client

4   Architectural Overview of a Web Surveillance System

4.1   Internet of Things Modifications for WebRTC

In a traditional WebRTC peer connection each the publisher and the subscriber components can initiate a connection and expect the other peer to respond with an answer. In more sophisticated implementations it is possible for both peers to join a room, which is the object that maintains the connections and ICE exchange state for both peers. This methodology is ideal for the use cases, where both peers try to engage in a video call and add the media track to the peer connection. However, in an IoT use case, which is depicted in Fig. 6, the publisher module is an embedded device with a camera module, which only captures and transmits the video. The subscriber module is a lightweight client, which only consumes the video. Therefore, we got the subscriber to trigger the `addTransceiver` method on `RTCPeerConnection` in order to create a `RTCRtpTransceiver` object and add it to the list of transceivers of the peer connection. The `RTCRtpTransceiver` object can have one of the following directions, which impact the behavior of Real-Time Transport Protocol (RTP) [16]:

- `sendrecv` represents the intention to both send and receive the RTP data if the offer is accepted by the other peer and responded with an answer.
- `sendonly` represents the intention to only send the RTP data if the offer is accepted by the other peer and responded with an answer.
- `recvonly` represents the intention to only receive RTP data if the offer is accepted by the other peer and responded with an answer.
- `inactive` represents neither to send nor to receive the RTP data from the remote peer.

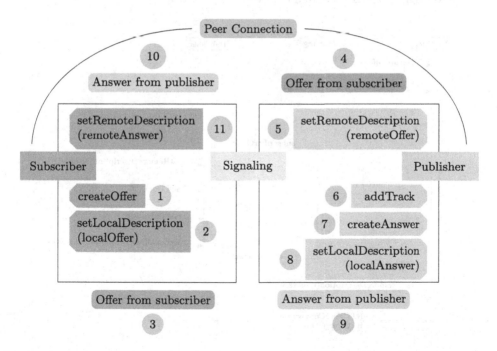

Fig. 7. The abstraction of the publish-subscribe model, which is needed to establish a P2P connection

In our prototype the subscriber only wants to receive the media stream. In order to start with the signaling procedure it initiates the `RTCPeerConnection` object and sets the direction of its `RTCRtpTransceiver` object to `recvonly`. Besides the publisher and the subscriber, we introduce a `mediator` for the orchestration. In accordance with the standard WebRTC specification we name it **Signaling** server in our implementation.

Now that we described all components of our architecture, we can focus on the big picture of the orchestration among our three fundamental building blocks. Figure 7 demonstrates the approach after we incorporate the **Signaling** component to mediate and act as a bridge between the publisher and subscriber. The procedure to establish a `RTCPeerConnection` is shown in Fig. 8 in form of a sequence diagram.

1. The *Subscriber* creates its offer with the asynchronous `createOffer` method on the `RTCPeerConnection`. The offer is an `RTCSessionDescription` object which encapsulates the information about an optional media track, all possible media codec information supported by the browser and any possible ICE candidate for establishing the peer connection.
2. The *Subscriber* configures the properties for the local end of the peer connection object by calling the method `setLocalDescription`. This method is triggered asynchronously and takes effect when negotiation is completed by both peers. Calling this method generates an `RTCIceCandidate` object and triggers the `icecandidate` event.

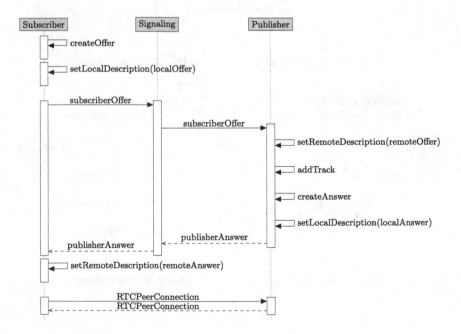

Fig. 8. Message flow to establish a peer connection

3. The *Subscriber* communicates its offer with the HTTP POST method to the *Signaling* server, which exposes a dedicated path for the *Subscriber* to reach out.

4. The *Signaling* server communicates the offer from the *Subscriber* to the *Publisher* via a dedicated path exposed by the *Publisher*'s web application for the *Signaling* server to reach out.

5. Upon receiving the offer, the *Publisher* triggers the `setRemoteDescription` method in order to set the properties of the remote end of the connection, which is the *Subscriber* from the perspective of the *Publisher*. This method is triggered asynchronously and only takes effect when negotiation is complete by both peers.

6. The *Publisher* instantiates the `MediaPlayer` API from the `aiortc` framework with the video interface and adds an instance of the `VideoStreamTrack` object to the peer connection object of its end.

7. The *Publisher* creates an answer to the offer it received from the *Subscriber* with the help of the `createAnswer` method of the peer connection object. The answer object is yet another session description encapsulating the information about the media stream that was added to the peer connection, like codec information it supports and any possible ICE candidate the peer connection has gathered so far.

8. The *Publisher* uses the `setLocalDescription` method in order to add the properties for its own end of the peer connection. This method is triggered asynchronously and only takes effect when negotiation is completed by both peers.

9. The *Publisher* sends its answer back to the *Signaling* server as an HTTP response.

10. Upon receiving an answer from the *Publisher*, the *Signaling* server sends the answer back to the *Subscriber* as an HTTP response.

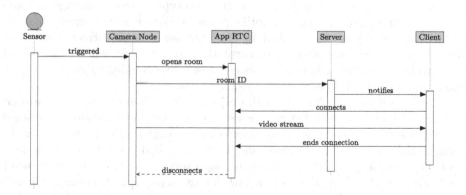

Fig. 9. The sequence used to react on sensor changes and run an AppRTC container if the sensor is triggered

11. Upon receiving the answer of the *Publisher* from the *Signaling* server, the *Subscriber* sets the properties of the remote end of its peer connection object with the answer object and the `setRemoteDescription` method.

12. At this point, all the asynchronous method invocations by both parties are fulfilled. As a result, both the *Publisher* and the *Subscriber* know their own configuration for the peer connection and the configuration for their relative remote peers. The `iceGatheringState` property for peer connections of both parties is set to be complete. Now, the *Subscriber* can directly consume the media stream captured and transmitted by the *Publisher*.

4.2   Video Surveillance Prototype

Our prototype is built on Docker [5] and Docker Compose to allow for easy deployment and management of dependencies and is made publicly available on Github under `uniba-ktr/iotrtc` [12] build with Github Actions as shown in Fig. 2. Both the camera and the necessary services for the server are completely "containerized" and can, therefore, be run on devices with only minimal preparation.

The system works as follows: One or more camera nodes are deployed and a sensor is connected to them. Once the sensor is triggered, the camera connects to a new AppRTC [2] room and sends the room ID to the signaling server. Any subscribed clients are notified and can watch the stream as shown in the sequence diagram of Fig. 9.

A *camera* node consists of a RPi 4, a USB camera and some sensor connected to the General Purpose Input/Output (GPIO) pins of the RPi. Whenever a trigger is detected on a selected pin, the node automatically initiates a video connection. As this behavior is based on Node-RED [9], the device can be configured easily. Once the connection has been triggered, the device automatically connects to an AppRTC [2] room and the room ID is sent to the signaling server.

The signaling *server* component of our prototype is used to deliver the web app to clients and to take care of notifications. A Node.js server serves all static HTML files and provides an API to send messages to subscribed clients. In the prototype only one device can currently subscribe and will be notified of changes for all cameras, however, this can easily be extended to allow for more subscriptions and/or subscriptions to specific cameras.

The Web Push API built into all major modern browsers has standardized how notifications are handled on the web. A web page can register a so-called *Service Worker*, basically a small JavaScript file that is allowed to run in the background under certain circumstances, that is called every time a new notification is available. Routing is done through servers provided by the browser company (e.g. Mozilla or Google), making it easy to implement messaging in web apps. Our server application delivers one single page to clients, which is used to subscribe to the service. Moreover, the server provides a simple API to receive messages from camera nodes and then send those messages to the users. Our prototype currently does not authenticate messages, anyone who knows about the API can send messages to subscribers.

As a security measure, browsers will only register a web app's service worker if the connection is encrypted. In our prototype, a simple Docker container acts as a TLS termination proxy, serving the web page using a self-signed certificate. To make it easier to start all components of the server, we provide a small micro-service stack as Docker Compose file with a bash startup script.

A *client* can be any device running a modern web browser that supports the Web Push API, H.264 encoded video, and WebRTC. First, the user subscribes to changes by visiting our subscription page, served by the server component of our prototype. Once subscribed, every trigger on any camera sends a message to the user, including the AppRTC room ID. The user can then click on that notification to be forwarded to the AppRTC room and watch the video stream. As we currently base our system on AppRTC, no development effort was necessary. Fortunately, AppRTC is open-source and could be integrated into our server as well, making the prototype independent from any outside systems.

The software of the camera node is based on *Node-RED* [9], *aiortc* [1], and *v4l2* [14], which interfaces with the USB camera. *Aiortc* is a Python library for WebRTC and Object Real-Time Communication (ORTC). The library is built with Python's built-in asynchronous programming framework *asyncio*. *Aiortc* implements the WebRTC specification without needing to invocate a web browser. Furthermore, *aiortc* uses *PyAV* [11], which is a Python wrapper for *FFmpeg* and offers a robust API to manipulate almost any kind of media on all popular platforms. *PyAV* offers access to media in many forms, e.g., containers, frames, streams, etc. with reasonable transformations creating a layer of abstraction over *FFmpeg*. In an embedded device running on Linux, *PyAV* can extract and record media from an attached camera module or even prior-recorded video files. We added the control for Docker containers to Node-RED [9], which can start and stop other processes on the device via the docker-cli.

5 Evaluation of the IoT Surveillance Prototype

We discussed our approach to build a prototypical application based on the propositions we made in order to consider WebRTC as a viable standardization framework for IoT. Now, we evaluate our application in light of the previously specified design goals for the framework, which is suitable for IoT environments.

- **Capability to handle P2P communication**
  The proposed solution is capable to establish a P2P communication session between concerned parties. The session is kept alive while both parties are engaged in active communication. The implementation of the publish-subscribe design pattern enables us to create a scalable and distributed architecture.
- **Capability to enable fast hardware-independent prototyping**
  Our prototype features an orchestration by the container virtualization platform Docker. Containers allow us to run the components of the application in an isolated containerized environment with all required dependencies. This

makes it possible to choose any machine, which supports container technology to host the application with minimal additional configuration.

– **Capability to support web-based applications**
  Our application prototype is inherently web-based. The subscriber module initiates the connection establishment procedure by generating its Session Description Protocol (SDP) object and subscribes to the signaling server over the network with the help of an HTTP POST POST method. Signaling server, in turn, transfers the SDP from the subscriber to the publisher over the network via HTTP POST POST methods. Similarly, the SDP object generated by the publisher as a response is communicated back to the subscriber with HTTP response messages.
– **Capability to feature component-based architecture**
  We tried to modularize the architecture of the prototype from ground up. We adapted a publish-subscribe pattern for distributed system design and created distinct building blocks for our implementation having specific responsibilities. Each of these components is executed in a separate container, which encapsulates its respective dependencies.

Now that we evaluated our prototypical application against the predefined design goals we want to draw a direct comparison of our solutions against similar works, which we reviewed earlier. Our solution attempts to address the issues we highlighted before. Our prototypical application is not dependent on a web browser in order to capture the camera feed and transmit it as a video stream. The `aiortc` [1] framework provides a native implementation of the WebRTC specification stack, which enables it to operate independently with the intervention of the web browser.

Our solution features hardware-independent fast prototyping with the help of the container-based virtualization platform Docker running on Linux systems. This not only enables our application to be executable on any Linux system having a Docker orchestration environment but also we can quickly scale our deployment with the addition or modification of new or existing services.

Our solution is not focused on particular use cases. We adapted the publish-subscribe design pattern of the distributed system in order to bring the values such as scalability, loose coupling, and security. Therefore, our prototype has the potential to be considered as a template in order to build complex web-based, component-oriented, loosely coupled, and secure P2P distributed applications.

The WebRTC specification does not provide any utility for a local peer to easily create a connection to a remote peer per default. It delegates the responsibility to create a channel of communication between the peers to the implementer of WebRTC. This channel of communication is encapsulated by the concept called *signaling* in WebRTC. This flexibility makes it possible for the implementers to go for their chosen option for implementing the signaling utility. Unfortunately, the `aiortc` [12] framework encapsulates its own implementation of the signaling server. It does not offer the interface to plug-in an alternate implementation for the signaling module. This design decision is rigid and does not follow the WebRTC specification.

We tested the application using a pre-recorded video feed, as well as, using a camera module. With our streaming evaluation framework, we chose reliable parameter for encoding the video stream and implemented our recommendations to use FFmpeg with the H.264 codec in our prototype to achieve a nearly real-time transmission of the camera feed on a RPi 4.

6   Conclusion and Future Work

We introduced the traditional and modern specifications of WebRTC while proposing it as a suitable standardization framework to build IoT solutions. We reviewed some of the recent contextual works on the subject matter, which feature the IoT focused solution based on WebRTC. Each of these applications was either focused on their specific use cases or inherently dependent on web browsers, which support the WebRTC specification stack. We analyzed the aforementioned limitations and set our objective to evaluate the potential of WebRTC as a standard framework to build IoT applications. We attempted to get rid of the web browser dependency of WebRTC since it is not optimal for IoT sensors to invoke browsers. We also made efforts to adapt one of the distributed system design patterns in order to develop a scalable and maintainable prototypical application. Finally, we evaluated our application with respect to the design goals, which we set earlier for a potential standardization framework for IoT.

On the implementation perspective, we created a component-based, scalable, and loosely coupled distributed IoT application. It is a web-based orchestration of three distinct functional modules having their dependencies self-contained inside respective containers. Therefore, they are executable in any environment supporting container virtualization, which contributes to the aspect of platform-independent fast prototyping. The publisher and the subscriber module establish a P2P connection with the help of the signaling server module as an intermediary decoupling agent in order to realize the WebRTC specification. The publisher no longer necessitates having a web browser, which implements the WebRTC specification stack. Our solution addresses the issues we highlighted while defining our goal for this study. Thus, we were able to create a strong argument in favor of WebRTC to be considered as a standardization framework for IoT.

Unfortunately, we encountered substantial challenges in the implementation phase, compromising the QoE guarantee. Severe downfalls in the performance of the video stream occurred while using the camera module. This resulted in a video stream, which was non-productive for real-world use cases. Within a few modifications, we were able to provide a first solution. However, further investigations with our measurement framework [13] on more codec settings, and a better signaling strategy to choose appropriate video encoding options should increase the expected QoE for different SBC models.

The current implementation features a signaling server running inside the same orchestration environment with a subscriber module. Furthermore, the signaling server needs to know the network address of the publisher. These could result in security loopholes for the entire application. In order to address these concerns, one could isolate the signaling server component on a separate host. Moreover, one could revise the implementation in such a way that the publisher needs to register with the signaling server with its own reachability information before the initiation of the P2P connection. This refines to the aspect of loose coupling and promotes security for the overall system.

Further possible improvements for our prototype may solve the current issue that if a *camera* node has entered an AppRTC [2] room, it will wait forever for a client to join. Of course, a timeout of, e.g., three minutes would make more sense, such that resources are not wasted. Lastly, we could replace Node-RED [9] for something more custom-built to save on resources of the SBC.

Currently, the signaling *server* only allows for one single subscription by one client device. This can be changed rather easily, as subscriptions can be saved in a database. Moreover, every device gets notified by every camera at the moment. Similarly to multiple subscriptions, this requires a database of cameras so that users can choose, which camera nodes will notify them. Lastly, the API needs to be secured such that no unauthorized third-party can send arbitrary notifications to users. AppRTC [2] is an open-source web app and could be integrated into our server component. Also, AppRTC could be modified to support more than one client streaming from a camera node at a time.

In light of our evaluation of WebRTC as a standardization framework for platform independent fast prototyping of IoT solutions, we conclude this study with the affirmative outcome having a note of the critical challenges, which are encountered and possible ways to mitigate them.

Acknowledgment. Mrs. Krolikowsky and Mr. Klinger contributed to the codec evaluation and enhanced the WebRTC prototypes developed by Mr. Sarkar, while they were working with the Computer Networks group at the University of Bamberg. The authors are very much indebted to their efforts for the implementation and publication of the measurement platform, as well as, the first prototype of the web-based surveillance system.

References

1. Aiortc. https://github.com/aiortc/aiortc
2. Apprtc. https://github.com/webrtc/apprtc
3. Cadvisor. https://github.com/google/cadvisor
4. Debian images for the raspberry pi. https://raspi.debian.net/tested-images/
5. Docker. https://www.docker.com/
6. Ffmpeg. https://ffmpeg.org/
7. Gstreamer - open source multimedia framework. https://gstreamer.freedesktop.org/
8. Kurento media server. https://github.com/Kurento/kurento-media-server
9. Nodered. https://nodered.org/
10. Open source machine emulator (qemu). https://www.qemu.org/
11. Pyav. https://github.com/PyAV-Org/PyAV
12. Rtc framework for the internet of things. https://github.com/uniba-ktr/iotrtc
13. Streaming trial framework. https://github.com/uniba-ktr/streaming

14. Video for linux. https://linuxtv.org/downloads/v4l-dvb-apis/
15. Vlc media player. https://www.videolan.org/vlc/index.de.html
16. Webrtc api. https://developer.mozilla.org/en-US/docs/Web/API/WebRTC_API
17. Al-Fuqaha, A., Guizani, M., Mohammadi, M., Aledhari, M., Ayyash, M.: Internet of things: a survey on enabling technologies, protocols, and applications. IEEE Commun. Surv. Tutor. **17**(4), 2347–2376 (2015). https://doi.org/10.1109/COMST.2015.2444095
18. Antunes, M., Silva, C., Barranca, J.: A telemedicine application using WebRTC. Procedia Comput. Sci. **100**, 414–420 (2016). ISSN 1877-0509, https://doi.org/10.1016/j.procs.2016.09.177, https://www.sciencedirect.com/science/article/pii/S1877050916323456, International Conference on ENTERprise Information Systems/International Conference on Project MANagement/International Conference on Health and Social Care Information Systems and Technologies, CENTER-IS/ProjMAN/HCist 2016
19. Blum, N., Lachapelle, S., Alvestrand, H.: WebRTC: real-time communication for the open web platform. Commun. ACM **64**(8), 50–54 (2021). ISSN 0001-0782, https://doi.org/10.1145/3453182
20. Großmann, M., Ioannidis, C.: Continuous integration of applications for ONOS. In: 2019 IEEE Conference on Network Softwarization (NetSoft), pp. 213–217 (2019). https://doi.org/10.1109/NETSOFT.2019.8806696
21. Großmann, M., Ioannidis, C.: Cloudless computing - a vision to become reality. In: 2020 International Conference on Information Networking (ICOIN), pp. 372 377 (2020). https://doi.org/10.1109/ICOIN48656.2020.9016441
22. Loreto, S., Romano, S.P.: Real-Time Communication with WebRTC: Peer-to-Peer in the Browser. O'Reilly Media, Inc., Sebastopol (2014)
23. Razzaque, M.A., Milojevic-Jevric, M., Palade, A., Clarke, S.: Middleware for internet of things: a survey. IEEE Internet Things J. **3**(1), 70 95 (2016)
24. Regola, N., Ducom, J.C.: Recommendations for virtualization technologies in high performance computing. In: 2010 IEEE Second International Conference on Cloud Computing Technology and Science, pp. 409–416 (2010). https://doi.org/10.1109/CloudCom.2010.71
25. Satyanarayanan, M.: The emergence of edge computing. Computer **50**(1), 30–39 (2017). https://doi.org/10.1109/MC.2017.9
26. Sulema, Y., Rozinaj, G.: WebRTC-based 3D videoconferencing system. In: 2017 International Symposium ELMAR, pp. 193–196 (2017). https://doi.org/10.23919/ELMAR.2017.8124466
27. Xavier, M.G., Neves, M.V., Rossi, F.D., Ferreto, T.C., Lange, T., De Rose, C.A.F.: Performance evaluation of container-based virtualization for high performance computing environments. In: 2013 21st Euromicro International Conference on Parallel, Distributed, and Network-Based Processing, pp. 233–240 (2013). https://doi.org/10.1109/PDP.2013.41

Short Papers

Improved Euclidean Distance
in the K Nearest Neighbors Method

Chérifa Boucetta(✉), Laurent Hussenet, and Michel Herbin

CReSTIC EA 3804, 51097, Université de Reims Champagne-Ardenne, Reims, France
{cherifa.boucetta,laurent.hussenet,michel.herbin}@univ-reims.fr

Abstract. The KNN algorithm is one of the most famous algorithms in data mining. It consists in calculating the distance between a query and all the data in the reference set. In this paper, we present an approach to standardize variables that avoids making assumptions about the presence of outliers or the number of classes. Our method involves computing the ranks of values within the dataset for each variable and using these ranks to standardize the variables. We then calculate a dissimilarity index between the standardized data, called the Rank-Based Dissimilarity Index (RBDI), which we use instead of Euclidean distance to find the K nearest neighbors. Finally, we combine the Euclidean distance and the RBDI index taking into account the advantage of both dissimilarity indices. In essence, the Euclidean distance considers the Euclidean geometry of the data space while RBDI is not constrained by distance or geometry in data space. We evaluate our approach using multidimensional open datasets.

Keywords: Euclidean distance · K nearest neighbors · Open datasets · Rank-based dissimilarity index

1 Introduction

Managing a data center that hosts virtual machines (VMs) can be a complex task, as there are multiple variables to consider in order to ensure optimal performance, energy efficiency, and cost-effectiveness. VMs are defined as data with various quantitative variables such as memory, CPU, GPU, and usage time, energy consumption, etc. As part of the DeMETeRE[1] project (Deployment of Territorial Micro-Environments for Student Success), we need to facilitate the energy management and pricing of VM hosting. The project consists of implementing a virtualization system for workstations for both URCA students and professionals. This solution aims to meet the techno-pedagogical needs by providing specific tools and software for each program, while ensuring equal access for all users, regardless of their workplace or equipment.

Different classes of VMs can be defined. When we need to deploy a new VM, it is assigned to one of these classes based on its requirements and specifications.

---

[1] https://www.univ-reims.fr/demetere.

© The Author(s), under exclusive license to Springer Nature Switzerland AG 2023
U. R. Krieger et al. (Eds.): I4CS 2023, CCIS 1876, pp. 315–324, 2023.
https://doi.org/10.1007/978-3-031-40852-6_17

This allows for easier management of the VMs as they can be grouped together based on their similarities and managed accordingly [1,8]. For example, VMs with high processing power requirements can be grouped together and hosted on servers with high-performance CPUs and GPUs [5]. Similarly, VMs with lower processing requirements can be hosted on servers with lower specifications to ensure optimal utilization of resources. In this context, this paper proposes a classification method that aims to assign a quantitative multidimensional data to a class by calculating the nearest neighbors. Finding the nearest neighbors is at the heart of many data analysis methods.

The K nearest neighbors (KNN) is the most classical method of classification [4,14]. The purpose of classification is to determine the class of new data within a set of reference data. The new data is called a query and the reference dataset is partitioned into classes. KNN consists in calculating the distance between a query and all the data in the reference set. We select the K nearest neighbors of the query. Each neighbor is assigned to its reference class. We predict the class of the query by assigning it the most represented class among its neighbors. The core of the method is to find the K nearest neighbors of the query.

Classically the search for the nearest neighbors is based on the Euclidean distance. However, the Euclidean distance requires prior standardization of the variables in the data space. The goal is to obtain comparable range values between the variables. So the standardisation is performed separately for each variable. In literature we have mainly two methods to standardise each variable. The first one is Min-Max method [2]. Its transforms each variable by subtracting the minimum value and dividing the result by the range value (maximum minus minimum). Thus the standardised variable lies between 0 and 1. These results depend on the minimum and maximum values. The Min-Max method is therefore not robust against outliers. The second one is a normalization called Z-score. Its is based on the mean and standard deviation of the variable within the reference set. So the transformed variable will have a mean of 0 and a variance of 1. This kind of normalization implicitly implies that we have only one class with a Gaussian distribution. Unfortunately, the classification assumes that the reference dataset has multiple classes.

In this paper, we propose a new way to standardize variables without making implicit assumptions about the absence of outliers or the number of classes. For each variable, we obtain the standardization using the ranks of the values within the dataset. If the dataset has n datapoint, then each standardised value is a rank that lies between 1 and n. After standardising variables, we compute a dissimilarity index between standardised data. This dissimilarity index is called Rank-Based Dissimilarity Index (RBDI). We use this index instead of Euclidean distance to search K nearest neighbors. Evaluation experiments are conducted under multidimensional open datasets. The objective is to validate the method by testing it on several open datasets and then apply it to virtual machine and data center data when they are ready. It should be noted that this paper is focused on the validation of our approach and does not address the actual management of a data center.

In the second section of this paper, we present the related work. Then in Sect. 3 we describe our standardisation method. We define RBDI rank and we apply this new index for searching the K nearest neighbor within several datasets. Then, we compute the number of errors in classification when using Euclidean distance and RBDI. Section 4 is devoted to the improvement of Euclidean distance using RBDI. In a concluding section, we provide a discussion of Euclidean distance improvement we propose.

2 Related Work

The k-nearest neighbors (KNN) algorithm is a well-known decision rule that is widely used in pattern classification and regression. There are several related works that have explored various aspects of the KNN algorithm, including its performance, optimization, and applications.

One area of research related to KNN is its performance in high-dimensional spaces. Studies have shown that the accuracy of KNN decreases as the dimensionality of the data increases [7]. Various techniques have been proposed to address this issue, such as dimensionality reduction and feature selection [3,16]. Another area of research is the optimization of the KNN algorithm. One approach is to use approximate nearest neighbor search methods, such as locality-sensitive hashing and tree-based methods, to improve the efficiency of KNN [11]. The KNN algorithm has also been applied to various domains, such as image recognition [12] and anomaly detection [15] and Cloud Data Centers [6]. Researchers have explored different variations of KNN to adapt it to these specific domains. In essence, the KNN algorithm can be used for applications that require high accuracy. The quality of the predictions depends on the distance measure. Therefore, the KNN algorithm is suitable for applications for which sufficient domain knowledge is available. This knowledge supports the selection of an appropriate measure.

There are many studies that have applied KNN in various ways in cloud data centers: resource allocation, task scheduling, and energy efficiency. Mazidi et al. proposed in [10] an approach based on MAPE-K loop to auto-scale the resources for multilayered cloud applications. They used KNN to analyze and label virtual machines and statistical methods to make scaling decision. Then, they described a resource allocation algorithm to allocate requests on the resources. KNN is also applied in [13] to optimize resource allocation in Network Functions Virtualization (NFV). The authors in [9] proposed an approach that analyzes virtual machine and physical machine models and applied the K-means clustering algorithm for unsupervised learning and the KNN classification algorithm for supervised learning to establish a dynamic hybrid resource deployment rule. Then, they defined an energy-aware resource deployment algorithm for cloud data centers based on dynamic hybrid machine learning based on the theory of machine learning. Another approach applied KNN to predict resource usage in each host and to minimize the number of active physical servers on a data center in order to reduce energy cost [6]. For the KNN algorithm, researchers have also made many improvements because the algorithm has some limitations such as the sensitive to noise and outliers in the data that can affect the accuracy of the algorithm. Furthermore, KNN can also be affected by imbalanced data, where one class of data is much more prevalent than another. Obviously, among the many proposed methods, the improvement of and the study of KNN is still a widely studied method. Hence, in this paper, we combine the euclidean distance and the RBDI index.

3   KNN with Rank-Based Method

Classically the search for the nearest neighbors is based on the Euclidean distance that requires prior standardization of variables. This section proposes a new way to standardize variables.

3.1   Rank-Based Standardisation

Let Ω be a dataset with n datapoints:

$$\Omega = \{X_1, X_2, X_3...X_n\}$$

Each datapoint is determined with p variables $v_1, v_2, v_3...v_p$. Thus each data is defined with:

$$X_i = (x_{i1}, x_{i2}, x_{i3}...x_{ip})$$

where $x_{ij} = v_j(X_i)$ with $1 \leq i \leq n$ and $1 \leq j \leq p$.

There are two classical methods to standardize the variables. Let v be a variable. Min-Max method needs for minimum value and maximum value of the variable with $min_v = \min_{1 \leq i \leq n} v(X_i)$ and $max_v = \max_{1 \leq i \leq n} v(X_i)$. The standardised variable is called v_m and defined with:

$$v_m = \frac{v - min_v}{max_v - min_v}$$

This standardisation depends on the maximum and minimum value. Unfortunately, outliers could affect the minimum and maximum values. This standardisation is therefore unsuitable in the event of possible outliers. Z-score method is another method that needs mean and standard deviation of the variable, respectively μ_v and σ_v. The standardised variable is called v_z and defined with:

$$v_z = \frac{v - \mu_v}{\sigma_v}$$

This method implicitly assumes that the data distribution is Gaussian. Unfortunately the dataset has generally multiple classes. Then the data distribution cannot be considered as Gaussian.

Table 1. Table of notation

Notation	Description
Ω	The dataset with n datapoints
X_i	The coordinates of the datapoint
v_m	The variable of X_i
v_z	The standardised variable
N_{Euclid}	The neighborhood of the query X
r_{ij}	The rank of x_{ij}

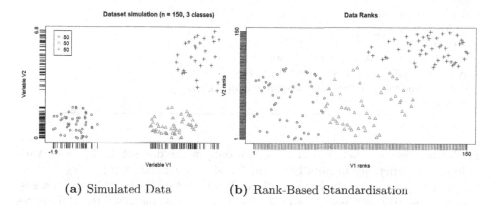

(a) Simulated Data   (b) Rank-Based Standardisation

Fig. 1. Standardisation of variables through RBS

We propose another approach of standardisation using the ranks. The values x_{ij} of data X_i with variable v_j is replaced by the rank of X_i within the dataset with variable v_j. Let r_{ij} be this rank:

$$r_{ij} = \text{rank of } x_{ij} \text{ among } x_{1j}, x_{2j}, x_{3j}...x_{nj}$$

Thus r_{ij} is an integer that lies between 1 and n. So the variables are standardised by values between 1 and n.

In Table 1, we provide a detailed description of the various variables utilized in the study.

We call this method Rank-Based Standardisation (RBS). Let us apply RBS with an example of 150 simulated data in dimension 2 (i.e. with two variables). Figure 1 shows simulated data without standardisation (see Fig. 1a) and through RBS standardisation (see Fig. 1b). RBS respects data ranks for each variable It does not fear outliers. It also makes no implicit assumption about the data distributions. But it does not take into account the geometry of data distribution in the initial dataspace. You can see that when comparing Figs. 1a and 1b.

3.2 Rank-Based Dissimilarity Index

When standardising data, RBS does not respect geometry. Therefore the difference between two data should not be evaluated by geometric distance like

Algorithm 1. Classification with K nearest neighbors through Rank-Based Dissimilarity Index (RDBI)

Require: Ω a set of n data in dimension p

$\Omega = \{X_1, X_2, X_3...X_n\}$ where $X_i = (x_{ij})$ with $1 \leq i \leq n$ and $1 \leq j \leq p$

Each data of Ω has one class assignment c_k with $1 \leq k \leq m$

X is a query where $X = (x_j)$ with $1 \leq j \leq p$

K is the number of Nearest Neighbors of X

Ensure: $c(X)$ the class assignment for the query X

    for $j \leftarrow 1$ to p **do**

        $(r_{1j}, r_{2j}, r_{3j}, ...r_{nj}, r_j) \leftarrow$ respective ranks of $(x_{1j}, x_{2j}, x_{3j}, ...x_{nj}, x_j)$

    end for

    for $i \leftarrow 1$ to n **do**

        $RBDI_i \leftarrow \frac{1}{p} \sum_{j=1}^{p} |r_j - r_{ij}|$

    end for

    $r_{RBDI}(X_i) \leftarrow$ rank of $RBDI_i$ where $1 \leq i \leq n$

    $N_{RBDI} \leftarrow \{X \in \Omega$ where $r_{RBDI}(X) \leq K\}$

    $c(X) \leftarrow$ the most represented assignment in N_{RBDI}

    return $c(X)$

Euclidean distance. Let X and Y be two data in the dataset Ω. For each variable v_j, the difference in rank between X and Y is defined by $|r_{Yj} - r_{Xj}|$ where r_{Yj} and r_{Xj} are respectively the ranks of Y and X for the variable v_j. To assess the dissimilarity between X and Y, we propose the mean of the differences according to the variables. Then we define the Rank-Based Dissimilarity Index (RBDI) by:

$$RBDI(X,Y) = \frac{1}{p} \sum_{j=1}^{p} |r_{Yj} - r_{Xj}|$$

We propose to use RBDI instead of classical Euclidean distance to evaluate the proximity between two data.

3.3 K Nearest Neighbors Through RDBI

Let us assess the proximity with RBDI in the framework of KNN classification. Let us consider a dataset and its partition into classes. Within the dataset, we can compute the proximity between a query and the other data. The most represented class among the neighbors of query is the one assigned to the query.

Algorithm 1 gives the algorithm we use to assign a class to a query through RBDI.

If the assigned class is not the effective class of the query, then we have an error in classification. In this paper we assume that the higher the number of misclassifications, the worse the proximity index.

Using this approach we compute the number of misclassifications on WINE dataset of UCI Learning Machine Repository. These data are described with 9 variables. The dimension of the data space is therefore equal to 9. In such

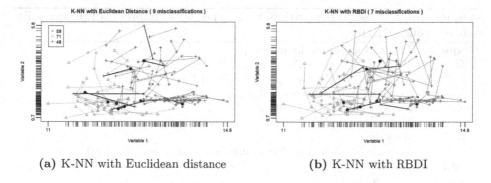

(a) K-NN with Euclidean distance   (b) K-NN with RBDI

Fig. 2. Classification using the K-NN method (K = 5) on the WINE dataset of the UCI repository. Bold black points indicate misclassifications. Lines indicate links with 1-NN (i.e. nearest neighbor). Black lines indicate misclassifications with 1-NN.

a high-dimensional data space, the geometry of objects can be very complex. Euclidean distance might not be well suited to analyze the geometry of such objects. Fearing such geometric complexity in WINE dataset, we propose to define KNNs with RBDI. Then, we compare the number of classification errors to the one obtained with Euclidean distance.

Figure 2 displays the projections of WINE data using the variables v_1 and v_2. The black bold points show the misclassified data using KNN classification with K = 5. When using Euclidean Distance, KNN gives 9 misclassifications (see Fig. 2a). When using RBDI, KNN gives 7 misclassifications (see Fig. 2b). In this case of complex geometry with apparent overlap between classes, RBDI gives fewer classification errors than Euclidean distance. We therefore consider that RBDI is better than the Euclidean distance for the KNN classification on the WINE dataset.

Moreover, RDBI generally looks better than Euclidean distance when using KNN classification (see Table 2). But the Euclidean distance can sometimes give much better results (see "WIFI localization" dataset in Table 2).

4   Improving Euclidean Distance with RBDI

This paper propose to take the advantage of both Euclidean distance and RBDI. On the one hand, the Euclidean distance takes into account the Euclidean geometry of the data space. On the other hand, RBDI is not constrained by distance or geometry in data space.

Let N_{Euclid} be the neighborhood of the query X (i.e. the K nearest neighbors of X) for the Euclidean distance. Let N_{RBDI} be the neighborhood of the same query X for RBDI. Thus, we propose to extend the neighborhood N_{Euclid} with RBDI considering the union of the two neighborhoods. Thus we propose to extend the neighborhood N_{Euclid} with RBDI considering the union of these two neighborhoods. Improving the Euclidean distance, the K nearest neighbors of X are then defined by:

Algorithm 2. Classification with K nearest neighbors improving Euclidean distance through RBDI

Require: Ω a set of n data in dimension p

$\Omega = \{X_1, X_2, X_3...X_n\}$ where $X_i = (x_{ij})$ with $1 \leq i \leq n$ and $1 \leq j \leq p$

Each data of Ω has one class assignment c_k with $1 \leq k \leq m$

X is a query where $X = (x_j)$ with $1 \leq j \leq p$

K is the number of Nearest Neighbors of X

Ensure: $c(X)$ the class assignment for the query X

    for $j \leftarrow 1$ to p **do**

        $(r_{1j}, r_{2j}, r_{3j}, ...r_{nj}, r_j) \leftarrow$ respective ranks of $(x_{1j}, x_{2j}, x_{3j}, ...x_{nj}, x_j)$

    end for

    for $i \leftarrow 1$ to n **do**

        $RBDI_i \leftarrow \frac{1}{p}\sum_{j=1}^{p} |r_j - r_{ij}|$

        $Euclid_i \leftarrow \sqrt{\sum_{j=1}^{p}(x_j - x_{ij})^2}$

    end for

    $r_{RBDI}(X_i) \leftarrow$ rank of $RBDI_i$ where $1 \leq i \leq n$

    $r_{Euclid}(X_i) \leftarrow$ rank of $Euclid_i$ where $1 \leq i \leq n$

    $N_{Improv} \leftarrow \{X \in \Omega$ where $r_{RBDI}(X) \leq K$ or $r_{Euclid}(X) \leq K\}$

    $c(X) \leftarrow$ the most represented assignment in N_{Improv}

    return $c(X)$

Table 2. Misclassifications through KNN in real datasets where n is the number of data, p is the number of variables (i.e. dimension of data space), c is the number of classes when using three ways: Euclidean distance (Euclid.), RBDI and Improvement of Euclidean distance with RBDI (Improv.)

dataset	n	p	c	Euclid	RBDI	Improv
Wine	178	13	3	9	7	4
Iris	150	4	3	7	8	7
Ecoli	336	7	8	50	52	36
Glass	214	9	6	77	66	46
Segmentation	210	19	7	34	20	13
Seeds	210	7	3	15	16	11
Banknote	1372	4	2	2	5	1
Social Network	400	2	2	43	40	31
WIFI localization	2000	7	4	29	40	16

$$N_{Improv} = N_{Euclid} \cup N_{RBDI}$$

In N_{Improv} the neighbors of X are either neighbor for the Euclidean distance or neighbor for RBDI. In the framework of classification, the class assigned to X is then the one most represented in N_{Improv}.

Algorithm 2 gives the algorithm we use to assign a class to a query when improving Euclidean distance through RBDI.

Table 2 displays the numbers of misclassifications we obtain when using N_{Euclid}, N_{RBDI} and N_{Improv}. The results are obtained using various datasets from UCI Repository and from Kaggle. N_{Improv} gives always the best results in terms of misclassifications (i.e. the lowest number of classification errors).

5 Discussion and Conclusion

This paper presents an improvement of the KNN algorithm. We proposed a classification scheme with K nearest neighbors through both rank based dissimilarity index and the Euclidean distance. The rank-based dissimilarity index plays a crucial role in capturing the preference relationships among instances. It assigns ranks to the attributes or features based on their values, taking into account the relative ordering rather than the absolute values. On the other hand, the Euclidean distance is a geometric measure that quantifies the numerical differences between attribute values. It calculates the straight-line distance between two instances in the feature space, considering all the attributes. This distance measure enables the comparison of instances in a geometrically meaningful way. The number of misclassifications indicates that the neighborhood approach using N_{Improv} is significantly more effective than either the geometric approach using Euclidean distance or the non-geometric approach using preferences with ranks alone. In essence, the integration of preference-based and geometric information enhances the accuracy and effectiveness of the classification scheme, offering a promising solution for various classification tasks. In a future work, we could replace the Euclidean distance of the geometric approach with another distance (such as Minkowski, etc.). We could also replace RBDI with another aggregation of preferences (i.e., aggregation of ranks, see our last year's communication [5] or social choice theory). It would also be possible to add other similarity indices between data in addition to these two approaches. On the other hand, our approach is quantitative and validated on small samples (a few thousand data) and modest dimensions (less than 100 variables). We would need to optimize the algorithm for larger samples or larger dimensions. The next phase of our research will be the application of this method in the context of data center management. Efficient management of a data center and its VMs is essential to ensure the smooth operation of the center and minimize costs. By grouping VMs into classes, energy management and pricing could be optimized, leading to a more cost-effective and efficient system.

References

1. Afzal, S., Ganesh, K.: Load balancing in cloud computing - a hierarchical taxonomical classification. J. Cloud Comput. **8** (2019)
2. Aquino, L.D.G., Eckstein, S.: Minmax methods for optimal transport and beyond: regularization, approximation and numerics (2020)
3. Arora, A., Sinha, S., Kumar, P., Bhattacharya, A.: HD-index: pushing the scalability-accuracy boundary for approximate KNN search in high-dimensional spaces. Proc. VLDB Endow. **11**(8), 906–919 (2018)
4. Belkasim, S., Shridhar, M., Ahmadi, M.: Pattern classification using an efficient KNNR. Pattern Recogn. **25**(10), 1269–1274 (1992)

5. Boucetta, C., Hussenet, L., Herbin, M.: Practical method for multidimensional data ranking. In: Phillipson, F., Eichler, G., Erfurth, C., Fahrnberger, G. (eds.) I4CS 2022. CCIS, vol. 1585, pp. 267–277. Springer, Cham (2022). https://doi.org/10.1007/978-3-031-06668-9_19

6. Farahnakian, F., Pahikkala, T., Liljeberg, P., Plosila, J.: Energy aware consolidation algorithm based on k-nearest neighbor regression for cloud data centers. In: 2013 IEEE/ACM 6th International Conference on Utility and Cloud Computing, pp. 256–259 (2013)

7. He, X., Cai, D., Niyogi, P.: Laplacian score for feature selection. In: Weiss, Y., Schölkopf, B., Platt, J. (eds.) Advances in Neural Information Processing Systems, vol. 18. MIT Press, Cambridge (2005)

8. Hussenet, L., Boucetta, C.: A green-aware optimization strategy for virtual machine migration in cloud data centers. In: 2022 International Wireless Communications and Mobile Computing (IWCMC), pp. 1082–1087 (2022)

9. Liang, B., Wu, D., Wu, P., Su, Y.: An energy-aware resource deployment algorithm for cloud data centers based on dynamic hybrid machine learning. Knowl.-Based Syst. **222**, 107020 (2021)

10. Mazidi, A., Golsorkhtabar, M., Tabari, M.: Autonomic resource provisioning for multilayer cloud applications with k-nearest neighbor resource scaling and priority-based resource allocation. Software: Practice and Experience 50 (04 2020)

11. Muja, M., Lowe, D.G.: Scalable nearest neighbor algorithms for high dimensional data. IEEE Trans. Pattern Anal. Mach. Intell. **36**(11), 2227–2240 (2014)

12. Ou, X., et al.: Hyperspectral image target detection via weighted joint k-nearest neighbor and multitask learning sparse representation. IEEE Access **8**, 11503–11511 (2020)

13. Su, J., Nair, S., Popokh, L.: EdgeGYM: a reinforcement learning environment for constraint-aware NFV resource allocation. In: 2023 IEEE 2nd International Conference on AI in Cybersecurity (ICAIC), pp. 1–7 (2023)

14. Taunk, K., De, S., Verma, S., Swetapadma, A.: A brief review of nearest neighbor algorithm for learning and classification. In: 2019 International Conference on Intelligent Computing and Control Systems (ICCS), pp. 1255–1260 (2019)

15. Xie, M., Hu, J., Han, S., Chen, H.H.: Scalable hypergrid K-NN-based online anomaly detection in wireless sensor networks. IEEE Trans. Parallel Distrib. Syst. **24**(8), 1661–1670 (2013)

16. Yu, C., Cui, B., Wang, S., Su, J.: Efficient index-based KNN join processing for high-dimensional data. Inf. Softw. Technol. **49**(4), 332–344 (2007)

AutoBookFinder: A Case Study of Automated Book Rack Identification in Library Through UGV

Udit Nath, Bhaskar Jyoti Medhi, Anuradha Deori, Maharaj Brahma, Mwnthai Narzary, and Pranav Kumar Singh(✉) ⓘ

Central Institute of Technology Kokrajhar, BTR, Kokrajhar, Assam 783370, India
p.singh@cit.ac.in

Abstract. The misplacement of books in libraries often results in wasted time when searching for a specific book on the wrong shelf. To address this issue, we created a novel, low-cost prototype Unmanned Ground Vehicle (UGV) equipped with a camera and Wi-Fi modules. The UGV wirelessly sends data to a local server, which uses image processing to determine the location of the book. A web user interface was created to enable users to easily locate the exact shelf of the desired book. This solution has not been previously explored and was tested in our Institute's library. The adoption of UGVs greatly improved the overall user experience, transforming the manual and time-consuming process of book-finding into an automated and time-saving operation.

Keywords: Smart library · UGV · Image processing · Flask · Arduino UNO

1 Introduction

The Central Library of Central Institute of Technology Kokrajhar (CITK), Assam, India has a collection of approximately 0.3 million books [1]. The library organizes each book into proper places based on its genre and category, and book issuing and returning activities are digitized. Users are required to use their library cards to perform any activity in the library, and the cards are provided by the library. The library patrons handle the entire process of issuing and returning books, while the library staff supervises. On an average day, the library receives approximately 300 visitors and processes about 150 issue requests. The library is divided into different shelves according to the department to which the book belongs, and each shelf has different racks where the library staff stores the books after they are returned by users. However, the problem arises when users search for a particular book. The books are randomly placed on a rack when returned, making it difficult for library users to find the required book in its place. Moreover, the library racks do not have a specific naming system, so library patrons spend a long time searching for books. It has also been found that sometimes users cannot locate a required book even when it is shown as available in the library database.

U. R. Krieger et al. (Eds.): I4CS 2023, CCIS 1876, pp. 325–333, 2023.
https://doi.org/10.1007/978-3-031-40852-6_18

The main objective of this project prototype is to create a system that informs library patrons of the precise location of a book by providing its rack number. This will be accomplished by using an Unmanned Ground Vehicle (UGV) [4] to inspect the library racks regularly and capture still images of them. The system will then process the images to extract book details and rack numbers, which will be fed into the database. The entire system will operate wirelessly, without requiring an internet connection. A user-friendly web interface has been developed to simplify the process of searching for a book name in the database, which will direct patrons to the appropriate shelf. This system will also assist the library in reducing its dependence on staff to manage library operations, such as locating and organizing books.

The remainder of the paper is structured as follows. Section 2 discusses related and relevant works. Section 3 outlines the materials and methods employed in this study. Section 4 provides a detailed description of our experimental setup. Section 5 presents our findings and provides a discussion of the results. Finally, in Sect. 6, we summarize our conclusions and offer suggestions for future research.

2   Related Works

In this section, we review the existing literature on book locating solutions in library racks and shelves. Automatic library book detection systems using book call numbers have shown to be effective, and various research works have been conducted in this area. For instance, Duan et al. [5] proposed a line segment detector with color segmentation and slanted angle removal techniques, which significantly enhanced the performance. The authors presented a modified contours clustering method to extract call numbers completely and achieved an accuracy of 97.70% using the proposed technique, compared to 87.77% accuracy with a combination of Hough and color. The authors also highlighted that smartphones cannot capture all books in a single row shelf.

Yang et al. [9] proposed the use of Convolutional Neural Networks (CNN) and Recurrent Neural Network (RNN) deep learning-based techniques for spine text information extraction. The authors achieved an accuracy of 92% and 91% on Tsai2011 (Text) dataset and their dataset, respectively, using a large physical library database. In another work, Ekram et al. [6] used image segmentation and OCR techniques to perform book indexing and organize mismatched library books. However, the authors noted that the OCR algorithm is unable to detect the book call number of images captured from different angles, achieving a 76.08% accuracy on a test set of 100 image samples. The authors suggested that the use of Hough transformation, lines, and contours for segmentation can lead to better results. Cao et al. [3] introduced BSRBOT, a book spine recognition framework that performs image acquisition, segmentation, call number recognition, and spine image matching from an existing database. The authors achieved an accuracy of more than 90% and an average time per spine of fewer than 300 milliseconds.

Previous work in this direction mainly focuses on using smartphones for image capturing and processing which are costly. They also focus on the use of book call number for book identification. However, in this work, we perform experiments on the physical library of CITK, where the books are not maintained by the call number. Instead, each book has a Radio Frequency Identification (RFID) chip [8] that is issued to issue and return the book through a self-kiosk machine. This is particularly challenging due to the non-existence of rack names and the lack of a mechanism to locate the misplaced book. Hence, in this work, we proposed low-cost solution that leverage the use of UGV to traverse the library area, existing OCR technology, and rack naming. The proposed solution works completely on a local server without the need for cloud processing or the internet. The overall objective of the work is to reduce the time wasted by the students in finding the books. To address this, we also provide a web interface to query the rack number using the book name.

3 Proposed Mechanism

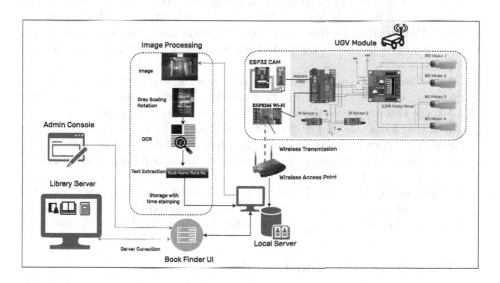

Fig. 1. System Architecture

The proposed UGV-based mechanism is depicted in Fig. 1. The UGV traverses the path around the bookshelves, taking pictures of the racks. The images are sent to the system wirelessly and stored in a local directory. The main system does routine checks on the database. The system requests images from the local directory. Upon locating the images, the system performs image processing and text extraction on the images. The resultant data is then fed to the local database. The system also provides a User Interface (UI) that allows us to search for a particular book. The system fetches the search result and displays the proper location and rack number of the entered book. The overall working principle of the prototype is divided into six steps, which are as follows:

1. **UGV Traversal and Image Capturing:** The UGV is turned on at a specific time of the day, and it traverses the path, behaving as a line follower. The UGV makes occasional calculated steps in front of the library racks taking images of the books in the racks. The UGV continues traversing and taking pictures of the racks until the entire path is traversed.
2. **Image Transfer and Storage:** The UGV has a Wi-Fi interface to connect to the Library Wi-Fi access point (AP). The images captured by the camera module mounted on UGV in step 1 are transferred to the local server connected with UGV wirelessly (having a fixed IP) via Library AP. The system receives the captured images and stores them in a local directory of system. The local server is designed to check for the images once a day at a specific time. The system checks for the directory wherein the images are stored and fetches them one by one to perform necessary image processing.
3. **Image Processing:** The local server applies the image processing techniques to find the best results and perform image enhancements on stored images captured in different lighting conditions and with varying book orientations.
4. **Text Extraction:** In this step, text extraction is applied to the processed images to get the book name and corresponding rack number in the text format.
5. **Data Cleaning and Storage:** Before feeding the extracted text to the database, it is crucial to ensure that the data is clean, readable, and correct. To serve this purpose, the local server uses a cleaning process to remove unwanted characters and digits and a spellchecker to correct the words. The cleaned and corrected text is stored in a separate database that contains the book name and corresponding rack name. A timestamp is also maintained to keep a record of the entry.
6. **Book Finding through UI:** After coming to the library, the user opens the UI to search for the book. Since the UI is connected to the backend database, it returns the corresponding rack number for the entered book by the user.

4   Experimental Setup Details

This section of the paper provides selected operational area details for our case study, UGV prototype, and software details that were used to conduct the experiment and demonstrate the effectiveness of the proposed solution.

4.1   Operational Area Details

The experiment was conducted around the Computer Science & Engineering (CSE) department shelf in the CITK digital library. It has a total area of 79.58 m^2 where the perimeter of each column is 27.648 m.

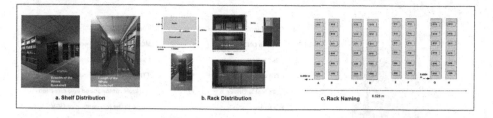

Fig. 2. Operational Area selected for the Experiment

1. **Shelf Distribution:** Each shelf has a length of 12.192 m and a height of 2.13 m. Figure 2a gives a better idea of the shelves.
2. **Rack Distribution:** The shelves in the CSE Department had 5 X 9 (5 rows, 9 columns) rack distribution concerning rows and columns. Each of the racks had a length of 1.91m and a width of 0.381 m, as depicted in Fig. 2b.
3. **Rack Naming System:** Since, at present the library does not utilize rack naming system hence, it is difficult to organize the book shelves. The proposed rack naming system was derived from the 2-D array-like structure of the racks, as depicted in Fig. 2c. Each of the shelves has been given a name A to H, and the format was decided as [shelf name][i][j], where i and j stand for rows and columns, respectively. To place the naming system physically we use sticky notes. We wrote various rack name and number using a black ink on yellow sticky notes and placed in all the shelves inside our operational area. This is done to improve the contrast.

4.2   UGV Prototype

The UGV prototype (Fig. 3a) developed for the experiment is of the autonomous kind. It was controlled via an Arduino UNO, mounted with an ESP32 camera module for capturing the images and transferring them via its Wi-Fi module. The UGV is lightweight and small, with a length of 0.11 m and a weight of 1.186 g. The camera mount had a Body-and-Arm in RR with an end effector. It is battery-powered and can be plugged into power after its complete traversal. The hardware components used in UGV are listed in Fig. 3b.

4.3   Software Details

We used various software to implement the entire operations, such as for UGV function automation (traversal, stoppage, image capturing, forwarding, etc.), image processing and text extractions, database design and user interface. The details are listed in Table 1.

5   Results and Discussion

The UGV traverses the operational area through a line follower path placed in the operational area as shown in Fig. 4a. It starts capturing images as shown

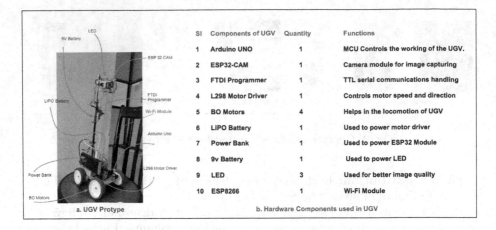

Fig. 3. UGV Prototype and its components

Table 1. Software Details

Sl No.	Software Name	Functions	Device
1	FTDI Programmer	Serial communications handling	UGV
2	Arduino Software (IDE)	Automate the entire UGV Operation	UGV
3	Tesseract	To detect orientation and script of image	Local Server
4	OpenCV [2]	Image Processing	Local Server
5	Easy OCR	Extraction of data	Local Server
6	Auto Correct	For spell checking purpose	Local Server
7	MySql	To design a database to hold the book name and rack name	Local Server
8	Flask [7]	To design the web interface	

in Fig. 4.b. The light quality in a closed indoor library environment affects the image quality. Hence, at the local server, we tried two image pre-processing techniques: grayscaling and binarization. The grayscale image is shown in Fig. 4c. We extract the rack name using Tesseract OCR. However, since the books are stacks in vertical fashion. For extracting the corresponding book name, we use Tesseract OCR to detect images containing in a vertically stacked fashion. Next, we check for the orientation of the image if it is vertical and then rotated in a counterclockwise direction. This image is then sent for text extraction. The extraction is performed by EasyOCR. The extracted book name by the OCR suffers from missing characters. To address this, we use a spell checker for OCR post-processing. The *Rack name* and *Book name* information are then stored in the relational database along with the timestamp.

(a) UGV Traversal in Operational Area   (b) Image Capturing   (c) Image Processing

Fig. 4. Results

AutoBookFinder: Automated Book Rack Identification in Library through UGV

Find Book

database system

Search

Results

SL. NO.	BOOK NAME	RACK NAME	TIMESTAMP
1	database system concepts	A00	13/11/2022 05:10 PM

Fig. 5. Web Interface of AutoBookFinder

For accessing the rack information of a particular book, we build a web application that fetches information from the local server. The web application is built using a python based flask framework and contains a search functionality using for book. The resultant rack name is then fetch from the database and shown to the user as depicted in Fig. 5. The UGV after traversing the operation area returns back to its starting location. Since physical libraries are very dynamic in nature and there is frequent book issue-return, we setup the UGV to be automatic traverse in the operational area in the time period when the library is less busy.

6   Conclusion

In this work, we present a novel solution for automatic book rack identification through the integration of UGV, image processing technologies, and a rack naming system. The proposed solution is cost-effective and efficient. It requires less human intervention and improves the library user experience.

In this case study, we have explored the bookshelf at the level reachable by the camera. However, the bookshelf can have multiple stacks (top to bottom). Images of such a bookshelf can be captured by an adjustable camera mounted on UGV. Lighting conditions greatly impact the OCR quality, and we address the issue through the use of LED and require prior adjustment based on the rack positions. Therefore, improvements in the camera and LED module can be made to improve the lighting and OCR performance. At present, the proposed system architecture does not consider a docking station for UGV. Hence, a docking system with automatic charging can improve UGV's productivity and lifecycle. In this work, we only extracted the book name along with the rack name. However, it can be extended to capture the associated publisher information. Another challenge that we will consider in our future work is how to deal with the improper orientation of a misplaced book. Furthermore, the web interface currently only allows for searching through book name. It can, however, be extended to support search through title and publisher information. Furthermore, CITK library books are tagged using RFID technology, and UGV mounted RFID reader can be used to read book name as done by Zhang et al. [10]. This approach is scalable when the books are kept in an unordered fashion as well.

References

1. Library, Central Institute of Technology Kokrajhar. http://centrallibrary.cit.ac.in/ (2022). Accessed 12 July 2022
2. Bradski, G.: The opencv library. Dr. Dobb's J. Softw. Tools Professional Program. **25**(11), 120–123 (2000)
3. Cao, L., Liu, M., Dong, Z., Yang, H.: Book spine recognition based on opencv and tesseract. In: 2019 11th International Conference on Intelligent Human-Machine Systems and Cybernetics (IHMSC), vol. 1, pp. 332–336 (2019). https://doi.org/10.1109/IHMSC.2019.00083
4. De Simone, M.C., Guida, D.: Identification and control of a unmanned ground vehicle by using arduino. UPB Sci. Bull. Ser. D **80**, 141–154 (2018)
5. Duan, X., Zhao, Q., Anwar, S.: Identifying books in library using line segment detector and contour clustering. In: 2012 7th International Conference on Computing and Convergence Technology (ICCCT), pp. 998–1003 (2012)
6. Ekram, M.A.U., Chaudhary, A., Yadav, A., Khanal, J., Asian, S.: Book organization checking algorithm using image segmentation and OCR. In: 2017 IEEE 60th International Midwest Symposium on Circuits and Systems (MWSCAS), pp. 196–199. IEEE (2017)
7. Grinberg, M.: Flask Web Development: Developing Web Applications with Python. O'Reilly Media, Inc. Sebastopol (2018)

8. Roberts, C.M.: Radio frequency identification (RFID). Comput. Secur. **25**(1), 18–26 (2006)
9. Yang, X., He, D., Huang, W., Ororbia, A., Zhou, Z., Kifer, D., Giles, C.L.: Smart library: identifying books on library shelves using supervised deep learning for scene text reading. In: 2017 ACM/IEEE Joint Conference on Digital Libraries (JCDL), pp. 1–4. IEEE (2017)
10. Zhang, J., et al.: An Rfid and computer vision fusion system for book inventory using mobile robot. In: IEEE INFOCOM 2022 - IEEE Conference on Computer Communications, pp. 1239–1248 (2022). https://doi.org/10.1109/INFOCOM48880.2022.9796711

AIoT Chances in Resource-Constrained Environments via Manual Pruning

Moritz Peter Weber[✉] [ID]

University of Applied Sciences Jena, Carl-Zeiß-Promenade 2, 07745 Jena, Germany
moritzpeterweber@gmail.com

Abstract. The challenges of AIoT devices in a resource-constrained environment are extensive. Even in areas where new AI opportunities are only being identified, an AIoT implementation can be more effective than traditional AI approaches. This paper proposes relevant solutions to address resource constraints, utilizing the pruning method. Furthermore, it presents a theoretical and strategic procedure for manual pruning, outlining how to navigate emerging challenges and identify potential limitations. To illustrate the efficacy of such applications and how they facilitate new AIoT use cases, the energy sector serves as an example scenario. The paper signify a foundation in tailoring AI applications to IoT devices with greater precision, establishing a solid foundation for future adaptations.

Keywords: Artifical Intelligence of Things · Machine learning · Deep learning · Big data analytics · Pruning

1 Motivation and Foundations

The adoption of Artificial Intelligence (AI) has become increasingly widespread across various industries. Typically, AI algorithms and models are kept separate from on-site operations and stored in the cloud, along with recorded data. However, the Internet of Things (IoT) has opened up new opportunities for AI models to be directly integrated into the process, commonly known as AIoT. This integration allows for enhanced efficiency and productivity while facilitating more informed decision-making [14].

AIoT, an acronym for Artificial Intelligence of Things, combines two technology areas. The first is IoT, which primarily collects various data sets through sensors. The second is Artificial Intelligence, which efficiently processes and analyzes data in existing systems. This integration enables prompt data analysis and facilitates the enhancement of current processes [14].

Nevertheless, Internet of Things use cases often do not offer the necessary prerequisites for using the possibilities of AI, which we name under the term resource-constrained environments in this paper. This term refers to specific technical requirements already existing based on typical Internet of Things systems. That would be needed, for example, to achieve successful implementation

U. R. Krieger et al. (Eds.): I4CS 2023, CCIS 1876, pp. 334–344, 2023.
https://doi.org/10.1007/978-3-031-40852-6_19

in the industrial environment. If we include AI algorithms as a further step, there are also additional challenges like security, big data storage, computational performance, reliability and more [1,2]. However, the advantage of implementing AI applications in IoT environments is very large and can greatly simplify processes by allowing a variety of tasks to be executed directly on the device.

The subsequent sections start by providing an explanation of AIoT and the extant challenges therein. Afterwards, the potential solution of pruning is introduced and a comprehensive description of a strategic and manual approach is employed. Lastly, the energy sector is presented as a paradigmatic use case, serving to summarize the outcomes achieved.

2 AIoT Potential in the Energy Sector

2.1 State of the Art

AIoT has been largely associated with **data management** at its source, yet this represents only a single facet of its potential applications. Researchers have also explored the development of intelligent services to foster a more refined and sophisticated AI-driven ecosystem [7]. The IoT has experienced significant growth, and with that, the potential applications of Artificial Intelligence of Things have expanded as well. Statista declares that the number of IoT devices reached nearly 30 billion in 2020, estimated to grow to 75 billion by 2025. However, many of these devices generate vast amounts of unused data due to outdated tools, flawed analytics, and strict processes. AIoT has emerged as a promising solution to address these challenges. While the exact classification and benefits of AIoT are still not being defined in some situations, it is a technology that shows great promise [3].

An potential application of AIoT devices is their ability to **leverage sensor data** to assess vehicle engine performance. This approach can be highly advantageous, as it helps minimize the necessary maintenance and allows for prompt interventions to extend the lifespan of engines. Rolls Royce, a renowned manufacturer of automobiles and turbines, has harnessed this technology to optimize their business operations [3].

A third use case is **predictive maintenance**. It is a valuable tool for industries that rely heavily on machine performance, such as pharmaceuticals and food production. By investigating machine data, companies can gain insights into possible equipment failures and take proactive actions to prevent downtime. This approach allows for precision planning of maintenance work, delivering detailed information on when a machine may experience technical problems, down to the hour or minute. The advantages of predictive maintenance are clear, offering a bold and efficient approach to equipment management that can improve productivity and minimize the risk of costly downtime [3]. The advantage using AIoT for this use case is, for example, the reduction of required infrastructure as the analyses can be carried out directly on the machines.

In order to gain a thorough comprehension of the potential of Artificial Intelligence of Things, it is recommendable to analyze hypothetical situations within the realm of IoT. The energy sector, for example, has numerous practical applications that can be effectively utilized. For example there are use cases in transmission and distribution (Distributed Energy Systems, Energy Management) or in demand side services (Smart Buildings, Demand Response) [9]. Applications can be therefore divided into four areas. Roughly summarized there is plant planning, which primarily includes the planning and construction of power generation as example. Furthermore, there is a topic for sales and various customer interfaces; that goal is to make the created products available to customers on the market (development of pricing strategies, customer service). There is maintenance, servicing, and plant management, which is based on an operational level. These include, for example, the procurement and provision of information on plants or the development. Fourthly there is the field of network and plant operation that deals with the provision of the final product to consumers, and further, it contains the management of the facilities [6]. These fields contain different use case which however can mostly be implemented using forecasting or computer vision. In the following, a computer vision use case is examined in more detail.

Numerous practical implementations of computer vision technology exist, including the ability to forecast the remaining service lifespan of equipment and optimize plant maintenance through sensor data. In addition, aerial photography can assist in the location of underground cables, resulting in improved operational efficiency. Lastly, image data analysis can automate the evaluation of damage classifications and equipment quantities, reducing repair time and enhancing overall productivity [6].

A fourth application is that the **marketing of photovoltaic systems** is usually done in an untargeted manner without addressing a suitable person in a targeted manner. This causes an issue meaning that the budget of the energy supplier, for example, could be used more efficiently to reach optimal customers. This use case focuses on finding more effective ways to reach customers with suitable areas. The final solution was to identify these suitable areas by analyzing satellite or aerial images. This approach makes it possible to target customers with the needed requirements in their possession [6].

2.2   Identification of Challenges

The first crucial step is to identify the challenges of a resource-constrained environment and address them in a targeted manner. It affects not only hardware components that need to accommodate more software but also crucial factors such as security, connectivity, efficiency, accuracy, scalability, robustness, and complexity must be considered in the environments [14]. Figure 1 shows some topics that must be considered to enable a successful implementation of the planned use case. To comprehensively understand a resource-constrained environment, we have partitioned it into two distinct components: software and hardware. Although these two elements are interdependent, we have prioritized addressing software challenges before initiating hardware modifications. This approach has enabled us to accurately identify and rectify specific requirements and obstacles before implementing solutions that may not have been necessary or effective in light of the current circumstances.

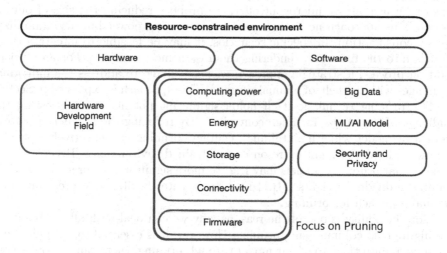

Fig. 1. AIoT Challenges in a ressource-constrained environment

The domain of "Hardware Development Field" encompasses the enhancement of hardware components, namely storage media, processors, flash layout, and RAM layout, alongside upgrades to sensors for IoT devices. If a computer vision application, for example, necessitates a higher image resolution to enable successful neural network training, it may become necessary to replace the camera. Moreover, the camera may need to capture images with greater precision without exceeding memory capacity. We may explore alternative options to meet our requirements depending on the use case. However, before implementing any hardware modifications, it is essential to consider optimizing the software to, for example, minimize production costs.

The project's software section encompasses various topics, with the rightmost column addressing key areas such as Big Data, ML/AI Models, and Security. While some topics related to connectivity as addition may also be relevant in this group, we have chosen not to focus on these areas in this paper because these concerns should already be declared at the beginning of a project. This paper will not discuss these topics that we count together to Edge Computing. Instead, we will focus on the challenges associated with the middle column, which are critical for successfully executing our AI model on a microcontroller using the pruning approach.

2.3   Focus on Pruning

Summarized for all the challenges in Fig. 1, there are different approaches and solutions. The key is not always one method alone but usually a combination of methods. This paper will focus on the pruning method since it can be used to address the challenges in the middle column. This effect is because the various points like memory and computing power correlate with each other. To optimize memory usage on the microcontroller, we propose reducing the size of our AI model. This approach not only conserves computing power but also minimizes energy consumption. In specific scenarios, it may be feasible to integrate these models into the firmware, rendering them even more compact. For an efficient solution process, a strategic approach was considered to address the individual challenges with the help of manual pruning. This approach is explained in Sect. 3.

The pruning technique itself holds significant potential in addressing the challenge of model size for microcontrollers. By reducing the number of parameters in a model while maintaining accuracy, pruning can effectively optimize the model for deployment on resource-constrained environments. Recent studies suggest that pruning channels may lead to more significant accuracy losses than pruning individual weights [11]. To achieve greater flexibility, we recommend a manual approach for pruning.

More flexibility is one of the reasons why we can deal with all the points in the highlighted column using pruning. However, it is essential to recognize that when we reduce the size of our model through pruning, there can be consequential impacts on other areas of the process and vice versa. It is also noteworthy that specific topics, such as big data and security, which will be again shortly highlighted in Sect. 3.4, are less susceptible to the effects of pruning. Big data management is a substantial challenge in its own right, while security heavily relies on the specific use case and required connectivity.

3   Strategic Manual Pruning

3.1   Process Approach

Figure 2 roughly illustrates our methodological approach. It could be made more comprehensive, but it makes remarkable progress by providing a better overview.

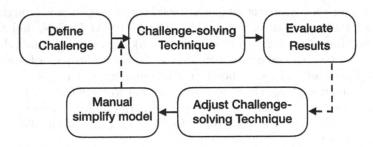

Fig. 2. Process approach for strategic pruning procedure

The process approach can be used once we have decided which problem to solve first. An example of this would be to first try to reduce the size of our model. To tackle this problem, we could employ pruning techniques to reduce its size. Once we have obtained some initial results, we must ensure that the model's accuracy remains consistent. Accuracy is paramount in this area, and reducing the model size should not be done at the expense of accuracy. If, after pruning, we find that the model size is still not satisfactory, we have two options to consider. Firstly, we could revise our solution technique, or secondly, we could manually adjust the neural network. It is crucial to remember the importance of adjusting the model's layers manually, as this will be necessary for the manual pruning that follows in subsequent chapters. This process affords us greater flexibility and knowledge of the neural network, which can be used to adjust the pruning process. This cycle can be repeated until the desired result is achieved.

3.2   Model Reduction

Based on our test cases manual pruning of neural networks boasts numerous advantages, including enhanced comprehension, heightened command, superior performance, and greater adaptability when converting to microcontrollers. In order to reduce the size of the neural network, a sequence of steps is taken centered around principles previously established in our specific use case. As a basis, it is necessary that our initial machine learning or deep learning project has been successfully completed. As a result, we have a functional model that has undergone all necessary preprocessing steps. These measures are imperative to guarantee a successful conversion of our model to a microcontroller.

Once the used environment has all the necessary foundations, the model pruning can start. There are, of course, different approaches to how the pruning can be done. Foremost, we refer to pruning using a threshold value. First, this approach aims to compress the model and reduce memory requirements and inference time. However, this reduction should be made without affecting the model accuracy too much. Furthermore, there are more complex ways to adjust the model, but the threshold fits very well as a starting point.

Step 1: Weights and Layers
To manually reduce the weights of the mesh, a loop can be created that checks all layers of the model as it passes through, whether they are convolutional layers or fully connected layers. During this loop, the result should be that a weight matrix is output for each layer. In order to retrieve the weights and biases of a designated dense layer within the Tensorflow platform, a specific set of steps must be followed. Firstly, it is necessary to determine the layer that requires reduction and subsequently extract the corresponding weights. This process can be applied to multiple layers simultaneously. Once the extraction is completed, it is recommended to convert the weights and biases into Numpy arrays to facilitate their usage.

When using threshold pruning, especially when manually accessing the individual layers, it is essential to note that in scenarios where the code is to be used efficiently, it is important to pay attention to how complex the model is. Extensive models can lead to time-consuming processes when each layer is checked individually. However, this contradicts the challenges of the optimal AIoT environment. Thus, the code must be implemented more efficiently, retrieving and updating the matrices of weights and biases simultaneously.

Step 2: Threshold and Granularity
Some of the weights can then be set to zero using a threshold θ, which corresponds that the input x_i of the i-th neuron does not affect the output y_j of the j-th neuron. The threshold is used in this process to adjust the sparsity or to control the proportion of weights to be trimmed. Depending on how the threshold is set, the process achieves different results regarding the resulting complexity of the neural network. If the value is set higher, more weights are pruned, resulting in the original neural network becoming sparser. With a lower value, it behaves on the contrary. Only a few weights are affected, and the model remains similar to its original design.

Pruning by a simple threshold is done relatively quickly and allows first successes. However, it is worth going more in-depth here to exploit possible chances to preserve the accuracy better. That is why we additionally use the granularity of sparsity. This point gives us finer control over sparsity patterns in our neural network. Only all weights below the threshold are pruned if we use a simple threshold. This process is done regardless of their position in the network. It can lead to a very irregular and unstructured sparsity pattern that is difficult to implement efficiently. This method also makes further optimizations difficult, especially for more complex models. Sparsity granularity, on the other hand, has the advantage that we can use more structured pruning patterns that preserve the connectivity and topology of the network. For example, in a convolutional layer, it may be more advantageous to prune entire channels or groups of filters that match certain features rather than individual weights. Further, the interpretability and generalization of the network can be improved, and its computational and memory requirements can also be reduced, thus directly addressing yet another challenge of AIoT in resource-constrained environments [5,12].

Step 2.5: Intermediate Step - Integration of further Approaches
The sparsity granularity approach effectively addresses various challenges, and its efficacy can be further amplified by incorporating additional techniques as intermediate steps. For instance, we can significantly reduce network size and complexity by integrating quantization, enabling manual pruning to integrate into a more sophisticated methodology seamlessly. Those seeking additional information on this subject are encouraged to consult Sect. 3.3.

Step 3: Apply the Pruning Mask
In summary, the first two steps restricts all weights of a weight matrix W to values greater than or equal to the simple threshold θ or combined with sparsity granularity. It is done by setting all weights smaller than θ to zero. Once all layers and corresponding weights have been adjusted as desired, these changes must now be exchanged with the original model's values, resulting in a sparse matrix W'.

Step 4: Evaluate the Model
Upon completion of the three key steps, the model should be evaluated based on predetermined criteria to ascertain its compliance with the set requirements. If any modifications are deemed necessary, they should be implemented without delay.

3.3 Enhancements and Complexity

The pruning process can be more intricate than a simple threshold-based approach. Threshold pruning, even if done manually, has several disadvantages. The biggest issue is that finding a suitable threshold value is usually very time-consuming. It is because setting the value is generally quite tricky as it significantly impacts the converted model and can, therefore, severely affect the model's actual performance if the value is set incorrectly. Also, the fact that the model is clipped too much or too little is a cause. The problem here is that everything is resolved from a single value. To avoid this problem, we can use other pruning techniques to improve our approaches. One of these possibilities is the Optimal Brain Surgeon (abbreviated OBS) pruning method [8]. There are several other ways in which pruning can be used as a solution. These are aimed at different needs and basics. Some can be divided into the following categories: the Magnitude based pruning methods, which are based on the view that local measures can determine the saliency of weights and neurons. Another group would be the quantization methods that reduce computations through the fact that they are based on using hashing, low precision, and binary representations of the weights [15]. Further important for the whole project is that the use case's requirements must be clarified before a pruning approach is selected. This is essential because there are already differences between the different pruning methods on a structural level [4].

3.4 Edge Computing

There are possibilities to make the pruning itself more complex and even more customized, but applying other principles and methods can be helpful, especially when developing an AIoT application for real-world implementation. It is crucial to consider various aspects beyond pruning approaches. These factors should be duly noted in the conclusion and consider the multitude of possibilities and diversity in this field. These include but are not limited to, points such as quantification, which reduces the precision with which parameter values are stored. The goal is to make the computations faster and to get deep-learning models running. They need to be reduced in size while containing the loss in accuracy [13]. To get even more technical in structuring the neural network to handle AIoT Use Cases, topics like improvements for the rectified linear unit and ternarisation, in general, are worth looking at.

Incorporating technical approaches is undoubtedly critical when implementing an AIoT use case. However, considering other factors, such as big data, is equally important. One of the primary obstacles that AI faces in IoT settings is the scarcity of data containing errors pertinent to a specific use case, commonly referred to as big data issues. It is especially problematic for computer vision scenarios to begin with. Besides solutions like anomaly detection, there is also the possibility of considering synthetically generated data. Of course, it depends on the use case and its data. However, there are many possibilities, for example, through image processing or 3D rendering processes, to process image data so that the data sets become more balanced. It can be beneficial at the beginning of a project where the amount of data is still minimal, but also to serve detailed or niche areas later [10].

4   Achievements

4.1   Energy Sector Perspectives

In order to gain a comprehensive understanding of the advantages of artificial intelligence of things, it is beneficial to provide practical illustrations from the energy sector. Apart from process enhancements, several opportunities can be leveraged, including increased efficiency, discovering chances and potential, better scalability, more far-sighted action and utilization of existing data.

As a more detailed example, we look at one use case specifically. The original final solution was to identify suitable solar places by recognizing suitable areas based on satellite or aerial images to reach the perfect customer. Nevertheless, in this case, these are all separate steps from collecting the images or video streams from different sources over the necessary infrastructure until the algorithms cluster the results. With the help of AIoT, the potential would be to analyze the images while collecting with a drone directly. It would be no need to send the data or even save the data. The system would take the image or video and directly analyze it on the same device. The good results could be transmitted to a location or saved when the drone's flight is finished. That would be a straightforward example of how AIoT can improve the process. With this, the costs for the whole project will be decreased, and the efficiency rise.

4.2   Outlook

From an outlook, there are naturally far more opportunities than the possibilities for AIoT and the pruning approach described in this paper. The approach around the presented strategic manual pruning can be refined with additional methods such as quantification and further steps regarding edge computing. These enhancements could address the requirements and challenges of the use case even more. Also, a comprehensive look at the hardware page is critical to consider use cases in a natural environment. In order to optimize the computer vision process, careful consideration must be given to selecting a camera compatible with the microcontroller. The camera's technical specifications are a crucial factor that can significantly impact the software and ultimately influence the size of the AI model being used. It is essential to carefully evaluate these factors to ensure that the camera can meet the specific requirements and demands of the project at hand. An example of this would be the resolution of the camera. The lower the quality of the photos, so naturally, the bumped storage on the microcontroller is much smaller. Even the eventually used neural network, which should be shrunk, has it more accessible to cope with images with low resolution than with high-quality images in an AIoT environment.

5 Conclusion

The findings are based on the new potential opportunities for application cases that can be improved with the help of artificial intelligence of things rather than conventional AI environments such as the cloud. The energy industry has been identified as having significant opportunities for improvement through the integration of AI methods. With a focus on direct AIoT use, these opportunities have undergone continuous testing to identify ways to enhance efficiency and productivity. A simple yet effective process has been developed for successful implementation renewal through the combination of use case detection and resource-constrained environment analysis. It further includes the strategic and manual application of the pruning method, which can be tailored to specific scenarios for greater customization and effectiveness rather than relying solely on pre-existing APIs. The process also lays the groundwork for addressing more complex models in the future.

Summarized this paper presents use cases, their chances for using artificial intelligence of things, and a pruning approach to solve their challenges in a resource-constrained environment. Further pruning enhancements for a more efficient implementation of AIoT use cases were named, and their potential for deployment in a real-world system has been discussed. Further possible next steps and opportunities for improvements were described.

References

1. Abdulkareem, N., Zeebaree, S., Sadeeq, M., Ahmed, D., Sami, A., Zebari, R.: Iot and cloud computing issues, challenges and opportunities: a review. 1, 1–7 (2021)
2. Ali, Z., Ali, H., Badawy, M.: Internet of Things (IoT): definitions, challenges, and recent research directions. Int. J. Comput. Appl. **128**, 975–8887 (2015)
3. Anna Sidyuk, A.M.: AIOT - IST das die zukunft von internet of things? (2021)
4. Blalock, D., Ortiz, J.J.G., Frankle, J., Guttag, J.: What is the state of neural network pruning? (2020)
5. Chen, T., Chen, X., Ma, X., Wang, Y., Wang, Z.: Coarsening the granularity: towards structurally sparse lottery tickets (2022)
6. der Energie-und Wasserwirtschaft e.V., B.B.: Künstliche intelligenz für die energiewirtschaft
7. Ding, Y., et al.: An efficient industrial federated learning framework for AIOT: a face recognition application (2022)
8. Frantar, E., Singh, S.P., Alistarh, D.: Optimal brain compression: a framework for accurate post-training quantization and pruning (2023)

9. Hossein Motlagh, N., Mohammadrezaei, M., Hunt, J., Zakeri, B.: Internet of things (IOT) and the energy sector. Energies **13**(2) (2020)
10. Jordon, J., et al.: Synthetic data - what, why and how? (2022)
11. Mao, H., et al.: Exploring the granularity of sparsity in convolutional neural networks. In: 2017 IEEE Conference on Computer Vision and Pattern Recognition Workshops (CVPRW), pp. 1927–1934 (2017)
12. Mao, H., et al.: Exploring the regularity of sparse structure in convolutional neural networks (2017)
13. Murshed, M.G.S., Murphy, C., Hou, D., Khan, N., Ananthanarayanan, G., Hussain, F.: Machine learning at the network edge: a survey (2019)
14. Sung, T.W., Tsai, P.W., Gaber, T., Lee, C.Y.: Artificial intelligence of things (AIOT) technologies and applications. Wirel. Commun. Mob. Comput. **2021**, 1–2 (2021)
15. Vadera, S., Ameen, S.: Methods for pruning deep neural networks (2021)

End-to-End Quality of Service Management in the Physical Internet: A Digital Internet Inspired Multi-domain Approach

Frank Phillipson[1,2(✉)]

[1] TNO, The Hague, The Netherlands
frank.phillipson@tno.nl
[2] Maastricht University, Maastricht, The Netherlands

Abstract. For the layer 'System Level Functionality' of the Phyisical Internet, it is needed to estimate end-to-end performance characteristics of transportations that visit multiple logistic domains. This paper proposes an approach based on a Digital Internet functionality: a combination of a Service Level Agreement registry and a Quality of Service processor. Existing SLA-calculus gives tools for the QoS-processor to combine the SLA-parameters for all possible end-to-end paths and gives the QoS-processor the possibility to propose the best path given the required performance. A realistic implementation is proposed using a multi objective/constraint approach and a related communication form between the domain owner and the QoS Processor.

Keywords: End-to-End QoS · Physical Internet · Logistic multi-domain network · Service Level Agreements · SLA registry

1 Introduction

The Physical Internet (PI) is a logistic concept that aims at realising full interconnectivity (information, physical and financial flows) of several (private) freight transport and logistics services networks and make them ready to be seamlessly used as one large logistics network [14]. The concept of the Physical Internet was introduced by [12]. The goal is to create an open global logistics system founded on physical, digital and operational interconnectivity through encapsulation, interfaces and protocols [13] to obtain a more efficient logistic system in terms of costs [20], carbon emissions and carbon-free city logistics [2,5]. A lot of work has been done on this topic since then, of which an overview can be found in the literature overviews of [15,17,18]. The PI does not directly manage physical goods but rather manages the shipping of containers that store goods, just as Digital Internet (DI) uses packets to store user data. For the PI to become full-fledged, numerous elements need to be coordinated, including physical objects, such as PI modular containers and PI transit centres, and more

© The Author(s), under exclusive license to Springer Nature Switzerland AG 2023
U. R. Krieger et al. (Eds.): I4CS 2023, CCIS 1876, pp. 345–355, 2023.
https://doi.org/10.1007/978-3-031-40852-6_20

abstract concepts, such as legislation and business models [18]. The Alice/Sense 'Roadmap to Physical Internet' in the [14] explains and describes the development of PI in the next years, using five specific areas:

1. PI Nodes - Roles of physical nodes and operational model for physical nodes;
2. PI Network Services - PI protocol stack and network management;
3. Governance - Governance concepts, bodies, regulations and trust building measures;
4. Access and Adoption - Benefits of PI and mental shift towards PI;
5. System Level Functionality - PI architecture, building blocks and information exchange.

Each of the areas in the roadmap has started in 2015–2020 and shows the possible developments in 'generations' until 2040. Generations define possible evolutions towards PI and can be scenarios or parts of PI-like implementations. PI-like operation will be established around 2030, the developments from 2030 to 2040 focus on improvements on the way to fully autonomous PI operation.

In this paper we will look at the highest level, the System Level Functionality. In the [14] is stated that the basic operational premise of the Physical Internet is similar to the one that has served the Digital Internet so well over its almost 50 years of operations and growth. That premise is that simplicity and openness must drive all system level protocols and controls. Such a premise provides users with the opportunity to innovate without burdening them with overhead that inhibits creativity. With respect to the PI, [14] states that this premise implies that the PI needs only a small amount of information concerning the shipments that are entrusted to it for delivery to ensure their delivery. The protocols to be employed by the PI also should reflect the minimalist nature of the protocols employed in the DI. While the DI's protocols have grown more complex over the years, the PI should attempt to start out as the DI did with an extremely simple protocol structure and allow circumstances to drive the modification of these originating control processes. As a starting point, the protocols for the PI should control how nodes forward shipments onwards, how costs are collected, how errors and exceptions are to be handled, how end-to-end control is to be maintained, how node-to-node control is to be maintained, how congestion is to be managed, how differing physical layers are to be managed, how QoS (Quality of Service) parameters should be handled, and how users can access data concerning each of these managed activities. The Alice roadmap in the [14] gives an example, in 12 steps, of how the PI could work. The first three steps are:

1. A shipper is interested in sending a consignment of goods from Barcelona to Hamburg. The shipper contacts their freight forwarder and asks the freight forwarder what the cost will be for the shipment providing the forwarder with delivery information, shipment information and required time of delivery.
2. The freight forwarder queries the PI to obtain an estimate of costs for the shipment, given the shipments characteristics and delivery time.
3. The PI examines the end-to-end route that the goods most likely will travel (based on historical information concerning origin-destination routings), integrates existing loads anticipated for the dates in question over the routes

considered, incorporates node costs, transport costs, and any other pertinent costs for handling along the most likely route, and any known maintenance information to arrive at a preliminary cost estimate for the shipment.

This end-to-end route, meaning the entire route from origin to destination, will make use of several transporters and their network. The network of each of the transporters will be named a domain, leading to the concept that the shipment, end-to-end, will be a multi-domain transportation. The freight forwarder organises this multi-domain end-to-end path, where every transporter will manage the part within their own domain.

The research question in this paper is how can we come to a realistic implementation of steps 2 and 3, where there is no prior proposal for these steps in the logistic Physical Internet community. In this paper a proposal will be outlined, which is inspired by an approach proposed for the DI, however newly designed and tailored for the Physical Internet case. For that, we start with [3], where a Service Level Agreement (SLA) registry is proposed for the DI, which provides Quality-of-Service (QoS) data. This data is handled by a QoS processor, based on SLA-calculus as proposed in [9–11], resulting in predictions of end-to-end QoS parameters used for selection and/or ranking actions for new session requests.

We will now give a realistic implementation of step 2 and 3, inspired by an approach proposed for the DI. In [3] a Service Level Agreement (SLA) registry is proposed which provides Quality-of-Service (QoS) data. This data is handled by a QoS processor, based on SLA-calculus as proposed in [9–11], resulting in predictions of end-to-end QoS parameters used for selection and/or ranking actions for new session requests. In the next section this original DI approach is explained in detail. Next, in Sect. 3 the proposed concept in the PI environment is elaborated on. An example implementation of this concept is shown in Sect. 4. The paper ends with some conclusions.

2   End-to-End QoS in Multi-domain Telecommunication Networks

In telecommunication multi-domain end-to-end QoS was a hot topic already in 2002 [7]. Each domain is a telecommunication network of a specific Service Provider (SP), each with its own characteristics, QoS-mechanism and service levels. For a specific service (for example Voice-over-IP) a connection has to be established over multiple domains between the origin and the destination of the call. The service provider of the originating domain wants some guarantee about the end-to-end QoS, as he promises some service level to his clients.

In [9] is stated that an effective and increasingly popular means to deal with QoS in multi-domain environments is to negotiate Service Level Agreements (SLAs) between the different domain owners. In this context, a key question to be addressed by a SP is "What combination of SLAs should be agreed upon by the SP and the respective network domain owners to achieve a certain predefined end-to-end QoS level?". Note that an SP would not subscribe to a costly premium service class in one of the intermediate backbone networks, when there appears to be an inevitable bottleneck with respect to the achievable end-to-end QoS in, e.g., the wireless access. An example of inter-domain dynamic service negotiation, which is an important step that must be considered prior to the physical resource provisioning, can be found in [7]. In more general terms, the service provider should try to distribute the involved 'performance budgets' (e.g., packet loss, delay) over the underlying domains, such that the envisioned end-to-end QoS level can be realised against minimal costs. It is clear that this 'cost optimisation' problem requires the ability to determine end-to-end QoS guarantees from the performance parameters specified in the SLAs. This mapping of a set of per-domain SLAs to an associated (achievable) end-to-end QoS level is called SLA calculus, examples of which can be found in [9–11,19]. These papers show for various services (voice-over-IP, web serving) what key performance indices (KPIs) per domain should be shared and how these can be translated to the end-to-end performance and in some cases to some perceived quality measure. This perceived quality measure is a prediction of how more technical parameters such as delay, response time etc., are perceived by the end-user and translated to a Mean Opinion Score (MOS), as in [21]. Additional, in the operational setting, call admission control can be used to guarantee the SLAs, as proposed in the framework of [4]. They present a framework to provision end-to-end QoS in heterogeneous multi-domain networks that was implemented in EuQoS system and tested in Pan-European research network.

If we know what information has to be shared to be able to calculate the end-to-end performance, the following questions arise: where this information is stored? Who can access this information/data to perform the calculations? For both questions the answer can be 'each domain owner individually', what we will call a distributed approach, and 'some orchestrator' what will be called a global approach. This leads to four main areas:

1. Distributed/Distributed: if both data and the calculation are distributed, for each call all possible used domains have to be contacted, leading to a huge overhead on communication.
2. Distributed/Global: if data is distributed and the calculation is done globally, some orchestrator has to take this role and communicate with all domains each time a request is made.
3. Global/Distributed: if data is global and the calculation is distributed, the domain owner can request the database and perform the calculation.
4. Global/Global: now all data is centralised and the domain owner gets a single answer to his request.

When data is shared, the question about confidentiality arises: do we want to share this data. Also, when there is a single orchestrator, it has to be trusted by all parties, both in data confidentiality as well in giving the best, unbiased, answer to the request.

In [3] a Global/Global system is described. Preconditions that are set in this work for a such system are:

1. Domain owners should be able to make their own decisions;
2. No new protocol should be needed for such a system;
3. The solution should be scalable;
4. Commercial Service Level Agreement (SLA) information must be kept confidential.

This system proposes a combination of a QoS processor and an SLA registry, predicting the end-to-end QoS value of the paths between the originating and destination location, based on the SLA information as stored in the SLA registry. The system ranks the relevant paths end-to-end QoS value order and selects the path(s) having the best end-to-end QoS prediction. The SLA information is kept confidential as the SLA registry does not exchange the SLA information itself, only the ranking and the information about the requested end-to-end QoS will be obtained. This information is given using a MOS value. The main reason that the system generates an ordered list instead of just prescribing the 'next to go' domain is that the QoS processor only calculated long-term predictions without taking into account the dynamics of the current status of each individual domain. This lack of dynamics is of course depending on the time interval of renewing the SLA information within the registry. The method can be implemented as a distributed database and processor, comparable to DNS servers in the DI. As indicated, this method promises confidentiality, but asks trust of the central orchestrator. As alternative, a decentral method based on secure multiparty computation can be used [6]. In that case, a method is used for parties to jointly compute a function over their inputs, while keeping those inputs private.

3   End-to-End QoS in Multi-domain Physical Internet

Comparable to the approach in [3] we propose a Global/Global system for the Physical Internet. Now, a domain is the logistic network of a single Logistic Service Provider (LSP) who offers transportation services within its network and as part of a multi LSP domain delivery. The main conditions we enforce for the QoS system are:

1. Domain owners should be able to make their own decisions;
2. The solution should be scalable;
3. Commercial Service Level Agreement (SLA) information must be kept confidential.

As explained in Sect. 1, the end-to-end route of the shipment will use several transporters and their network. Each network of a transporter is named a domain. The freight forwarder is responsible for the end-to-end shipment, however, he has no control over how each transporter handles the shipment within their domain. For the first condition, each transporter, or domain owner, can decide on its own how the shipment travels through its network, as long as the

SLA is complied to. The second conditions asks for scalability. Given the huge number of shipments, transporters, paths, the curse of dimensionality is lurking. The system should be able to handle all these dimensions. Lastly, to persuade transporters to cooperate, commercial data should be kept confidential.

For this we propose an SLA database or registry in which domain owners upload their SLA parameters and a QoS processor which processes the QoS related parameters from the SLA registry for predicting an end-to-end QoS value that is representative for the path between the originating location and the destination location. In many cases there will be (a plurality of) alternative paths between the originating location and the destination location. Then the QoS processor is adapted for predicting a plurality of end-to-end QoS values. The QoS processor calculates (predicts) the end-to-end QoS value of the paths between the originating and destination location, based on the SLA information as stored in the (common) SLA registry and ranks the relevant paths end-to-end QoS value order or, alternatively, selects the path having the best end-to-end QoS prediction. This action can be done on request, meaning each time an LSP demands an end-to-end QoS value. However, as [3] also proposes, an alternative approach can be calculating and storing QoS values for all or a selection of paths in advance or store path values in the SLA registry when calculated on request. This leads to a situation where for a specific request the information can be retrieved from the database directly. Re-computation of the end-to end QoS predictions for some paths may then be needed only when a domain's SLA changes.

The implementation of the QoS processor depends on the chosen SLA parameters. One could think of average, minimal and maximal delivery times, order accuracy[1], number of modality changes, cost, CO_2 emissions, delivery on time percentage etc. How the convolution of the SLA parameters is done over multiple domains also depends on the specific parameter and the assumed underlying (mathematical) model. In some cases simple addition and subtraction is sufficient or sums of stochastic variables can be calculated easily in the case of assumed underlying (log) normal or Poisson distributions. In other cases more sophisticated techniques are required, when more complex probability distributions are assumed, for example in the form of queuing systems with batch arrivals, modelling the handling by ships or trains within a domain. Techniques from [19] can be of inspiration here. The QoS processor then calculates the convolution value of all the n SLA parameters per end-to-end path resulting in the vector $(x_1, ..., x_n)$, where x_i is the resulting end-to-end SLA parameter for the i-th SLA parameter.

In the DI case, there exists a single value, MOS, that depicts the perceived quality determined by multiple underlying, physical SLA parameters. In logistics, there does not exist such a single (perceived) quality parameter. Therefor, a multi objective/constraint approach is proposed, where the domain owner can select and define:

---

[1] Order accuracy measures the amount of orders that are processed, shipped and delivered without any incidents on its way.

1. SLA parameters that have to be of a certain minimum/maximum value, the constraints, and
2. SLA parameters that have to be optimised, asking for coefficients to weight their perceived relative importance, the objectives.

If we have n SLA parameters, we propose to define the input for the QoS processor in the form:

$$C = (C_1, ..., C_n)$$

where C_i is the QoS processor command for SLA parameter i. This command can be '$= c_i$', '$> c_i$', '$\geq c_i$', '$< c_i$' or '$\leq c_i$' in the case of a constraint parameter and '$w = w_i$' in the case of a objective parameter. If we separate all SLA parameters into the sets I_o for the objective parameters and $I_{c=}$, $I_{c<}$, $I_{c\leq}$, $I_{c>}$ and $I_{c\geq}$, then the formal optimisation problem based on C equals:

$$\max \sum_{i \in I_o} w_i x_i,$$

under the constraints

$$x_i = c_i \quad \forall i \in I_{c=},$$
$$x_i < c_i \quad \forall i \in I_{c<},$$
$$x_i \leq c_i \quad \forall i \in I_{c\leq},$$
$$x_i > c_i \quad \forall i \in I_{c>},$$
$$x_i \geq c_i \quad \forall i \in I_{c\geq}.$$

As example, the command

$$C = (= 10, > 20, w = 5, w = 1)$$

will result in the optimisation problem

$$\max 5x_3 + x_4,$$

under the constraints

$$x_1 = 10, \quad x_2 > 20.$$

This proposed methodology meets the conditions that we requested in the beginning of this section. The ranking and the composed results make sure that the first and last condition are met: domain owners can make their own decisions and the SLA information is kept confidential. The scalability can be realised by pre-processing and storing paths, reducing the update frequency of SLA parameters and distributed implementation of the SLA registry and QoS processor, in the same way this is done for the DI. To make this work, it should be integrated in a Internet-of-Things service-oriented architecture environment, as proposed in [8,16], or [1].

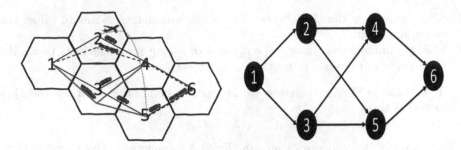

Fig. 1. Example logistic network with six domains and the schematic representation

4   Example of a Multi Objective QoS Processor

In this section we give a small but illustrative example of the proposed methodology. Looking at the operations in logistics, examples of important SLA parameters are cost, on time delivery and CO_2 emissions. This means that in practice a combination of these SLA parameters is used for steering decisions and indeed a multi objective problem is defined, where the solutions give a score on all the SLA parameters and their total score is a weighted combination. We assume a network of domains as depicted in Fig. 1. Note that domains do not require to be geographically separated, a domain stands for the logistic network of a specific LSP. The owner of domain 1 wants to ship a container to domain 6. Each domain owner should register in the SLA registry for each pair of neighbouring domains:

- the cost for shipping a container via its domain between the neighbouring domains;
- the CO_2 emissions for shipping a container via its domain between the neighbouring domains;
- the average and variance transportation time, assuming normal distributed transportation times per domain.

In the case of a multi objective environment, it will not suffice for domain owner to report a single SLA value for each pair of neighbouring domains. Instead, a number of Pareto efficient solutions per pair should be determined. A Pareto efficient (or Pareto optimal) solution is a solution for a multi-objective problem where there is no other solution with a better score for one of the objectives, without a worse score for one of the other objectives. If we assume that cost and CO_2 emissions have positive correlation, meaning that a more expensive solution, e.g., trucking, has a higher CO_2 emission than a less expensive solution, e.g., transport by barge, and that they both have a negative correlation with transportation time, it suffices to report the solution with the lowest cost and the solution with the lowest transportation time per domain. An example is found in Table 1. Here each intermediate node in the network of Fig. 1 reports two Pareto efficient solutions per connection.

Table 1. Items of SLA register; multiple lines per pair of neighbouring domains

				Transportation Time (TT)	
Path	Objective	Costs (€)	CO_2 (kg)	Average (h)	Variance
2→4	TT	100	100	24	4
	Costs	80	60	35	12
2→5	TT	90	90	20	4
	Costs	80	70	36	16
3→4	TT	120	110	26	4
	Costs	100	50	50	15
3→5	TT	70	90	16	6
	Costs	90	70	36	16
4→6	TT	75	60	20	10
	Costs	70	50	25	15
5→6	TT	80	55	18	5
	Costs	75	40	22	10

Table 2. Resulting ranking of QoS Processor and indication of allowed solutions

Rank	Weighted cost	Path	Cost	Emission	Probability	
1	134	2 4 6	150	110	50%	✗
2	137	2 5 6	155	110	65%	✓
3	139	3 5 6	145	130	100%	✓
4	141	2 4 6	155	120	86%	✓
5	142	3 4 6	170	100	0%	✗
6	143	3 5 6	165	110	65%	✓
7	146	2 5 6	160	125	90%	✓
8	148	3 5 6	150	145	100%	✓
9	149	3 4 6	175	110	2%	✗
10	151	2 5 6	165	130	100%	✓
11	152	3 5 6	170	125	90%	✓
12	160	2 5 6	170	145	100%	✓
13	162	2 4 6	170	150	99%	✓
14	169	2 4 6	175	160	100%	✓
15	178	3 4 6	190	160	98%	✓
16	185	3 4 6	195	170	100%	✓

Based on this input, the QoS Processor is able to calculate the total costs, CO_2 emission and the probability density of the transportation time. Assume that the owner of domain 1 communicates to the QoS processor that he wants to ship a container to domain 6, having preference weights for cost and emission of $w_1 = \frac{3}{5}$ and $w_2 = \frac{2}{5}$ respectively, and a transportation time of less than 60 h with 60% probability, $(w_1 = \frac{3}{5}, w_2 = \frac{2}{5}, > 60\%)$, the QoS could rank the paths as depicted in Table 2. Here one could consider to translate the weighted cost into a value that cannot be traced back to the original SLA parameter values.

The solution with the lowest cost is not allowed. This solution does not meet the transportation time probability. The best, allowed, solutions can now be communicated to the owner of domain 1.

5   Conclusions

The Physical Internet concept needs to be completed in the next decades, following the 'Roadmap to Physical Internet' [14]. For the layer 'System Level Functionality', the PI needs to estimate end-to-end performance characteristics of transportations that visit multiple LSP domains. Where Physical Internet is inspired by the Digital Internet, also for this function an DI inspired approach is chosen: a combination of a SLA registry and a QoS processor, both on the global level of the PI. SLA-calculus gives tools for the QoS-processor to combine the SLA-parameters for all possible end-to-end paths and gives the QoS-processor the possibility to propose the best path given the required performance. A realistic implementation is proposed using a multi objective/constraint approach and a related communication form between the domain owner and the QoS Processor. Note that the proposed methodology is only a small part in the entire PI concept. Only two steps in the envisioned way of working in the System Level Functionality, as presented by the [14]. Next step here is the integration of the proposed methodology within the SENSE framework, such as the tendering phase and the operational phase. For future research, we propose to look at this integration and the scalability of the concept. A trial project is foreseen on this topic. In this trial not only the technology should be considered, also the acceptance of the methodology and sharing of commercial, confidential information with the system has to be evaluated and discussed with the transporters.

References

1. Acciaro, M., Renken, K., El Khadiri, N.: Technological change and logistics development in European ports. In: Carpenter, A., Lozano, R. (eds.) European Port Cities in Transition. SS, pp. 73–88. Springer, Cham (2020). https://doi.org/10.1007/978-3-030-36464-9_5
2. Ballot, E., Liesa, F., Franklin, R.: Improving logistics by interconnecting services in a physical internet: potential benefits, barriers and developments. J. Supply Chain Manag. Logist. Procurement **1**(2), 178–192 (2018)
3. Blom, M., Phillipson, F.: System and method for processing quality-of-service parameters in a communication network (2011). uS Patent 8,046,489
4. Burakowski, W., et al.: Provision of end-to-end qos in heterogeneous multi-domain networks. Ann. Telecommun.-annales des télécommunications **63**(11–12), 559–577 (2008)

5. Ciprés, C., de la Cruz, M.T.: The physical internet from shippers perspective. In: Müller, B., Meyer, G. (eds.) Towards User-Centric Transport in Europe. LNM, pp. 203–221. Springer, Cham (2019). https://doi.org/10.1007/978-3-319-99756-8_14
6. Cramer, R., Damgård, I., Nielsen, J.: Secure Multiparty Computation. Cambridge University Press, Cambridge (2015)
7. Kamienski, C.A., Sadok, D.: Strategies for provisioning end-to-end qos-based services in a multi-domain scenario. In: Teletraffic Science and Engineering, vol. 5, pp. 1031–1040. Elsevier (2003)
8. Kim, D.-S., Tran-Dang, H.: An information framework of internet of things services for physical internet. In: Industrial Sensors and Controls in Communication Networks. CCN, pp. 259–281. Springer, Cham (2019). https://doi.org/10.1007/978-3-030-04927-0_19
9. Kooij, R., et al.: Sla calculus for end-to-end qos of tcp-based applications in a multi-domain environment. In: Proceedings World Telecommunications Congress (2006)
10. van der Mei, R., Meeuwissen, H.: Modelling end-to-end quality-of-service for transaction-based services in multi-domain environments. In: 2006 IEEE International Conference on Web Services (ICWS 2006), pp. 453–462. IEEE (2006)
11. van der Mei, R., Meeuwissen, H., Phillipson, F.: User perceived quality-of-service for voice-over-ip in a heterogeneous multi-domain network environment. In: Proceedings of ICWS (2006)
12. Montreuil, B.: Toward a physical internet: meeting the global logistics sustainability grand challenge. Logist. Res. 3(2–3), 71–87 (2011)
13. Montreuil, B., Meller, R., Ballot, E.: Physical internet foundations. In: Borangiu, T., Thomas, A., Trentesaux, D. (eds.) Service Orientation in Holonic and Multi Agent Manufacturing and Robotics. Studies in Computational Intelligence, vol. 472, pp. 151–166. Springer, Heidelberg (2013). https://doi.org/10.1007/978-3-642-35852-4_10
14. SENSE-project: Roadmap to physical internet. Technical report, Alice, London (2019)
15. Sternberg, H., Norrman, A.: The physical internet-review, analysis and future research agenda. Int. J. Phys. Distrib. Logist. Manag. 47, 736–762 (2017)
16. Tran-Dang, H., Krommenacker, N., Charpentier, P., Kim, D.S.: Towards the internet of things for physical internet: perspectives and challenges. IEEE Internet Things J. 7, 4711–4736 (2020)
17. Treiblmaier, H., Mirkovski, K., Lowry, P.: Conceptualizing the physical internet: literature review, implications and directions for future research. In: 11th CSCMP Annual European Research Seminar, Vienna, Austria, May (2016)
18. Treiblmaier, H., Mirkovski, K., Lowry, P., Zacharia, Z.: The physical internet as a new supply chain paradigm: a systematic literature review and a comprehensive framework. Int. J. Logist. Manag. 31, 239–287 (2020)
19. Vastag, S.: SLA calculus. Ph.D. thesis, Technischen Universität Dortmund (2014)
20. Venkatadri, U., Krishna, K.S., Ülkü, M.A.: On physical internet logistics: modeling the impact of consolidation on transportation and inventory costs. IEEE Trans. Autom. Sci. Eng. 13(4), 1517–1527 (2016)
21. Yamamoto, L., Beerends, J.: Impact of network performance parameters on the end-to-end perceived speech quality. In: In Proceedings of EXPERT ATM Traffic Symposium (1997)

Author Index

© The Editor(s) (if applicable) and The Author(s), under exclusive license
to Springer Nature Switzerland AG 2023
U. R. Krieger et al. (Eds.): I4CS 2023, CCIS 1876, pp. 357–358, 2023.
https://doi.org/10.1007/978-3-031-40852-6

Printed in the United States
by Baker & Taylor Publisher Services